COCAINE

JÜRGEN BUCHENAU, Series Editor

The Americas in the World series publishes cutting-edge scholarship about the Americas in global and transnational history, politics, society, and culture as well as about the impact of global and transnational actors and processes on the hemisphere. The series includes both works on specialized topics as well as broad syntheses. All titles aim at a wide audience.

Also available in The Americas in the World:

Embracing Autonomy: Latin American–US Relations in the Twenty-First Century by Gregory Weeks

The Dollar: How the US Dollar Became a Popular Currency in Argentina by Ariel Wilkis and Mariana Luzzi

North American Regionalism: Stagnation, Decline, or Renewal? edited by Eric Hershberg and Tom Long

THE GLOBAL REACH OF THE
WORLD'S MOST LUCRATIVE
ILLICIT DRUG

Edited by SEBASTIÁN A. CUTRONA

and JONATHAN D. ROSEN

University of New Mexico Press
Albuquerque

© 2025 by the University of New Mexico Press
All rights reserved. Published 2025
Printed in the United States of America

ISBN 978-0-8263-6820-1 (cloth)
ISBN 978-0-8263-6821-8 (paper)
ISBN 978-0-8263-6822-5 (ePub)

Library of Congress Control Number: 2025006424

Founded in 1889, the University of New Mexico sits on the traditional homelands of the Pueblo of Sandia. The original peoples of New Mexico—Pueblo, Navajo, and Apache—since time immemorial have deep connections to the land and have made significant contributions to the broader community statewide. We honor the land itself and those who remain stewards of this land throughout the generations and also acknowledge our committed relationship to Indigenous peoples. We gratefully recognize our history.

Cover image courtesy of Wikimedia Commons
Designed by Isaac Morris
Composed in Change, Proxima Nova, and Veneer

Contents

vii	**ACKNOWLEDGMENTS**
1	**INTRODUCTION.** The Cocaine Supply Chain Sebastián A. Cutrona and Jonathan D. Rosen
27	**CHAPTER 1.** The Andean Cocaine Trade: Global Reach and Local Impacts Susan Brewer-Osorio
66	**CHAPTER 2.** Organized Crime and Cocaine Trafficking: Counterintuitive Routes, and Consolidated and New Markets Carolina Sampó and Valeska Troncoso
87	**CHAPTER 3.** Cocaine and Criminal Governance in Colombia Héctor Alarcón Barrera and Juan Albarracín
110	**CHAPTER 4.** Cocaine in Brazil: The Emergent Center of a Globalized Market Michael Jerome Wolff
129	**CHAPTER 5** Cocaine Trafficking in Ecuador and Its Crossroads Daniel Pontón C.
155	**CHAPTER 6.** Changing Dynamics of Cocaine Trafficking: The Caribbean in the Global Matrix Ivelaw Lloyd Griffith
177	**CHAPTER 7.** Central America's *Maras*: A Negative Case of DTO Evolution Michael Ahn Paarlberg

202	**CHAPTER 8.**	Cocaine in Mexico: The Forgotten Drug and Its Implications
		Nathan P. Jones and Gary Hale
233	**CHAPTER 9.**	Cocaine in the United States: A Brief History
		Marten Brienen
255	**CHAPTER 10.**	Cocaine Trafficking in Europe
		Alberto Aziani
281	**CHAPTER 11.**	Cocaine Trafficking and Criminal Organizations in Africa
		Caroline Agboola
305	**CHAPTER 12.**	The Cocaine Trade in Asia
		Molly Charles
331	**CHAPTER 13.**	Cocaine Trafficking and Criminal Organizations in Oceania
		Jose Sousa-Santos
348	**CONCLUSION**	
		Jonathan D. Rosen and Sebastián A. Cutrona
358	**SELECTED BIBLIOGRAPHY**	
365	**LIST OF CONTRIBUTORS**	
373	**INDEX**	

Acknowledgments

We extend our sincere gratitude to the peer reviewers, whose insightful comments and constructive feedback significantly strengthened the manuscript. We are deeply indebted to Michael Millman, senior acquisitions editor at the University of New Mexico Press, for his invaluable guidance and unwavering support throughout this project. We also wish to express our profound appreciation to Norman Ware for his exceptional editorial expertise and meticulous work during the editing stage. Finally, thanks to our respective institutions for their support

INTRODUCTION

The Cocaine Supply Chain

Sebastián A. Cutrona and
Jonathan D. Rosen

After discovering a twenty-two-meter narco-submarine carrying roughly three tons of cocaine off the coast of Galicia, Spanish authorities announced in April 2023 the uncovering of "Europe's largest-ever cocaine-manufacturing laboratory" in Pontevedra, a province in the northwest of the Iberian Peninsula. The National Police seized 150 kilos of cocaine, 1,300 kilos of *pasta* (paste) base, and 25,000 liters of chemical precursors.[1] The clandestine laboratory was prepared to refine 200 kilos of cocaine hydrochloride on a daily basis. Facilities manufacturing cocaine from pasta base had previously been found in Europe, suggesting that Latin America no longer harbors all stages of the production process. Cocaine manufacturing outside the Andean Ridge is also suspected in distant territories such as India. According to India's Narcotics Control Bureau (NCB), Mumbai has become "India's cocaine capital," especially after authorities seized approximately 300 kilos of the illicit drug in December 2018. Anecdotal evidence in this Asian country also suggests that various cocaine processing facilities are likely operational within its territory,[2] although the identities of those behind these activities remain largely speculative.

Official statistics confirm that the cocaine market worldwide is expanding rapidly. According to the United Nations Office on Drugs and Crime (UNODC), the supply of cocaine has reached historic levels. Not only did coca bush cultivation soar by 35 percent from 2020 to 2021, but also the manufacturing of hydrochloride cocaine became more efficient in the Andean Ridge.[3] In 2020, almost two thousand tons of cocaine were manufactured, continuing a dramatic uptick that began in 2014.[4] As the COVID-19 restrictions were slowly lifted, cocaine started flowing smoothly to consolidated markets such as North America, Europe, and Australia while also expanding to new regions. In effect, increasing seizures in nontraditional markets such as Africa and Asia reveal that cocaine trafficking is becoming a global phenomenon.[5] Researchers suggest that South Africa, for example, could use up to twenty tons of pure cocaine annually, meaning that its per capita consumption rates are not far from the cocaine prevalence registered in large and consolidated markets such as Australia.[6] As a result, the worldwide use of cocaine is currently above prepandemic levels. The evidence demonstrates that both the absolute number of users and the prevalence rates have increased steadily since around 2005.[7]

As the cocaine market expands, the criminal world is also experiencing profound transformations. Unlike the 1980s and 1990s, when just a few drug cartels—notably Colombian and then Mexican—dominated the cocaine supply chain internationally, the underworld has become increasingly fragmented. Drug cartels, small criminal groups, subcontractors, and brokers coexist in a highly interconnected, competitive, and specialized global cocaine market. While the evidence shows that the underworld remains largely territorial, a condition that favors a certain division of labor, the expansion of criminal organizations such as the Primeiro Comando da Capital (PCC; First Command of the Capital) and the 'Ndrangheta suggests that national borders are still vulnerable. In 2008, for example, an Italian parliamentary anti-mafia commission sustained that approximately 80 percent of the transatlantic cocaine trafficking to Europe was controlled by 'Ndrangheta groups.[8] Furthermore, research highlights that a similar percentage of the continental routes are also operated by the Calabrian mafia,[9] although other scholars sustain that claims about their monopolistic power should be tempered with caution.[10]

This volume seeks to change the way the cocaine trade is analyzed. Unlike most scholarly works, which disintegrate the stages of the supply chain into country-specific analyses or the study of individual criminal organizations, this work focuses on the global dimensions of the cocaine market. From describing coca cultivation by campesinos in the Andean Ridge to examining street dealers in New York, Abuja, Rotterdam, Mumbai, or Sydney, our contributors depict the processes and mechanisms that interconnect the cocaine supply chain by looking at the various ways criminal organizations have expanded their trafficking activities across countries and regions. In doing so, this volume shows the empirical and theoretical relevance of better understanding how the phases of the cocaine supply chain are intertwined, and identifies the major driving forces that favor international mobility, overseas relocation, and/or cooperation among criminal organizations.

The remainder of this introduction is structured as follows. First, we concisely discuss our approach to the global cocaine market, paying special attention to the theoretical contributions that nurture the concept of "supply chain." Second, focusing on the various ways market segments are articulated within transnational production structures, we then trace back the major transformations in the cocaine supply chain since the late 1970s. Third, we explore how criminal organizations have contributed and adapted to the expansion of the cocaine market, showing the growing interconnectedness, competitiveness, and specialization within each phase of the supply chain. Finally, this introduction concludes by providing an overview of the chapters.

The Global Supply Chain

World-systems theory has explored extensively the various ways commodities accumulate value as they move from production to consumption stages in fragmented networks.[11] Drawing on the notions of core and periphery, scholars such as Immanuel Wallerstein have explained how vertically integrated structures of production and consumption create an international division of labor that favors capital-intensive segments of the economy as opposed to those focused on labor.[12] This perspective posits that phases of greater added value are concentrated in the core, or Global North, of the world economy, whereas the rent in places where extractive and agricultural goods are sourced is limited.[13] As a result, the value of products within the commodity chain is expected to increase as it moves away from the production phase toward consumption markets. Sidney Mintz, for example, explored sugar production in British dependencies and its use in the United Kingdom during the past 350-odd years.[14] This anthropologist emphasizes the economic constraints posed by a transnational production structure, showing how the supply of sugar was associated with slavery and colonialism in the evolution of world capitalism.

More recent contributions elucidate the linkages between production and consumption by focusing on firms or industries rather than on the historical processes of structural transformation.[15] Analysis of "global commodity chains"[16] and "global value chains,"[17] largely developed by economic geographers and economists, has yielded valuable insights into the classic approach of world-systems theory. According to Phillip A. Hough, this group of studies has shed light on commodity-specific chain dynamics in the contemporary era, incorporating into the analysis the role of key factors such as governance structures, barriers to entry, quality standards, transaction costs, leading firms, and upgrades to production capacities.[18]

Jennifer Bair claims that despite the fact that global commodity chains and global value chains have their own history, theoretical and disciplinary affinities, and empirical concerns, they can nevertheless be regarded as originating from a single intellectual lineage.[19] Indeed, the global commodity chains framework was born out of Terence Hopkins and Immanuel Wallerstein's world-systems theory, and the global value chains grew out of the former. Not surprisingly, an understanding of production and consumption in terms of a chain linking both agents and activities, in which commodities accumulate value as they move along different stages, is a recurring assumption among a voluminous group of scholars studying international trade and production networks.

Yet the commodity chain model has been also subject to criticism. New strands of relevant theorizing have noted that commodity relations are more complex than the classic deterministic, linear, structurally rigid, and weak-on-gender approaches of the past.[20] In a theme issue of the journal *Environment and Planning A: Economy and Space* coordinated by Jennifer Bair and Marion Werner, different contributors have noted "the challenge of rethinking commodities through disarticulations via research into the linking and unmooring of people and places to and from transnational circuits of commodity production."[21] This critical approximation understands that not all territories become equally connected to commodity chains. By contrast, transnational circuits also reproduce the subjects and places included and excluded from the global commodity production. Christian Berndt and Marc Boeckler, for example, studied an agro-commodity, the tomato, across two paradigmatic north-south border contexts—Morocco/European Union and Mexico/United States—to understand how the free trade logic translates into concrete integration realities.[22] Drawing on a perspective informed by the performativity approach of economic analysis, the authors maintain that the creation of commodity chains involves framing and the management of related overflows. Moreover, in the tomato trade, this process contributes to reproducing uneven power geographies.

Notwithstanding recent criticisms, commodity chain scholarship has informed works from various fields including geography, political science, sociology, history, and anthropology. In the rest of this introduction, we draw on the logic of commodity chains to illuminate how each phase of the global cocaine market has been organized and interconnected through the years, from coca cultivation in the Andes to sales on the streets of established and emerging markets around the world. In doing so, we also seek to highlight some of the limitations of the commodity chain perspective in understanding the global cocaine market.

From Coca Fields in the Andes to the World

Similar to other illicit drugs, the cocaine supply chain is characterized by economies of scale, as retail prices are extraordinarily high compared to production costs.[23] Recent studies show that the total retail value of the cocaine market is between $94 and $143 billion.[24] The profits, however, are not equally distributed among all participants. While wholesalers and traffickers accumulate a great deal of the revenues, other actors along the cocaine supply chain do not receive the same economic benefits. It is estimated, for example, that coca leaf accounts for between 0.01 and 2 percent of cocaine's market value.[25] Although campesinos receive a minimum percentage of the profits, the rent in illegal economies is not always concentrated in the north.[26] Unlike the tenets of world-systems theory, the structure of the cocaine supply chain allows participants in the so-called peripheries to accumulate large amounts of money.

The cocaine supply chain is often described as encompassing four broad activities: production, international trafficking, retailing, and the domestic distribution network that connects imports to street or retail sales.[27] Scholarly works and government reports alike have typically labeled countries as "producers," "manufacturers," "trafficking hubs," "suppliers of precursor chemicals," or "consumer markets" of cocaine. Nonetheless, the lines that separate each of the phases of the cocaine supply chain have become increasingly blurred over the years. As Juan Gabriel Tokatlian sustains, this type of segmentation often obscures the real complexity of the global cocaine market, its ongoing expansion, and its capacity for adaptation and mutation.[28]

Yet a relatively high degree of segmentation existed at the time the cocaine market gained momentum. By the mid-1980s, Peru was producing approximately 65 percent of the world's supply of coca leaf, whereas Bolivia and Colombia produced roughly 25 percent and 10 percent, respectively.[29] This labor-intensive activity has been historically led by campesinos, who have been growing coca for approximately seven thousand years.[30] They work largely in nonmetropolitan areas such as the Alto Huallaga Valley and the VRAEM region in Peru,[31] the Yungas and Chapare Valleys in Bolivia, and the departments of Nariño, Norte de Santander, and Putumayo in Colombia. Since cultivation and harvesting do not require a great amount of care or knowledge, tens of thousands of campesinos have been involved in coca production for economic survival, often in contexts of economic hardship and state absence. In the case of Bolivia, *sindicatos* (unions) have organized the local coca economy, distributing land, imposing sanctions, and facilitating supplies for the public works in their communities.[32]

The other agro-industrial activity within the cocaine supply chain is manufacturing. After coca leaves are harvested by campesinos, they are processed into cocaine paste. Until the 1980s, this activity was largely conducted in Peru and Bolivia, especially in regions where coca leaves were produced. Compared to the final processing stage, the manufacturing of cocaine paste requires neither in-depth knowledge nor a sophisticated infrastructure.[33] A person with limited work experience, often known as a "cook," can oversee the process in the same coca fields. Nevertheless, a higher connectivity with other phases of the supply chain is warranted, as this rudimentary activity requires chemical precursors to transform coca leaves into cocaine paste.

Laboratories finalize the manufacturing process. Colombia has historically harbored the vast majority of these establishments, particularly in relatively isolated regions that are distant from the main metropolitan areas. Francisco E. Thoumi notes that cocaine manufacturing requires a complex organization, as it includes human capital with chemistry training, chemical precursors, access to electrical lines or generators, microwave ovens, and a few other materials.[34] Unlike the production of coca leaves, this phase of the supply chain is not labor intensive. Only a small number of individuals are required to transform pasta base into cocaine hydrochloride. Nonetheless, the value of the product and the risks associated are higher at this stage, a situation that favors the intervention of criminal actors to provide protection.

Cocaine trafficking from laboratories in the Andean Ridge to consumer markets is accomplished by sea, land, and air. The evidence suggests that multiple means are available in each modality. In maritime trafficking, for example, containerized shipments allow large quantities of cocaine to be transported in single consignments, whereas go-fast boats are typically used for trafficking smaller quantities over short stretches and fishing vessels along longer distances.[35] Irrespective of the trafficking modality, this stage in the supply chain involves critical activities such as storing and smuggling product and corrupting government officials. Criminals are hence required to master a wide variety of sophisticated skills, including secreting goods in shipping containers, altering electronic records, operating planes and semisubmersibles, and building tunnels and airfields, among others.[36] As criminal organizations anticipate detection, corruption also becomes a central mechanism to guaranteeing that cocaine reaches its final destination. It is therefore not surprising that criminals at this stage accumulate large amounts of wealth compared to other participants in the cocaine supply chain.

Yet trafficking routes have largely changed over the years. Despite other factors such as the availability of subcontractors, logistical infrastructure, and the presence or not of other criminal organizations in the region, most of the main transformations in trafficking routes have been a consequence of interdiction efforts.[37] The Medellín and Cali cartels, for instance, initially trafficked cocaine into the United States through the Caribbean. The creation of the South Florida Task Force in 1982, however, pushed cocaine trafficking toward Central America and the Pacific route. Recent research shows that criminal organizations are prioritizing nontraditional ports in the Southern Cone due to the porosity of borders, the lack of controls, and the possibility of exploiting the region's lack of history in cocaine trafficking.[38] Increasing seizures in major seaports such as Rotterdam[39] and Antwerp[40] illustrate the relevance of the Parana-Paraguay waterway system in connecting Europe with South America.

Once in the destination market, the distribution of cocaine takes a relatively long time and typically involves sales between independent buyers and sellers. Considering that the size of the initial import determines the number of actors involved, it is often expected that each importer will sell cocaine to high-level domestic dealers, each of whom in turn will sell to a larger number of middle-level dealers.[41] Jonathan P. Caulkins and colleagues have demonstrated that the distribution of cocaine within countries often involves three or four transactions.[42] The actors involved, however, have been described in different ways. While some scholars claim that individuals are often part of structured criminal organizations,[43] others depict the retail underworld landscape as largely disorganized, where individuals operate independently from each other.[44] Either way, consumption markets are highly competitive, meaning that wealth is distributed among several low-skilled actors who earn a limited percentage of the cocaine profits.

The United States has historically been the world's most lucrative market for cocaine. Although the illicit drug has been available since the late nineteenth century, its demand skyrocketed during the 1970s.[45] Of the four major drug epidemics of the twentieth century, two were associated with cocaine: cocaine powder in the mid-1970s and crack cocaine in the 1980s. In effect, the long-term picture indicates that cocaine prevalence rates increased since the inception of the first epidemiological studies, peaking in the late 1970s and then falling during the 1980s.[46] With cocaine use in the United States decreasing or stabilizing in the 1990s, other markets gained momentum toward the end of the century, suggesting that the drug's consumption is no longer an "American disease," as David F. Musto claimed in his groundbreaking book *The American Disease: Origins of Narcotics Control*.[47] Various countries in Europe and Oceania in particular have witnessed increasing prevalence rates over the past two to three decades.[48] Furthermore, the available evidence indicates that cocaine markets have also expanded across several South American countries, and seizures in Africa and Asia are at record levels.[49] Paul Gootenberg contends that this trend reverses the course of cocaine's previous half-century historical march to the north, as the illicit drug started "shifting south" in 2005.[50]

Cocaine production also experienced profound transformations. In the 1990s, the cocaine supply chain became more integrated, as Peru and Bolivia increased their refining capabilities while Colombia became the world's primary coca producer.[51] Yet interdiction and eradication policies implemented in Peru and Bolivia, as well as the rise of drug cartels and then left-wing guerrilla organizations, transformed Colombia into the world's epicenter of cocaine production. The Andean country eventually harbored all stages of the agro-industrial phase of the cocaine supply chain. Furthermore, Colombian criminal organizations controlled large segments of the retail market within US territory after eliminating many of their Cuban counterparts in states like Florida.[52] By 2003, Colombia was supplying approximately 90 percent of the cocaine used in the United States despite the adoption of Plan Colombia, a $10 billion counterdrug initiative promoted by the US government in the Andean Ridge.[53] This process, however, did not last long. As part of the so-called balloon effect, coca cultivation shifted back to Peru, and that country became the world's leading coca cultivator in 2013.[54] And more recently, the deceleration of Plan Colombia has contributed to transforming the latter country again into the world's largest producer of coca.

Criminal Organizations

Criminal organizations and other non-law-abiding actors are the glue binding together all segments of the cocaine supply chain. Nevertheless, since the illicit psychoactive substance commonly travels large distances to reach consumer markets, criminal organizations are not expected to carry out all the activities within the global supply chain. Unlike the centralized model prevailing in the 1980s and 1990s in which a limited number of criminal organizations—notably Colombian cartels—controlled almost the entire cocaine supply chain, a division of labor has emerged among actors in the criminal underworld. Today, smaller groups and various criminals cooperate across borders to bring the cocaine manufactured in the Andean Ridge to the streets of major cities such as New York, Abuja, Rotterdam, Mumbai, and Sydney, albeit some theories posit that the actors involved do not have a unique or typical form.[55]

The organization of the underworld has experienced profound transformations over the past several decades. In the 1980s and early 1990s, Colombian criminal organizations dominated critical segments of the cocaine supply chain. By using violence and threats, drug cartels deterred the development of other export-oriented organizations in Colombia while also limiting competition in Peru and Bolivia. When coca production decreased in the other two Andean countries because of more stringent eradication and interdiction policies, the Medellín and Cali cartels filled the vacuum and started supplying domestically most of the coca leaves to the laboratories they already controlled in Colombia. By the early 1990s, these large organizations not only were responsible for the production of coca leaves, the manufacturing of cocaine hydrochloride, and international trafficking operations, but they also got involved in retail activities inside the United States, after the so-called *paisas*[56] who had migrated to South Florida in the 1970s largely eliminated Cuban mafias in places like Miami.[57] At the peak of their power, Colombian cartels trafficked approximately 90 percent of the cocaine used in the United States.[58]

Colombia's criminal organizations expanded their trafficking operations during the early 1990s. As the cocaine demand in the United States stagnated, the Medellín and Cali cartels established links with different criminal groups operating in Europe.[59] With cocaine production increasing and prices experiencing the opposite trend, transatlantic trafficking became a strategic option to mitigate the cartels' losses in their traditional market. Not only European criminals—who contribute to expanding cocaine demand across their own territories—gained relevance during the 1990s, but also Mexican drug cartels, a trend favored by the shift of trafficking routes from the Caribbean to Central America and the Pacific. Their rapid expansion, however, eventually came to a halt. The death of Pablo Escobar in 1993 and the imprisonment and extradition to the United States of the Rodríguez Orejuela brothers ended the era of Colombia's large drug cartels.

Smaller organizations emerged after the demise of the Medellín and Cali cartels. The evidence suggests that approximately three hundred drug-trafficking organizations, known as *cartelitos* (small cartels), surfaced to fill the vacuum left by Colombia's large drug syndicates.[60] Led by more educated criminals, these organizations followed a low, pro-business profile, often being reluctant to use violence.[61] Meanwhile, the cultivation of coca leaves and the manufacture of cocaine became increasingly controlled by the Fuerzas Armadas Revolucionarias de Colombia (FARC; Revolutionary Armed Forces of Colombia), especially after the dissolution of the Soviet Union had shrunk their funding opportunities; and, more importantly, by the right-wing Autodefensas Unidas de Colombia (AUC; United Self-Defense Forces of Colombia). Although the AUC demobilized in 2006, smaller criminal actors known as *bandas criminales* (BACRIM), together with the Ejército de Liberación Nacional (ELN; National Liberation Army), ex-FARC groups, and other actors, have filled the gap.[62]

Mexican drug cartels gained salience during the late 1990s. The demise of Colombia's large cartels and the emergence of new trafficking routes provided criminal organizations such as the Tijuana, Jalisco, and Gulf cartels with unprecedented profits. Unlike the years when the Guadalajara Federation led by Miguel Ángel Félix Gallardo dominated Mexico's underworld, each of these organizations controlled specific trafficking corridors toward the United States, thereby favoring competition and violence. As Laura H. Atuesta and Yocelyn Samantha Pérez-Dávila note, the fragmentation of drug cartels was not only the result of militarized policing but also the strategy adopted by criminals pursuing different interests or deciding to expand their dominion to new territories.[63] By the 2010s, for example, there were around twelve drug cartels associated with cocaine trafficking.[64] Similar to the strategies developed by Colombian groups during the 1990s and the AUC in the 2000s, Mexican criminal organizations also established contacts with the 'Ndrangheta.[65] According to a report elaborated by the UNODC and Europol, the Calabrian mafia started forging links with Mexican groups after the dissolution of the AUC, an event that allegedly culminated in their monopoly in the transatlantic cocaine trade.[66]

Militarizing the drug war not only resulted in the fragmentation of Mexico's organized crime landscape but also favored the displacement of trafficking routes toward other Latin American regions. The Southern Cone in particular became a critical transshipment hub for the cocaine trafficked to West Africa and Europe.[67] As a result, criminal organizations in countries like Brazil and, to a lesser extent, Argentina became increasingly exposed to the profits of the cocaine trade. The evidence shows that the Brazilian PCC and Comando Vermelho (CV) monopolized the growing retail markets in São Paulo and Rio de Janeiro, respectively, and across the country while also transforming Brazil into a transshipment hub for the cocaine trafficked to Europe.[68] These criminal organizations also engaged in basic governing functions such as providing security and welfare.[69] This trend, however, is not limited to the Southern Cone. Other nontraditional routes have also gained increasing relevance, favoring the strengthening of criminal organizations involved in cocaine trafficking in countries such as Ecuador and Venezuela.

Until recently, the relevance of criminal organizations involved in cocaine trafficking was relatively limited outside Latin America. Pierre Tremblay, Maurice Cusson, and Carlo Morselli argue that the incentives for organizational growth for criminals operating where marketing opportunities are most rewarding (i.e., destination points) are relatively limited.[70] Yet since around 2010 this situation seems to have changed substantially. Driven by significantly higher prices and allegedly lower risks of interdiction and imprisonment, the cocaine retail market in several European countries is becoming increasingly populated by criminal organizations. Albanian gangs, for instance, are using contacts with Latin American cartels and their relationship with more traditional criminal organizations such as the 'Ndrangheta to smuggle cocaine from northern seaports—notably Rotterdam in the Netherlands and Antwerp in Belgium—to different countries across Europe.[71] In effect, their logistical infrastructure, strategic location, and embeddedness with licit trade flows made seaports critical spaces for criminal groups operating across the last stages of the cocaine supply chain.[72] As criminals evade authorities[73] or corrupt security checkpoints,[74] the maritime trafficking modality largely explains the growing connection between Latin America's supply and Europe's cocaine market.

Outside Europe, the situation in other consolidated cocaine markets such as Australia is not that different. While the presence of criminal organizations of Italian origin such as the 'Ndrangheta has been widely documented in Australia,[75] local groups largely control the retail segment of the cocaine supply chain there. Caitlin E. Hughes, David A. Bright, and Jenny Chalmers demonstrate that trafficking organizations are involved in multiple illicit drugs. Although these criminal groups have employed different approaches to diversifying their products (e.g., collaboration with other syndicates and outsourcing services), in all cases there is a division of labor by drug type, and all these groups feature a clear management structure.[76] Meanwhile, less developed markets such as in Africa and Asia, albeit presenting their own peculiarities, show similar features: hierarchical organizations with a single command are largely absent.[77] Instead, the evidence reveals that local criminal groups are relatively small and primarily devoted to midlevel and dealer operations, often relying on brokers or contractors who provide logistical services to connect them with international trafficking organizations. Unlike the criminal networks responsible for international trafficking operations, groups involved in street-level distribution often remain in conditions of poverty and marginalization.[78]

The expansion of the cocaine supply chain beyond traditional markets and the increasing role of criminal groups operating outside Latin America suggest that the underworld has become more fragmented, specialized, and interconnected. The evidence suggests that even powerful criminal organizations rely on affiliated groups or subcontracted brokers, service providers, and independent contractors to perform various logistical activities (e.g., shipping, concealment, transportation, and protection) outside their stronghold territories. In Colombia, for example, relatively large organizations are still responsible for the manufacturing of cocaine, but they subcontract other groups to perform specific activities across other segments of the supply chain. The Clan del Golfo (Gulf Clan) is illustrative of this trend. While this criminal organization controls certain hubs of production and manufacture of cocaine, other activities such as trafficking outside South America, protection of the illicit substance, and street dealing are outsourced to multiple groups. Nonetheless, as Enrique Desmond Arias and Thomas Grisaffi point out, the various participants in the global supply chain are not necessarily aware of the role and activities of others in the chain.[79] This means that criminals often build unstable contacts and relationships with other members of the supply chain, suggesting that actors or groups can be easily substituted if imprisoned or killed.

Yet some criminal organizations have either resisted or attempted to reverse the fragmentation of the cocaine supply chain. For example, associates of Mexican drug cartels like Jalisco Nueva Generación (CJNG; Jalisco New Generation) and Sinaloa are regularly present in Colombia to oversee the manufacture of cocaine and its transport to Mexico before being trafficked into the United States, a core activity that they still largely control.[80] As noted above, other criminal organizations such as the Brazilian PCC,[81] the Italian 'Ndrangheta,[82] the Colombian *traquetos*,[83] and Nigerian criminal groups[84] have expanded their cocaine trafficking operations beyond their stronghold territories. While scholars such as Manuel Castells claim that technological developments—especially in communication and transportation—have helped criminal organizations migrate easily across national borders,[85] the chapters in this book largely demonstrate the contrary. The criminal world around the cocaine supply chain, albeit with certain exceptions, remains predominately territorial. Despite a relatively limited number of organizations such as the Brazilian PCC having recently attempted to seize the opportunity and encompass more than one activity, fragmentation, specialization, and interconnection better describe the ongoing nature of the cocaine supply chain.

Structure of the Book

This edited volume is intended to sharpen our understanding of the actors, processes, and trends in the global cocaine supply chain briefly discussed in this introduction. This work consists of thirteen chapters and a conclusion. Chapter 1 examines the history and structure of cocaine production in the Andes. Susan Brewer-Osorio shows that the rapid expansion of the Andean illicit cocaine industry has been a central factor in shaping regional and country-level relations with the world and especially the United States. Brewer-Osorio emphasizes how cocaine production in the Andes links marginalized rural communities to global markets and how these links affect the population where cocaine is produced. She also demonstrates that criminal organizations and their impacts in the region are diverse. While nonstate armed groups facilitate illicit coca production in Peru and Colombia by protecting and regulating markets in exchange for rents, in Bolivia the absence of an internal armed conflict and the roles of various intermediary actors help to explain the absence of large criminal groups and the relatively low level of drug-related violence.

Law enforcement initiatives have certainly shaped activities across all the stages of the cocaine supply chain. In chapter 2, Carolina Sampó and Valeska Troncoso explore the proliferation of "counterintuitive" routes used by various criminal organizations to export cocaine toward consolidated and new markets. They reveal that these routes, which do not respond exclusively to a lowest cost–greatest profit dynamic, expose criminal organizations to fewer risks than traditional routes and often utilize nontraditional ports of departure. By analyzing the cases of China, South Korea, India, Nepal, and Japan, Sampó and Troncoso show that counterintuitive routes are increasingly playing a key role in the supply of new markets.

Colombia, the world's leading cocaine producer, is analyzed in chapter 3. Héctor Alarcón Barrera and Juan Albarracín explore how the country went from being a negligible player in the global cocaine supply chain before the 1970s to becoming the epicenter of the Andean cocaine trade and the central concern and target of US antidrug efforts in the 1990s and 2000s. Despite Colombia still producing more cocaine than any other country in the world, Alarcón Barrera and Albarracín show that the fragmentation of the country's large cartels has favored the Mexican criminal organizations now controlling major drug-trafficking routes, particularly those that connect the cocaine-producing Andes with the United States. They look at key aspects of the criminal governance of the cocaine supply chain in which Colombian organizations are embedded, including the control of illicit markets and the regulation of social life.

Chapter 4 examines the rise of prison gangs in Brazil and their role in transforming the country into the epicenter of cocaine trafficking destined for Europe, Africa, and Asia. Michael Jerome Wolff effectively demonstrates how the PCC and, to a lesser extent, the CV have sought to control all segments of the cocaine supply chain in order to reduce transactional costs and ensure product supply. By investing in coca-leaf cultivation at its source, eliminating middlemen and competitors along the region's cocaine routes, taking control of major seaports, increasing their presence in other countries' prison facilities, and establishing new partnerships with criminals abroad, Wolff shows that the PCC has successfully transformed itself into a large transnational criminal organization. While the FARC's demobilization in Colombia favored the international expansion of the PCC, prison overcrowding in Brazil, media fame, and ineffective security policies provided ripe conditions for the proliferation of criminal organizations at home.

Drawing on political economy analysis, Daniel Pontón shows in chapter 5 that Ecuador continues to be a transit country in the cocaine supply chain. Despite allegations that Ecuador is increasingly supplying cocaine, the manufacture of the psychoactive substance remains marginal. What has changed, however, is the volume of cocaine passing through the country. Pontón defines this as the "territorial specialization" of Ecuador, a trend that has contributed to transforming the country into a center for the collection and shipment of cocaine abroad through maritime and air routes. It has become, indeed, the main port of departure to Europe. According to Pontón, Ecuador's new role in the cocaine supply chain has been driven by domestic and systemic forces that ultimately favor the development of an economy of criminal services, exacerbating various conflicts among a new generation of criminal gangs such as Los Choneros. Ecuador's current security crisis is illustrated not only by the presence of unprecedented homicide rates but also by the use of violent tactics such as prison massacres, the hanging of corpses, and systematic attacks of public buildings.

The Caribbean's long role in the movement of cocaine from South America to North America and, to a lesser extent, Europe, Africa, and Asia is analyzed in chapter 6. Ivelaw Griffith draws on the "Geonarcotics Framework"—an approach based on the interaction of narcotics, geography, power, and politics—to assess the multiple dimensions and changing dynamics of the cocaine business in the Caribbean. According to Griffith, trafficking dramatizes the importance of geography as a geonarcotics factor in the region. Its proximity to South America, the major cocaine supply source, and to North America, the biggest consumer market, makes the Caribbean a major maritime pathway for cocaine trafficking. Ivelaw shows, however, that Europe is increasingly becoming a major destination for the so-called criminal movers and shakers—state and nonstate actors in charge of cocaine trafficking in the Caribbean. While corrupt police, military, customs, and other state officials participate in trafficking operations, cocaine flows are largely controlled by nonstate actors, both individuals and organized groups.

In chapter 7, Michael Ahn Paarlberg analyzes cocaine trafficking in Central America. He argues that the gangs of the Northern Triangle, the most powerful criminal organizations operating in the region, present a unique negative case in the evolution of drug-trafficking organizations. Mara Salvatrucha (MS-13) and Barrio 18 (18th Street) in particular have played a minor role in the cocaine supply chain. According to Paarlberg, these criminal organizations often support other gangs or cartels already established in the drug trade, although their connections are always brokered with contacts outside of the *maras*. Even in areas where they control territory outright, they have failed to participate in transport activities or handle money above the street level, at best working as intermediaries or distributors for other cartels. Paarlberg explains that their limited role in lucrative transnational criminal enterprises such as cocaine trafficking is a result of the reactive and nearly accidental nature of their geographical expansion, their decentralized and localized structure, and their youthful membership profiles.

Nathan P. Jones and Gary Hale show in chapter 8 how Mexican cartels have become major players in the cocaine supply chain. Mexican organizations gained prominence in the 1990s after increased US pressure on Caribbean trafficking routes and their renegotiation with Colombian traffickers who were no longer in charge of entering the US wholesale and retail cocaine markets. Jones and Hale also demonstrate that the drug war has fragmented organized crime in Mexico, leading to smaller groups, who also diversified their criminal portfolios. They argue, however, that Mexico still harbors a "bipolar criminal structure" with two dominant cartels: the Jalisco New Generation and Sinaloa cartels—the most transnationalized organized crime groups.

The United States, the world's biggest cocaine market, is analyzed in chapter 9. Marten Brienen traces back the origins of cocaine's popularity to the late nineteenth century, when pharmaceutical companies and traders launched the product in various forms. While the psychoactive substance largely disappeared from the US marketplace after World War I, it slowly resurged during the counterculture movement of the 1960s largely as a result of supply increases, price drops, and the establishment of Miami as a hub for cocaine distribution. After analyzing major counterdrug initiatives, especially those developed during the Richard Nixon administration, Brienen demonstrates that cocaine exploded into the public consciousness in 1984, when crack cocaine consumption skyrocketed. According to Brienen, the punitive atmosphere of American politics and US foreign policy efforts aimed at tackling the cocaine supply are a "testament to the self-defeating nature" of that exercise. Indeed, although the focus has been redirected toward the fentanyl crisis, cocaine has not diminished in popularity since the panic of the late 1980s and early 1990s, and the threat the psychoactive substance poses to the American public is still present.

The European cocaine market is analyzed in chapter 10. Due to increasing prevalence rates and the high value of the psychoactive substance, Alberto Aziani shows that cocaine trafficking has become one of the most profitable illegal activities in Europe. The evidence presented by Aziani indicates that not only has Europe become the second-largest market for cocaine in the world, but several countries also export cocaine to other continental destinations as well as the Middle East and Australia. Large European seaports are key hubs of multiple trafficking routes, which constantly adapt due to enforcement pressure. Interestingly, Aziani demonstrates that no single criminal organization exerts monopolistic power across any of the most significant cocaine markets in Europe, a phenomenon largely demonstrated by the continuous decline in cocaine prices over the past decades. By contrast, various actors—including mafia-like organizations—engage in mutually beneficial partnerships across various stages of the cocaine supply chain. While large and structured groups such as the 'Ndrangheta have established extensive distribution networks in Italy and other European countries, often collaborating with Latin American criminal organizations, they tend to be based in Europe and only to a lesser extent operate from departure and transit countries.

The evidence suggests that cocaine is expanding into new markets. In chapter 11, Caroline Agboola addresses Africa's growing role in the cocaine supply chain. Due to its transit and storage capabilities, Africa has become, particularly since the 2000s and 2010s, a key trafficking route for the cocaine produced in Latin America and destined for Europe. While geographic considerations are critical to understanding Africa's central role, Agboola sustains that weak law enforcement, corruption, and lax security have certainly aided the growth of cocaine trafficking within the region. West Africa in particular has become a storage, transit, and consumer constituent in the cocaine supply chain, especially countries such as Nigeria, Guinea-Bissau, Ghana, and Mali. This region is a key distribution point within and outside Africa, including the Asia-Pacific region, the Middle East, and Europe. The widely heterogeneous criminal actors that dominate cocaine trafficking activities in Africa, including Nigerian networks and Mali's armed groups, are loose and transactional structures largely incapable of the complex planning required for cocaine trafficking via maritime routes. Yet Agboola also demonstrates that Nigerian criminal actors are also present in Brazil, although they have not formed large organizations as they often engage in solo work as cocaine traders or in collaboration with other middlemen or criminal groups such as the PCC.

In chapter 12, Molly Charles traces back the cultivation of the coca plant and the manufacture of cocaine in Asia to the operations of Dutch and German manufacturers in Java during the late nineteenth century. Although other countries such as Japan were also actively involved and the cocaine industry prospered between the world wars, the illicit drug has not gained a strong foothold in Asia. However, Charles claims that the region is slowly witnessing new cocaine trafficking routes and emerging markets. The trafficking of large quantities of cocaine is largely routed through the African continent, where Nigerian criminal organizations play a major role. Yet Charles sustains that even if cocaine is more available today than it was a few decades ago, it is very unlikely that it will become the favorite drug of Asia. Cocaine's limited social embeddedness, its higher price vis-à-vis other illicit substances, and other key economic and geographic factors are critical to understanding its limited relevance in Asia.

Cocaine trafficking in Oceania is analyzed in chapter 13. Jose Sousa-Santos shows that the region has become a principal transshipment hub for drugs, with significant implications for populations and local communities. Asian criminal syndicates, Italian mafia groups, and Mexican and South American criminal organizations have benefited from highly lucrative markets in Australia and New Zealand, where the street value of cocaine is among the highest in the world. Through protectionist activities, local criminal organizations such as the Commission have controlled the cocaine market in Australia. Sousa-Santos also demonstrates that although cocaine trafficking in the Pacific islands is comparatively low, Australian and New Zealand outlaw motorcycle gangs have increasingly expanded their criminal activities in the region.

Notes

1. Patricia Ortega Dolz, "La intervención en Galicia del mayor laboratorio de cocaína de Europa confirma que los narcos quieren producir en el continente europeo," *El País* (Madrid), April 13, 2023, https://elpais.com/espana/2023-04-13/la-intervencion-en-galicia-del-mayor-laboratorio-de-cocaina-de-europa-confirma-que-los-narcos-quieren-producir-en-el-continente-europeo.html.

2. Shishir Gupta, "NCB Red-Flags Mumbai as Cocaine Capital of India," *Hindustan Times* (New Delhi), April 2, 2021, https://www.hindustantimes.com/india-news/ncb-red-flags-mumbai-as-cocaine-capital-of-india-101617347061903.html.

3. United Nations Office on Drugs and Crime, *Global Report on Cocaine 2023* (Vienna: United Nations, 2023).

4. United Nations Office on Drugs and Crime, *Global Report on Cocaine 2023*.

5. United Nations Office on Drugs and Crime, *World Drug Report 2021* (Vienna: United Nations, 2021).

6. Jason Eligh, "A Powder Storm: The Cocaine Markets of East and Southern Africa," Global Initiative Against Transnational Organized Crime, December 2022, https://globalinitiative.net/wp-content/uploads/2022/12/Jason-Eligh-A-Powder-of-Storm-The-cocaine-markets-of-East-and-southern-Africa-GI-TOC-2022.pdf.

7. United Nations Office on Drugs and Crime, *Global Report on Cocaine 2023*.

8. Douwe den Held, "The 'Ndrangheta: Versatile Middlemen in the Cocaine Pipeline to Europe," InSight Crime, November 23, 2022, https://insightcrime.org/investigations/ndrangheta-versatile-middlemen-cocaine-pipeline-to-europe/.

9. Francesca Calandra, "Between Local and Global: The 'Ndrangheta's Drug Trafficking Route," *International Annals of Criminology* 55, no. 1 (2017): 78–98.

10. See Alberto Aziani's chapter in this volume, "Cocaine Trafficking in Europe."

11. See, for example, Terence K. Hopkins and Immanuel Wallerstein, "Patterns of Development of the Modern World-System," *Review* 1, no. 2 (1977): 111–45.

12. Immanuel Wallerstein, *The Modern World-System I: Capitalist Agriculture and the Origins of the European World-Economy in the Sixteenth Century* (New York: Academic Press, 1974).

13. Anayansi Dávila, Nicholas Magliocca, Kendra McSweeney, and Ximena Rueda, "Spatialising Illicit Commodity Chains: Comparing Coffee and Cocaine," *Area* 53, no. 3 (September 2021): 501–10.

14. Sidney W. Mintz, *Sweetness and Power: The Place of Sugar in Modern History* (Harmondsworth, England: Penguin, 1986).

15. Jennifer Bair and Marion Werner, "Commodity Chains and the Uneven Geographies of Global Capitalism: A Disarticulations Perspective," *Environment and Planning A: Economy and Space* 43, no. 5 (2011): 988–97.

16. Gary Gereffi and Miguel Korzeniewicz, *Commodity Chains and Global Capitalism* (Westport, CT: Greenwood Press, 1994).

17. Peter Gibbon and Stefano Ponte, *Trading Down: Africa, Value Chains, and the Global Economy* (Philadelphia: Temple University Press, 2005); and Gary Gereffi, John Humphrey, and Timothy Sturgeon, "The Governance of Global Value Chains," *Review of International Political Economy* 12, no. 1 (2005): 78–104.

18. Phillip A. Hough, "Disarticulations and Commodity Chains: Cattle, Coca, and Capital Accumulation Along Colombia's Agricultural Frontier," *Environment and Planning A: Economy and Space* 43, no. 5 (2011): 1016–34.

19. Jennifer Bair, "Global Commodity Chains: Genealogy and Review," In *Frontiers in Commodity Chain Research*, ed. Jennifer Bair (Stanford, CA: Stanford University Press, 2009), 1–34.

20. Benjamin Neimark, Sango Mahanty, and Wolfram H. Dressler, "Mapping Value in a 'Green' Commodity Frontier: Revisiting Commodity Chain Analysis," *Development and Change* 47, no. 2 (March 2016): 240–65.

21. Bair and Werner, "Commodity Chains and the Uneven Geographies of Global Capitalism," 993.

22. Christian Berndt and Marc Boeckler, "Performative Regional (Dis)Integration: Transnational Markets, Mobile Commodities, and Bordered North-South Differences," *Environment and Planning A: Economy and Space* 43, no. 5 (2011): 1057–78.

23. Peter H. Reuter, *Disorganized Crime: The Economics of the Visible Hand* (Cambridge, MA: MIT Press, 1983).

24. Channing May, *Transnational Crime and the Developing World* (Washington, DC: Global Financial Integrity, 2017).

25. Kathryn Ledebur, "Bolivia: Clear Consequences," in *Drugs and Democracy in Latin America: The Impact of U.S. Policy*, ed. Coletta A. Youngers and Eileen Rosin (Boulder, CO: Lynne Rienner, 2005), 143–84; and Menno Vellinga, "The Political Economy of the Drug Industry: Its Structure and Functioning," in *The Political Economy of the Drug Industry: Latin America and the International System*, ed. Menno Vellinga (Gainesville: University Press of Florida, 2004), 3–22.

26. Philippe Bourgois, "Decolonising Drug Studies in an Era of Predatory Accumulation," *Third World Quarterly* 39, no. 2 (2018): 385–98.

27. Jonathan P. Caulkins, Emma Disley, Marina Tzvetkova, Mafalda Pardal, Hemali Shah, and Xiaoke Zhang, "Modeling the Structure and Operation of Drug Supply Chains: The Case of Cocaine and Heroin in Italy and Slovenia," *International Journal of Drug Policy* 31 (2016): 64–73.

28. Juan Gabriel Tokatlian, preface to *Drogas, política y actores sociales en la Argentina democrática*, by Sebastián A. Cutrona (Buenos Aires: Editorial Universitaria de Buenos Aires), i–vii.

29. Bruce Michael Bagley, "Drug Trafficking and Organized Crime in the Americas: Major Trends in the Twenty-First Century," Woodrow Wilson International Center for Scholars, Latin American Program, August 2012, https://www.wilsoncenter.org/sites/default/files/media/documents/publication/BB%20Final.pdf.

30. Enrique Obando, "U.S. Policy Toward Peru: At Odds for Twenty Years," in *Addicted to Failure: U.S. Security Policy in Latin America and the Andean Region*, ed. Brian Loveman (Lanham, MD: Rowman and Littlefield, 2006), 169–96.

31. The VRAEM encompasses the valley of the Apurímac, Ene, and Mantaro Rivers.

32. Ledebur, "Bolivia: Clear Consequences."

33. Paul Gootenberg, *Andean Cocaine: The Making of a Global Drug* (Chapel Hill: University of North Carolina Press, 2008).

34. Francisco E. Thoumi, *Illegal Drugs, Economy, and Society in the Andes* (Washington, DC: Woodrow Wilson Center Press; Baltimore: Johns Hopkins University Press, 2003).

35. United Nations Office on Drugs and Crime, *Global Report on Cocaine 2023*.

36. Enrique Desmond Arias and Thomas Grisaffi, "Introduction: The Moral Economy of the Cocaine Trade," in *Cocaine: From Coca Fields to the Streets*, ed. Enrique Desmond Arias and Thomas Grisaffi (Durham, NC: Duke University Press, 2021), 1–40.

37. Sebastián A. Cutrona, "El desertor latino: Cómo la Argentina rechazó el modelo norteamericano de la guerra contra las drogas," *Desarrollo Económico* 58, no. 226 (January–April 2019): 399–432; and Sebastián A. Cutrona, *Challenging the U.S.-Led War on Drugs: Argentina in Comparative Perspective* (New York: Routledge, 2017).

38. Carolina Sampó and Valeska Troncoso, "Cocaine Trafficking from Non-Traditional Ports: Examining the Cases of Argentina, Chile, and Uruguay," *Trends in Organized Crime* 26, no. 1 (January 2022): 235–57.

39. Robby Roks, Lieselot Bisschop, and Richard Staring, "Getting a Foot in the Door: Spaces of Cocaine Trafficking in the Port of Rotterdam," *Trends in Organized Crime* 24, no. 2 (June 2021): 171–88.

40. Marleen Easton, "Policing Flows of Drugs in the Harbor of Antwerp: A Nodal-Network Analysis," in *Maritime Supply Chains*, ed. Thierry Vanelslander and Christa Sys (Amsterdam: Elsevier, 2020), 115–34.

41. Peter H. Reuter and Mark A. R. Kleiman, "Risks and Prices: An Economic Analysis of Drug Enforcement," *Crime and Justice* 7 (1986): 289–340.

42. Caulkins et al., "Modeling the Structure and Operation of Drug Supply Chains."

43. Francesco Calderoni, "The Structure of Drug Trafficking Mafias: The 'Ndrangheta and Cocaine," *Crime, Law and Social Change* 58, no. 3 (December 2012): 321–49.

44. Peter H. Reuter and John Haaga, *The Organization of High-Level Drug Markets: An Exploratory Study* (Santa Monica, CA: RAND Corporation, 1989); and Reuter, *Disorganized Crime*.

45. J. Bryan Page, "Coca, Cocaine, and Consumption: Trends and Antitrends," in *Drug Trafficking, Organized Crime, and Violence in the Americas Today*, ed. Bruce Michael Bagley and Jonathan D. Rosen (Gainesville: University Press of Florida, 2015), 27–42.

46. Thomas M. Mieczkowski, "The Prevalence of Drug Use in the United States," *Crime and Justice* 20 (1996): 349–414.

47. David F. Musto, *The American Disease: Origins of Narcotics Control* (New York: Oxford University Press, 1999).

48. United Nations Office for Drug Control and Crime Prevention, *Global Illicit Drug Trends 2001* (Vienna: United Nations, 2001); and United Nations Office for Drug Control and Crime Prevention, *Global Illicit Drug Trends 2000* (Vienna: United Nations, 2000).

49. United Nations Office on Drugs and Crime, *Global Report on Cocaine 2023*.

50. Paul Gootenberg, "Shifting South: Cocaine's Historical Present and the Changing Politics of the Drug War, 1975–2015," in *Cocaine: From Coca Fields to the Streets*, ed. Enrique Desmond Arias and Thomas Grisaffi (Durham: Duke University Press, 2021), 287–316.

51. Thoumi, *Illegal Drugs, Economy, and Society*.

52. Guy Gugliotta and Jeff Leen, *Kings of Cocaine* (New York: HarperCollins, 1990).

53. María Clemencia Ramírez Lemus, Kimberly Stanton, and John Walsh, "Colombia: A Vicious Circle of Drugs and War," in *Drugs and Democracy in Latin America: The Impact of U.S. Policy*, ed. Coletta A. Youngers and Eileen Rosin (Boulder, CO: Lynne Rienner, 2005), 99–142.

54. Jonathan D. Rosen, "The War on Drugs in Colombia: A History of Failure," in *New Approaches to Drug Policies: A Time for Change*, ed. Marten W. Brienen and Jonathan D. Rosen (New York: Palgrave Macmillan, 2015), 58–72; and Bagley, "Drug Trafficking and Organized Crime."

55. Peter H. Reuter, "Drug Markets and Organized Crime," in *The Oxford Handbook of Organized Crime*, ed. Letizia Paoli (New York: Oxford University Press, 2014), 359–80.

56. The term *paisa* refers to the culture prevailing in the Department of Antioquia, especially its capital city, Medellín.

57. Havana was a major trafficking hub until 1959. After the Cuban Revolution, some of the criminal actors involved in the cocaine industry moved to Miami, where they established new trafficking networks.

58. As of 2024, 90 percent of the cocaine arriving in the United States still comes from Colombia. For more information, see Drug Enforcement Administration, "Drug Fact Sheet," April 2020, https://www.dea.gov/sites/default/files/2020-06/Cocaine-2020_1.pdf; Michael Kenney, "The Architecture of Drug Trafficking: Network Forms of Organisation in the Colombian Cocaine Trade," *Global Crime* 8, no. 3 (2007): 233–59; and Bruce Michael Bagley, "Colombia and the War on Drugs," *Foreign Affairs* 67, no. 1 (Fall 1988): 70–92.

59. Francisco E. Thoumi, "Illegal Drugs in Colombia: From Illegal Economic Boom to Social Crisis," in *The Political Economy of the Drug Industry: Latin America and the International System*, ed. Menno Vellinga (Gainesville: University Press of Florida, 2004), 70–84.

60. Bagley, "Drug Trafficking and Organized Crime."

61. Thoumi, "Illegal Drugs in Colombia."

62. Bilal Y. Saab and Alexandra W. Taylor, "Criminality and Armed Groups: A Comparative Study of FARC and Paramilitary Groups in Colombia," *Studies in Conflict and Terrorism* 32, no. 6 (2009): 455–75; and David Maher and Andrew Thomson, "A Precarious Peace? The Threat of Paramilitary Violence to the Peace Process in Colombia," *Third World Quarterly* 39, no. 11 (2018): 2142–72.

63. Laura H. Atuesta and Yocelyn Samantha Pérez-Dávila, "Fragmentation and Cooperation: The Evolution of Organized Crime in Mexico," *Trends in Organized Crime* 21, no. 3 (September 2017): 235–61.

64. Bagley, "Drug Trafficking and Organized Crime."

65. Patrick Corcoran, "Italy's 'Ndrangheta Mafia: A Powerful Ally for the Zetas," InSight Crime, August 10, 2011, https://insightcrime.org/news/analysis/italys-ndrangheta-mafia-a-powerful-ally-for-the-zetas/.

66. United Nations Office on Drugs and Crime and Europol, *Cocaine Insights 1: The Illicit Trade of Cocaine from Latin America to Europe; From Oligopolies to Free-for-All?* (Vienna: United Nations, 2021), https://www.unodc.org/documents/data-and-analysis/cocaine/Cocaine_Insights_2021.pdf.

67. Frank O. Mora, "Victims of the Balloon Effect: Drug Trafficking and U.S. Policy in Brazil and the Southern Cone of Latin America," *Journal of Social, Political, and Economic Studies* 21, no. 2 (Summer 1996): 115–40.

68. Michael Jerome Wolff, "Organized Crime and the State in Brazil," in *The Criminalization of States: The Relationship Between States and Organized Crime*, ed. Jonathan D. Rosen, Bruce Michael Bagley, and Jorge Chabat (Lanham, MD: Lexington Books, 2019), 323–40.

69. Benjamin Lessing and Graham Denyer Willis, "Legitimacy in Criminal Governance: Managing a Drug Empire from Behind Bars," *American Political Science Review* 113, no. 2 (May 2019): 584–606; and Enrique Desmond Arias, *Drugs and Democracy in Rio de Janeiro: Trafficking, Social Networks, and Public Security* (Chapel Hill: University of North Carolina Press, 2006).

70. Pierre Tremblay, Maurice Cusson, and Carlo Morselli, "Market Offenses and Limits to Growth," *Crime, Law and Social Change* 29, no. 4 (1998): 311–30.

71. José Luis Gil Valero, "The Western Balkan Organised Crime at European Union: The Albanian Mafia—Does It Pose a Real Threat?," *European Law Enforcement Research Bulletin* 22 (Summer 2022): 79–99.

72. Roks, Bisschop, and Staring, "Getting a Foot in the Door"; Anna Sergi, "Playing Pac-Man in Portville: Policing the Dilution and Fragmentation of Drug Importations Through Major Seaports," *European Journal of Criminology* 19, no. 4 (July 2022): 674–91; and Vincenzo Ruggiero, "Organised and Transnational Crime in Europe," in *The Routledge Handbook of European Criminology*, ed. Sophie Body-Gendrot, Mike Hough, Klára Kerezsi, René Lévy, and Sonja Snacken (Abingdon, Oxon., England: Routledge, 2014), 154–67.

73. Damián Zaitch, "From Cali to Rotterdam: Perceptions of Colombian Cocaine Traffickers on the Dutch Port," *Crime, Law and Social Change* 38, no. 3 (2002): 239–66; and Edward Kleemans, Marten Brienen, Henk van de Bunt, Ruud Kouwenberg, G. Paulides,

and J. Barensen, *Georganiseerde criminaliteit in Nederland: Tweede rapportage op basis van de WODC-Monitor* (The Hague: Ministerie van Justitie, 2002).

74. For the Netherlands, see Renushka Madarie and Edwin Kruisbergen, "Transit-criminaliteit en logistieke knooppunten in Nederland," *Justitiële Verkenningen* 45, no. 5 (December 2019): 29–51. For Belgium, see Easton, "Policing Flows of Drugs"; and Freja de Middeleer, Stephan Van Nimwegen, Rik Ceulen, Sabine Gerbrands, Elke Roevens, Antonius Spapens, Letizia Paoli, Cyrille Fijnaut, Benny Van Camp, Brice de Ruyver, and Charlotte Colman, *Illegale drugsmarkten in België en Nederland: Communicerende vaten?* (Brussels: Belgian Science Policy Office, 2018).

75. Anna Sergi, "Polycephalous 'Ndrangheta: Crimes, Behaviours and Organisation of the Calabrian Mafia in Australia," *Australian and New Zealand Journal of Criminology* 52, no. 1 (March 2019): 3–22; and Anna Sergi, "The Evolution of the Australian 'Ndrangheta: An Historical Perspective," *Australian and New Zealand Journal of Criminology* 48, no. 2 (June 2015): 155–74.

76. Caitlin E. Hughes, David A. Bright, and Jenny Chalmers, "Social Network Analysis of Australian Poly-Drug Trafficking Networks: How Do Drug Traffickers Manage Multiple Illicit Drugs?," *Social Networks* 51 (2017): 135–47.

77. United Nations Office on Drugs and Crime, *Transnational Organized Crime in West Africa: A Threat Assessment* (Vienna: United Nations, 2013); and Vanda Felbab-Brown, "The Political Economy of Illegal Domains in India and China," *International Lawyer* 43, no. 4 (2009): 1411–28.

78. Molly Charles, K. S. Nair, Gabriel Britto, and Anthony A. Das, "The Bombay Underworld: A Descriptive Account and Its Role in Drug Trade," in *Globalisation, Drugs and Criminalisation: Final Research Report on Brazil, China, India and Mexico*, ed. Christian Geffray, Guilhem Fabre, and Michel Schiray (Marseille: UNESCO, 2002).

79. Arias and Grisaffi, "Introduction: The Moral Economy of the Cocaine Trade."

80. United Nations Office on Drug and Crime, *Global Report on Cocaine 2023*.

81. See Michael Jerome Wolff's chapter in this volume, "Cocaine in Brazil: The Emergent Center of a Globalized Market." See also Ana Isadora Meneguetti and Marcos Alan Ferreira, "Transnational Gangs in South America: The Expansion of the Primeiro Comando da Capital to Paraguay," *Urban Crime: An International Journal* 1, no. 2 (November 2020): 29–53; Marcos Alan Ferreira, "Brazilian Criminal Organizations as Transnational Violent Non-State Actors: A Case Study of the Primeiro Comando da Capital (PCC)," *Trends in Organized Crime* 22, no. 61 (June 2019): 148–65; and Mariano César Bartolomé and Vicente Ventura Barreiro, "Narcotráfico en América del Sur más allá del bloque andino: Los casos de Argentina y Brasil," *Revista de Relaciones Internacionales, Estrategia y Seguridad* 14, no. 1 (2020): 205–22.

82. Federico Varese, "How Mafias Migrate: Transplantation, Functional Diversification, and Separation," *Crime and Justice* 49, no. 3 (June 2020): 289–337; Rocco Sciarrone and Luca Storti, "The Territorial Expansion of Mafia-Type Organized Crime: The Case of the Italian Mafia in Germany," *Crime, Law and Social Change* 61, no. 1 (February 2014): 37–60; Calderoni, "The Structure of Drug Trafficking Mafias"; and Federico Varese, *Mafias on the Move: How Organized Crime Conquers New Territories* (Princeton, NJ: Princeton University Press, 2011).

83. Damián Zaitch, *Trafficking Cocaine: Colombian Drug Entrepreneurs in the Netherlands* (The Hague: Kluwer Law International, 2002).

84. United Nations Office on Drugs and Crime, *Global Report on Cocaine 2023*; Jude Roys Oboh, *Cocaine Hoppers: Nigerian International Cocaine Trafficking* (Lanham, MD: Lexington Books, 2021); Stephen Ellis, *This Present Darkness: A History of Nigerian Organized Crime* (New York: Oxford University Press, 2016); and Phil Williams, "Nigerian Criminal Organizations," in *The Oxford Handbook of Organized Crime*, ed. Letizia Paoli (New York: Oxford University Press, 2014), 254–69.

85. Manuel Castells, *The Information Age: Economy, Society and Culture*, vol. 3, *End of Millennium* (Hoboken, NJ: Blackwell, 1998).

CHAPTER 1

The Andean Cocaine Trade

Global Reach and Local Impacts

Susan Brewer-Osorio

The Andean countries of Bolivia, Colombia, and Peru have monopolized the production of illicit cocaine for global consumption since the 1940s. As such, this region of northwestern South America is central to the global cocaine trade and international efforts to combat it, with consequences for regional development, security, and politics. To understand these dynamics, this chapter examines the history and structure of cocaine production in the Andes, emphasizing how cocaine production links marginalized communities to global markets and how these links in turn affect the communities where cocaine is produced. The chapter starts with an overview of the history of coca and cocaine production in the region, followed by a description of the complex Andean cocaine supply chain. Finally, the chapter concludes with a discussion of the twenty-first-century boom in global cocaine consumption and implications for the Andean region.

History and Trends

An Andean Crop

The modern drug cocaine is made from an alkaloid of the ancient coca leaf, a benign herbal stimulant native to the Andean region of South America. Thousands of years before the discovery of the potent drug cocaine hydrochloride (HCl) in 1859, Andean people cultivated and consumed raw coca as a cultural practice and to stave off hunger and fatigue.[1] Coca was cultivated throughout the Inca Empire (1438–1533), spanning contemporary Peru and Bolivia and parts of Colombia, Ecuador, Argentina, and Chile.[2] Later, Spanish colonial authorities encouraged large-scale coca production on haciendas, particularly in present-day Bolivia, to supply the Indigenous workers of the great silver mines of Potosí, which was linked by trade routes to the Yungas of La Paz, Bolivia's largest coca-growing region.[3]

In contemporary Bolivia, coca remains an important cash crop that is legally produced and consumed by hundreds of thousands of Bolivians, usually by chewing the raw leaf or as herbal tea.[4] In contrast, Peru and Colombia have very small markets for legal coca, which is consumed in smaller and more marginalized Indigenous communities. Outside of these legal markets, the vast majority of coca produced in present-day Bolivia, Colombia, and Peru supplies the illicit global cocaine trade. Indeed, these three Andean nations have a monopoly on illicit cocaine production.

While similarly positioned in the global cocaine supply chain, Andean countries have distinct historical and cultural relationships with coca and cocaine, with implications for how each country affects and is affected by the cocaine industry. In Bolivia, coca is woven into the cultural fabric of the nation and regarded as sacred by the majority Indigenous population of the western highlands.[5] Hence, Bolivia has a long history of coca production but did not engage in global cocaine production and export until the late 1950s.[6] Moreover, in Bolivia there is more social resistance to drug control efforts to suppress coca compared to Colombia and Peru.[7]

In contrast, in contemporary Peru the coca leaf is not strongly linked to national identity and is instead associated with marginalized Indigenous identities. However, Peru was central to early cocaine trade circuits and was the first Andean country to establish the domestic production of legal (and later illegal) cocaine for export.[8] Finally, Colombia did not produce significant coca or cocaine prior to the 1970s. However, while a latecomer to the cocaine industry, Colombia emerged as the world's largest supplier of both illicit raw coca and cocaine by the mid-1990s and held that position for most of the early twenty-first century.[9]

Global Cocaine

While coca is a native Andean crop, the potent drug cocaine hydrochloride (HCl) was first produced in Germany in 1859. There, the chemist Albert Niemann created powder HCl by chemically isolating the cocaine alkaloid of a Peruvian coca leaf.[10] Two decades later, Niemann's discovery led to a global boom in research on coca and cocaine, which in turn generated a boom in legal Peruvian coca and cocaine production for global markets.[11] In the late nineteenth century, leading pharmaceutical firms like Merck and Bayer promoted cocaine as a topical anesthetic.[12] At the same time, raw Peruvian coca was exported and used as a stimulant additive for popular tonics like Coca-Cola and the French elixir Vin Mariani, consumed throughout North America and Europe.[13]

Despite cocaine's early popularity, the period from 1890 through the 1920s saw a wave of anticocaine sentiment in the United States and Europe, the largest markets for coca and cocaine products, followed by increasingly punitive national legislation to restrict sales and use.[14] The anticocaine movement started with medical communities raising concerns about cocaine toxicity in a context of reduced demand for medical cocaine after the discovery of a safer synthetic alternative, Novocain.[15] Beyond the medical community, antivice social organizations and nativist groups in the United States associated coca and cocaine use to moral decline and to crime within immigrant and Black communities.[16] Finally, at the international level, the League of Nations extended its long-standing campaign against the opium trade to include coca and cocaine during the 1920s, and later the United Nations took on the League's international anticoca and anticocaine efforts.[17]

The prohibitionist movement supported progressively more punitive domestic laws prohibiting coca and cocaine production, sale, and use.[18] Indeed, by the time legal cocaine was internationally banned under the 1961 UN Single Convention on Narcotic Drugs, national laws for prohibiting cocaine and eradicating coca were already widespread. This national legislation drove the cocaine industry underground and across borders, laying the groundwork for the global illicit cocaine trade.[19] Moreover, Peru and later Bolivia emerged as the world's sole suppliers for this emerging illicit trade after German and Dutch efforts to root coca export economies in colonial Taiwan and Java collapsed during World War II.[20]

While the Andes claimed an early monopoly on cocaine production, cocaine had very a minor position in the global drug trade prior to the late twentieth-century illicit cocaine boom. During the 1960s and 1970s, Chilean and Cuban smugglers dominated the nascent cocaine trade, which mainly consisted of transporting small, suitcase-sized shipments from Andean source countries to markets in North America and Europe.[21] However, Cuban and Chilean trafficking networks were stifled by the 1959 Cuban Revolution and later the 1973 Chilean coup.[22] These changes generated a space for Colombian smugglers to respond to skyrocketing demand for illegal recreational cocaine, mainly in the United States.

During the 1970s and 1980s, booming demand for pure and tempered (crack) cocaine, particularly in the United States, galvanized a rapid expansion of the Andean illicit cocaine industry, with Colombia as the main producer and smuggler of cocaine made from Peruvian and Bolivian coca leaf. Between 1980 and 1985, cocaine consumption in the United States tripled from about thirty-four to one hundred metric tons a year.[23] Colombian smugglers capitalized on several advantages for making and trafficking cocaine, including proximity to coca production in neighboring Peru, the availability of precursor chemicals for making cocaine in Colombia, and established smuggling routes and distribution networks in the United States previously used for trafficking luxury goods and marijuana.[24] During the 1980s, Colombian cocaine smugglers consolidated under two hierarchical cartels based in the cities of Medellín and Cali.[25] Finally, beyond market advantages, both cartels employed assassins and paramilitaries to violently remove market competitors and dissuade government efforts to suppress the cocaine industry.[26]

Finally, while the Colombian cartels wielded enormous power, their dominion did not extend to the production of coca and *pasta básica de cocaína* (PBC; cocaine paste), an intermediary material between raw coca and cocaine base.[27] Instead, these activities were, and largely remain, peasant cottage industries in remote areas where economic opportunities are limited and state presence is weak.[28] Colombian cartels purchased coca and PBC in Peru and Bolivia until the early 1990s, when Colombian coca production surpassed that of Peru and Bolivia.[29] By the late 1990s, Colombia had become the world's largest source country for illicit coca and cocaine, a standing that it mostly maintained during the first two decades of the twenty-first century.

Cocaine Prohibition in the Andes

The Andean region's critical role in cocaine production has been a central factor shaping regional and country-level relations with the world and especially the United States. In the 1980s, the US government began framing cocaine production as a national security threat[30] and advocating for punitive drug control interventions including bolstering the security forces of the Andean producer countries and supporting the forced eradication of coca crops.[31] These punitive policies often come at the expense of human rights and democratic governance.[32] Moreover, Andean countries waver in their responses to US pressures, resulting in different national drug control strategies.

In the case of Peru, the government response has been mostly cooperative with US-supported punitive approaches but has also softened over time.[33] In the early 1980s, Peru capitulated to US pressure to eradicate coca and later conducted air raids on cocaine labs and airstrips. These measures did little to reduce cocaine production and galvanized significant social resistance.[34] Moreover, Peru cooperated with the 1989 Andean Regional Initiative (ARI), a US foreign aid package to combat the Andean cocaine trade. The ARI had some success dismantling the airbridge linking Colombian traffickers to Peruvian coca, resulting in a proliferation of coca farms in neighboring Colombia.[35] Since the 1990s, Peru has asserted more national autonomy over its drug control policy in part because it has reduced dependence on international aid.[36] This shift resulted in more emphasis on unusually comprehensive alternative development (AD) programs with some notable success.[37]

In contrast to Peru, Bolivia has become more resistant to the US strategy due to domestic pressure to protect coca leaf as an important cash crop and a symbol of national identity. Bolivian resistance began as a response to nearly two decades of cooperation with US-supported forced eradication of coca in the 1980s and 1990s outside the areas where coca is traditionally cultivated for legal consumption. The forced eradication effectively reduced Bolivia's coca output from 25 percent of global production in 1990 to about 16 percent in 2005, and is linked to human rights violations and the destruction of livelihoods.[38]

In the late 1990s, Bolivia's so-called nontraditional coca farmers and allied social movements formed a new political party called Movimiento al Socialismo (MAS; Movement Toward Socialism). In 2005, MAS leader Evo Morales Ayma (2006–2019) was elected president of Bolivia. After evicting the US ambassador and the Drug Enforcement Administration (DEA) from the country, the new MAS government implemented a sweeping reform called "Coca Yes, Cocaine No" (CYCN) that decriminalized coca cultivation while prioritizing human rights.[39] In 2017, CYCN was deepened under a new coca law that expanded legal production from twelve thousand to twenty-two thousand hectares.[40] These reforms significantly reduced illicit coca cultivation,[41] even while Bolivian farmers continue to participate in the cocaine trade.[42] Moreover, the reforms galvanized new social resistance from the traditional coca farmers who backed the unconstitutional removal of President Morales in 2019.[43]

Finally, of the three Andean countries, Colombia has been the most consistent US ally in the drug war and a leading recipient of US military aid. In 2000, the US and Colombian governments initiated Plan Colombia, a US foreign aid and military initiative at the center of US-Colombian bilateral counterdrug cooperation. Initially construed as a counternarcotics initiative, Plan Colombia (2000–2015) was expanded after 2001 to include counterinsurgency aid to fight so-called narcoguerrillas, or leftist insurgents with ties to the drug trade.[44] During the first five years of Plan Colombia, the United States spent US$5 billion to equip and train the Colombian army and antinarcotics battalions and to support aerial fumigation of coca plants with herbicide.[45]

Plan Colombia is celebrated for significantly reducing coca production in targeted areas,[46] but these gains were more than offset by a "balloon effect" wherein eradication caused cultivation to spread to other areas of Colombia and Peru.[47] Moreover, Plan Colombia controversially bolstered the Colombian military despite its poor human rights record and recognized collusion with violent narco-paramilitaries.[48] Indeed, Plan Colombia funds were implicated in a human rights scandal in which Colombian military units executed some five thousand civilians and posed them as guerrilla fighters in order to access performance bonuses.[49] In 2015, the US government repackaged Plan Colombia as "Peace Colombia," reflecting reduced military spending and more emphasis on institution building and development.[50]

The US-led war on drugs has thus far failed to destroy the cocaine industry in the Andes, but it has contributed significantly to its transformation over time.[51] For example, US-led efforts to close the Caribbean route to Colombian cocaine traffickers in the 1980s weakened the Medellín cartel but also pushed cocaine routes west, elevating the role of violent Mexican cartels[52] and aggravating gang-related security threats in Central America.[53] Moreover, while US support was central to Colombian security forces' takedown of the Medellín and Cali cartels, these victories merely contributed to decentralizing control of the cocaine trade across more than two hundred Colombian crime groups that are more difficult to detect and dismantle.[54]

In the twenty-first century, Andean cocaine production was again transformed by declining cocaine consumption in the United States combined with an unprecedented boom in cocaine consumption in Europe, South America, Africa, Asia, and the Middle East.[55] As occurred in the past, market adaptations to global market change have expanded the harmful impacts associated with the cocaine industry and repressive efforts to combat it to new areas and populations. At the same time, the recent boom triggered new innovations in Andean cocaine production and trafficking that have reduced barriers to participation while rendering punitive policies even less effective.

The Cocaine Supply Chain

The global cocaine trade that emerged in the twentieth century is organized around an international division of labor, with asymmetrical power between the Andean source countries that produce, wholesale, and traffic cocaine, and the consumer countries, historically in the Global North, that retail, deal, and launder money internationally.[56] This section describes cocaine production in the Andes from the cultivation of raw coca leaf to processed PBC, and finally to pure cocaine hydrochloride.[57] In Peru, Bolivia, and Colombia, these upstream activities employ hundreds of thousands of farmers, processors, merchants, smugglers, and crime bosses. Similar to global relations between producer and consumer countries, relations between actors at the lowest and highest levels of the cocaine production chain are shaped by extreme power imbalances, with profits concentrating at the top.[58]

Raw Coca

The global cocaine industry starts with the production of raw coca leaf in remote areas of Peru, Bolivia, and Colombia, where coca cultivation constitutes a peasant cottage industry. Most coca farmers plot less than two hectares of coca, and most coca plots are in areas where remoteness, poor infrastructure, and deficient public services are obstacles to making a living from legal agricultural production.[59] Indeed, while coca farmers claim only a miniscule share of cocaine profits, income from coca still far exceeds that of other cash crops in most of these areas.[60] In this way, Andean integration into the global cocaine trade is rooted in the political and economic marginalization of large numbers of rural Andean inhabitants.

In the twenty-first century, much Andean coca is still cultivated in the traditional zones of the western highlands, or in areas where coca production predates the nineteenth-century discovery of cocaine by at least a few hundred years and is mainly for legal domestic sale and consumption. In addition, some coca is grown legally outside traditional zones for both licit and illicit markets. For example, Bolivian law allows up to twenty-two thousand hectares of legal coca cultivation for farmers in traditional zones,[61] and in other designated areas for farmers with union membership.[62] Likewise, Peruvian farmers can register to legally cultivate and market coca through the state agency Empresa Nacional de la Coca (ENACO; the National Coca Company).[63]

However, despite some coca production for legal domestic use, since the mid-twentieth century, the vast majority of coca produced in the Andes is cultivated illicitly to supply the illicit cocaine market.[64] Farmers shifted to illegal coca cultivation in the mid- to late twentieth century mainly because markets for legal coca and other agricultural commodities were and remain comparably small and unprofitable.[65] The shift to the illicit expanded coca cultivation from the western highlands to the more remote agricultural frontiers of the eastern Andes including the Peruvian Ene Valley, the Bolivian Chapare, and the Colombian Amazon and eastern llanos.[66] The expansion of illicit coca in the Andes was supported by five coalescing factors: state abandonment, rising external demand for cocaine, ease of coca production, economic crisis, and internal armed conflict in the cases of Peru and Colombia.

First, the Andean state played a key role in generating favorable conditions for illicit coca cultivation to flourish. In the context of the Cold War and the US-funded Alliance for Progress, Andean governments implemented development projects to encourage the colonization of their eastern agricultural frontiers, including land grants, subsidies, and highway construction.[67] In Peru and Bolivia, state-led colonization followed sweeping top-down agrarian reforms that caused land overcrowding in western coastal Peru and the Bolivian highlands.[68] In Colombia, state-led colonization of the southern and eastern frontiers is not associated with agrarian reforms but was instead a strategy to deflate demand for land redistribution by making public lands available to landless peasants from the highlands.[69] In all three countries, state-led colonization spurred population growth in the remote eastern frontiers. However, most accompanying development projects either failed or were abandoned, leaving the newly arrived *colonos* (colonizers) in relatively isolated areas and without economic prospects.[70]

Second, state abandonment of the eastern frontier coincided with the burgeoning of the global cocaine industry in the 1960s and 1970s, which caused a steep rise in coca prices. Moreover, beyond robust prices, a third factor in the expansion of illicit coca was its appeal as an ideal cash crop requiring little skill or capital. Coca is nonperishable, grows easily in diverse soil alongside other crops, and is easily stored, transported, and marketed to eager buyers.[71] In addition, coca shrubs begin producing within a relatively short twelve to fifteen months and produce for an impressive fifteen years, yielding three or four harvests annually.[72]

The Peruvian case illustrates the link between illicit coca and state abandonment in a context of rising cocaine demand. In Peru, coca first expanded in two regions (the Upper Huallaga [UHV] and adjacent Monzón Valleys), both located in San Martín on the eastern slopes of Huánuco Province northeast of Lima, and in the valley of the rivers Apurímac, Ene, and Mantaro (VRAEM) a high jungle region southeast of Lima. The UHV and Monzón have a history of coca production for Peru's legal coca industry.[73] However, in the 1970s a failed state-managed cooperative farming experiment left thousands of newly arrived settlers economically destitute.[74] Consequently, when cocaine demand began to rise, the abandoned settlers turned to cultivating illicit coca, expanding the area planted with coca from 10,000 hectares in 1973 to about 120,000 hectares in the UHV alone by the early 1990s.[75]

Like Peru, Bolivia's illicit coca market emerged from the combined effects of state-led colonization and the cocaine boom. In Bolivia, coca cultivation concentrates in three regions: in Apolo and Yungas of La Paz in the western highlands, and east in the Chapare of Cochabamba. However, while Yungas and Apolo are traditional cultivation zones, the Chapare is a colonization zone where illicit coca expanded in the twentieth century in response to rising cocaine demand. In 1953, the Bolivian government implemented an agrarian reform that caused a proliferation of *minifundios* (small holdings) in the western highlands with limited production capacity. With US support, the Bolivian government addressed land overcrowding in the west with planned settlements in the east, including the Chapare.[76]

At first, peasant settlers in the Chapare introduced only small-scale coca cultivation alongside other crops for local consumption. However, during the 1960s, large landowners in the neighboring departments of Santa Cruz and Beni, facing a collapse of the agricultural export sector, transformed their vast estates into hubs for cocaine trafficking and production, and began purchasing wholesale coca in the Chapare.[77] In this way, Chapare colonos were integrated into the global cocaine circuit, and by the late 1970s the region surpassed the Yungas of La Paz in hectares of planted coca.[78]

Finally, the delayed onset of illicit coca production in 1980s Colombia is also linked to the legacy of failed state-led colonization projects, but the more immediate factor in Colombia was the counterdrug effort.[79] Beginning in the 1940s, the Colombian government initiated the colonization of the country's southern and eastern frontiers in response to the increased radicalization of peasant organizations in more economically integrated areas. Moreover, in the 1950s, interparty warfare between the country's Liberal and Conservative Parties displaced entire peasant communities to the frontier. Subsequently, the Colombian government worked to incorporate these populations by offering loans for purchasing land, but the absence of an infrastructure for accessing the market left settlers in a vicious debt cycle. Hence, in the 1970s, the Medellín cartel encountered abandoned and economically destitute frontier settlers eager to earn a livelihood by planting coca.[80]

In contrast to Peru and Bolivia, in Colombia the presence of multiple and competing trafficking groups in different areas resulted in more dispersed coca cultivation.[81] Hence, by the 1990s, illicit coca had spread to new areas including southwestern Putumayo, where coca provided relief from declining commodity booms in petroleum and rubber.[82] Later in the early twenty-first century, aerial fumigation of coca plants under Plan Colombia further dispersed production to the eastern departments of Arauca, Santander, and Norte de Santander and to the Pacific coastal departments of Cauca, Nariño, and Chocó.[83] However, by 2022, production had consolidated so that two-thirds of Colombia's coca crops were planted in just three frontier departments: Nariño, Norte de Santander, and Putumayo.[84]

Beyond failed state-led development and eradication, the spread of illicit coca into Colombia was also the result of market adaptations to US and Andean counterdrug campaigns. For example, US-supported counternarcotics campaigns that caused the demise of the Medellín and Cali cartels and the shutdown of the coca trafficking airbridge between Peru and Colombia elevated the risks and costs of cross-border coca smuggling. Hence, the collapse of the two-cartel system gave way to smaller cocaine trafficking operations, which encouraged more coca cultivation within Colombian borders.[85] Colombia's participation in raw material production fully integrated the country into the cocaine supply chain, making it the world's largest producer of both illicit coca and cocaine by 1998.[86] By 2001, coca cultivation in Colombia had increased by 500 percent to 169,800 hectares.[87]

Finally, the fourth and fifth factors supporting illicit coca production in the Andes were economic crisis in Peru and Bolivia, and internal armed conflict in Peru and Colombia. With respect to economic crisis, during the 1980s, the nascent democratic governments of Peru and Bolivia faced severe economic depression, which was partially offset by unofficial government tolerance of the then-thriving cocaine industry. For example, Bolivia's economic recession of the early 1980s, linked to plummeting tin prices, triggered renewed migration to the Chapare, where the coca boom provided employment to thousands of jobless miners, thereby supporting Bolivia's economic recovery.[88] By decade's end, coca production had expanded to an estimated fifty-five thousand hectares in Bolivia.[89] Likewise, during the economic crisis in 1980s Peru, the cocaine industry emerged as "a dynamic enclave in an otherwise dysfunctional economy."[90] As the Peruvian economy toppled, PBC production skyrocketed to 65-70 percent of global production, generating employment for up to 279,000 Peruvians by the late 1980s.[91] Moreover, in Peru, economic depression drew new regions into coca production. For example, farmers in the VRAEM hardly produced any coca until prices for traditional agricultural commodities collapsed in the 1980s, pushing farmers into the illicit market.[92] For three decades, the VRAEM remained an important but secondary coca source region. However, during the early twenty-first century, state-led eradication in the UHV and Monzón Valleys,[93] combined with shifting trafficking routes, transformed the VRAEM into Peru's largest producer of illicit coca, accounting for about 44 percent of national production by the late 2010s.[94]

Finally, in Peru and Colombia, nonstate armed groups facilitated illicit coca production by protecting and regulating markets in exchange for rents. In the Peruvian case, the Maoist insurgent group Sendero Luminoso (SL; Shining Path) expanded its territorial presence into coca-producing regions during the 1980s. In the VRAEM, coca farmers and cocaine traffickers responded to the extreme brutality of the SL by underwriting government-supported armed civilian defense groups.[95] After expelling the SL, the VRAEM civilian defense groups continued to participate in and protect the flourishing local cocaine industry.[96] In contrast, in the UHV, the SL forged strong ties with the population by protecting farmers against predatory traffickers, and protecting the traffickers' shipments and airstrips against counterdrug operations, in exchange for rents and recruits.[97] Meanwhile, the state's violent efforts to eradicate coca only strengthened social support for the SL. However, after 1989 the Peruvian military strategically abandoned counternarcotics operations to forge an alliance with coca farmers and local civilian defense groups against the SL.[98] This "hearts and minds" counterinsurgent strategy, in addition to a decline in coca prices, the 1992 capture of SL leader Abimael Guzmán, and an amnesty offer for cooperating SL fighters, resulted in a military defeat of the SL.[99]

Like Peru, in Colombia nonstate armed groups also supported coca production by providing protection in exchange for rents. In the early 1980s, Colombia's largest rebel group, the Fuerzas Armadas Revolucionarias de Colombia–Ejército del Pueblo (FARC-EP; Revolutionary Armed Forces of Colombia–People's Army) started protecting coca farmers, taxing coca sales, and selling protection services to traffickers for airfields, smuggling routes, and cocaine labs.[100] Over time, some FARC-EP fronts integrated into the cocaine trade as coca merchants, and some even participated in cross-border cocaine smuggling. As the FARC-EP expanded into economically integrated regions, Colombian agrarian elites began colluding with drug cartels to underwrite right-wing self-defense or paramilitary groups.[101]

During the 1990s, the paramilitary groups formed a national organization called the Autodefensas Unidas de Colombia (AUC; United Self-Defense Forces of Colombia) and expanded into FARC-controlled coca zones by integrating local cocaine traffickers as AUC front commanders, thereby fusing the Colombian paramilitary movement with the cocaine trade.[102]

In contrast to Peru, the Colombian armed conflict is ongoing, though the country has taken significant steps toward peace. In 2002, peace talks between Colombian president Álvaro Uribe (2002–2010) and the AUC resulted in the demobilization of thirty thousand combatants.[103] However, while security conditions significantly improved, some three thousand AUC combatants formed new narcotrafficking groups called *bandas criminales* (BACRIM; criminal bands).[104] In addition, in 2016, the Colombian government and the FARC-EP signed a peace agreement that included an ambitious national plan for substituting coca with legal crops. However, that plan was derailed by incoming president Iván Duque (2018–2022), who opposed the peace accord. As had occurred with the AUC, the FARC's demobilization did not weaken the cocaine industry. In fact, Colombia's coca production expanded after 2016, and the areas formally controlled by the FARC were mostly consumed by violent competition among drug-trafficking groups seeking to fill the vacuum of authority left by the FARC's disarmament.[105]

Finally, the absence of internal armed conflict in Bolivia helps explain, along with other factors, the relatively low level of drug-related violence there compared to Peru and Colombia. However, Bolivia's powerful coca farmer unions perform functions similar to those of nonstate armed actors in Peru and Colombia with respect to protecting the illicit coca economy. These powerful unions emerged in the wake of Bolivia's 1952 revolution and subsequent agrarian reform that, in the case of the coca-growing regions, divided large estates where coca had been produced since colonial times into small farms.[106] The emerging communities of small producers formed local agrarian unions, which controlled access to land and to the coca markets.[107] For example, by the mid-1980s, the unions in Yungas of La Paz, the largest area of traditional coca production, regulated access to producer licenses required for selling coca on the legal market.[108] In contemporary Bolivia, the coca growers' unions stand officially opposed to the cocaine trade. However, particularly in the Chapare, union leaders regularly facilitate and protect the trade by restricting state access to the region to give cover for illicit market activities.[109]

Pasta Básica de Cocaína (PBC)

The creation of HCl entails a two-step chemical process that starts with the production of PBC, a crude substance made from soaking coca leaf in a chemical mix. Later, the PBC is again processed with chemicals to create powder cocaine. Most of the time, PBC and pure cocaine production are carried out at different locations and by different actors. This is because PBC production is low skill and low capital, and mostly controlled by coca farmers, about 44 percent of whom process PBC. Meanwhile, cocaine production requires expensive chemical additives and highly skilled chemists (*químicos*) typically employed by powerful drug-trafficking organizations.[110]

Andean farmers first began processing PBC as early as the 1970s, but the practice became widespread, forming a cottage industry in the 1980s.[111] Most farmers process raw coca into PBC by making maceration pits near their farms.[112] The coca leaves are macerated, or softened, using an acid solution made of lime or sodium carbonate and then left to soak in a pit covered by a plastic tarp. After gathering the PBC from the pit, farmers usually sell to exporters and wholesalers, who prefer the more expensive paste to the bulkier (and more detectable) coca leaf.[113] From there, PBC passes from wholesalers to smugglers, who then sell to traffickers.[114]

Peasant participation in PBC production is higher risk with respect to criminal penalties and potential violence.[115] However, processed PBC captures higher profits than raw coca while requiring little skill and modest investment in additives such as cement lime, sodium bicarbonate, gasoline, and sulfuric acid.[116] During the 1980s, about 80 percent of PBC production took place in Peru and Bolivia, but today Colombia also produces significant PBC.[117] In the Peruvian UHV, PBC production doubled between 1985 and 1988.[118] Initially, Huallaga farmers sold PBC to local gangs controlled by about seven or eight Colombian trafficking groups, which smuggled the PBC to cocaine labs in Colombia.[119] However, Peru's cocaine trafficking landscape has since diversified to include Peruvian, Mexican, and Brazilian buyers. In addition, in contrast to Huallaga and most other coca zones, the Peruvian VRAEM also houses some small-scale cocaine labs near coca farms.[120] The presence of cocaine labs was facilitated by the local economy, which developed around the cocaine industry to include, for example, an unwarranted number of gas stations, local stores well stocked with fertilizers and pesticides, and local pharmacies carrying imported precursor chemicals for processing cocaine.[121]

In the Bolivian Chapare, much PBC is still produced in maceration pits and sold to middlemen, locally known as *pichacateros*, who process crude cocaine.[122] However, in recent years, decentralized and clandestine production in maceration pits has been slowly replaced by well-organized and larger-scale PBC workshops that process large quantities of locally purchased and stockpiled coca leaf into PBC using more advanced techniques and machinery.[123] The establishment of PBC processing facilities was expedited by the powerful Chapare coca unions, which block state access, thereby giving cover to the workshops. According to some analysts, by the early 2000s, PBC was among Bolivia's principal commodity exports.[124]

In Colombia, the drug traffickers who introduced coca seeds to peasant farmers in the 1970s concealed the method for producing PBC from geographically isolated peasant farmers to maximize control over the supply chain and profits. However, later the FARC-EP facilitated coca farmers' access to information on transforming their coca harvest into PBC, resulting in a peasant-controlled cottage industry by the mid-1980s.[125] By 2008, approximately 65 percent of coca farmers in Colombia participated in PBC production on or near their farms.[126]

Finally, while the vast majority of coca farmers end participation in cocaine production at PBC production, the decentralization of the industry since the 1990s has created lucrative opportunities for famers and other low-level workers to participate higher up the chain as smugglers of chemical precursors and PBC.[127] Particularly in the Bolivian Chapare, PBC workshops employ low-level smugglers, usually taxi drivers, to deliver chemical precursors, hired hands to carry coca and heavy machinery, and sometimes *pisa-cocas* to stomp on the chemical mixture in the absence of machine-driven mixers.[128]

Cocaine Hydrochloride

While peasant farmers dominate coca and PBC production, they seldom participate directly in the processing of HCl.[129] The process of transforming PBC into HCl is complex and requires a well-equipped lab, skillful chemists, and capital for equipment and costly additives like acetone, ether, and potassium permanganate.[130] Hence, this process tends to fall under the control of more organized and sophisticated crime groups. Historically, Peru was the first Andean country to produce crude cocaine—outside a pharmaceutical lab—and by the 1940s Peru and Chile were producing some illicit cocaine for global markets. Meanwhile, Bolivia became a source country for cocaine in the 1960s and Colombia in the 1970s.

Between 1886 and about 1900, legal cocaine was among Peru's most important exports. Moreover, Peru was the "unrivaled producer" of cocaine for global markets for medicinal and recreational use.[131] However, several factors including cocaine cultivation in colonial Asia, mounting anticocaine sentiment in the United States, and the onset of an international antidrug crusade caused a demise in Peruvian legal cocaine production after 1910.[132] In the 1920s and 1930s, Peruvian cocaine production for licit markets was reduced to a small regional enclave in the backwater province of Huánuco, including the Upper Huallaga Valley. There, an illicit cocaine industry formed in the 1940s but remained nascent until the global illicit cocaine industry began to boom in the 1970s.[133]

During the 1970s, Peru's illicit cocaine industry was controlled by Colombian traffickers, who purchased raw coca and PBC in the Huánuco to supply cocaine labs in Colombia.[134] However, by the late 1980s, a decline in coca prices and weakening Colombian cartels created space for some Peruvians to establish cocaine labs in Peru and even smuggle small quantities of cocaine to Colombia under constant threat of violence from competitors and police raids.[135] Still, while Peru integrated into small-scale cocaine production and smuggling, the cocaine industry did not organize under an elite group of prominent traffickers or "narco-bourgeoisie" as occurred in Bolivia and Colombia.[136] Hence, Peruvian production remained low at about 12 percent of Andean cocaine output by decade's end compared to 26 percent and 54 percent in Bolivia and Colombia, respectively.[137]

In the 1990s, Colombian control over the Peruvian cocaine industry eroded even more due to the closing of the airbridge, the collapse of the Colombian cartels, and the emergence of smaller Colombian operations supported by increased coca cultivation in Colombia. As Colombian organizations lost their hold on Peru's coca markets, Peruvian nationals organized more sophisticated cocaine "firms" and established cocaine labs in the Upper Huallaga to produce and move larger quantities of cocaine.[138] By decade's end, Peruvian cocaine production surpassed that of Bolivia. Indeed, Peru surpassed Colombia in cocaine production if only briefly during 2012–2013.[139] In the twenty-first century, the Peruvian cocaine industry emerged as highly complex, competitive, and decentralized, with relatively low barriers to entry. Peruvian cocaine firms and their networks, largely held together by personal ties, are in constant flux with high turnover of actors over time.[140] For these reasons, it is a precarious industry where large sums of money are made and lost quickly.

In contrast to Peru's long history with cocaine, Bolivia hardly produced or exported any cocaine prior to the 1960s. Before that, Bolivian participation in the global cocaine trade was limited to the sale of raw coca to supply Chilean traffickers.[141] However, beginning in the late 1960s, Bolivia's military government began to encourage the country's small but politically powerful class of wealthy ranchers and agribusiness elites in eastern Beni and Santa Cruz Departments to invest in cocaine processing and smuggling operations, as a remedy for declining agricultural prices.[142] Hence, in Bolivia it was the political and economic elites who integrated the country into the global cocaine circuit from the top down, with Beni and Santa Cruz as the national epicenters for cocaine processing and trafficking.[143]

In contrast to Peru, where initial Colombian control gave way to a fragmented and violently competitive cocaine industry, Bolivia's state-led integration into the global cocaine industry supported the early formation of an insular and politically protected narco-bourgeoisie. Hence, the Bolivian cocaine industry was more cooperative, and consequently less violent.[144] In the 1970s, the most infamous Bolivian drug capo, Roberto Suárez, endeavored to maximize cooperation within the Bolivian cocaine business, which primarily supplied the Medellín cartel, by creating La Corporación (the Corporation) as a business and umbrella organization that centrally coordinated cocaine market activities among raw material producers, smugglers, and traffickers.[145] Through La Corporación, Suárez invested in land near the Chapare for cocaine labs to benefit smugglers and contracted pilots called *maruchos* to transport PBC from the Chapare to the labs.[146] US and Bolivian counternarcotics operations resulted in Suárez's exit from the cocaine trade in 1984 and subsequent arrest, which brought about the collapse of La Corporación.[147]

The early establishment of a Bolivian narco-bourgeoisie precluded the formation of cocaine cartels, but it did not preclude market decentralization after the downfall of Roberto Suárez. The contemporary Bolivian cocaine industry remains under the control of a few "family clans," but with greater specialization in specific tasks such as processing, importing chemical precursors, or cross-border smuggling. Hence, while twentieth-century Bolivian coca farmers sold large quantities of raw coca directly to traffickers, twenty-first-century farmers tend to supply smaller quantities to *acopiadores* or PBC processors. The acopiadores, in turn, employ low-level smugglers to move the PBC by road to cocaine labs in the dense jungle areas near the Chapare under the protection of the coca unions.[148] Hence, rather than spur violent competition, the decentralization of Bolivia's cocaine industry into specialized tasks has demanded greater coordination among market actors, which further contributes to lower violence in Bolivia.[149]

Finally, Colombia has been the world's largest producer of pure cocaine since the late 1970s. Colombian dominance in cocaine processing is tied to the emergence of the Colombian cartels in the 1980s and the early establishment of a monopoly over the US cocaine market. During the 1980s and 1990s, the Medellín and Cali cartels operated cocaine laboratories in the Colombian jungles, often with protection from illegal armed groups like the FARC-EP.[150] Initially, the cartels processed cocaine hydrochloride with PBC smuggled from Peru and Bolivia, but contemporary organizations mainly rely on Colombian PBC. After the collapse of the cartel system in the 1990s, which caused a brief decline in Colombian cocaine production, the cocaine industry reorganized around smaller and more networked organizations, including a small number of "micro and small entrepreneurs" who might also be coca farmers and PBC producers, who participate in lesser tasks such as chemical smuggling as part of a "complex system of contracting and subcontracting."[151]

Cross-Border Cocaine Trafficking

The last link in the Andean cocaine supply chain is cross-border cocaine trafficking. Indeed, most cocaine produced in the Andes is destined for distant markets resulting in lucrative, albeit high-risk, smuggling opportunities. Andean cocaine moves to foreign markets through a complex system of global crime networks. While Colombian organizations initially dominated cocaine trafficking, the decline of the two-cartel system generated opportunities for Peruvian and Bolivian organizations like what occurred with cocaine processing. Moreover, Colombian organizations have lost position to organizations outside the Andes, especially Mexican drug-trafficking organizations. In the twenty-first century, Colombian organizations work to supply European and emerging markets in response to changes in global demand, and to circumvent the Mexican cartels that control access to the US market but not to European and emerging markets. Meanwhile, Peruvian and Bolivian organizations also participate in cross-border cocaine trafficking, though more on a regional level and certainly on a much smaller scale than Colombia.

In Peru, the decline of the Colombian cartels gave way to numerous small Peruvian "firms" or drug-trafficking groups that mainly smuggle cocaine by land into neighboring Colombia, Bolivia, Ecuador, Argentina, and Brazil, but rarely beyond. Typically, multiple firms occupy Peruvian coca and cocaine production zones. The upper ranks of firms include some large-scale cocaine smugglers called *traqueteros*, but firms also contract numerous independent smugglers known as *burros* to move smaller quantities of cocaine. At the top of the firms are *patrones* or "bosses" who are typically locals who started off as burros and became self-made men. Indeed, in Peru the cocaine trafficking business offers a rare opportunity for social mobility but one that entails extreme risk, as smugglers are under constant threat from law enforcement, interfirm feuds, robberies, and assaults.[152]

In the Peruvian cocaine industry, small-scale cocaine smuggling is a common practice. However, while burros regularly work as independent entrepreneurs who purchase cocaine from local *firmas*, most residents smuggle only intermittently when they need fast cash. These intermittent smugglers include many coca farmers and women who are contracted by firms for a single job, usually to move cocaine to a specific location for a fixed price. Small-scale smugglers might deliver cocaine to Lima or cross a national border for a much higher payout. In this way, Peruvian firms outsource and disperse much of the risk of cocaine trafficking to small-scale smugglers. Indeed, the high risk of violence or arrest, particularly with respect to land smuggling, contributes to high turnover within firms and among contracted smugglers.[153]

In Bolivia, state-led integration into the global cocaine industry gave powerful agrarian elites a lead role in cocaine trafficking. For example, Roberto Suárez was the wealthy heir of Casa Suárez, a rubber firm founded in the 1890s that controlled 6.5 million hectares of land. Hence, when Bolivia's military government created incentives for integrating into the global cocaine trade, Suárez converted part of his extensive land into airstrips used to transport PBC to his associates in Medellín.[154] After the collapse of the Suárez cocaine empire, cocaine smuggling declined and decentralized. However, in the early 2000s, Bolivian cocaine production and trafficking increased in response to booming demand in neighboring Argentina and Brazil and more smuggling of precursor chemicals from Argentina and raw coca from Peru. Nevertheless, the recent boom in the Bolivian cocaine industry, while benefiting small-scale Bolivian trafficking clans, has also brought foreign crime groups—mainly from Brazil—into Bolivian territory to set up operations. This has raised concern over potential increased drug-related violence in Latin America's least violent cocaine-producing country.[155]

Finally, in sharp contrast to Bolivia, Colombian cocaine trafficking was established "from the bottom up" by crime syndicates in the 1970s.[156] Colombian smugglers such as Pablo Escobar and Carlos Lehder used established networks and routes for marijuana smuggling to form the Medellín cartel with a near monopoly on cocaine trafficking.[157] Later, five independent criminal organizations in Cali merged to form a second, less hierarchical, megacartel. Between the late 1970s and early 1990s, about 70 to 80 percent of cocaine entering the United States passed through the Medellín or Cali cartels.[158] Much of this cocaine entered through the Caribbean mainly by light aircraft, but also by sea.[159] Finally, within the United States, the Medellín cartel exploited personal ties to the community of *paisas*, or Colombians from Medellín, who migrated to South Florida in the 1970s, to control the downstream distribution of cocaine in the eastern United States.[160] To a lesser extent, Andean cocaine was smuggled south through Brazil, where the coastal city of Rio de Janeiro became a cocaine transit hub in the 1980s.[161]

In Colombia, the presence of powerful crime syndicates that were fully integrated into the cocaine trade favored violent competition and state repression, contributing to greater violence. Both the Medellín and Cali cartels were notorious for using gratuitous violence, but the Medellín cartel is particularly associated with using terrorist tactics and employing a throng of professional assassins or *sicarios* to eliminate competitors and punish meddling politicians.[162] During the early 1990s, Colombian efforts to dismantle the cartels escalated into a war with organized crime, causing a spike in reactionary violence.[163] Meanwhile, the Medellín cartel faced threats from successful US, French, Dutch, and British military operations that significantly affected cocaine smuggling routes in the Caribbean.[164] However, while the government offensive and international interdiction were impactful, the Medellín cartel ultimately collapsed due to internal divisions. Fearing disloyalty, Escobar initiated a violent internal purge that caused breakaway factions like People Persecuted by Pablo Escobar (aka Los Pepes), led by the brothers Fidel, Carlos, and Vicente Castaño, who later formed the AUC paramilitary group. Los Pepes allied with Colombian security forces to find and execute Escobar in 1993, bringing an end to the debilitated Medellín cartel.[165]

After the Medellín cartel collapsed, the Cali cartel became the world's most powerful drug-trafficking organization for a short time.[166] Indeed, the suppression of the Caribbean route shifted cocaine's path west through the Pacific and US-Mexican borderlands, thereby benefiting the Cali cartel on the Pacific coast as well as Mexican drug cartels. However, in 1995, Colombian law enforcement arrested the leaders of the Cali cartel, thereby concluding the reign of the two-cartel system.[167] In the end, Mexican trafficking organizations were the chief beneficiaries of cocaine's westward drift, as most cocaine now entered the United States across the Mexican-US border.[168]

The demise of the Colombian cartels fragmented the cocaine industry into smaller, low-profile crime groups.[169] In the twenty-first century, Andean cocaine might pass through three hundred such organizations before reaching its final market.[170] During the 1990s, some of these trafficking groups merged with the Colombian paramilitary organization AUC in a way that further blurred the line between armed conflict and organized crime. Indeed, the Colombian paramilitary movement was tied to the cocaine industry from the moment the Medellín cartel underwrote the first paramilitary structure called Muerte a Secuestradores (MAS; Death to Kidnappers) in 1981. Moreover, the infamous leaders of the AUC, Fidel and Carlos Castaño, hailed from a wealthy landowning family and worked for the Medellín cartel before breaking ties to form Los Pepes.[171] After the AUC signed a peace agreement in 2002, several midlevel AUC commanders, already deeply entrenched in the cocaine trade, mobilized new drug-trafficking groups. The criminal bands that emerged from the old AUC include groups such as Los Urabeños and Los Gaitanistas.

The Andes in the Twenty-First Century Global Cocaine Boom

Despite decades of strong-arm interventions to destroy the cocaine trade, the Andean region experienced an unprecedented boom in cocaine production in the late 2010s, with production doubling between 2014 and 2019 and continuing to rise (albeit more slowly) in the early 2020s.[172] In addition to increased cocaine production in the traditional source countries of Peru, Bolivia, and Colombia, the new boom has led to nascent coca cultivation in Andean Venezuela and in Honduras, two countries with no history of coca production.[173] While in many ways the recent production increase echoes the mid-twentieth-century boom, it is distinct due to changes in global demand with implications for production sites and actors, trade routes, technologies, and a blurring of upstream and downstream market activities. This section describes the twenty-first-century cocaine boom and its implications for the Andean region.

To begin, in contrast to the twentieth-century boom, which was mainly driven by rising US demand, the twenty-first-century cocaine production boom has been responding to rising cocaine demand in Europe and in new Global South markets. In fact, the US market shrank by nearly 40 percent between 2000 and 2008, but the loss was offset by a twofold increase in Andean cocaine smuggled to European markets.[174] Since 2008, European demand has continued to rise such that the quantity of cocaine entering Europe in 2020 nearly equaled that entering the United States.[175] During the COVID-19 pandemic, global cocaine demand declined in response to the shuttering of bars and nightclubs as well as travel restrictions, but by 2022 European demand had rebounded to prepandemic levels.[176]

The increased flow of Andean cocaine to Europe contributed to a broader globalization of cocaine consumption as new markets embedded in the transit countries that were part of the new cocaine trade circuit, predominantly in the Global South.[177] For example, Brazil emerged early in the twenty-first century as the second-largest cocaine consumer market in the world after the United States.[178] Consumption also rose in Argentina, Chile, and Uruguay.[179] Finally, areas outside Latin America that became major transit sites between the Andes and Europe such as West and North Africa saw their previously small or nonexistent cocaine markets expand.[180]

In addition to embedding new consumer markets, the increased flow of Andean cocaine to Europe strengthened Andean organized crime groups through economic benefits, less law enforcement, an enhanced position vis-à-vis other crime groups within the global cocaine trade, and advances in smuggling technology and networks. The chief advantage for Andean organized crime has been higher prices for cocaine in Europe, which results from the greater risks of moving cocaine over longer distances and across an ocean. Hence, in 2021, a kilogram of cocaine sold for about US$28,000 in the United States compared to $40,000–$80,000 in Europe, depending on the location.[181] This means that the value of the European cocaine market nearly equaled that of the United States as early as 2011, even while US consumption remained slightly higher.[182]

A second advantage for Andean producers in Europe is weaker law enforcement compared to the heavily patrolled route north to the United States. There is a general perception that European authorities deprioritize policing drug trade activities. While European countries significantly expanded their law enforcement response in the 2010s with cocaine seizure rates reaching half of estimated shipments, they still lagged behind the United States.[183] Moreover, ramped-up law enforcement in Europe did not slow cocaine smuggling but merely shifted routes south to involve West African countries as new "transit sites," where law enforcement efforts are stifled by weak and corrupt state institutions.

Third, Europe is advantageous for Andean crime groups because it has helped these groups to reclaim status relative to other crime organizations within the cocaine trade. For Andean drug traffickers, the European market offered a way around dependence on mainly Mexican cartels that control access to the western United States,[184] and to a lesser extent dependence on Caribbean groups that mediate access to some markets in the eastern United States.[185] Indeed, the eagerness of cocaine traffickers, particularly from Colombia, to expand their networks and invest heavily in new technologies such as submarines to supply Europe is partly a lagged effect of US and international efforts to obstruct cocaine shipments through the Caribbean in the 1980s.[186]

Finally, Andean crime groups benefited from incentives to develop sophisticated smuggling technologies and practices to send ever larger shipments longer distances in the absence of a land bridge. Prior to the twenty-first-century cocaine boom, relatively small quantities of cocaine were sent from the Andes to Europe by commercial air carriers, usually within or attached to human passengers, and to a lesser extent by fishing vessels or go-fast boats.[187] However, the increased European demand during the 2010s forced Andean smugglers to innovate, using shipping containers to send much larger quantities of cocaine by sea.[188] In addition, while containers remain the dominant method, in recent years crime groups in Latin America and Europe have deployed submarines to move unprecedent amounts of cocaine to and within Europe,[189] through the Caribbean Sea and across the Pacific Ocean, and through the river system of the Brazilian Amazon.[190] As drug traffickers' technological capabilities expand, so too does their capacity for evading law enforcement.

Beyond better smuggling technologies, cocaine traffickers have also innovated with diversified smuggling routes to Europe to evade law enforcement. In addition to well-established northern routes, cocaine increasingly has moved south through Brazil to the Iberian Peninsula and through West and North Africa to reach European markets.[191] Cocaine's shift south expanded production opportunities for the Andean countries of Peru and Bolivia, which are better linked to southern routes through Brazil, Argentina, Paraguay, and Chile than Colombia, which is instead better linked to northbound routes.[192] For example, while Bolivia and Peru continue to trail Colombia in cocaine output, the two countries have increased production in response to European demand.[193] Importantly, some of the increase in coca cultivation in 2020 and 2021 was likely due to impacts from the COVID-19 pandemic, which caused a halt in government eradication and blocked buyer access to coca zones, contributing to coca overproduction and a price bust.[194] However, after 2021, coca prices rebounded slightly in response to the rebound in global cocaine demand. That year, Peruvian and Bolivian product accounted for less than 2 percent of cocaine consumed in the United States but a substantial 30 percent of cocaine consumed in Europe.[195]

In addition to increased production, Bolivia also elevated its role as a vital transit country for southbound Colombian cocaine and as a market and processing point for Peruvian coca and PBC. Bolivia's comparative advantage in the new boom is shared borders with Brazil, Argentina, and Chile, three countries with consumer markets for cocaine and ports for trafficking to Africa, Asia, and Europe.[196] Bolivia's elevated role has attracted an increased presence of Colombian and Brazilian crime groups with operations in Bolivia, where they capitalize on lower violence and weaker law enforcement than in Peru and Colombia.[197]

In Peru, the recent cocaine boom resulted in a 23 percent increase in coca cultivation during 2020–2021 to reach 80,681 hectares nationally.[198] The production spike effectively reversed Peru's progress in reducing coca cultivation and weakening criminal groups in the early 2000s.[199] While much of the expansion in Peru concentrated in the VRAEM, there are at least five new coca production sites in the isolated Amazonian departments of Loreto and Puno that border Brazil and Bolivia, respectively.[200] Finally, while Peruvian traffickers still process significant quantities of cocaine,[201] increasingly Peruvian coca and PBC either gets smuggled into Bolivia, where it sells at a lower price than Bolivian coca and PBC, or gets smuggled and sold directly to Brazilian cocaine traffickers.[202]

While Peru and Bolivia benefited from the southern shift in cocaine circuits, Colombia remains the world's largest supplier of coca, PBC, and pure cocaine. Between 2015 and 2020, Colombia accounted for 60–70 percent of global coca cultivation and between one-third and one-half of total manufactured cocaine.[203] Moreover, Colombia's more decentralized and highly competitive cocaine industry has contributed to production innovations such as new agricultural techniques that support denser planting of coca shrubs and production of coca leaf with a higher concentration of cocaine alkaloid in addition to advances in cocaine processing that permit more alkaloid extraction from smaller quantities of leaf. Hence, after 2016, the overall area of planted coca in Colombia declined while output of manufactured cocaine increased.[204] These innovations likely contributed to the recent overproduction of coca, which in turn caused Colombian coca markets to collapse in 2023. Other factors contributing to collapsing prices include halted aerial fumigation in 2015, increased coca production in Peru and Bolivia, and law enforcement successes in combating the crime groups that regulate coca production. While the collapse is likely temporary, it contributed to a humanitarian crisis including food shortages in Colombian coca-producing regions.[205]

Finally, cocaine's shift south changed the landscape of organized crime with sometimes violent consequences for both transit and producing countries. For example, new cocaine routes expanded organized crime in the most affected transit countries such as Brazil, where the cocaine trade sustains violent and competitive criminal groups such as the Comando Vermelho and the Primeiro Comando da Capital (PCC).[206] Both the Comando Vermelho and the PCC, along with Italian, Mexican, Colombian, and Argentine crime groups, established cocaine production and smuggling operations in Bolivia to capitalize on increased production. Meanwhile, several Mexican and European groups moved into Colombia.[207] Moreover, the Italian mafia, historically at the forefront of European organized crime, has established in-house brokers in Colombia, Venezuela, Costa Rica, Peru, and the Dominican Republic to profit from some upstream market activities. The Italian groups are also known to work with the Brazilian PCC.[208] To a lesser extent, Andean cocaine smugglers, such as the Colombian criminal organization Los Urabeños, moved downstream to directly participate in cocaine wholesaling and money laundering markets in Europe.[209]

Conclusion

The early integration of Andean countries as the source of global illicit cocaine results from complex historical, cultural, and political processes that generate propitious conditions for an illicit market to thrive. As this chapter shows, the Andes has a deep historical and cultural relationship with the benign coca leaf, the primary material for producing cocaine. Moreover, poor governance in the form of failed development projects targeting remote frontiers created conditions of impoverishment and state neglect, which gave rise to, and continue to fuel, coca and cocaine production. Subsequently, state repression in the form of coercive antinarcotics policies helped armed actors engaged in illegal activities to gain footholds in these areas by selling armed protection, which in turn helped the cocaine industry to survive government attacks. Finally, at the international level, the United States' and the United Nations' steadfast commitment to a failed punitive framework for combating illicit cocaine exacerbates the social injustices underlying participation in illicit cocaine markets and associated violence.

The above factors intersected with the globalization of cocaine consumption to support a thriving Andean cocaine industry in the twenty-first century. Indeed, after six decades of coercive interventions, the Andean cocaine industry remains robust and deeply embedded in Andean societies. It employs hundreds of thousands of Andean workers at every level of the supply chain. And while demonized at the international level, the Andean communities that survive from the cocaine trade experience it as a normalized and necessary part of daily life. They navigate through the complex moral economy that defines relations between market actors and try to circumnavigate the risks borne from market competition and state repression. Given this reality, dismantling the Andean cocaine industry will require more thoughtful and compassionate approaches that engage market actors in formulating policy solutions that focus on root causes of their participation in the production of cocaine.

Notes

1. Susan Virginia Norman, "Narcotization as Security Dilemma: The FARC and Drug Trade in Colombia," *Studies in Conflict and Terrorism* 41, no. 8 (2018): 640.

2. Paul Gootenberg, "Peruvian Cocaine and the Boomerang of History," *NACLA Report on the Americas* 47, no. 2 (Summer 2014): 48-49.

3. Susan Brewer-Osorio, "Turning Over a New Leaf: A Subnational Analysis of 'Coca Yes, Cocaine No' in Bolivia," *Journal of Latin American Studies* 53, no. 3 (August 2021): 573-600; and Angélica Durán-Martínez, "Cocaine Smuggling: Between Geopolitics and Domestic Power Struggles," in *The Routledge Handbook of Smuggling*, ed. Max Gallien and Florian Weigand (Abingdon, Oxon., England: Routledge, 2022), 184.

4. Zoe Pearson, "Bolivia, Coca, Culture and Colonialism," in *Research Handbook on International Drug Policy*, ed. David R. Bewley-Taylor and Khalid Tinasti (Cheltenham, Glos., England: Edward Elgar, 2020), 283-300; and Brewer-Osorio, "Turning Over a New Leaf."

5. Pearson, "Bolivia, Coca, Culture and Colonialism"; Paul Gootenberg, "Orphans of Development: The Unanticipated Rise of Illicit Coca in the Amazon Andes, 1950-1990," in *The Origins of Cocaine: Colonization and Failed Development in the Amazon Andes*, ed. Paul

Gootenberg and Liliana M. Dávalos (Abingdon, Oxon., England: Routledge, 2018), 5; Brewer-Osorio, "Turning Over a New Leaf"; and Thomas Grisaffi, *Coca Yes, Cocaine No: How Bolivia's Coca Growers Reshaped Democracy* (Durham, NC: Duke University Press, 2019).

6. Gootenberg, "Orphans of Development," 5.

7. Brewer-Osorio, "Turning Over a New Leaf"; and Grisaffi, *Coca Yes, Cocaine No*.

8. Paul Gootenberg, *Andean Cocaine: The Making of a Global Drug* (Chapel Hill: University of North Carolina Press, 2008), 55–56; Gootenberg, "Orphans of Development," 5; and Grisaffi, *Coca Yes, Cocaine No*, 582.

9. Francisco Ferreira, "De-Demonizing the VRAEM: A Peruvian-Cocalero Area," *Substance Use and Misuse* 51, no. 1 (2016): 43; and Gootenberg, "Orphans of Development," 5.

10. Gootenberg, *Andean Cocaine: The Making of a Global Drug*, 22–23.

11. Gootenberg, *Andean Cocaine: The Making of a Global Drug*, 53.

12. Gootenberg, *Andean Cocaine: The Making of a Global Drug*; and Peter Andreas, *Smuggler Nation: How Illicit Trade Made America* (New York: Oxford University Press, 2013), 254–56.

13. Gootenberg, *Andean Cocaine: The Making of a Global Drug*, 25–31; Brewer-Osorio, "Turning Over a New Leaf"; and Durán-Martínez, "Cocaine Smuggling," 184.

14. Gootenberg, *Andean Cocaine: The Making of a Global Drug*, 191–98; and Andreas, *Smuggler Nation*, 251–64.

15. Gootenberg, *Andean Cocaine: The Making of a Global Drug*, 191–98; and Andreas, *Smuggler Nation*, 256–57.

16. Andreas, *Smuggler Nation*, 256–57.

17. David R. Bewley-Taylor, *International Drug Control: Consensus Fractured* (Cambridge: Cambridge University Press, 2012).

18. Andreas, *Smuggler Nation*, 262–65.

19. Andreas, *Smuggler Nation*, 262–65.

20. Gootenberg, *Andean Cocaine: The Making of a Global Drug*, 30; Durán-Martínez, "Cocaine Smuggling," 184; and Paul Gootenberg, "Shifting South: Cocaine's Historical Present and the Changing Politics of Drug War, 1975–2015," in *Cocaine: From Coca Fields to the Streets*, ed. Enrique Desmond Arias and Thomas Grisaffi (Durham, NC: Duke University Press, 2021), 287–316.

21. Francisco E. Thoumi, "International Drug Conventions, Balanced Policy Recipes, and Latin American Cocaine Markets," in *Dual Markets: Comparative Approaches to Regulation*, ed. Ernesto U. Savona, Mark A. R. Kleiman, and Francesco Calderoni (Cham, Switzerland: Springer, 2017), 88; and Gootenberg, "Shifting South," 288.

22. Durán-Martínez, "Cocaine Smuggling."

23. Amy E. Bellone, "The Cocaine Commodity Chain and Development Paths in Peru and Bolivia," in *Latin America in the World-Economy*, ed. Roberto Patricio Korzeniewicz and William C. Smith (Westport, CT: Praeger, 1996), 33–52.

24. Ray Henkel, "The Bolivian Cocaine Industry," in *Drugs in Latin America: Studies in Third World Societies*, ed. Edmundo Morales (Williamsburg, VA: Department of Anthropology, College of William and Mary, 1986), 54; Bellone, "The Cocaine Commodity Chain," 42; and Thoumi, "International Drug Conventions," 82.

25. Francisco E. Thoumi, "Organized Crime in Colombia: The Actors Running the Illegal Drug Industry," in *The Oxford Handbook of Organized Crime*, ed. Letizia Paoli (New York: Oxford University Press, 2014), 183; and Tim Boekhout van Solinge, "Global Cocaine Flows, Geographical Displacement, and Crime Convergence," in *The Evolution of Illicit Flows: Displacement and Convergence Among Transnational Crime*, ed. Ernesto U. Savona, Rob T. Guerette, and Alberto Aziani (Cham, Switzerland: Springer, 2022), 65.

26. Thoumi, "International Drug Conventions," 84; and Boekhout van Solinge, "Global Cocaine Flows," 64.

27. Bellone, "The Cocaine Commodity Chain," 39.

28. Bellone, "The Cocaine Commodity Chain," 35–36; and Gootenberg, "Orphans of Development."

29. Bellone, "The Cocaine Commodity Chain," 37.

30. Bewley-Taylor, *International Drug Control*; David R. Bewley-Taylor, "Coca and Cocaine: The Evolution of International Control," in *Roadmaps to Regulation: Coca, Cocaine, and Derivatives*, ed. Amanda Feilding (Oxford: Beckley Foundation, 2016), 9–20; and Peter Andreas and Ethan Nadelmann, *Policing the Globe: Criminalization and Crime Control in International Relations* (New York: Oxford University Press, 2008), 37–45.

31. Vanda Felbab-Brown, *Shooting Up: Counterinsurgency and the War on Drugs* (Washington, DC: Brookings Institution Press, 2010); Jonathan D. Rosen, *The Losing War: Plan Colombia and Beyond* (Albany: State University of New York Press, 2014); and John Lindsay-Poland, *Plan Colombia: U.S. Ally Atrocities and Community Activism* (Durham, NC: Duke University Press, 2018).

32. Rosen, *The Losing War*; Lindsay-Poland, *Plan Colombia*; and Andreas and Nadelmann, *Policing the Globe*, 37–45.

33. Luciana Grillo, Allison Kendra, Alvaro Pastor, and Hernán Manrique, "Addressing Socio-Environmental Challenges and Unintended Consequences of Peruvian Drug Policy: An Analysis in Two Former Cocalero Valleys," *Journal of Illicit Economies and Development* 3, no. 1 (2021): 97–117; and Cynthia McClintock, "The War on Drugs: The Peruvian Case," *Journal of Interamerican Studies and World Affairs* 30, nos. 2–3 (Summer–Autumn 1988): 127–42.

34. Edmundo Morales, *Cocaine: White Gold Rush in Peru* (Tucson: University of Arizona Press, 1989); Bruce H. Kay, "Violent Opportunities: The Rise and Fall of 'King Coca' and Shining Path," *Journal of Interamerican Studies and World Affairs* 41, no. 3 (Autumn 1999): 104; and McClintock, "The War on Drugs," 131.

35. Raphael F. Perl, "United States Andean Drug Policy: Background and Issues for Decisionmakers," *Journal of Interamerican Studies and World Affairs* 34, no. 3 (Autumn 1992): 13–35; and Stella M. Rouse and Moises Arce, "The Drug-Laden Balloon: U.S. Military Assistance and Coca Production in the Central Andes," *Social Science Quarterly* 87, no. 3 (September 2006): 540–57.

36. Grillo et al., "Addressing Socio-Environmental Challenges," 101.

37. Carolina Navarrete-Frías, "Drug Crop Eradication and Alternative Development in the Andes," CRS Report for Congress, Congressional Research Service, Library of Congress, November 18, 2005, https://www.everycrsreport.com/files/20051118_RL33163_fffd90b57747 d5ca59ec7286e5876ffb5445e090.pdf; McClintock, "The War on Drugs," 130; Kay, "Violent Opportunities," 114; and Frank Casas and Mariana Ramírez, "Actores y escenarios como determinantes clave de la política de drogas en Perú: El caso de la implementación del control de hoja de coca en el valle del Monzón (2010–2015)," *Revista de Ciencia Política y Gobierno* 4, no. 7 (2017): 41.

38. Gabriela Valdivia, "Coca's Haunting Presence in the Agrarian Politics of the Bolivian Lowlands," *GeoJournal* 77, no. 5 (2012): 615; and Brewer-Osorio, "Turning Over a New Leaf."

39. Grisaffi, *Coca Yes, Cocaine No*; and Brewer-Osorio, "Turning Over a New Leaf."

40. Grisaffi, *Coca Yes, Cocaine No*; and Brewer-Osorio, "Turning Over a New Leaf."

41. Grisaffi, *Coca Yes, Cocaine No*.

42. Grisaffi, *Coca Yes, Cocaine No*, 579.

43. Susan Brewer-Osorio, "MAS Relations with Social Movements: The Yungas Cocaleros and the 2019 Crisis," *Bolivian Studies Journal* 30 (November 2024): 127–58.

44. Winifred Tate, *Drugs, Thugs, and Diplomats: U.S. Policymaking in Colombia* (Stanford, CA: Stanford University Press, 2015), 31.

45. Tate, *Drugs, Thugs, and Diplomats*, 31.

46. Forrest Hylton, "Plan Colombia: The Measure of Success," *Brown Journal of World Affairs* 17, no. 1 (Fall-Winter 2010): 99–115; White House Office of the Press Secretary, "Fact Sheet: Peace Colombia—A New Era of Partnership Between the United States and Colombia," February 4, 2016, https://obamawhitehouse.archives.gov/the-press-office/2016/02/04/fact-sheet-peace-colombia-new-era-partnership-between-united-states-and; and Alexander Rincón-Ruiz, Harold Leonardo Correa, Daniel Oswaldo Léon, and Stewart Williams, "Coca

Cultivation and Crop Eradication in Colombia: The Challenges of Integrating Rural Reality into Effective Anti-Drug Policy," *International Journal of Drug Policy* 33 (June 2016): 56–65.

47. Rincón-Ruiz et al., "Coca Cultivation and Crop Eradication in Colombia"; Rouse and Arce, "The Drug-Laden Balloon"; and Menno Vellinga, "The Illegal Drug Industry in Latin America: The Coca-Cocaine Commodity Value Chain," *Iberoamericana: Nordic Journal of Latin American and Caribbean Studies* 37, no. 2 (June 2007): 93–94.

48. Michael Evans, "Paramilitaries as Proxies: Declassified Evidence on the Colombian Army's Anti-Guerrilla 'Allies,'" National Security Archive, October 16, 2005, https://nsarchive2.gwu.edu/NSAEBB/NSAEBB166/index.htm; and Hylton, "Plan Colombia: The Measure of Success."

49. Lindsay-Poland, *Plan Colombia*.

50. White House Office of the Press Secretary, "Fact Sheet: Peace Colombia."

51. Vellinga, "The Illegal Drug Industry in Latin America," 97.

52. Gootenberg, "Shifting South," 289.

53. Jonathan D. Rosen and Hanna Samir Kassab, "Gangs and Counter-Gang Strategies," in *Drugs, Gangs, and Violence* (Cham, Switzerland: Palgrave Macmillan, 2019), 91–116.

54. Norman, "Narcotization as Security Dilemma."

55. Jeremy McDermott, James Bargent, Douwe den Held, and Maria Fernanda Ramírez, "The Cocaine Pipeline to Europe," InSight Crime, February 2021, 12, https://insightcrime.org/wp-content/uploads/2021/09/The-cocaine-pipeline-to-Europe-GI-TOC-InsightCrime.pdf.

56. Durán-Martínez, "Cocaine Smuggling," 187.

57. Vellinga, "The Illegal Drug Industry in Latin America," 91.

58. Durán-Martínez, "Cocaine Smuggling," 187.

59. Henkel, "The Bolivian Cocaine Industry"; Clare Hargreaves, *Snow Fields: The War on Cocaine in the Andes* (New York: Holmes and Meier, 1992); Morales, *Cocaine: White Gold Rush in Peru*; Bellone, "The Cocaine Commodity Chain"; Ursula Durand Ochoa, *The Political Empowerment of the Cocaleros of Bolivia and Peru* (New York: Palgrave Macmillan, 2014); Norman, "Narcotization as Security Dilemma"; and Brewer-Osorio, "Turning Over a New Leaf."

60. Christoph Heuser, "The Effect of Illicit Economies in the Margins of the State: The VRAEM," *Journal of Illicit Economies and Development* 1, no. 1 (2019): 27.

61. Valdivia, "Coca's Haunting Presence," 619.

62. Grisaffi, *Coca Yes, Cocaine No*; and Brewer-Osorio, "Turning Over a New Leaf."

63. Grillo et al., "Addressing Socio-Environmental Challenges," 97; and Heuser, "The Effect of Illicit Economies," 27.

64. Grillo et al., "Addressing Socio-Environmental Challenges," 97.

65. Grillo et al., "Addressing Socio-Environmental Challenges," 97; and Heuser, "The Effect of Illicit Economies," 27.

66. Vellinga, "The Illegal Drug Industry in Latin America," 91; and Norman, "Narcotization as Security Dilemma," 641.

67. Valdivia, "Coca's Haunting Presence," 619; Bellone, "The Cocaine Commodity Chain," 35; and Liliana M. Dávalos, Karina M. Sanchez, and Dolors Armenteras, "Deforestation and Coca Cultivation Rooted in Twentieth-Century Development Projects," *BioScience* 66, no. 11 (September 2016): 974–82.

68. Gootenberg, "Orphans of Development," 2–3.

69. Catherine LeGrand, *Frontier Expansion and Peasant Protest in Colombia, 1830–1936* (Albuquerque: University of New Mexico Press, 1986); Dávalos, Sanchez, and Armenteras, "Deforestation and Coca Cultivation"; and Norman, "Narcotization as Security Dilemma."

70. Gootenberg, "Orphans of Development," 5; Dávalos, Sanchez, and Armenteras, "Deforestation and Coca Cultivation"; and Ferreira, "De-Demonizing the VRAEM," 42.

71. Camilo Acero and Frances Thomson, "'Everything Peasants Do Is Illegal': Colombian Coca Growers' Everyday Experiences of Law Enforcement and Its Impacts on State Legitimacy," *Third World Quarterly* 43, no. 11 (2022): 2674–92; Vellinga, "The Illegal Drug Industry in Latin America," 91–94; and Gootenberg, "Orphans of Development," 1–4.

72. Vellinga, "The Illegal Drug Industry in Latin America," 92; Norman, "Narcotization as Security Dilemma," 645; and Gootenberg, "Shifting South," 584.

73. Gootenberg, *Andean Cocaine: The Making of a Global Drug*; and Grillo et al., "Addressing Socio-Environmental Challenges."

74. Kay, "Violent Opportunities"; and Grillo et al., "Addressing Socio-Environmental Challenges," 101.

75. McClintock, "The War on Drugs," 128; Mirella van Dun, "'It's Never a Sure Deal': Drug Trafficking, Violence, and Coping Strategies in a Peruvian Cocaine Enclave (2003–2007)," *Journal of Drug Issues* 44, no. 2 (March 2014): 182; Ferreira, "De-Demonizing the VRAEM," 42; and Kay, "Violent Opportunities," 101.

76. Valdivia, "Coca's Haunting Presence," 62.

77. Gootenberg, *Andean Cocaine: The Making of a Global Drug*, 274.

78. James Painter, *Bolivia and Coca: A Study in Dependency* (Boulder, CO: Lynne Rienner, 1994), 3–4; Eric Dante Gutierrez, "Criminal Entrepreneurs as Pioneers, Intermediaries, and Arbitrageurs in Borderland Economies," *International Journal of Drug Policy* 89 (March 2021): 5; Gonzalo Flores and José Blanes, *Dónde va el Chaparé?* (Cochabamba, Bolivia: Centro

de Estudios de la Realidad Económica y Social, 1984); and Valdivia, "Coca's Haunting Presence," 620.

79. Gootenberg, "Orphans of Development," 3; and Norman, "Narcotization as Security Dilemma," 640.

80. Norman, "Narcotization as Security Dilemma," 639, 641.

81. Gootenberg, "Orphans of Development," 4.

82. Gootenberg, "Orphans of Development," 4; and Acero and Thomson, "Everything Peasants Do Is Illegal," 2681.

83. Tate, *Drugs, Thugs, and Diplomats*; Rincón-Ruiz et al., "Coca Cultivation and Crop Eradication in Colombia"; Rouse and Arce, "The Drug-Laden Balloon"; and Vellinga, "The Illegal Drug Industry in Latin America," 93–94.

84. Alejandro Reyes Posada, *Tierras: Balance de la contribución del CNMH al esclarecimiento histórico* (Bogotá: Centro Nacional de Memoria Histórica, 2018), https://centrodememoria historica.gov.co/tierras-balance-de-la-contribucion-del-cnmh-al-esclarecimiento-historico/.

85. Norman, "Narcotization as Security Dilemma," 641; and Vellinga, "The Illegal Drug Industry in Latin America," 92.

86. Norman, "Narcotization as Security Dilemma," 641; and Gootenberg, "Orphans of Development," 4.

87. Norman, "Narcotization as Security Dilemma," 641.

88. Alain Labrousse, "Dependence on Drugs: Unemployment, Migration and an Alternative Path to Development in Bolivia," *International Labour Review* 129, no. 3 (1990): 333–48; and Gootenberg, "Shifting South," 585.

89. Bellone, "The Cocaine Commodity Chain," 36; Madeline Barbara Léons, "Risk and Opportunity in the Coca/Cocaine Economy of the Bolivian Yungas," *Journal of Latin American Studies* 25, no. 1 (February 1993): 121–57; Valdivia, "Coca's Haunting Presence," 620; and Gootenberg, "Orphans of Development," 3–4.

90. Kay, "Violent Opportunities," 97.

91. Kay, "Violent Opportunities," 101.

92. Heuser, "The Effect of Illicit Economies," 26–27.

93. Grillo et al., "Addressing Socio-Environmental Challenges," 98, 102–6.

94. Ferreira, "De-Demonizing the VRAEM," 41; Gootenberg, "Orphans of Development," 4; Scott Mistler-Ferguson, "How Peru's Coca Production Is Helping the Global Cocaine Boom," InSight Crime, September 27, 2022, https://insightcrime.org/news/four-takeaways-peruvian-coca-cultivation-report/; and Heuser, "The Effect of Illicit Economies," 26–27.

95. Heuser, "The Effect of Illicit Economies," 26.

96. Heuser, "The Effect of Illicit Economies," 28.

97. Kay, "Violent Opportunities," 102–3; and McClintock, "The War on Drugs," 138.

98. Kay, "Violent Opportunities," 105, 115–17; and Ferreira, "De-Demonizing the VRAEM," 41.

99. McClintock, "The War on Drugs," 137; Kay, "Violent Opportunities," 106, 111–17; and Richard Kernaghan, *Coca's Gone: Of Might and Right in the Huallaga Post-Boom* (Stanford, CA: Stanford University Press, 2009).

100. Norman, "Narcotization as Security Dilemma," 648.

101. Norman, "Narcotization as Security Dilemma," 646; and Gutierrez, "Criminal Entrepreneurs as Pioneers, Intermediaries, and Arbitrageurs," 5.

102. Norman, "Narcotization as Security Dilemma," 642, 649–50; and Gutierrez, "Criminal Entrepreneurs as Pioneers, Intermediaries, and Arbitrageurs," 4.

103. Gutierrez, "Criminal Entrepreneurs as Pioneers, Intermediaries, and Arbitrageurs," 5; and Norman, "Narcotization as Security Dilemma," 652–53.

104. Norman, "Narcotization as Security Dilemma," 652–53; and McDermott et al., "The Cocaine Pipeline to Europe," 20.

105. Acero and Thomson, "Everything Peasants Do Is Illegal," 2681.

106. Herbert S. Klein, "Coca Production in the Bolivian Yungas in the Colonial and Early National Periods," in *Coca and Cocaine: Effects on People and Policy in Latin America*, ed. Deborah Pacini and Christine Franquemont (Cambridge: Cultural Survival, 1986), 53–64; and Valdivia, "Coca's Haunting Presence," 19.

107. Grisaffi, *Coca Yes, Cocaine No*; Alessandra Pellegrini Calderón, *Beyond Indigeneity: Coca Growing and the Emergence of a New Middle Class in Bolivia* (Tucson: University of Arizona Press, 2016); and Thomas Grisaffi, "Why Is the Drug Trade Not Violent? Cocaine Production and the Embedded Economy in the Chapare, Bolivia," *Development and Change* 53, no. 3 (May 2022): 579, 587.

108. Brewer-Osorio, "Turning Over a New Leaf"; and Ana María Lema, "The Coca Debate and Yungas Landowners During the First Half of the Twentieth Century," in *Coca, Cocaine, and the Bolivian Reality*, ed. Barbara Madeline Leóns and Harry Sanabria (Albany: State University of New York Press, 1997), 99–116.

109. Grisaffi, "Why Is the Drug Trade Not Violent?," 590.

110. Durán-Martínez, "Cocaine Smuggling," 187.

111. McClintock, "The War on Drugs," 128.

112. Van Dun, "It's Never a Sure Deal," 183.

113. Bellone, "The Cocaine Commodity Chain," 39.

114. Vellinga, "The Illegal Drug Industry in Latin America," 93.

115. Vellinga, "The Illegal Drug Industry in Latin America," 94.

116. Gootenberg, "Orphans of Development," 3–4; Vellinga, "The Illegal Drug Industry in Latin America," 94; and Bellone, "The Cocaine Commodity Chain," 39.

117. Bellone, "The Cocaine Commodity Chain," 39.

118. McClintock, "The War on Drugs," 128.

119. McClintock, "The War on Drugs," 128; and Kay, "Violent Opportunities," 101.

120. Heuser, "The Effect of Illicit Economies," 27–29.

121. Heuser, "The Effect of Illicit Economies," 28.

122. Léons, "Risk and Opportunity in the Coca/Cocaine Economy."

123. Grisaffi, "Why Is the Drug Trade Not Violent?," 584–85.

124. Grisaffi, "Why Is the Drug Trade Not Violent?," 577.

125. Norman, "Narcotization as Security Dilemma," 641.

126. Daniel Mejía and Daniel Mauricio Rico, "La microeconomía de la producción y el tráfico de cocaína en Colombia," in *Políticas antidroga en Colombia: Éxito, fracasos y extravíos*, ed. Alejandro Gaviria Uribe and Daniel Mejía Londoño (Bogotá: Universidad de los Andes, 2011), 17.

127. Bellone, "The Cocaine Commodity Chain"; and Grisaffi, "Why Is the Drug Trade Not Violent?"

128. Grisaffi, "Why Is the Drug Trade Not Violent?," 584–85.

129. Vellinga, "The Illegal Drug Industry in Latin America," 90.

130. Grisaffi, "Why Is the Drug Trade Not Violent?," 592.

131. Gootenberg, *Andean Cocaine: The Making of a Global Drug*, 55–60.

132. Gootenberg, *Andean Cocaine: The Making of a Global Drug*, 143.

133. Gootenberg, *Andean Cocaine: The Making of a Global Drug*.

134. McClintock, "The War on Drugs," 128.

135. Van Dun, "It's Never a Sure Deal," 128.

136. McClintock, "The War on Drugs," 129.

137. McClintock, "The War on Drugs," 128–29.

138. Kay, "Violent Opportunities," 110.

139. Heuser, "The Effect of Illicit Economies."

140. Van Dun, "It's Never a Sure Deal," 181–82, 187.

141. Gootenberg, "Orphans of Development," 4.

142. Valdivia, "Coca's Haunting Presence," 620; and Allan Gillies, "Theorising State-Narco Relations in Bolivia's Nascent Democracy (1982–1993): Governance, Order and Political Transition," *Third World Quarterly* 39, no. 4 (2018): 734–35.

143. Valdivia, "Coca's Haunting Presence," 620; Gootenberg, *Andean Cocaine: The Making of a Global Drug*, 4; and Gillies, "Theorising State-Narco Relations," 734–35.

144. Gillies, "Theorising State-Narco Relations."

145. Gutierrez, "Criminal Entrepreneurs as Pioneers, Intermediaries, and Arbitrageurs," 6–7.

146. Gutierrez, "Criminal Entrepreneurs as Pioneers, Intermediaries, and Arbitrageurs," 6–7.

147. Gutierrez, "Criminal Entrepreneurs as Pioneers, Intermediaries, and Arbitrageurs," 8; and Painter, *Bolivia and Coca*, 27–28.

148. Grisaffi, "Why Is the Drug Trade Not Violent?," 589.

149. Grisaffi, "Why Is the Drug Trade Not Violent?," 579.

150. Norman, "Narcotization as Security Dilemma," 641.

151. Vellinga, "The Illegal Drug Industry in Latin America," 96.

152. Van Dun, "It's Never a Sure Deal," 184–90.

153. Van Dun, "It's Never a Sure Deal," 184–90.

154. Gutierrez, "Criminal Entrepreneurs as Pioneers, Intermediaries, and Arbitrageurs," 5.

155. Alessandro Ford, "What Lies Behind Bolivia's Expanding Cocaine Trade?," InSight Crime, October 25, 2022, http://insightcrime.org/news/what-lies-behind-bolivias-expanding-cocaine-trade/.

156. Thoumi, "International Drug Conventions," 82; and Boekhout van Solinge, "Global Cocaine Flows," 63–64.

157. Norman, "Narcotization as Security Dilemma," 650.

158. Vellinga, "The Illegal Drug Industry in Latin America," 100.

159. Thoumi, "Organized Crime in Colombia," 183; Boekhout van Solinge, "Global Cocaine Flows," 65; and McDermott et al., "The Cocaine Pipeline to Europe," 38.

160. Vellinga, "The Illegal Drug Industry in Latin America," 97, 100.

161. Enrique Desmond Arias, "The Impacts of Differential Armed Dominance of Politics in Rio de Janeiro, Brazil," *Studies in Comparative International Development* 48, no. 3 (September 2013): 269.

162. Thoumi, "International Drug Conventions," 84; and Boekhout van Solinge, "Global Cocaine Flows," 64.

163. Vellinga, "The Illegal Drug Industry in Latin America," 97.

164. Boekhout van Solinge, "Global Cocaine Flows," 67.

165. McDermott et al., "The Cocaine Pipeline to Europe," 30; Boekhout van Solinge, "Global Cocaine Flows," 65; and Vellinga, "The Illegal Drug Industry in Latin America," 92, 96–97.

166. US Drug Enforcement Administration, "Cali Cartel: The New Kings of Cocaine," US Department of Justice, Office of Justice Programs, 1994, https://ojp.gov/ncjrs/virtual-library/abstracts/cali-cartel-new-kings-cocaine.

167. Boekhout van Solinge, "Global Cocaine Flows," 67; and Kay, "Violent Opportunities," 110.

168. Boekhout van Solinge, "Global Cocaine Flows," 66.

169. McDermott et al., "The Cocaine Pipeline to Europe," 30; Boekhout van Solinge, "Global Cocaine Flows," 65; and Vellinga, "The Illegal Drug Industry in Latin America," 92, 96–97.

170. Vellinga, "The Illegal Drug Industry in Latin America," 97.

171. Nazih Richani, *Systems of Violence: The Political Economy of War and Peace in Colombia*, 2nd ed. (Albany: State University of New York Press, 2013), 196–215; and Gutierrez, "Criminal Entrepreneurs as Pioneers, Intermediaries, and Arbitrageurs," 2.

172. Mistler-Ferguson, "How Peru's Coca Production Is Helping the Global Cocaine Boom."

173. Mistler-Ferguson, "How Peru's Coca Production Is Helping the Global Cocaine Boom"; and Seth Robbins, "Coca Growing, Cocaine Production Reach New Heights in Honduras," InSight Crime, April 19, 2022, https://insightcrime.org/news/coca-growing-cocaine-production-reach-new-heights-in-honduras/.

174. Gootenberg, "Shifting South"; James T. Bradford, "Twenty-First Century Global Drug Trades and Consumption," in *The Oxford Handbook of Global Drug History*, ed. Paul Gootenberg (New York: Oxford University Press, 2022), 637; and Boekhout van Solinge, "Global Cocaine Flows," 60.

175. McDermott et al., "The Cocaine Pipeline to Europe," 1; and Boekhout van Solinge, "Global Cocaine Flows," 58.

176. United Nations Office on Drugs and Crime, *Global Report on Cocaine 2023: Local Dynamics, Global Challenges* (Vienna: United Nations, 2023).

177. Bradford, "Twenty-First Century Global Drug Trades," 637; and Mistler-Ferguson, "How Peru's Coca Production Is Helping the Global Cocaine Boom."

178. Parker Asmann, "Rising Seizures and Consumption in Argentina—The Next Brazil?," InSight Crime, June 27, 2017, https://insightcrime.org/news/analysis/amid-rising-seizures-consumption-argentina-following-brazil/; and Gootenberg, "Shifting South," 295.

179. Asmann, "Rising Seizures and Consumption in Argentina."

180. United Nations Office on Drugs and Crime, *Global Report on Cocaine 2023*, 104, 121–22, 129, 132, 135.

181. McDermott et al., "The Cocaine Pipeline to Europe," 1.

182. Boekhout van Solinge, "Global Cocaine Flows," 60; and Vellinga, "The Illegal Drug Industry in Latin America," 97.

183. McDermott et al., "The Cocaine Pipeline to Europe," 1, 11.

184. Vellinga, "The Illegal Drug Industry in Latin America," 100–101; and Monica Medel and Francisco E. Thoumi, "Mexican Drug 'Cartels,'" in *The Oxford Handbook of Organized Crime*, ed. Letizia Paoli (New York: Oxford University Press, 2014), 205.

185. Boekhout van Solinge, "Global Cocaine Flows," 65; and Vellinga, "The Illegal Drug Industry in Latin America," 101.

186. Vellinga, "The Illegal Drug Industry in Latin America," 101; and McDermott et al., "The Cocaine Pipeline to Europe," 8, 11, 13.

187. Vellinga, "The Illegal Drug Industry in Latin America," 98; and McDermott et al., "The Cocaine Pipeline to Europe," 38.

188. McDermott et al., "The Cocaine Pipeline to Europe," 3–4, 18, 38; and Boekhout van Solinge, "Global Cocaine Flows," 63.

189. McDermott et al., "The Cocaine Pipeline to Europe," 3–4, 18, 38; and Boekhout van Solinge, "Global Cocaine Flows," 63, 74.

190. Boekhout van Solinge, "Global Cocaine Flows," 68; and Vellinga, "The Illegal Drug Industry in Latin America," 99.

191. McDermott et al., "The Cocaine Pipeline to Europe," 31; and Boekhout van Solinge, "Global Cocaine Flows," 65.

192. Boekhout van Solinge, "Global Cocaine Flows," 57.

193. McDermott et al., "The Cocaine Pipeline to Europe," 12; and Mistler-Ferguson, "How Peru's Coca Production Is Helping the Global Cocaine Boom."

194. United Nations Office on Drugs and Crime, *Global Report on Cocaine 2023*, 50.

195. United Nations Office on Drugs and Crime, *Global Report on Cocaine 2023*, 52.

196. "Peru and Bolivia Are Unlikely Allies in the War on Drugs," *The Economist*, August 18, 2018.

197. Grisaffi, "Why Is the Drug Trade Not Violent?," 591–92; and Marten W. Brienen, "Throwing Away the Key: *Mano Dura* with Bolivian Characteristics," in *Mano Dura Policies in Latin America*, ed. Jonathan D. Rosen and Sebastián A. Cutrona (New York: Routledge, 2023), 119.

198. Mistler-Ferguson, "How Peru's Coca Production Is Helping the Global Cocaine Boom."

199. Casas and Ramírez, "Actores y escenarios como determinantes," 35.

200. Mistler-Ferguson, "How Peru's Coca Production Is Helping the Global Cocaine Boom."

201. Navarrete-Frías, "Drug Crop Eradication and Alternative Development in the Andes."

202. Mistler-Ferguson, "How Peru's Coca Production Is Helping the Global Cocaine Boom."

203. United Nations Office on Drugs and Crime, *Global Report on Cocaine 2023*, 50.

204. United Nations Office on Drugs and Crime, *Global Report on Cocaine 2023*, 50.

205. Adam Isacson, "Crisis and Opportunity: Unraveling Colombia's Collapsing Coca Markets," Washington Office on Latin America, August 24, 2023, https://www.wola.org/analysis/crisis-opportunity-unraveling-colombias-collapsing-coca-markets/.

206. McDermott et al., "The Cocaine Pipeline to Europe," 31, 40; and Boekhout van Solinge, "Global Cocaine Flows," 62, 69, 70.

207. Brienen, "Throwing Away the Key," 119.

208. McDermott et al., "The Cocaine Pipeline to Europe," 5, 22–23.

209. Vellinga, "The Illegal Drug Industry in Latin America," 101; and McDermott et al., "The Cocaine Pipeline to Europe," 20.

CHAPTER 2

Organized Crime and Cocaine Trafficking

Counterintuitive Routes, and Consolidated and New Markets

Carolina Sampó and
Valeska Troncoso

Latin America is the only region of the world where coca crops are cultivated and cocaine is produced. Even though Colombia, Peru, and Bolivia almost monopolize production, recently, authorities from Ecuador, Panama, Honduras, Guatemala, and Mexico have seized a significant number of illegal plantations in their respective countries. According to various sources, particularly in Honduras and Guatemala, a record number of eradications were made during the first month of 2023.[1] Even when production is absolutely residual, criminal organizations seem to be trying to expand their very profitable business to new territories, mainly located closer to consumer markets.

Technology is also playing an increasingly important role, not only because it increases the productivity of coca crops from traditional producers but also because it can help develop better-quality cultivations in countries where growers have been trying to produce coca crops that can be used to manufacture cocaine. Small-scale coca crop cultivation has been present in the aforementioned countries for more than a decade now. Nevertheless, there is not enough information about the quality of the coca leaf and whether it is possible to produce cocaine from it or not.[2]

However, authorities have begun to seize considerable amounts of coca bushes,[3] trying to prevent the production of cocaine from the coca-leaf cultivation in those territories. Since 2014, coca bush cultivation and cocaine production have proliferated enough to flood South America.[4] According to a United Nations Office on Drugs and Crime (UNODC) 2022 report, in 2014 in Colombia, Peru, and Bolivia 140,000 hectares were cultivated with coca bush, while in 2020, around 234,000 hectares were reported, representing an increase of more than 70 percent in only six years. As a result, drug-trafficking organizations produced a spillover effect beyond the producing countries and, in addition to using traditional routes, began to employ counterintuitive routes to export as much cocaine as possible.[5] Counterintuitive routes are understood as routes that escape traditional logic, from a state-based perspective, and do not necessarily correspond to the lowest cost–greatest profit dynamic. On the contrary, these routes take advantage of land, river, or sea routes that make no apparent geographical or economic sense. Nevertheless, counterintuitive routes are often preferred by criminal organizations because they provide greater security in avoiding law enforcement agencies.[6] This reflects the adaptability and flexibility of criminal organizations in employing more innovative and less predictable routes for cocaine trafficking, thus evading state surveillance. These counterintuitive routes offer significant incentives due to porous borders, lack of control at ports, and the ability to exploit a country's lack of reputation as a drug exporter, allowing cocaine to be reexported undetected. In this way, drug-trafficking organizations can deceive law enforcement institutions at ports of entry. This strategy reflects the continuing evolution of cocaine trafficking in response to international pressures and market opportunities.

Not only do these counterintuitive routes supply traditional markets, but they have also become a key aspect in provision to the so-called new markets. Cocaine seized in Africa and Asia reinforces the idea that those new markets are on the rise. Since 2015, on both continents, seizures have increased dramatically (except for 2020, due to the COVID-19 pandemic), highlighting the use of counterintuitive routes that defy the traditional logic of authorities. For example, unlike the usual trafficking across the Pacific Ocean from countries such as Mexico or Peru, recent seizures in Asia have revealed that routes have shifted to the south, using nontraditional Chilean ports as exit points and showing a complex combination of land and maritime routes.[7]

Two trends can be identified from this scenario: first, it is clear that criminal organizations tend to produce more, even when that means trying to expand coca crop production to soils that are not ideal for production; and second, since money is not a problem, criminal organizations are investing in new technologies to increase the production of cocaine, in order to fulfill the growing demand worldwide. As a result, not only can we find new countries of coca bush production, but it is also easy to identify an increase in the productivity of coca leaf.[8] As the 2023 UNODC report points out: "Between 2016 and 2020, the average quantity of cocaine hydrochloride obtained from one hectare under productive coca bush cultivation during a given year increased from 6.5 kg to 7 kg in Colombia."[9] In 2020, the global production of cocaine of 100 percent purity was calculated to be around 2,000 tons, which means that the productivity rate has increased by 11 percent since 2019, even when hectares under cultivation remain the same. In 2021, the production of cocaine reached over 2,200 tons, and the trend continues to move in that direction. As Concepción Anguita Olmedo highlights: "Both the range of drugs and the drug markets are expanding and diversifying as never before."[10] In short, the cocaine supply chain has changed recently because the increase in coca bush cultivation allows wider cocaine production, democratizing its commercialization.[11] We could be facing the future of cocaine production: if cocaine markets continue to grow at the speed they have been growing over the past ten years, more sources of coca leaf will be needed. Criminal organizations seem to be preparing the business for future demand—a demand they are nurturing by adding new markets to the supply chain of this global business.

The objective of this chapter is to discuss how counterintuitive routes for cocaine trafficking, as we will define them below, are used to supply both consolidated and new markets of cocaine consumption. We focus on the Latin American routes and on methods used to take cocaine out of South America, as well as on the provision of new markets, particularly those located in Asia. Considering their size and population, we decided to look at China, India, Nepal, Japan, and South Korea. The use of counterintuitive routes to supply consolidated and new markets reduces risks and maximizes profitability for criminal organizations,[12] so they gain importance in a low risk–high return scheme.[13]

This chapter will be divided into three parts. First, we will define concepts such as "counterintuitive routes," and "consolidated" and "new" markets. Second, we will briefly discuss the role of consolidated markets and describe the situation of some of the new markets, particularly those located in Asia. Finally, we will draw some conclusions from the data presented in the chapter.

Counterintuitive Routes, and Consolidated and New Markets

The routes preferred by criminal organizations reflect a rational choice related to a high level of planning and a low risk–high return equation.[14] Even when criminal organizations count on a portfolio of routes from which to choose to smuggle their illicit goods, they use the most convenient route and smuggling method for every moment. Considering the risk involved, the use of counterintuitive routes seems to be gaining importance.

A route can be considered counterintuitive, as we point out elsewhere, when it escapes conventional governmental logic and does not "respond exclusively to the lowest cost–most profit dynamic. Rather, [criminal structures] benefit from the inconveniences of routes that are not very accessible,"[15] which can be a strategic advantage. These inconveniences, "whether due to natural, political, or economic factors, . . . although they may imply a higher economic cost, provide greater security, avoiding police and customs controls."[16]

Counterintuitive routes expose criminal organizations to fewer risks than traditional routes, especially because the latter have been identified by authorities and seizures can take place at any moment. Compared to traditional routes, counterintuitive routes "are not the closest geographically, the shortest in terms of time, nor necessarily the cheapest routes,"[17] but they provide safety to criminal activities. In sum, those routes do not make geographical or economic sense, and yet they enable a low-risk operation that can be conducted by air, water, or land.[18]

According to Anna Sergi, routes and ports work together but may change constantly: "Indeed, a safer (that is, less patrolled) journey by sea—with a less controlled route—might justify using another port, even one that is far away."[19] Since risk is the most important variable that criminal organizations must analyze, they might modify their routes from one operation to another, and mix and match different smuggling methods.

Counterintuitive routes work in conjunction with nontraditional ports of departure, "understood as those ports that are not located in coca bush producing countries"[20] such as Colombia, Peru, or Bolivia. These ports have not "been identified as clear transit areas."[21] On the contrary, "they are located in countries where the government does not recognize transnational drug trafficking as a real problem."[22] Examples of these ports include Buenos Aires in Argentina, San

Antonio in Chile, and Montevideo in Uruguay. Besides, these nontraditional ports are not frequently monitored by international authorities, which makes them strategic points for cocaine exports; and ships leaving these ports do not raise red flags in their arrival ports.

The use of counterintuitive routes and nontraditional ports is part of a carefully planned strategy by criminal organizations to deceive authorities, maximize efficiency, and minimize risks in drug trafficking. The purpose of this strategy is to facilitate the reexport of cocaine and ensure its safe transportation. Earlier, we argued that reexport "is a way to launder the cargo and disguise the origin of the drugs"[23] by using ports and routes that are not typically associated with drug trafficking. This process involves shipping cocaine through countries that do not have an established reputation as drug exporters,[24] taking advantage of the perception that these countries are not involved in drug trafficking. By doing so, criminal organizations can "launder" the shipment, making it appear to come from a country with a "clean" reputation.[25] This reduces the likelihood that authorities at ports of entry will search for and detect the drugs, as these countries are not expected to be departure points for cocaine trafficking.

On the other hand, consolidated markets are those identified by the international community as having the highest cocaine prevalence. The United States is a well-known consolidated market. In recent years, Europe and Brazil have also become consolidated markets. The rise of Brazil as the world's second-biggest consumer of cocaine is related to its role as a transshipment point. Thus, we can learn from these examples, especially when we analyze what seems to be the rise of new markets, such as in some African and Asian countries. In the case of Africa, as for Brazil, its role as a transshipment point is directly related to its consolidation as a consumer market. Europe and Asia respond to a different logic because the demand for cocaine has increased dramatically in both continents.

Consolidated and New Cocaine Markets: The Use of Counterintuitive Routes

As we mentioned above, consolidated markets are those identified by national and international authorities as regular markets for cocaine consumption. The Americas exemplify the demand for cocaine, with more than 11 million users. The United States and Brazil are the main consumers. In absolute terms (i.e., by the number of consumers), the United States continues to be the world's most important market with 4.8 million people having used cocaine at least once during a recent twelve-month period.[26] Brazil is in second place among countries, while Europe as a whole reached 5.2 million consumers during the same time period. Finally, Asian consumers are increasing in number and reached 2.04 million during that twelve-month period. Yet if we consider how many people live in Asia, the number of cocaine consumers per capita is almost insignificant.

As a result, it is important to highlight that the most appealing market for criminal organizations has moved from the Americas to Europe. This is not only because the demand in Europe has continued to grow, but also because the continent has become the entry point to different regions in Asia.

Consolidated Markets and Counterintuitive Routes

How do criminal organizations move cocaine from the producing countries to the demanding markets? They do so by various routes that are not limited to a single mode of transport. These routes can be developed by land, air, river, or sea, allowing criminal organizations to adapt their methods according to the specific circumstances of each operation. Even when criminal organizations are fragmented and it is difficult to identify their actions, it is necessary to highlight the importance of three specific Latin American organizations that seem to have a global presence and work with organizations from outside the region, such as different mafias. These are the Sinaloa cartel and the Cártel de Jalisco Nueva Generación (CJNG; the Jalisco New Generation cartel) from Mexico, and the Brazilian Primeiro Comando da Capital (PCC; First Command of the Capital).[27]

Criminal organizations use air routes and commercial flights (using mules[28]), private flights, and even former commercial-conditioned planes to move drug shipments. Land routes are common, particularly in Latin America, as transporting cocaine there is not difficult; borders are porous, states are weak, and criminal organizations do not use established border crossings because they count on other route options in their portfolio.[29] Finally, fluvial and maritime routes allow them to smuggle cocaine especially outside the region.

Criminal organizations use many methods to smuggle cocaine by sea from Latin America to demanding markets. First, they may use semisubmersibles built and outfitted to carry the drug.[30] "Narco-submarines" are used frequently on the Pacific coast routes (Panama, Colombia, Ecuador, Peru, and Chile). On the Atlantic coast, they help connect routes from Colombia, Venezuela, and Brazil to Europe, as well as from Mexico to the United States. They can carry up to five tons of cocaine and are crewed by two or three crew members.[31]

Second, the most popular method deployed by criminal organizations to carry cocaine out of Latin America is using ship containers, taking advantage of commercial routes of legitimate international trade. There are at least three ways to use the containers: rip-off modality, reefers, and containers contaminated at source.[32]

A third option is to weld the drugs in metal containers to the hull of ships.[33] Specialized divers are required, and most of the time neither the transport company nor the crew are involved.[34] In fact, some countries are hiring professional divers to check ships' hulls before departure.

Fourth, smugglers use vessels specially prepared to cross the ocean, particularly from northern South America to Europe. Good sea conditions can allow criminal organizations to use their own vessels to approach a port near a demanding market or a transit point, as deliveries to some countries of West and North Africa demonstrate.

Finally, small ships are commonly utilized to fill mother ships in the high seas.[35] There are various methods to enhance this process. However, fishing vessels and small private boats are the most prevalent, as they can depart from private ports with a significant amount of cocaine and transfer it to a fully charged mother ship, which then delivers it to its final destination.

In sum, the ability to use diverse routes allows criminal organizations to adapt quickly to pressures and changes in the international security environment. For example, if a country increases its controls and surveillance, organizations can redirect their shipments through counterintuitive routes and less monitored nontraditional ports. Although it may appear that smuggling cocaine via these routes takes longer and is slower than air trafficking, such routes are commonly exploited. The need to diversify routes also fosters innovation in transportation methods, such as the use of narco-submarines, private planes, contaminated cargo containers, bulk carriers, and more. This tactical shift not only reduces the risk of seizure but also disperses the efforts of authorities, making it more difficult for them to predict and stop trafficking operations.

In this context, Africa must be considered because it is a consolidated transshipment point and also an increasingly important consumer market. It is a counterintuitive route of cocaine trafficking to Europe, Asia, and Oceania. In an earlier work, Carolina Sampó argued that West Africa has become a transshipment point to Europe, and she identified four hubs: first, the Atlantic Coast (Guinea-Bissau, Guinea, and Senegal); second, the Sahel (Mauritania, Mali, and Niger); third, North Africa (Morocco, Algeria, Libya, and Egypt); and finally, the Gulf of Guinea.[36] The latter follows the coastlines of Ghana, Togo, Benin, Nigeria, and Cameroon, and from those countries, most of the drug cargo is redistributed, in many cases via land or air routes. A UNODC report on cocaine trafficking adds South Africa, Ethiopia, and Kenya to the list of transit countries, but these are reached by air and serve as transshipment points to Asia.[37]

New Markets

New markets for cocaine rise constantly; because criminal organizations produce more cocaine, this creates pressure to find these new markets. Asia, on the one hand, is the source of precursor chemicals used to produce drugs in the Americas and is also the origin of some synthetic drugs such as fentanyl.[38] On the other hand, Asia has become an increasingly important cocaine market at least since 2015. Some Asian countries such as China, South Korea, and India show a close relationship with Latin American countries, as well as the greatest volume of container movement in the world. These Asian countries provide easy and cheap transportation for cocaine trafficking. Air routes to Asia are also important, especially coming from Europe and East Africa. But sea routes, whether from the Indian Ocean or the Pacific, are key to understanding the provision of cocaine from Latin America.

The Pacific maritime route has become increasingly important for global cocaine trafficking. Countries like Colombia, Chile, Ecuador, Guatemala, Honduras, Mexico, and Peru have been identified as the departure points for this route from South America.[39] The drugs may also pass through other countries like Japan, Thailand, China, the Philippines, and Vietnam[40] before reaching their final destinations, which include Australia, China, Hong Kong, Macau, and other parts of Asia.[41] As a result, many Asian countries have become transshipment points, and some of them have become consumers. Even if levels of cocaine consumption remain low (though probably underestimated), it is possible to identify a trend toward the use of cocaine in Asia.

China

Even though it is very difficult to access Chinese government data, recent drug seizures have shown that a route for cocaine is open there, especially because of the key role China is playing in the production of different drugs as the main exporter of precursor chemicals to Latin America. It is also important to understand that China's international maritime commerce routes indeed facilitate the smuggling of cocaine. According to World Bank data, in 2021, Chinese shipping moved 262,605,700 twenty-foot equivalents (TEUs), the highest number in the world and four times what the United States moved in that year.[42] From those containers, 58,669,478 TEUs were bound for Latin America and the Caribbean. China is also the most important commercial partner of many Latin American countries, such as Mexico and Chile. Commerce between China and Latin America, mainly maritime, reached US$4.5 billion in 2021.[43]

Having easy access and cheap transportation—thanks to the container traffic—as well as extremely high prices for cocaine on the other side of the world is an incentive for drug-trafficking organizations trying to enter a new, profitable market. From the limited information available on drug movements in China, we know that cocaine seizures in 2022 totaled 176.6 kilograms, most of which had been transported directly from South America.[44] Yet in previous years, bigger cargoes had been seized. For example, in 2018, altogether 1.3 tons of cocaine were discovered by Chinese authorities,[45] and in 2021, 700 kilos were seized by the Hong Kong police.[46] Hong Kong has also shown an increasing number of cocaine seizures, proving that both the route and the market for the drug exist. According to the UNODC, from 2018 to 2023, seizures in China, Hong Kong, and Macau tripled.[47] From less than one ton of cocaine seized in 2016, seizures increased to more than three tons in 2021. According to the Organized Crime Global Index, China is becoming a key transshipment node for cocaine coming from South America along a route that connects with Oceania.[48]

South Korea

Previously known as a "drug-free country," South Korea has become a significant hub for cocaine trafficking. The country has witnessed a noticeable surge in drug-related crimes, and the quantity of drugs seized has risen even with fewer enforcement operations to seize them since 2016.[49] Concerns have risen regarding the actual amount of cocaine circulated in South Korea, which might be significantly higher than what the official data suggests. Additionally, authorities are worried about the rise in domestic consumption.

A significant amount of drugs being distributed in South Korea comes from Southeast Asia, China, the United States, and South America.[50] When it comes to the rise in cocaine trafficking, there are two critical factors to keep in mind. First, criminal organizations focus on South Korea because the retail cost of drugs there is higher than in other Asian countries, with an average cost of US$341 per gram.[51] Second, law enforcement faces challenges in controlling drug trafficking. Korean police cannot simply arrest someone suspected of dealing drugs; they must first pretend to be customers.[52]

According to the Organized Crime Global Index, South Korea is mainly a transit country for cocaine going to Oceania, China (including Hong Kong and Macau), and other parts of Asia.[53] Seizures indicate that the port of Busan plays an important role in cocaine's arrival in South Korea. The port is located along the Pacific route of cocaine trafficking, connecting Latin America and Asia.

Organized Crime and Cocaine Trafficking — 75

Busan is a key hub for logistical transport in Northeast Asia and ranks sixth in global importance, moving 29.786 billion total TEUs of cargo per year; it is responsible for 80 percent of South Korea's container traffic. Although the port of Busan has modern infrastructure, customs authorities have acknowledged the port's deficiencies and its inability to control drug trafficking.[54] Authorities have determined that cocaine is trafficked from Latin American ports in Colombia, Chile, Ecuador, Guatemala, Honduras, and Mexico.[55]

India

Even though the cocaine market in India seems to be still quite small, according to the Organized Crime Global Index, cocaine smuggling has risen in recent years due to criminal organizations using the web for sales, payments, and distribution.[56] According to the UNODC, the most important ports for cocaine departure seized in India are located in countries such as Panama, South Africa, and Brazil,[57] proving the existence of the counterintuitive routes we mentioned above. Nevertheless, it is important to remember that India is the world's second-biggest producer of fentanyl and has commercial ties with Mexico, opening the door for the delivery of cocaine in the ships coming back from the Americas.

Cocaine movement has risen dramatically in India, as seizures show. In fiscal year 2018–2019, only 1.93 kilos were seized, while in fiscal year 2021–2022, more than 300 kilos were seized, showing a clear trend, despite the small amount of cocaine seized. According to the Directorate of Revenue Intelligence (DRI), Indian authorities have made "large seizures of cocaine, several of them from containerized cargo, indicating a new trend of trafficking of large quantities of cocaine to India via sea.[58]

According to a DRI report, most narcotics seizures "have been made on commercial trade routes. There has been a surge in seizures of narcotics along the maritime route on the west coast of India."[59] Intelligence officials note that some of the last seizures had come from Panama, transited via the ports of Antwerp (Belgium) and Colombo (Sri Lanka) before reaching Tuticorin in India.[60] Moreover, the use of air routes is also on the rise. In June 2023, a Brazilian national coming from São Paulo was detained with 3.22 kilos of black cocaine.[61] In 2020, another Brazilian was detained with eighty capsules full of high-purity cocaine in his stomach.[62] These are only a few examples of what seems to be a trend related to cocaine smuggling to India.

Nepal

Nepal, despite being a landlocked country, remains a significant transit hub for cocaine trafficking.[63] The Narcotics Control Bureau (NCB) reports that criminal groups use complex maritime and air routes to transport cocaine to Kathmandu, the capital.[64] These routes originate from various South American countries including Bolivia, Brazil, and Peru.[65] Cocaine has mainly entered Nepal via air travel from Qatar, Dubai, Mozambique, and South Africa, with its ultimate destination being India, Hong Kong, South Korea, Thailand, and Australia.[66] It is important to note that cocaine is trafficked in both directions between Nepal and India, across the porous border along land routes. Indeed, the evidence suggests that drugs are largely trafficked along the land border.

Nepal is a transit and consumer country for cocaine. Official reports indicate that people have started using cocaine and other stimulant drugs, leading to changes in the types and modes of drug use.[67] Although the cost of a gram of cocaine in Nepal is relatively high at US$222,[68] demand continues to grow. Part of the demand for cocaine can be attributed to tourism, mainly coming from Europe and the United States,[69] probably due to consumers having the resources to pay big prices.

Japan

Even though the UNODC has recently identified Japan as an emerging market for cocaine, the truth is that the data does not seem to confirm that statement. The UNODC indicates that a domestic market has existed for a long time, even if a small one.[70] A UNODC report on cocaine highlights that, between 2015 and 2020, cocaine seizures in Japan have increased approximately sevenfold. Nevertheless, official Japanese data shows that in 2021 seizures dropped dramatically to fourteen kilos.[71] These seizures were the result of thirty-four different cases, showing that the quantity seized in each operation is not significant.

Drug seizures have risen over time: 9.2 tons of drugs were seized in 4,280 separate cases between 2017 and 2021.[72] Nonetheless, cocaine use remains at very low levels. During the same five-year period, there were only 195 cases, with a total of 1.53 tons of cocaine seized, mostly from Latin America.[73] During 2019–2020, the number of cases decreased by 48 percent, according to official sources.[74]

Although most containers entering Japan pass through the port of Tokyo, authorities have identified the port of Yokohama as the main entry point for cocaine from Brazil, Colombia, Chile, Ecuador, Mexico, Panama, and Peru.[75] In spite of Yokohama being recognized by the World Bank as Asia's most efficient container port,[76] the largest cocaine shipment in Japan's history was seized there. And despite the importance of the 2020 seizures, there is a story behind them. First, a seized container coming from Ecuador was supposed to land in another Asian country.[77] Second, that container held 722 kilos of cocaine, which means that more than 88 percent of 2020 seizures was accounted for by that single operation. Something similar happened in 2019: of the 638 total kilos of cocaine seized in that year, 400 kilos were seized in one operation in the port of Yokohama,[78] while the other 236 kilos were seized in fifty-one other operations.[79]

Apart from shipping routes from Latin American countries with Pacific coastlines such as Ecuador, Colombia, Guatemala, Peru, Chile, and Mexico, air routes from Europe are also being used to deliver cocaine to Japan.[80] The market nevertheless remains small, and it does not seem to be a matter of great concern to Japanese authorities. Harsh penalties[81] and moral judgment from Japanese society likely explain why consumption is not increasing to the same degree that it is in other Asian countries.

In conclusion, even if it is tempting to think of Japan as a new cocaine market that can be reached through different counterintuitive routes, there is not enough data to sustain the statement. Even though the cocaine market has gone global, not every single country in the world has a demand to be exploited.

Conclusion

Ever since cocaine smuggling expanded to create a genuine global market, Latin American criminal organizations, as well as other organizations that may be producing, smuggling, and distributing cocaine from that region, have generated some remarkable changes in the cocaine market.

First, the production of cocaine continues to rise. The use of technological resources to increase the productivity of coca leaf, as well as the cultivation of coca crops beyond the borders of the traditional producers, show how the business is expanding. Second, the use of nontraditional ports to export cocaine with the objective of lowering the risk of detection proves that criminal organizations are rational actors whose business decisions result from a low risk–high return equation. In that sense, counterintuitive routes provide safety to shipments by avoiding law enforcement in departure and arrival ports, especially because shipments originating in nontraditional ports do not raise red flags. Third, criminal organizations continue to feed consolidated cocaine markets and at the same time exert pressure to open up new ones. As a result, Africa and Asia are shifting from exclusively transshipment points to consumer markets in their own right. Counterintuitive routes play a key role in the supply of these new markets. In Asia, the use of different methods and routes to smuggle cocaine is reflected in the seizures reported by authorities.

The countries we have analyzed in this chapter do not necessarily repeat the same trends. Cultural values, greater availability of other drugs, and harsh penalties play an important role in deterring potential consumers of cocaine in some countries, such as Japan and possibly South Korea. Additionally, the prominence of synthetic drugs may explain why it is not so easy for criminal organizations to open a cocaine market in a given region. Nevertheless, tourism and Western influence—and soft power—may play an important part in increasing cocaine consumption.

Cocaine trafficking continues to mutate. Criminal organizations are clearly focused on profit and run their business as rational actors. Nowadays, new markets seem to present a big business opportunity, but consolidated markets cannot be left unattended. The United States and Brazil at the regional level, as well as Europe as a whole, are consolidated markets that provide tremendous profit to criminal organizations. The future of cocaine trafficking may still be in those markets, especially Europe, since the volume of cocaine consumption continues to grow. Nonetheless, a bet on new markets might provide big revenues in the near future, explaining why criminal organizations choose to diversify their business. Counterintuitive routes provide safety to drug shipments and the criminal organizations that arrange them, and they will continue to be used and adjusted to guarantee the global provision of cocaine supply. Criminal organizations will continue to increase the productivity of this unique and extremely desirable drug, and Latin America will adapt and adjust according to the demands of the cocaine market.

Notes

1. Gavin Voss, "Coca May Have Permanently Taken Root in Central America," InSight Crime, March 15, 2023, https://insightcrime.org/news/coca-permanently-taken-root-central-america/.

2. US Department of State, *2021 International Narcotics Control Strategy Report*, vol. 1, *Drug and Chemical Control*, Bureau of International Narcotics and Law Enforcement Affairs, March 2, 2021, https://www.state.gov/2021-international-narcotics-control-strategy-report/.

3. Between January 1 and May 25, 2023, Honduran authorities destroyed three million coca bushes, dismantled sixteen drug laboratories, and seized eleven coca fields. Lorena Baires, "Honduras Combats Coca Cultivation," *Diálogo Américas*, June 20, 2023, https://dialogo-americas.com/articles/honduras-combats-coca-cultivation/. Also, Guatemala destroyed almost nine hundred thousand bushes before March 12, 2023. Voss, "Coca May Have Permanently Taken Root in Central America." Regarding Ecuador, more than seven hundred hectares with coca leaf are been cultivated in different regions. Renato Rivera-Rhon and Carlos Bravo-Grijalva, "Crimen organizado y cadenas de valor: El ascenso

estratégico del Ecuador en la economía del narcotráfico," *URVIO: Revista Latinoamericana de Estudios de Seguridad*, no. 28 (September–December 2020): 8–29.

4. Carolina Sampó and Marcos Alan Ferreira, "De la fragmentación de las estructuras criminales a una proto-mafia: Un análisis del Primeiro Comando da Capital (PCC) en Sudamérica," *Revista de Estudios en Seguridad Internacional* 6, no. 2 (2020): 101–15.

5. Carolina Sampó and Valeska Troncoso, "Cocaine Trafficking from Non-Traditional Ports: Examining the Cases of Argentina, Chile and Uruguay," *Trends in Organized Crime* 26, no. 1 (January 2022): 235–57.

6. Sampó and Troncoso, "Cocaine Trafficking from Non-Traditional Ports."

7. Antonio González, "Incautan cocaína avaluada en más de $3 mil millones escondida en Zinc con destino a Corea del Sur," BioBioChile, January 17, 2023, https://www.biobiochile.cl/especial/el-narco-en-chile/noticias/2023/01/17/incautan-cocaina-avaluada-en-mas-de-3-mil-millones-escondida-en-zinc-con-destino-a-corea-del-sur.shtml.

8. United Nations Office on Drugs and Crime, *World Drug Report 2022* (Vienna: United Nations, 2022), 154.

9. United Nations Office on Drugs and Crime, *World Drug Report 2023* (Vienna: United Nations, 2023).

10. Concepción Anguita Olmedo, "Dynamics of Organized Crime in the European Union in the Context of Global Insecurity," in *The Routledge Handbook of European Security Law and Policy*, ed. E. Conde, Zhaklin V. Yaneva, and Marzia Scopelliti (Abingdon, Oxon., England: Routledge, 2020), 179.

11. Sampó and Ferreira, "De la fragmentación de las estructuras criminales," 111–15.

12. Damián Zaitch, "From Cali to Rotterdam: Perceptions of Colombian Cocaine Traffickers on the Dutch Port," *Crime, Law and Social Change* 38, no. 3 (2002): 239–66.

13. Sampó and Troncoso, "Cocaine Trafficking from Non-Traditional Ports."

14. Sampó and Troncoso, "Cocaine Trafficking from Non-Traditional Ports."

15. Sampó and Troncoso, "Cocaine Trafficking from Non-Traditional Ports," 240.

16. Sampó and Troncoso, "Cocaine Trafficking from Non-Traditional Ports," 240.

17. Sampó and Troncoso, "Cocaine Trafficking from Non-Traditional Ports," 240.

18. Sampó and Troncoso, "Cocaine Trafficking from Non-Traditional Ports," 240.

19. Anna Sergi, "Playing Pac-Man in Portville: Policing the Dilution and Fragmentation of Drug Importations Through Major Seaports," *European Journal of Criminology* 19, no. 4 (July 2022): 683.

20. Sampó and Troncoso, "Cocaine Trafficking from Non-Traditional Ports," 240.

21. Sampó and Troncoso, "Cocaine Trafficking from Non-Traditional Ports," 240.

22. Sampó and Troncoso, "Cocaine Trafficking from Non-Traditional Ports," 240.

23. Sampó and Troncoso, "Cocaine Trafficking from Non-Traditional Ports," 251.

24. Sampó and Troncoso, "Cocaine Trafficking from Non-Traditional Ports," 251.

25. Sampó and Troncoso, "Cocaine Trafficking from Non-Traditional Ports," 251.

26. National Institute on Drug Abuse, "Cocaína: Abuso y adicción—Reporte de investigación ¿Cuál es el alcance del consumo de cocaína en los Estados Unidos?," 2023, https://nida.nih.gov/es/publicaciones/serie-de-reportes/cocaina-abuso-y-adiccion/cual-es-el-alcance-del-consumo-de-cocaina-en-los-estados-unidos.

27. Nathan P. Jones, "The Strategic Implications of the Cártel de Jalisco Nueva Generación," *Journal of Strategic Security* 11, no. 1 (Spring 2018): 19–42; Marcos Alan Ferreira, "Brazilian Criminal Organizations as Transnational Violent Non-State Actors: A Case Study of the Primeiro Comando da Capital (PCC)," *Trends in Organized Crime* 22, no. 61 (June 2019): 148–65; Sampó and Ferreira, "De la fragmentación de las estructuras criminales"; and Valentin Pereda and David Décary-Hetu, "Illegal Market Governance and Organized Crime Groups' Resilience: A Study of the Sinaloa Cartel," *British Journal of Criminology* 64, no. 2 (March 2024): 326–42.

28. Mules are people who carry cocaine inside their bodies during a flight.

29. Sampó and Troncoso, "Cocaine Trafficking from Non-Traditional Ports."

30. Patricia Ortega Dolz, Nacho Carretero, Artur Galocha, and Mariano Zafra, "26 días de travesía en un narcosubmarino," *El País* (Madrid), December 16, 2019, https://elpais.com/politica/2019/12/13/actualidad/1576232797_250425.html.

31. "Narcosubmarinos: Hechos en masa, en secreto, en la selva y con el toque del artesano fabricante," Infobae, August 27, 2020, https://www.infobae.com/america/mexico/2020/08/27/narcosubmarinos-hechos-en-masa-en-secreto-en-la-selva-y-con-el-toque-del-artesano-fabricante/.

32. "Rip off" is "a concealment methodology whereby a legitimate shipment, usually containerised, is exploited to smuggle [cocaine] from the country of origin or the transshipment port to the country of destination," according to the UNODC. "Reefers" are refrigerated containers used to ship perishable goods, and due to the density of these products, some scanners are not able to identify cocaine among the licit goods. Containers are "contaminated at source" when the cocaine is hidden inside before the container is sealed. Fiscalía de Chile, *Observatorio del narcotráfico: Informe 2020* (Santiago: Ministerio Público, 2020).

33. Juan Manuel Díaz C., "Las redes del narcotráfico acechan sistema portuario," *La Prensa* (Panama City), November 2, 2020, https://www.prensa.com/impresa/panorama/las-redes-del-narcotrafico-acechan-sistema-portuario/.

34. Ana Lilia Pérez, *Mares de cocaína: Las rutas náuticas del narcotráfico* (Mexico City: Editorial Grijalbo, 2014).

35. Pérez, *Mares de cocaína*.

36. Carolina Sampó, "El tráfico de cocaína entre América Latina y África Occidental," *URVIO: Revista Latinoamericana de Estudios de Seguridad* 24 (June 2019): 187–203.

37. United Nations Office on Drugs and Crime, *Global Report on Cocaine 2023* (Vienna: United Nations, 2023).

38. Vanda Felbab-Brown, "China and Synthetic Drugs: Geopolitics Trumps Counternarcotics Cooperation," Brookings Institution, March 7, 2022, https://www.brookings.edu/articles/china-and-synthetic-drugs-geopolitics-trumps-counternarcotics-cooperation/.

39. González, "Incautan cocaína avaluada en más de $3 mil millones"; Global Initiative Against Transnational Organized Crime (GI-TOC), *Global Organized Crime Index 2021: Korea* (Geneva: GI-TOC, 2021); and Elizabeth Shim, "South Korea Raises Concerns About Drug Smuggling in New Report," United Press International, August 19, 2021, https://www.upi.com/Top_News/World-News/2021/08/19/south-korean-spy-report-drug-smuggling/1061629396703/.

40. United Nations Office on Drugs and Crime, *Global Report on Cocaine 2023*.

41. GI-TOC, *Global Organized Crime Index 2021: Korea*.

42. World Bank Group, "Container Port Traffic (TEU: 20 Foot Equivalent Units): China," Trading Economics, 2023, https://tradingeconomics.com/china/container-port-traffic-teu-20-foot-equivalent-units-wb-data.html.

43. Luz María Gallardo Castro, "Latinoamérica: ¿Una región en disputa entre China y Estados Unidos?," *Foreign Affairs Latinoamérica*, October 6, 2022, https://revistafal.com/latinoamerica-una-region-en-disputa-entre-china-y-estados-unidos/.

44. "China Drug Situation Report, 2022," Consulate General of the People's Republic of China, Los Angeles, 2022.

45. Agence France-Presse, "China Seizes Record 1.3 Tons of Cocaine," *Hürriyet Daily News* (Istanbul), April 25, 2018, https://www.hurriyetdailynews.com/china-seizes-record-1-3-tons-of-cocaine-130859.

46. United Nations Office on Drugs and Crime, *Global Report on Cocaine 2023*.

47. United Nations Office on Drugs and Crime, *Global Report on Cocaine 2023*, 122.

48. Global Initiative Against Transnational Organized Crime (GI-TOC), *Organized Crime Global Index 2022* (Geneva: GI-TOC, 2022).

49. GI-TOC, *Organized Crime Global Index: Korea 2021*.

50. Kang Yoon-seung, "Customs Agency Seizes Record Amount of Drugs Through April," *Yonhap News Agency*, May 18, 2023, https://en.yna.co.kr/view/AEN20230518001300320; and GI-TOC, *Organized Crime Global Index: Korea 2021*.

51. United Nations Office on Drugs and Crime, *Global Report on Cocaine 2023*.

52. Kim Jae-heun, "Korea Is No Longer 'Drug Free' Country," *Korea Times*, December 9, 2023, https://www.koreatimes.co.kr/www/nation/2023/09/113_280018.html.

53. GI-TOC, *Organized Crime Global Index: Korea 2021*.

54. Jang Seob Yoon, "Container Throughput at Busan Port in South Korea from 2013 to 2023," *Statista*, October 21, 2024, https://www.statista.com/statistics/954655/busan-port-throughput-container-south-korea/.

55. González, "Incautan cocaína avaluada en más de $3 mil millones"; GI-TOC, *Organized Crime Global Index: Korea 2021*; and Shim, "South Korea Raises Concerns About Drug Smuggling."

56. Global Initiative Against Transnational Organized Crime (GI-TOC), *Global Organized Crime Index 2021: India* (Geneva: GI-TOC, 2021).

57. United Nations Office on Drugs and Crime, *Global Report on Cocaine 2023*, 128.

58. Directorate of Revenue Intelligence, *2021–2022 Smuggling in India Report*, November 2022, xxiv, https://dri.nic.in/writereaddata/2021_2022%20REPORT%20FINAL_14.pdf.

59. Directorate of Revenue Intelligence, *2021–2022 Smuggling in India Report*, xxiv.

60. "DRI Seizes 300 kg Cocaine Worth Rs 2,000 Crore at Tuticorin Port in Tamil Nadu," *Economic Times* (Mumbai), April 22, 2021, https://economictimes.indiatimes.com/news/india/dri-seizes-300-kg-cocaine-worth-rs-2000-crore-at-tuticorin-port-in-tamil-nadu/articleshow/82191478.cms?from=mdr.

61. "In Rare Seizure, 'Black Cocaine' Worth ₹32 Crore Recovered in Ahmedabad," *India News*, June 21, 2023, https://www.ndtv.com/india-news/in-rare-seizure-black-cocaine-worth-rs-32-crore-recovered-in-ahmedabad-4140868.

62. Vijay Kumar Yadav, "Brazilian Man Caught with ₹2.38-cr Capsules of Cocaine in His Stomach," *Hindustan Times* (New Delhi), February 26, 2020, https://www.hindustantimes.com/mumbai-news/brazilian-man-caught-with-2-38-cr-capsules-of-cocaine-in-his-stomach/story-ioG8jjeJ8FKsfPTMctTNSL.html.

63. Global Initiative Against Transnational Organized Crime (GI-TOC), *Global Organized Crime Index 2021: Nepal* (Geneva: GI-TOC, 2021), 3.

64. Narcotics Control Bureau, *Magazine 2072: Annual Publication*, 2022, https://ncb.nepalpolice.gov.np/media/filer_public/52/6b/526b40ac-f9c7-4802-8318-a18c44f105aa/ncb-magazine-2072-cover.pdf.

65. "Two Foreigners Held with 5.6kg Cocaine," *Himalayan Times* (Kathmandu), December 24, 2022, https://thehimalayantimes.com/nepal/two-foreigners-held-with-56kg-cocaine; and National Statistics Office, *Drugs and Persons in Trafficking in Nepal* (Kathmandu: National Statistics Office, 2022), 6.

66. Shuvam Dhungana, "Nepal May Be Becoming a New Transit Point for Drug Smugglers," *Kathmandu Post*, January 4, 2020, https://kathmandupost.com/national/2020/01/04/nepal-may-be-becoming-the-new-transit-point-for-the-drug-smugglers; and "Nepal Becoming Transit Hub for Drug Peddlers," *Himalayan Times* (Kathmandu), August 30, 2021, https://thehimalayantimes.com/nepal/nepal-becoming-transit-hub-for-drug-peddlers.

67. Government of Nepal, Ministry of Home Affairs, *Nepal Drug Users Survey 2076*, June 2020, 18, https://nepalindata.com/media/resources/items/20/bNepal_Drug_Users_Survey_2076.pdf.

68. United Nations Office on Drugs and Crime, *Global Report on Cocaine 2023*, 95.

69. Anbarasan Ethirajan, "Nepal Steps Up Battle Against Drug Traffickers," BBC News, April 4, 2013, https://www.bbc.com/news/business-21963600.

70. United Nations Office on Drugs and Crime, *Global Report on Cocaine 2023*.

71. Customs and Tariff Bureau, Government of Japan, *Trends in Smuggling in Japan ("White Powder and Black Firearms" Report)*, 2022 ed. (Tokyo: Ministry of Finance, 2022).

72. Customs and Tariff Bureau, Government of Japan, *Trends in Smuggling in Japan*, 2022 ed..

73. Customs and Tariff Bureau, Government of Japan, *Trends in Smuggling in Japan*, 2022 ed..

74. Customs and Tariff Bureau, Government of Japan, *Trends in Illicit Drugs Smuggling* (Tokyo: Ministry of Finance, 2021).

75. "Aduanas decomisa cerca de dos toneladas de cocaína impregnada en madera originaria de Bolivia en Puerto de Arica," Portal Portuario, July 27, 2023, https://portalportuario.cl/aduanas-decomisa-cerca-de-dos-toneladas-de-cocaina-impregnada-en-madera-originaria-de-bolivia-en-puerto-de-arica/; Customs and Tariff Bureau, Government of Japan, *Trends in Smuggling in Japan ("White Powder and Black Firearms" Report)*, 2020 ed. (Tokyo: Ministry of Finance, 2020); Customs and Tariff Bureau, Government of Japan, *Trends in Smuggling in Japan ("White Powder and Black Firearms" Report)*, 2021 ed. (Tokyo: Ministry of Finance, 2021); and "Japan Record 115 kg of Cocaine Seized in Yokohama," *Tokyo Reporter*, August 31, 2018, https://www.tokyoreporter.com/crime/japan-record-100-kg-of-cocaine-seized-in-yokohama/.

76. World Bank Group, *Transport Global Practice: The Container Port Performance Index 2021* (Washington, DC: International Bank for Reconstruction and Development, 2022), https://thedocs.worldbank.org/en/doc/66e3aa5c3be4647addd01845ce353992-0190062022/original/Container-Port-Performance-Index-2021.pdf.

77. "Record 700 kg of Cocaine Seized at Yokohama Port," Kyodo News, April 16, 2020, https://english.kyodonews.net/news/2020/04/52065fd2f6a9-record-700-kg-of-cocaine-seized-at-yokohama-port.html.

78. "Record 700 kg of Cocaine Seized at Yokohama Port."

79. Customs and Tariff Bureau, Government of Japan, *Trends in Smuggling in Japan ("White Powder and Black Firearms" Report)*.

80. United Nations Office on Drugs and Crime, *Global Report on Cocaine 2023*.

81. For cocaine possession, according to the Japanese National Police Agency, a person can be sentenced up to five years in prison.

CHAPTER 3

Cocaine and Criminal Governance in Colombia

Héctor Alarcón Barrera and
Juan Albarracín

Colombia's centrality in the global cocaine supply chain today and in the past decades, often emphasized by the prevalence of Colombian criminal characters in US cultural production about the "war on drugs,"[1] can blur the dramatic transformations experienced by the country since the 1960s: after the US-led drug prohibitionist regime firmly established itself in the second half of the twentieth century—making cocaine markets illicit across the globe—Colombia was a negligible player, almost entirely off the radar of US authorities in the Andean cocaine trade.[2] Yet within a few decades, the country became the epicenter of the Andean cocaine trade and the central concern and target of US antidrug efforts.[3] In recent years, while remaining the leading global cocaine producer, the country's drug-trafficking groups have lost preeminence in the control of the cocaine trade to the United States vis-à-vis Mexican criminal organizations.

In this chapter, we track the rise and transformation of Colombia as one of the central nodes of the global cocaine supply chain. We focus initially on describing key aspects of Colombia's changing position in this illicit market and the relevant actors involved. We show how, in the 1970s and 1980s, Colombian criminal groups transformed the country into the leading processor of Peruvian and Bolivian cocaine paste and dominated trafficking to the United States. This position changed in the mid- to late 1990s with the explosion of coca-bush cultivation and the ensuing vertical integration of the cocaine industry in Colombia. At the same time, the country's leading drug-trafficking organizations collapsed, giving way to a more fragmented landscape of criminal actors and an increasing loss of relevance—relative to Mexican organizations—in the control of drug-trafficking networks, particularly those that connect the cocaine producing Andes with the United States.

This initial description is necessary to understand key aspects of the criminal *governance* of the cocaine supply chain—from production to trafficking and laundering—in Colombia. Instead of focusing on the (changing) criminal organizations involved in drug production and trafficking in isolation, we look at the broader *governance* patterns in which they are embedded. Unlike some illicit activities, like theft, the cocaine production and trafficking chain requires a level of informal regulation—the enforcement of a framework of rules—to be able to function. Importantly, the criminal governance of cocaine is shaped by government choices and policies but also, crucially, by the (informal) involvement of state actors in criminal governance. It is state actors who provide valuable resources for the market to operate, like protection.[4]

While exploring overall changing patterns of cocaine governance, we also distinguish patterns of governance *along* the cocaine supply chain. Criminal governance can involve the regulation of illicit markets and/or the regulation of social life beyond the illicit market.[5] In the case of cocaine in Colombia, as persuasively argued by Gustavo Duncan, criminal groups do not always engage in the same modes of criminal governance in every step of the cocaine chain.[6] In some cases, they control populations and exercise armed control of territories, while on other points of the chain they engage in a more functional form of criminal governance, focusing mostly on the regulation of illicit markets.

The dizzying and changing number of actors and modes of criminal governance precludes a detailed analysis of each of them over an extended time period. However, by providing an overview of changing patterns of governance, we offer an analytical framework to explore a rich and growing literature on drug production and trafficking in Colombia.

Colombia's Evolving Position in the International Cocaine Supply Chain

This section maps Colombia's trajectory from a marginal to a central actor in the global cocaine supply chain in three important phases. In the first phase, Colombia became the leading refiner of Peruvian and Bolivian cocaine paste. The tremendous growth in cocaine production achieved by Colombian criminal organizations was matched by their control of trafficking to and distribution in the largest cocaine consumer market, the United States. In the second phase, there was a vertical integration of the cocaine industry in Colombia with the rapid growth of coca-leaf cultivation in the country. At the same time, the crackdown on larger drug-trafficking organizations—the Medellín and Cali cartels—initiated a process of fragmentation of criminal groups and the greater involvement of other actors, such as guerrilla and paramilitary groups, in the cocaine business.

Although the Colombian government engaged in aggressive coca crop eradication strategies and enjoyed some partial successes in containing production, recent years have seen a growth in coca-bush cultivation. The fragmentation of criminal actors has increased throughout the past few decades, propelled by the (partial) demobilization of paramilitary groups during the Álvaro Uribe administration (2002–2010) and of the Fuerzas Armadas Revolucionarias de Colombia (FARC) after the signing of the peace agreement in 2016. This growing fragmentation has weakened Colombian drug-trafficking organizations' position in the cocaine trade to the United States, with organizations from other countries, particularly Mexico, gaining a more prominent role. Despite these changes, one constant remains: Colombia is still a leading global producer of cocaine (see figure 3.1).

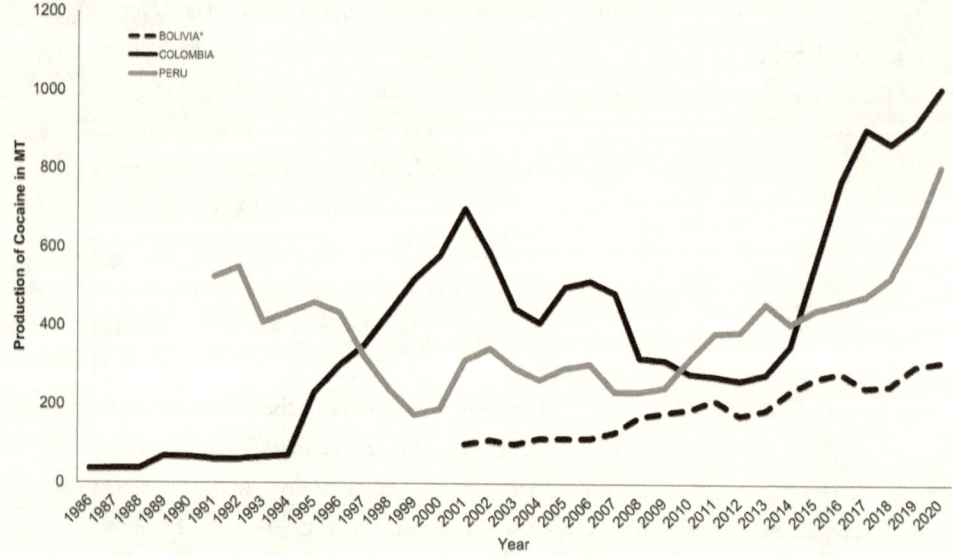

Figure 3.1. Potential pure cocaine production in Colombia, Bolivia, and Peru, 1986–2020. Source: US Department of Justice, *Special Report: Worldwide Cocaine Trafficking Trends* (Washington, DC: US Department of Justice, 1985); Bureau of International Narcotics and Law Enforcement Affairs, *International Narcotics Control Strategy Report 1995* (Washington, DC: US Department of State, 1995); and Bureau of International Narcotics and Law Enforcement Affairs, *International Narcotics Control Strategy Report 2022* (Washington, DC: US Department of State, 2022). *Information available in the case of Bolivia is since 2000, due to revisions in the estimates before 2000.

Colombia's Rise to a Global Cocaine Producer and Preeminence in Drug Trafficking to the United States

As cocaine transformed globally from a licit to an illicit commodity after the Second World War, Colombia was a conspicuously absent player. Production and trafficking centered in other countries: Peru, Bolivia, Chile, Cuba, and Argentina.[7] Colombia's first inroad into drug production and trafficking revolved around the marijuana industry, which emerged in the late 1960s in the Sierra Nevada and Guajira areas on Colombia's Caribbean coast.[8] The Bonanza Marimbera (Marijuana Boom) ushered in Colombia's participation in the global narcotics trade. After crackdowns on Mexican marijuana production, Colombia quickly filled the market void to become the main supplier of the United States.[9]

As the marijuana boom peaked, cocaine production started making its way into Colombia. Mostly nameless Colombian traffickers already had developed links to traffickers from the Southern Cone, and through these connections they engaged in trafficking of (relatively) small amounts of cocaine.[10] However, the marginal position of Colombian traffickers dramatically changed when traffickers from the Southern Cone, particularly Chilean traffickers, faced government crackdowns. Colombian traffickers rapidly filled the void in the global cocaine supply chain left by their Chilean counterparts, who became the target of government crackdowns following the 1973 coup.[11]

As the global cocaine supply chain was shifting due to state efforts in Chile, marijuana became the first target of President Richard Nixon's (now declared) war against drugs in the United States. The marijuana industry in Colombia was also the target of government policies of crop eradication and traffic suppression. These efforts initially led to changes in the governance of marijuana markets, which became more competitive and violent, and at the same time marijuana production and export became less profitable.[12] Simultaneously, consumer patterns in the United States shifted toward the trendier and more glamorous cocaine.[13] The growing demand and higher rentability of cocaine compared to marijuana incentivized the Colombian drug cartels to shift gears and invest in the processing of cocaine paste.[14]

Colombian drug traffickers were well positioned to take advantage of the country's geography to become a central hub of the global cocaine supply chain. They connected the coca-cultivating and cocaine paste–producing regions of Peru and Bolivia with "laboratories" for the refinement of cocaine paste to cocaine in eastern Colombia, for subsequent trafficking to consumer markets.[15] These traffickers quickly transformed the rather artisanal refinement of paste to cocaine into a process of industrial scale.[16] The infamous processing compound known as Tranquilandia in the Yari Plains of eastern Colombia was a symbol of the country's new role in the global cocaine chain. By the time the compound was dismantled by Colombian authorities, it consisted of nine labs and eight landing strips.[17] Between 1975 and 1980, Colombian traffickers went from placing an estimated 4 tons to 100 tons of cocaine annually in the US market.[18] By 1995, Colombia had an estimated capacity of annual production of 600–720 metric tons of cocaine.[19]

Colombia's growing role in the cocaine supply chain was not limited to cocaine production. Colombian traffickers quickly became dominant in the trafficking and distribution of cocaine in US markets, displacing other groups who had previously controlled these markets, for example those of Cuban origin in South Florida. The presence of a Colombian diaspora in key US cities like New York and Miami aided in the building of networks that connected the cocaine-producing regions with consumer markets.[20]

Moreover, as Colombian drug traffickers' position in the market grew and they started moving greater quantities of cocaine to the United States, they perfected trafficking routes and strategies. Traffickers coalesced into syndicates, frequently referred to as cartels, in which they pooled important resources (for example, trafficking routes and protection from law enforcement) and shared the risk of moving tons of cocaine to consumer markets.[21] The Medellín and Cali cartels transported tons of cocaine along Caribbean routes and later—when US interdiction efforts in the 1980s blocked these routes—through Central America and Mexico.[22] In short, within a decade, Colombia went from being a marginal player in the global cocaine supply chain to being the central player in this global market. Colombian criminal organizations—coalescing into powerful criminal syndicates—controlled the production, trafficking, and distribution of cocaine in the largest consumer markets.

Vertical Integration of Cocaine Production and the Demise of the Large Cartels

In the 1980s, Colombia became the key center for the processing of cocaine paste coming from Bolivia and Peru, but not for the cultivation of coca bush. Based on information from Mauricio Reina,[23] table 3.1 shows a comparison of the estimated production of coca leaf for Bolivia, Colombia, and Peru between 1980 and 1990. Although coca cultivation slowly increased in Colombia during the 1980s—and in 1990 it was more than eight times the production in 1980—Colombia remained far behind the other two Andean countries.

In the first phase of Colombia's insertion in the global cocaine supply chain, it was more advantageous for Colombian traffickers to process paste from Peru and Bolivia because the quality of coca leaves from these countries, in terms of alkaloid content, was higher than it was in Colombia.[24] This would change, however, in the late 1980s and early 1990s because of crop eradication programs in Bolivia and the interdiction of the aerial route connecting the paste-producing regions of Peru with Colombia.[25] During the 1990s, Colombia experienced a continued increase in the cultivation of coca crops and went from being the world's third-biggest producer of coca leaves in 1990 after Peru and Bolivia to the first by the end of the decade (see figure 3.2).

The increased coca cultivation in Colombia during the 1990s and 2000s intensified the presence of the plant in the Amazonian regions—where cocaine paste was already being processed in the 1980s—and bordering regions. Figure 3.3 maps areas of high coca cultivation density in 2002, with a marked presence near the border with Ecuador (departments of Nariño and Putumayo), the border with Venezuela (departments of Norte de Santander and Arauca), and the Amazonian and Orinoquía regions (departments of Caquetá, Guaviare, Meta, and Vichada).

This explosion in coca cultivation facilitated the vertical integration of the cocaine industry in the country, as Colombian traffickers were no longer dependent on Bolivian and Peruvian producers as the source of cocaine paste. This process of vertical integration transformed the industry in Colombia, with new actors getting involved. Cultivation required the incorporation of a rural labor force—peasants and other rural workers—as well as mechanisms to regulate relationships with these actors and, more broadly, govern rural populations. At the same time, armed actors of Colombia's long civil war, guerrilla groups like the

Table 3.1. Coca Leaf Production (thousands of tons)

Year	Bolivia	Colombia	Peru	Total
1980	52.5	4	50	106.5
1981	55	2.5-3.0	50	107.5-108
1982	25-60	–	50	110-115
1983	25-40	11.2	100	136.5-151
1984	49.2	11	100	100.2
1985	42-53.2	12.4	95.2	149.6-160.8
1986	44-52.9	12-13.6	95-120	151-186.5
1987	46-67	18.23	98-121	162-211
1988	57.4-78.3	19-24.2	97-124	173.4-223.5
1989	66	33.5	124	223.5
1990	64	33.4	108.5	205.9

Source: Mauricio Reina, "Economía política y estrategia antidrogas: ¿Un esfuerzo fallido?"; and Bureau of International Narcotics and Law Enforcement Affairs, *International Narcotics Control Strategy Report 1995*.

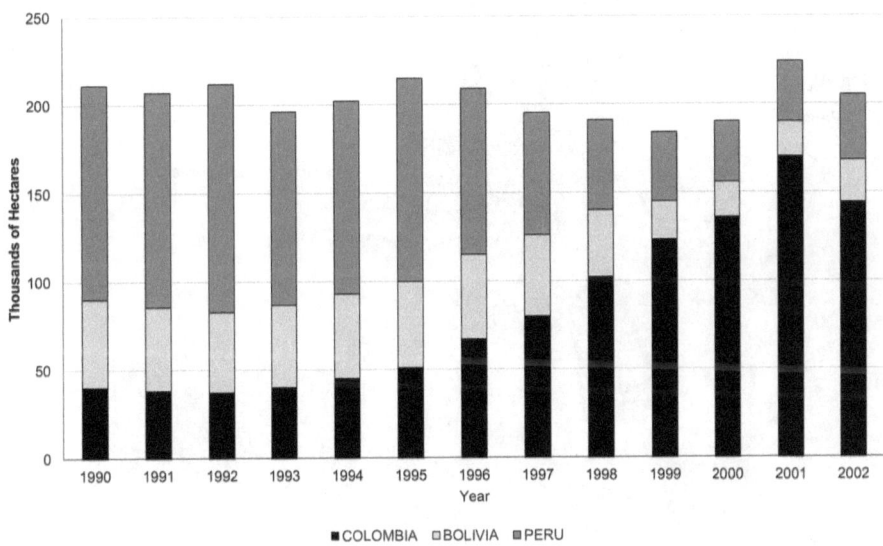

Figure 3.2. Coca cultivation (hectares), 1990–2002. Source: Adam Isacson, "Crisis and Opportunity: Unraveling Colombia's Collapsing Coca Markets," Washington Office on Latin America, August 24, 2023, https://www.wola.org/analysis/crisis-opportunity-unraveling-colombias-collapsing-coca-markets/.

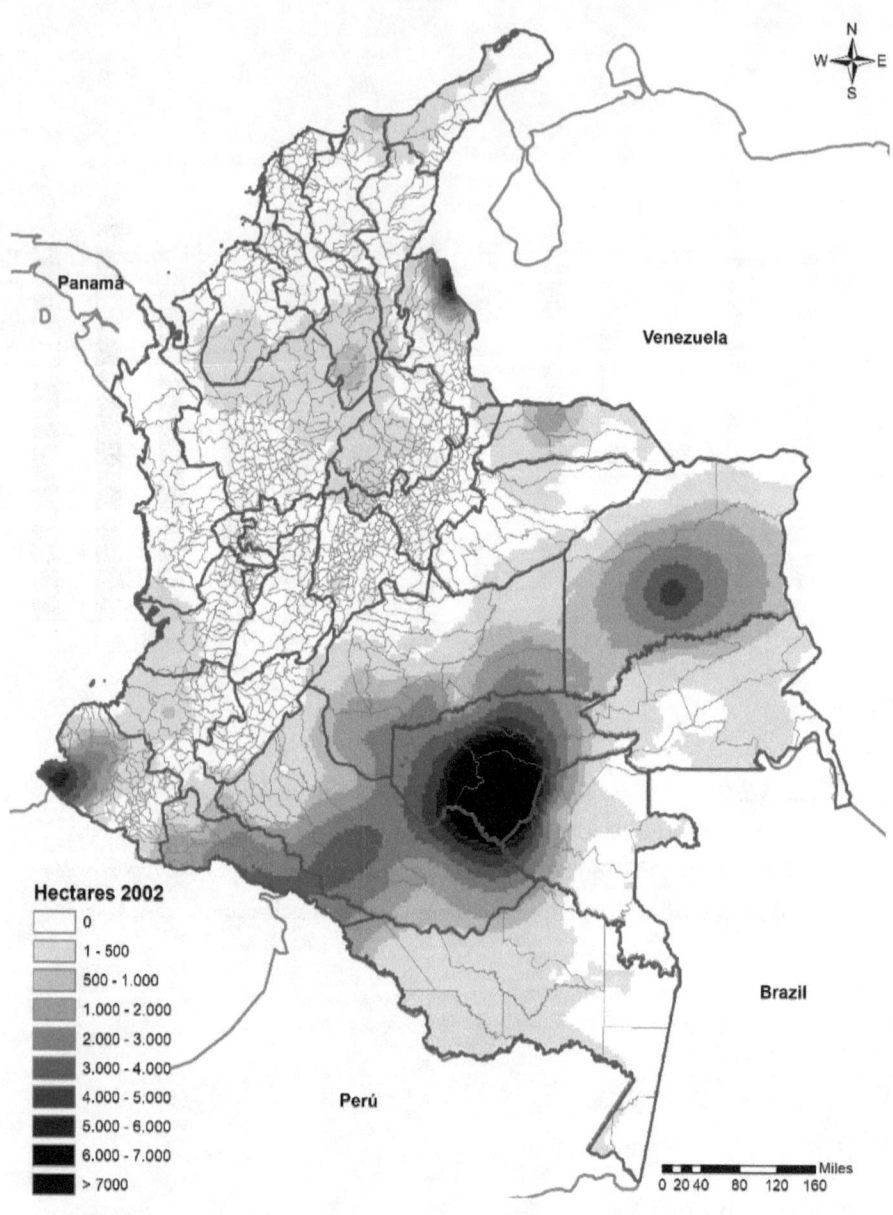

Figure 3.3. Colombia coca density map, 2002. Source: Original map using data from the Observatorio de Drogas de Colombia, Ministerio de Justicia y del Derecho.

FARC and paramilitaries, became more actively engaged in the cocaine economy: by providing protection, and by regulating production indirectly (e.g., through taxation) or directly (managing production and trafficking).[26] This evidently had an impact on internal conflict dynamics and prompted the involvement of external actors like the United States. For example, by the end of the 1990s, some estimates indicate that the FARC was earning around US$400 million annually for drug trafficking, thus providing a substantial source of income that enhanced the group's capabilities.[27] This participation in drug trafficking, however, does not imply that Colombia's civil war could be reduced to a manifestation of drug trafficking.[28]

As Colombia was transitioning to the vertical integration of cocaine production, its role in trafficking and distribution—particularly to the United States—started changing. Already in the 1980s, the Colombian state was responding to US pressure and to actions by drug traffickers (e.g., the assassination of high-profile politicians) and beginning to crack down on cocaine production and trafficking. The crackdown targeted the largest drug-trafficking network, the Medellín cartel, and its most visible figure, Pablo Escobar, resulting in an intense state-cartel conflict that took a tremendous toll in human life and destruction. The Cali cartel filled the void left by the collapse of the Medellín cartel but retained its preeminence among drug-trafficking organizations for only a short time. Unlike the Medellín cartel, it sought to influence Colombian political leadership through bribery rather than conflict.[29] However, substantial pressure from the United States, especially after the scandal surrounding the cartel's financial support for President Ernesto Samper's campaign in the 1994 election (known as Proceso 8000), and the decertification of Colombia in 1995, 1996, and 1997 by the US government,[30] prompted efforts to disarticulate the Cali cartel.

At the end of the 1990s, Colombia's large cartels were mostly dismantled and replaced by smaller cartels (for example, the Norte del Valle cartel) and the increasing involvement of paramilitary groups (which in some cases were almost indistinguishable from drug-trafficking organizations, or DTOs) and guerrillas in the production and trafficking of cocaine.[31] The fragmentation of Colombian DTOs weakened their position vis-à-vis their Mexican counterparts in the control of cocaine traffic to the United States. As a result of the Caribbean interdiction efforts of the 1980s, by 1999, an estimated 60 percent of the cocaine entering the United States was smuggled across the Mexico-US border.[32] The growing relevance of Mexico as the most important route for cocaine trafficking to the United States, coupled with the growing fragmentation of Colombian DTOs, led to the latter's progressive loss of importance. However, despite waning influence in the control of trade, Colombia, as the world's greatest coca cultivator and cocaine producer, kept its status as a threat to US national security and remained a focal point of the United States' drug control policies.

Fleeting "Victories"

The election of Álvaro Uribe as Colombia's president in 2002 on a law-and-order platform promising to defeat the FARC, after a notoriously failed peace process during the previous Andrés Pastrana administration (1998–2002), intensified the already militarized, US-sponsored antidrug policy known as Plan Colombia. Undoubtedly, involvement in cocaine production and trafficking provided a valuable source of income for the FARC,[33] enabling it to continue its war against the Colombian state even after guerrilla movements elsewhere in the hemisphere had disappeared. For the Uribe administration, curbing coca cultivation and cocaine production was seen as a critical component in the strategy to defeat the FARC. After the 9/11 attack on the United States, Uribe could successfully frame the fight against the FARC, drug trafficking, and international terrorism as one and the same—hence the strategic use of the term "narcoterrorism" by the Colombian government—leading to a stronger relationship with the George W. Bush administration in the context of its "war against terror."[34]

A central component of Uribe's strategy was coca eradication. In 2003, there was an estimated cultivated area of 114,000 hectares in Colombia, more than double the number of hectares in Peru and Bolivia combined (see figure 3.4). Not surprisingly, coca eradication—primarily through aerial aspersion of herbicides using the controversial glyphosate, but also with manual forced eradication and crop substitution programs—was a cornerstone of Uribe's antidrug policy.[35] As the first decade of the twentieth century progressed, the cultivated area decreased significantly, but never to the levels observed before the mid-1990s (see figure 3.4).

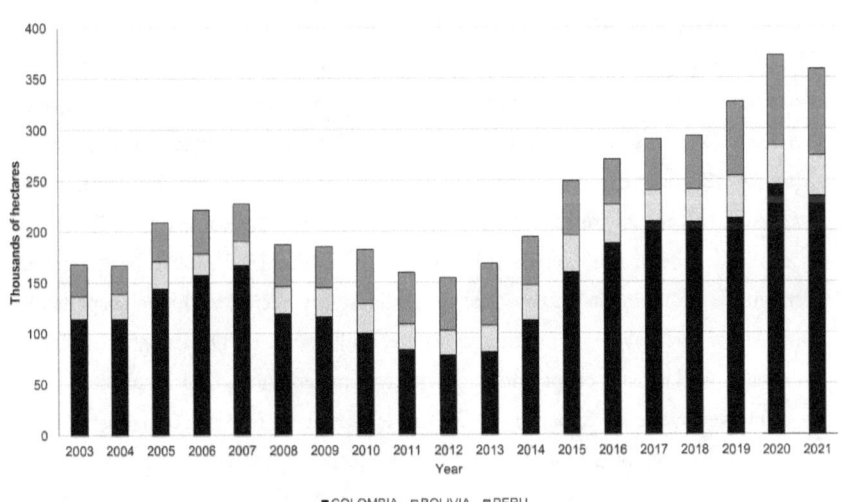

Figure 3.4. Coca cultivation (hectares), 2003–2021. Source: Adam Isacson, "Crisis and Opportunity: Unraveling Colombia's Collapsing Coca Markets," Washington Office on Latin America.

Uribe's security strategy, known as Seguridad Democrática or Democratic Security, also had an important effect on drug-trafficking dynamics in Colombia. This policy was successful in significantly weakening the FARC. At the same time, Uribe's administration promoted the demobilization of paramilitary groups, which were deeply involved in drug trafficking. However, the demobilization of paramilitary groups was incomplete, and a significant number of paramilitaries remilitarized.[36] The remilitarized armed groups, including the Rastrojos and the Autodefensas Gaitanistas (also known as the Clan del Golfo), rapidly became central players in the drug-trafficking market.

The reduction in cultivated coca areas was short lived and a sharp increase occurred after 2014, as negotiations that ultimately led to the 2016 peace agreement between the Colombian government led by President Juan Manuel Santos (2010–2018) and the FARC were nearing their end. The peace agreement crystallized a new approach by fostering a voluntary crop substitution program.[37] In the second decade of the twenty-first century, the Colombian government started moving away from its most coercive eradication policies, with the suspension in 2015 of aerial aspersion with glyphosate, a substance that destroyed beneficial crops as well as coca crops and had negative consequences on human health.[38]

However, the anticipation of the implementation of new coca substitution policies that involved monetary incentives became a powerful motivator behind the sharp increase in coca cultivation after 2014. As Juan Felipe Ladino, Santiago Saavedra, and Daniel Wiesner point out, increasing the area of coca cultivation was a rational strategy for peasants—especially in FARC-controlled areas—as these cultivated areas would benefit from the monetary eradication benefits that the FARC and the Colombian government negotiated.[39]

The growth in coca cultivation in recent years—reaching an all-time high in cultivated area in 2020 and 2021—motivated the Colombian government under President Iván Duque (2018–2022) to seek the reversal of the suspension of aerial aspersion. This was systematically blocked by Colombian courts. After years of crop eradication strategies and some transient successes, Colombia today has the historically largest coca-cultivated areas (figure 3.4) and cocaine production capacity (figure 3.1). Furthermore, the geography of coca cultivation has changed only slightly as well (see figure 3.5): while some earlier hotspots in Colombia's east are less significant than before, Putumayo and Nariño Departments (which border Ecuador) and Norte de Santander Department (bordering Venezuela) concentrate a significant portion of Colombia's cultivation of coca cultivation areas, similarly to 2002.

The FARC's demobilization after the peace agreement in 2016 also intensified the fragmentation of and competition among drug-trafficking organizations. FARC rebels were central to drug production and trafficking, and the void left was filled by smaller organizations, some of them so-called FARC dissident groups (i.e., groups that either never demobilized or that remilitarized after demobilization). Together with the recent weakening of some post-paramilitary groups—like the Clan del Golfo—the more fragmented landscape of Colombian DTOs has enabled Mexican DTOs to have a stronger presence in Colombia and become the central actors in drug trafficking to the United States, relegating their Colombian counterparts to the status of junior partners. At the same time, the growing power of Venezuelan criminal organizations (like the Tren de Aragua) and the involvement of Venezuelan state actors in drug trafficking, in particular members of its armed forces,[40] have made Venezuela (and its border with Colombia) an important route of Colombian cocaine.

Cocaine Criminal Governance

The global cocaine chain requires a level of informal regulation—the enforcement of a framework of rules—to be able to function at each one of its links. Although analyses of the cocaine industry in Colombia have frequently focused on forms of criminal organization,[41] we take a step back and look at the criminal governance of cocaine in Colombia (i.e., the set of interactions and often informal rules that regulate the cocaine supply chain in its different stages). This necessarily implies looking at criminal groups and networks but also incorporating other actors in the analysis, especially state actors. State actors are crucial in shaping forms of regulation of illicit markets, through the constraints placed by state policy on those markets and/or the active involvement of state actors in the (informal) regulation of illicit markets and populations under the control of organized criminal groups.[42] Complex criminal industries are not the product of state absence or failure, as has commonly been assumed for drug production and trafficking, but on the contrary are the product of state policies and involvement: there is

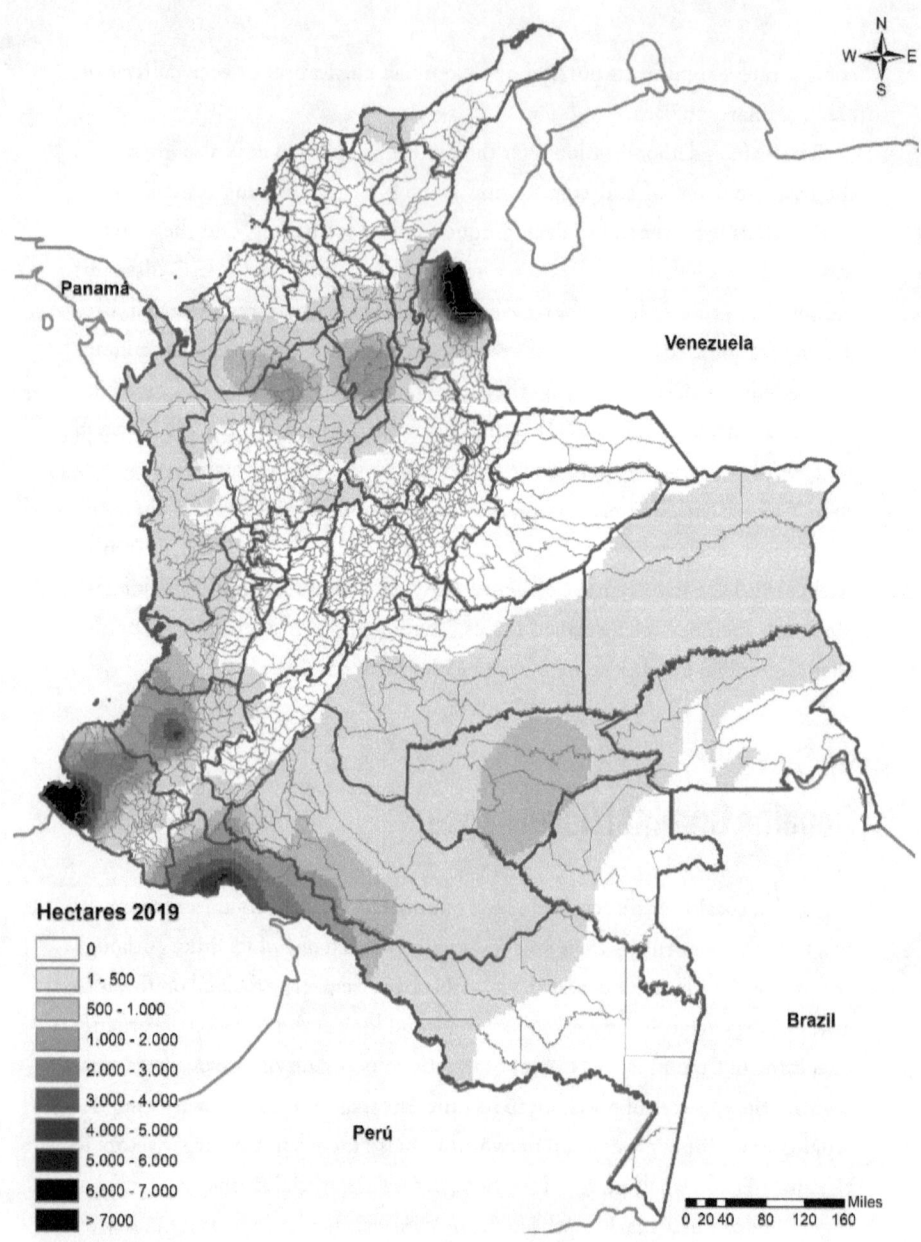

Figure 3.5. Colombia coca density map, 2019. Source: Original map using data from the Observatorio de Drogas de Colombia, Ministerio de Justicia y del Derecho.

no organized crime without the state.[43] In this sense, the varying relationship between state and criminal actors—ranging from antagonism to cooperation[44]—is seen as a key variable in explaining forms of criminal governance,[45] and the level of violence surrounding the industry.

With this in mind, we present two propositions regarding criminal governance of cocaine in Colombia: first, cocaine, as well as other drug industries with high levels of complexity, developed in Colombia as a product not of state failure but rather of state action. The emergence of the marijuana industry in the mid-1960s[46] and of coca/cocaine[47] are consequences of state developmental and state-building projects that "opened-up" drug-producing regions and sought to "integrate" them into the nation. At the same time, the central state—unwilling to incur the costs of state governance of peripheral communities—delegated to local elites, including criminal elites, the provision of social and political order.[48] While far from the ideal type of the Weberian rational-legal state that aspires to monopolize violence, the Colombian state *strategically* delegated to criminal actors the construction of social order in some of the country's peripheries. However, although the Colombian state had incentives to allow these forms of extralegal governance in the peripheries, it also established redlines that actors engaged in illicit activities should not cross. On occasion, when those lines were crossed—for example, when criminal groups targeted high-profile politicians—the state responded by cracking down on trafficking groups.[49]

Colombian policies—either based on the government's own motivations or in response to pressure from the United States—to crack down on drug-trafficking groups have led to an ever-growing fragmentation of these groups, altering existing governance mechanisms and increasing (violent) competition between groups, in the cases of both the marijuana industry[50] and the cocaine industry. Naturally, state action is not the only source of change in relationships between criminal actors. For example, while early generations of drug traffickers from Cali cooperated with Pablo Escobar and used his routes to traffic cocaine to the United States, conflicts over profit distribution and the availability of new routes through the Pacific transformed the original division of labor among *narcos*.[51] Yet state action remained a primary factor impacting the relationship *between* criminal groups. This had important repercussions on the level of violence that surrounded the industry. The fragmentation of criminal groups incentivized higher levels of violence.[52] Crackdowns meant to decimate the Medellín cartel resulted in the onset of an extremely violent state-cartel war.[53] While the use of (usually targeted) violence is a feature of criminal governance, extremely high levels of violence tend to be the result of the breakdown of criminal governance.

Our second proposition regarding criminal governance of cocaine in Colombia, following Gustavo Duncan,[54] maintains that the form of cocaine governance varies dramatically depending on the specific point on the cocaine supply chain. The myth of the omnipresent and all-powerful cartels paints them as actors who completely regulate the social and political life of communities under their control, from small towns to large cities. While criminal governance of communities is a characteristic of some areas affected by the cocaine industry—usually peripheral areas where coca is cultivated and cocaine is produced, and smaller towns along trafficking routes—this is not the case in larger cities.[55] In smaller, particularly peripheral areas, the state has delegated to local actors the provision of social order. These criminal actors engage in the (costly) exercise of providing order because it enables them to regulate the labor and guarantee the social stability that are needed for drug production. In larger cities, Colombian drug-trafficking groups are interested in securing influence and access to the state, which enables them to conduct crucial aspects of their business, like money laundering.[56] The less conspicuous behavior, more sophisticated money-laundering methods, and diverse investment portfolios of a new generation of Colombian drug traffickers seem to follow this logic.[57] Thus, criminal governance in these areas is less about ruling people and controlling territory and more about functionality (i.e., regulating an illicit market), in a manner akin to the forms of criminal governance observed in Uruguay and Chile.[58] Although there are sporadic episodes in which criminal groups directly challenge the state in large Colombian cities (e.g., the state-cartel war in the 1980s and early 1990s), these are extremely unusual events.[59]

Conclusion

This short overview of cocaine and cocaine criminal governance in Colombia has shown how Colombia went from being a marginal player to a central cog in the global cocaine economy. Since the 1980s, the country has remained a leading producer—if not *the* leading producer—of cocaine. Coca cultivation was an initially limited activity that has grown exponentially, despite the crop eradication efforts of the Colombian government since the 1990s. Finally, Colombian drug-trafficking organizations' control over the trafficking and distribution of cocaine in consumer markets (particularly the United States) has waned. Today, Colombian organizations are junior partners to Mexican cartels, and foreign criminal organizations—mainly Mexican, but also Venezuelan—have a growing presence in the country.

Although the growth of the cocaine industry in Colombia has frequently been associated with the weakness or absence of the Colombian state, the emergence of this and other drug industries was in fact the product of state policies and development projects. The Colombian state continues to shape the dynamics of this industry and the characteristics of its governance along the different links of the cocaine industry. Gustavo Petro (2022–), Colombia's first leftist president, has frequently criticized previous drug policies and has promised a new policy prioritizing human rights and the environment.[60] While a window of opportunity for new, alternative policies opens at the national level—with the historic low prices of coca leaf in some regions[61]—and while some flexibility exists at international level, the fundamental structure of the international prohibitionist regime remains untouched. New national drug policies can either bring about decisive transformations with respect to Colombia's place in the global cocaine supply chain, or—if poorly conceived and implemented—set the stage for the return of more radically militarized approaches.

Notes

1. Jason Ruiz, *Narcomedia: Latinidad, Popular Culture, and America's War on Drugs* (Austin: University of Texas Press, 2023).

2. Paul Gootenberg, *Andean Cocaine: The Making of a Global Drug* (Chapel Hill: University of North Carolina Press, 2008); and Paul Gootenberg, "Cocaine's Long March North, 1900–2010," *Latin American Politics and Society* 54, no. 1 (Spring 2012): 159–80.

3. Bruce Michael Bagley, "The Evolution of Drug Trafficking and Organized Crime in Latin America," *Sociologia, problemas y práticas*, no. 71 (2013): 99–123; and Gootenberg, "Cocaine's Long March North."

4. Guillermo Trejo and Sandra Ley, *Votes, Drugs, and Violence: The Political Logic of Criminal Wars in Mexico* (Cambridge: Cambridge University Press, 2020).

5. Benjamin Lessing, "Conceptualizing Criminal Governance," *Perspectives on Politics* 19, no. 3 (September 2021): 854–73. See also Gabriel Feltran, *The Entangled City: Crime as Urban Fabric in São Paulo* (Manchester: Manchester University Press, 2020).

6. Gustavo Duncan, *Beyond "Plata o Plomo": Drugs and State Reconfiguration in Colombia* (Cambridge: Cambridge University Press, 2022).

7. Gootenberg, *Andean Cocaine: The Making of a Global Drug*.

8. Lina Britto, *Marijuana Boom: The Rise and Fall of Colombia's First Drug Paradise* (Oakland: University of California Press, 2020); and Hernando José Gómez R., "La economía ilegal en Colombia: Tamaño, evolución, características e impacto económico," *Coyuntura Económica* 18, no. 3 (September 1988): 93–113.

9. Britto, *Marijuana Boom*.

10. Gildardo Vanegas Muñoz, *La saga del narcotráfico en Cali, 1950–2018* (Cali: Programa Editorial Universidad del Valle, 2021).

11. Gootenberg, "Cocaine's Long March North."

12. Britto, *Marijuana Boom*.

13. Gootenberg, "Cocaine's Long March North."

14. Gómez R., "La economía ilegal en Colombia."

15. Gootenberg, "Cocaine's Long March North."

16. Vanegas Muñoz, *La saga del narcotráfico en Cali*.

17. "El complejo cocalero de Tranquilandia," *El Espectador* (Bogotá), September 3, 2016, https://www.elespectador.com/colombia/mas-regiones/el-complejo-cocalero-de-tranquilandia-article-652853/.

18. Gootenberg, "Cocaine's Long March North."

19. Bureau of International Narcotics and Law Enforcement Affairs, *International Narcotics Control Strategy Report 1995* (Washington, DC: US Department of State, 1995).

20. Vanegas Muñoz, *La saga del narcotráfico en Cali*.

21. Michael Kenney, "The Evolution of the International Drugs Trade: The Case of Colombia, 1930–2000," in *Routledge Handbook of Transnational Organized Crime*, ed. Felia Allum and Stan Gilmour (Abingdon, Oxon., England: Routledge, 2012), 201–16.

22. Bagley, "The Evolution of Drug Trafficking."

23. Mauricio Reina, "Economía política y estrategia antidrogas: ¿Un esfuerzo fallido?" *Colombia Internacional* 8 (1989): 12–16.

24. Gómez R., "La economía ilegal en Colombia."

25. Bagley, "The Evolution of Drug Trafficking"; and Francisco E. Thoumi, "Illegal Drugs in Colombia: From Illegal Economic Boom to Social Crisis," *Annals of the American Academy of Political and Social Science* 582, no. 1 (July 2002): 102–16.

26. Thoumi, "Illegal Drugs in Colombia."

27. Bruce Michael Bagley, "Drug Trafficking, Political Violence, and U.S. Policy in Colombia Under the Clinton Administration," in *Elusive Peace: International, National, and Local Dimensions of Conflict in Colombia*, ed. Cristina Rojas and Judy Meltzer (New York: Palgrave Macmillan, 2005), 21–52.

28. Bagley, "Drug Trafficking, Political Violence, and U.S. Policy in Colombia." For a recent analysis of the impact of the FARC's involvement in drug trafficking and rebel governance, see Zachariah Mampilly and Jose Antonio Gutierrez, "A Tax Like Any Other? Rebel Taxes on Narcotics and War Time Economic Order," *International Politics* (2023).

29. Benjamin Lessing, *Making Peace in Drug Wars: Crackdowns and Cartels in Latin America* (Cambridge: Cambridge University Press, 2018).

30. Jonathan Rosen, *The Losing War: Plan Colombia and Beyond* (Albany: State University of New York Press, 2014).

31. Bagley, "The Evolution of Drug Trafficking."

32. United Nations Office for Drug Control and Crime Prevention, *Global Illicit Drug Trends* (Vienna: United Nations, 1999).

33. Thoumi, "Illegal Drugs in Colombia."

34. Bagley, "The Evolution of Drug Trafficking"; Elvira María Restrepo, "Colombia and Its Wars Against Drug Trafficking, 1970–2010," in *Drug Trafficking, Organized Crime, and Violence in the Americas Today*, ed. Bruce Michael Bagley and Jonathan Rosen (Gainesville: University Press of Florida, 2015), 139–60; and Jonathan D. Rosen and Roberto Zepeda Martínez, "La guerra contra las drogas y la cooperación internacional: El caso de Colombia," *Revista CS*, no. 18 (January–April 2016): 63–84.

35. Hernando Zuleta, "Coca, Cocaine and Drug Trafficking," Documento CEDE no. 2019-09, Universidad de los Andes, Bogotá, February 14, 2019, https://papers.ssrn.com/sol3/papers.cfm?abstract_id=3334538.

36. Sarah Zukerman Daly, *Organized Violence After Civil War: The Geography of Recruitment in Latin America* (Cambridge: Cambridge University Press, 2016).

37. Francisco Gutiérrez Sanín, "The Politics of Peace: Competing Agendas in the Colombian Agrarian Agreement and Implementation," *Peacebuilding* 7, no. 3 (June 2019): 314–28.

38. Adriana Camacho and Daniel Mejía, "The Health Consequences of Aerial Spraying of Illicit Crops: The Case of Colombia," Working Paper no. 408, Center for Global Development, Washington, DC, June 1, 2015, https://www.cgdev.org/publication/health-consequences-aerial-spraying-illicit-crops-case-colombia-working-paper-408.

39. Juan Felipe Ladino, Santiago Saavedra, and Daniel Wiesner, "One Step Ahead of the Law: The Net Effect of Anticipation and Implementation of Colombia's Illegal Crops Substitution Program," *Journal of Public Economics* 202 (October 2021).

40. InSight Crime Venezuela Investigative Unit, "Venezuela's Cocaine Revolution," InSight Crime, April 2022, https://insightcrime.org/wp-content/uploads/2022/05/Venezuelas-Cocaine-Revolution-InSight-Crime-Apr-2022.pdf.

41. Michael Kenney, "The Architecture of Drug Trafficking: Network Forms of Organisation in the Colombian Cocaine Trade," *Global Crime* 8, no. 3 (2007): 233–59.

42. Lessing, "Conceptualizing Criminal Governance."

43. Trejo and Ley, *Votes, Drugs, and Violence.*

44. Nicholas Barnes, "Criminal Politics: An Integrated Approach to the Study of Organized Crime, Politics, and Violence," *Perspectives on Politics* 15, no. 4 (December 2017): 967–87.

45. Enrique Desmond Arias, *Criminal Enterprises and Governance in Latin America and the Caribbean* (New York: Cambridge University Press, 2017).

46. Britto, *Marijuana Boom.*

47. María-Clara Torres, "The Making of a Coca Frontier: The Case of Ariari, Colombia," in *The Origins of Cocaine: Colonization and Failed Development in the Amazon Andes*, ed. Paul Gootenberg and Liliana M. Dávalos (Abingdon, Oxon., England: Routledge, 2018), 133–59.

48. Fernán E. González González and Silvia Otero, "La presencia diferenciada del estado: Un desafío a los conceptos de gobernabilidad y gobernanza," in *Gobernanza y conflicto en Colombia: Interacción entre gobernantes y gobernados en un contexto violento*, ed. Claire Launay-Gama and Fernán E. González González (Bogotá: Cinep, 2010), 28–36.

49. Lessing, *Making Peace in Drug Wars.*

50. Britto, *Marijuana Boom.*

51. Vanegas Muñoz, *La saga del narcotráfico en Cali*.

52. Angélica Durán-Martínez, *The Politics of Drug Violence: Criminals, Cops, and Politicians in Colombia and Mexico* (New York: Oxford University Press, 2017).

53. Lessing, "Conceptualizing Criminal Governance."

54. Duncan, *Beyond "Plata o Plomo."*

55. Vanegas Muñoz, *La saga del narcotráfico en Cali*. Urban peripheries in cities are interesting cases. In some cities, like Medellín, criminal groups have established forms of criminal governance that regulate social life in urban communities; see Christopher Blattman, Gustavo Duncan, Benjamin Lessing, and Santiago Tobón, "Gang Rule: Understanding and Countering Criminal Governance," Working Paper no. 28458, National Bureau of Economic Research, Cambridge, MA, February 2021, https://www.nber.org/system/files/working_papers/w28458/w28458.pdf. In other cities, like Cali, local criminal groups that control retail drug sales are organizationally incapable of engaging in these forms of governance. When criminal governance of urban peripheries occurs, however, it is usually with the (tacit) delegation of authority from the state.

56. Duncan, *Beyond "Plata o Plomo."*

57. Jeremy McDermott, "The 'Invisibles': Colombia's New Generation of Drug Traffickers," InSight Crime, March 14, 2018, https://insightcrime.org/investigations/invisibles-colombias-new-generation-drug-traffickers/.

58. Andreas E. Feldmann and Juan Pablo Luna, *Criminal Politics and Botched Development in Contemporary Latin America* (Cambridge: Cambridge University Press, 2023).

59. Lessing, *Making Peace in Drug Wars*.

60. Luis Benito, "Gustavo Petro presentará oficialmente su política antidrogas en El Tambo, Cauca," Infobae, October 3, 2023, https://www.infobae.com/colombia/2023/10/03/gustavo-petro-presentara-su-politica-antidrogas-en-el-tambo-cauca/.

61. Adam Isacson, "Crisis and Opportunity: Unraveling Colombia's Collapsing Coca Markets," Washington Office on Latin America, August 24, 2023, https://www.wola.org/analysis/crisis-opportunity-unraveling-colombias-collapsing-coca-markets/.

CHAPTER 4

Cocaine in Brazil

The Emergent Center of a Globalized Market

Michael Jerome Wolff

On May 5, 2023, staff workers at a Nespresso coffee processing plant in Fribourg, Switzerland, discovered sacks of mysterious white powder hidden within several shipping containers carrying fresh coffee beans from Brazil. Swiss police later confirmed the powder to be highly refined cocaine, rated at 80 percent purity and weighing in at more than half a ton. They estimated the load's market value to exceed US$50 million.[1] The discovery was anything but a one-off event, although it did reflect something new in the world of transnational drug smuggling. Less than a decade earlier, most cocaine made its way onto the European continent in piecemeal fashion, dropped from speedboats along the Iberian coastline or hidden among the personal items of air travelers. Today, the lion's share of white powder sails into the ports of Antwerp and Rotterdam in northern Europe, hidden inside large shipping containers amid any manner of legally traded goods,[2] like construction equipment, household appliances, or, in this case, fresh coffee beans.

Unsurprisingly, the shift in smuggling methods and routes has coincided with an increase in the availability of cocaine across Europe. It also coincides with a dramatic increase in the cultivation of coca leaf itself, the baseline ingredient in refined cocaine, which, according to the United Nations Office on Drugs and Crime (UNODC), has more than doubled since 2013.[3] What is surprising, and perplexing, is that these changes have occurred despite a concurrent fragmentation and weakening of those very transnational criminal organizations—particularly the Fuerzas Armadas Revolucionarias de Colombia (FARC; Revolutionary Armed Forces of Colombia), Ejército de Liberación Nacional (ELN; National Liberation Army), and various cartel groups in Colombia—that had been most responsible for moving cocaine from its primary source of production in South America to consumer markets in the Global North. In other words, at the very moment we might have expected a steep decline in the availability of cocaine globally, precisely the opposite has happened. Indeed, not only is there more cocaine in North America and western Europe, it is also beginning to boom in eastern Europe, Africa, and even Asia.

The answer to this puzzle may be found in Brazil, where over the course of just a few decades a handful of once highly localized prison gangs have succeeded in transforming themselves into some of the largest and most effective transnational criminal organizations on historical record. The most powerful among them, the São Paulo–based Primeiro Comando da Capital (PCC; First Command of the Capital), today has more than thirty thousand members in Brazil alone and maintains operational bases to control cocaine production and trade throughout South America and, more recently, along both the west and east coasts of Africa as well. In short, they have sought to control all ends of the cocaine supply chain in order to reduce transactional costs and ensure product supply, while proactively seeking to establish new transnational partnerships and expand consumer markets abroad. The rapid ascension of the PCC and other Brazilian crime syndicates has, in this way, acted as a gravitational force pulling the operational epicenter of the global cocaine trade southward to Brazil, where today the majority of Europe-, Africa-, and Asia-bound cocaine departs South America from major seaports in São Paulo, Rio de Janeiro, and Recife, hidden in large shipping containers aboard transoceanic vessels.[4]

This chapter examines the rise of Brazilian crime syndicates and their role in placing Brazil at the center of the global cocaine trade. I begin with a cursory history of cocaine in Brazil, with a focus on a critical time in the 1980s and 1990s when embryonic prison gangs first sought to control and expand the cocaine trade domestically. I then turn my focus on the PCC specifically, which by the mid-2000s had consciously set itself on a course of strategic and operational transnationalization while retaining its membership base and identity as a prison-based organization fighting for "Peace, Justice, and Liberty," as their gang slogan insists. Lastly, I attempt to measure the consequences of the PCC's organizational expansion with respect to political stability in Brazil as well as for the control of illicit drugs worldwide.

Cocaine and the Rise of Prison Gangs in Brazil

The history of cocaine in Brazil most likely dates back as far as the 1890s, when a legally sanctioned boom in cocaine exports from Peru satisfied emerging consumer demand in urban centers across much of the Western world. Only in the late 1950s, however, did the Brazilian government begin treating cocaine as a serious threat to public security and social order. Police seizures of cocaine shipments multiplied in the latter half of that decade (although, by today's standards, these were minuscule amounts), and in March 1960, Brazil went as far as to host the first-ever UN-sponsored "Inter-American Conference on the Illicit Traffic in Coca Leaf and Cocaine."[5] From this point on, Brazil has played a prominent role in propagating and enforcing what had by then become a full-fledged international prohibition regime on cocaine usage and trafficking.

Cocaine usage then apparently declined in Brazil—or at least did not significantly increase—during the following two decades (1964–1984), which were marked by military rule and cultural isolationism. However, as the military's hold on power fell into decline in the early 1980s, cocaine usage exploded in Brazil's major cities. At that time, after years of government censorship and restriction, liberalizing reforms suddenly opened Brazilians to the world politically, economically, and culturally, and the sudden shift provoked radical changes to youth culture that favored the astronomic rise of cocaine usage.[6] In booming metropolises like Rio de Janeiro and São Paulo, the potent white powder came to define a new generation of young people coming of age in a new era of capitalist democracy.

Concurrent to these consumption trends, violent crime was also on the rise during the 1980s. Over the course of the previous three decades, Brazil had transitioned from a predominantly rural agricultural society to a semi-industrialized and predominantly urban one.[7] Now in the midst of so persistent an economic crisis that the 1980s came to be known as "the lost decade," a new generation of poor urban youth with high expectations and few prospects of gainful employment embraced crime as an alternative.[8] Something of a moral panic among Brazil's middle and upper classes then ensued, ushering in an era of heavy-handed police crackdowns that quickly led to a ballooning of the country's prison population, a trend that has continued to the present day. This is important because, as we shall see, by the end of the decade overcrowded prisons would give birth to powerful gangs that would soon become the organizational pulse of a rapidly expanding domestic cocaine market.

The first of Brazil's notorious prison gangs to emerge from the political, economic, and cultural transformations of the 1980s was the Comando Vermelho (CV; Red Command). An iconic legacy of the military regime's waning years, the CV initially fashioned itself as an inmate advocacy organization inspired by the ideologies and rhetoric of political prisoners with whom its members cohabitated during the 1970s at the now defunct Cândido Mendes prison on Ilha Grande, an island off the coast of Rio de Janeiro. To this end, the organization successfully used tactics such as hunger strikes, media outreach, and legal action to negotiate better living conditions at the prison while also organizing spectacular prison escapes. In order to pay for such actions, CV members who were freed from prison—yet still bound by loyalty and obligation to the organization—robbed banks and other sources of concentrated wealth, channeling the proceeds back to the prison-based leadership. These actions tended to be spectacular affairs that drew nationwide media attention, which itself generated a profound popular allure (as well as paranoia) around the CV that would end up contributing to the organization's growing strength.[9]

By the mid-1980s, however, armed robbery as a primary source of income had proved to be too high-risk and too low-yield to sustain the organization, and CV leaders began looking into alternative sources of cash. What they soon discovered, and arguably could not resist, was a booming demand for cocaine and cannabis on the streets of Rio de Janeiro, a highly lucrative black market that disciplined prison gangs were uniquely well suited to take over.[10] This moment marked a consequential point of convergence between two rising trends in Brazil's criminal underworld—skyrocketing cocaine usage and prison gangs—that would shape the political economy of criminal violence and drug trafficking for decades to come.

The resulting change in the structure of the drug trade was particularly profound. At the time of the CV's transition from an inmate advocacy organization funded by armed robberies to a full-blown prison gang committed to the illegal drug trade, most cocaine suppliers and retail distributors in Brazil were still independent operators working in a remarkably decentralized marketplace. Solo opportunists, often corrupted military officers tasked with policing Brazil's northwestern borderlands, smuggled small shipments to personal contacts in the favelas of Rio de Janeiro and São Paulo.[11] There in the favelas, independent drug dealers maintained small-scale retail operations with little organizational cohesion or operational scope.[12] Within just a few years, however, the CV would fundamentally transform these structures and effectively monopolize the narcotics retail market in Rio de Janeiro. Since this market was (and still is) geographically rooted in the city's sprawling favelas, the CV then set out on a strategic campaign to kill or co-opt community leaders and drive out all independent drug dealers in these spaces, which are home to one-fifth of Rio's population.[13] By 1987, the organization reportedly controlled no less than 70 percent of the city's favelas.[14]

The CV's quasi-monopoly of the drug retail market in Brazil's cocaine capital did not last very long. By the early 1990s, rifts in the CV leadership led to the formation of several rival gangs, also based in the state's overcrowded prisons, which have been violently contesting the CV's favela-centered control of the local drug trade ever since. Visitors to Rio de Janeiro today can still see these rifts play out in real time, as rival factions frequently invade one another's territories, armed to the teeth with automatic rifles, hand grenades, and ballistics vests.[15] Still, the CV helped to generate a unique organizational culture and a strategic blueprint that, since its apogee in the late 1980s, would ultimately shape criminal collective action not only in Rio de Janeiro but across the entirety of Brazil. As we shall see, in the decades since the CV's founding, inmate advocacy organizations turned criminally oriented prison gangs, most of them boasting almost identical rhetoric and organizational structure, have emerged in virtually all twenty-seven of Brazil's federative states.[16]

The nationwide spread of prison-based gangs, or crime syndicates, was at first slow and limited to Brazil's major urban centers, particularly Rio de Janeiro and São Paulo, where police crackdowns on drug trafficking and violent crime caused prison overcrowding as far back as the 1980s. By the mid-1990s, however, a new trend in cocaine consumption would lay the ground conditions for the emergence of prison gangs across the country: crack, as the smokable cocaine derivative is popularly called, hit the streets of towns and cities across Brazil during the last decade of the millennium and changed everything. Highly decentralized and perilously unstable, the dynamics of the crack trade—as well as the desperation and volatility of its user base—produced a crime wave that by the mid-2000s would mark Brazil as the most homicidal country in the world. The crisis was especially severe in the impoverished north and northeastern regions, where once-quiet cities like Salvador de Bahia, Recife, Maceió, and Manaus now found themselves competing over the dubious moniker of Brazil's "murder capital."[17] Unsurprisingly, this crime wave fueled a concurrent growth in the prison population, and just as had occurred elsewhere, prison overcrowding again provided ripe conditions for the emergence of more prison gangs.

Both the introduction of crack into new domestic markets and the emergence of prison gangs across the country can be loosely traced back to the CV in Rio de Janeiro, as well as to similar prison-based gangs in São Paulo such as the PCC, which I will return to later in this chapter. Crack cocaine itself was pioneered by both organizations, and by the early 1990s, the more business savvy among their ranks sought to expand their retail ventures into the untapped markets of the North and the Northeast. This was a natural market for them, too, as many among the CV and PCC membership base had migrated from those regions as children, or otherwise maintained direct family relations there.[18]

But the emergence and development of new prison gangs was also directly influenced by the previously existing Comandos. This was in part due to their media fame, which provided counterculture youth around the country with an alluring symbology and criminal culture to emulate. More directly, it was also the unintended consequence of poorly devised prison policies. In an effort to weaken prison gangs in Rio de Janeiro and São Paulo, state authorities repeatedly transferred prominent gang leaders to distant prisons in other states, hoping to isolate them. Unfortunately, transferred gang leaders tended to bring their organizational knowledge with them, and they often created new prison gangs wherever they found themselves.[19] The ever-increasing growth of the inmate population across the country[20] ensured that they would have no shortage of captive recruits eager to fill their ranks.[21]

Prison gangs have since rendered counterproductive the great bulk of the country's drug war and public security policies writ large. This is because, quite simply, the primary tool employed by the state to combat crime—incarceration—tends to increase the ability of prison gangs to recruit new members, govern and tax illicit economies inside prisons, and eventually extend their coercive power far beyond prison walls and govern illicit markets more broadly.[22] This has been exceptionally true of Brazil's most notorious prison-based crime syndicates, particularly the CV and the PCC, which, despite their modest origins as localized inmate advocacy organizations, have today become the primary motor of organized criminal expansion within and far beyond national borders. And while these crime syndicates have certainly diversified their market portfolios over time, branching out into an ever-expanding array of legal and illegal business ventures, cocaine continues to be at the heart of it all.

All that said, however, their transition from inmate advocacy organizations to regionally significant prison gangs to full-fledged transnational criminal actors that would fundamentally reshape the global cocaine trade—a transition that became evident only since around 2010—was never a foregone conclusion. To better understand how this happened, it is useful to examine the rise of Brazil's largest and most powerful crime syndicate today, and the first to extend its operational reach across national borders in a strategic and systematic way: the Primeiro Comando da Capital.

The PCC:
From Prison Gang to
Transnational Criminal Organization

More than a decade after the formation of the CV in Rio de Janeiro, a small group of inmates at the infamous Taubaté prison complex in São Paulo resolved a soccer brawl by sitting down and hashing out a written constitution meant to regulate inmate behavior, avoid conflict among themselves, and direct their collective energies toward improving the living conditions of all prisoners.[23] The year was 1993, and the inmates at Taubaté had good reason to organize. Not only were intergroup rivalries making life in prison dangerous and wearisome, but the state itself seemed to be hunting them down. Less than two years earlier, state police slaughtered as many as 111 people at the nearby Carandiru prison in response to a rebellion there. Now, the inmates swore to never let such a tragedy happen again. They called themselves the Primeiro Comando da Capital, or PCC, and by the end of the millennium they would become a household name across Brazil.

Emulating much of the strategy and rhetoric of the CV from a generation earlier, the PCC immediately set out to consolidate its control of the Taubaté prison while expanding its operational reach into other state and federal prisons in São Paulo. In 1995, hoping to compel the state government to recognize their organization and begin negotiating with them, they initiated their first of many so-called mega-rebellions, wherein inmates from two separate prison complexes coordinated simultaneous uprisings.

It appeared at first that these uprisings were a failure, as state authorities continued to refuse to recognize or negotiate with the PCC and even publicly denied the group's existence altogether. But within the prison system, and just as importantly out in the slum communities where growing numbers of young men expected to find themselves behind bars eventually, the PCC had begun to make a name for itself.[24] Consequently, the organization continued to grow and expand, taking control of inmate populations in more and more prisons across the state such that, in 2001, when the PCC organized its second mega-rebellion, simultaneous uprisings shook the walls of no fewer than twenty-nine prison complexes. After dozens were killed both inside the rebelling prisons and out in the streets, São Paulo's governor, Geraldo Alckmin, publicly recognized the existence of the PCC for the first time.[25]

In response to the 2001 rebellions, the state government introduced measures to isolate the PCC leadership by removing them from the larger population of inmates affiliated with the organization, either placing them in solitary confinement (known in Brazil as *regime disciplinar diferenciado*—RDD) or transferring them to prisons outside of São Paulo State.[26] By this time, however, such tactics were ineffective or even counterproductive. The PCC's decentralized modality of communications and decision making made a moot point of the state's attempts to isolate individual leaders, while out-of-state inmate transfers, as mentioned in the previous section, in fact facilitated the expansion of the PCC into other states, and of prison gang dominance across the country.[27] Coincident to this expansion was, interestingly, a temporary alliance agreed upon between the PCC and the CV in 2001, which in the short term resulted in a boom in Brazil's illegal drug and small arms markets.[28]

Further attempts by the São Paulo state government to isolate the PCC leadership continued over the following half decade and eventually provoked a decision by the prison-based crime syndicate to launch yet another mega-rebellion in May 2006. This time, inmates unleashed simultaneous rebellions in a total of fifty-one prisons across the state, constituting around 95 percent of all of São Paulo's correctional facilities. As if this were not testament enough to the PCC's power as an organization, the prison-based leadership also ordered their members out in the streets to attack police officers and public institutions wherever they could. The ultimate tally of death and destruction will never be exact, but within just a few days of the uprising, reportedly some forty-two police officers had been murdered, ninety public buses had been burned in the streets, seventeen banks had been bombed, and as many as three hundred other attacks had targeted public institutions.[29] Coordinated criminal violence on this scale had no precedent in Brazil, and the week-long orgy of violence left both government officials and the civilian populace in shock.

The state's response to this frontal assault on its authority was no less brutal, however, and within a week, São Paulo's police forces had outright killed upward of 451 people who were suspected of helping to carry out the rebellion in the streets.[30] Moreover, rather than inciting a general revolt against the state as the PCC may have hoped, the Brazilian public largely condemned the organization's violence, which gave state authorities broad license to clamp down even tighter on the PCC leadership, even at the cost of skirting constitutional protections of human rights.[31] Indeed, any victory the PCC may have claimed by successfully carrying out such a massive coordinated rebellion might well have been Pyrrhic, as its very success provided state authorities with all the justification they needed to destroy the organization by any means necessary.

However, it was at this point that the PCC, now under the control of its most visionary of original founders, Marcos Willians Herbas Camacho (aka "Marcola"), abruptly changed course. Instead of digging in his heels to fight the state head-to-head, as the PCC's counterparts in the CV had long been doing in Rio de Janeiro, Marcola now sought to redirect the PCC's mission both inward—in effect, to pacify itself and eschew state repression as much as possible—while also focusing it outward, toward new economic horizons in a seemingly limitless global market for illicit goods, particularly cocaine.[32] Over the course of the following decade, these changes would be profound and remarkably successful.

Internally, the PCC began institutionalizing procedural mechanisms for collective decision making, the carrying out of "criminal justice," the provision of welfare services for members and their families, and even the workings of an elaborate public transportation system to facilitate visitation at PCC-controlled prisons. At the same time, they pioneered a rare consignment-based system for managing the domestic drug retail market that allowed for significant capital accumulation[33] while reducing the incidence of territorial conflict among drug dealers. In effect, the PCC was transitioning from a brutish prison gang reliant on overt violence to a complex corporate organization that derived its legitimacy from a predominantly nonviolent, Weberian form of rational-bureaucratic governance.[34]

Externally, the post-2006 shift in the PCC's mission was just as—or perhaps even more—consequential. Realizing that a confrontational approach to dealing with state authorities was, in the long term, likely to be counterproductive to their underlying goal of improving the living conditions of Brazil's inmate population, Marcola sought an alternative strategy: to focus the PCC's energies on becoming extremely rich. To do this, he calculated that it would be necessary to control as much of the cocaine supply chain as possible. This was no small endeavor. The plan entailed a risky investment in coca-leaf cultivation at its source far outside Brazil's borders, the elimination of so many entrenched middlemen along the transnational cocaine highway by which refined cocaine is trafficked into Brazil, and finally, the taking of control of major seaports to enable the transatlantic shipment of cocaine to continental Europe, Africa, and elsewhere.

The PCC's expansionist market agenda would take more than a decade to fully materialize, but its strategic efforts to control the cocaine supply chain began right away. By late 2006, reports emerged of significant numbers of PCC conversions in the prisons of neighboring Paraguay, a key trafficking hub for both cocaine and illegal firearms, while Brazilian PCC members increased their presence on important smuggling points along the Brazil-Paraguay border. Around the same time, PCC members were sent to Colombia to be trained in kidnapping and special combat operations by experienced FARC guerrillas. The skills (and weapons) they brought back would later be put to the test as the PCC set out to eliminate its rivals in Paraguay. In 2010, they failed in their attempt to assassinate Roberto Acevedo, a Paraguayan senator who had been active in blocking the PCC's expansion west of Brazil. In 2016, however, a paramilitary unit of more than one hundred PCC mercenaries succeeded in killing Paraguay's top drug lord, Jorge Rafaat (aka "O Turco"), during a nighttime ambush.[35] By the following year, it was clear that the PCC had near full control over the so-called Rota Caipira, the cocaine smuggling route that connects Andean cocaine to ports in southeastern Brazil via Paraguay.[36]

As the PCC was consolidating its control of the Rota Caipira, it was also seeking to invest in coca-leaf production itself. As early as 2013, the Bolivian police reported that the PCC had already established cocaine processing plants there,[37] and by the following year, reports of PCC-controlled cultivation and cocaine processing were emerging in Colombia and Peru as well.

At the same time, the PCC sought to control the highly lucrative and rapidly developing smuggling superhighway through the Brazilian Amazon known as the Rota Solimões, after the Solimões River basin through which unmeasurable amounts illicit trade passes on its way to the rest of Brazil and into the global marketplace. It was at this point, however, that the PCC's expansionist agenda finally met with stiff resistance from another powerful prison gang based in the Amazonian capital of Manaus, the Familia do Norte (FDN; Family of the North), whose leaders had already claimed the Rota Solimões for themselves.

The ensuing conflict was ruthless. On January 1, 2017, the seventeen-thousand-member FDN launched coordinated rebellions in dozens of prisons across the North and Northeast of Brazil in an effort to stop PCC encroachment in the region. When order was restored two weeks later, authorities reported the deaths of 130 inmates, most of whom were PCC members or others suspected to be affiliated with the gang from São Paulo.[38] Simultaneously, FDN leaders forged an alliance the CV in Rio de Janeiro, promising to share the wealth of the Rota Solimões in exchange for the CV's help in fending off PCC expansion. The subsequent gang war wracked Brazil for the better part of 2017, with prison riots and street violence erupting in cities across the country.

Despite its ferocity and scale, the FDN's strategy of containment by confrontation ultimately backfired. Before the year was out, the CV/FDN alliance had fallen apart, and worse still, the FDN itself split into multiple rival factions.[39] Remnants of the organization then scattered, some forming small, highly localized criminal groups, while others joined ranks with their former rivals. At the end of the day, the PCC succeeded in establishing its dominance over a large chunk of the Rota Solimões, and in doing so definitively affirmed its status as Brazil's—and South America's—most powerful criminal organization, a title that it still holds today more firmly than ever.

Brazilian Crime Syndicates Go Global

The PCC initiated its plan to control a dominant part of the cocaine supply chain in South America as early as 2006, but it was not until 2016 that this objective suddenly became a realistic one. In November of that year, a national referendum in Colombia led to the ratification of a peace agreement between the government and the FARC. Almost immediately, the twenty-thousand-member rebel organization officially disbanded and began the process of demobilization, effectively ending a civil war that had persisted for more than half a century. It marked the end of something else, too, however. During the three decades prior to 2016, the FARC and other large and well-organized armed groups in Colombia had dominated the cocaine supply chain at its source and dictated its terms of trade for export to foreign markets. In the wake of the peace accords, however, those organizations quickly fragmented and as a consequence lost their ability to bring large quantities of cocaine to the global market.[40] It was an unforeseeable circumstance, and it generated both challenges and opportunities for buyers in the global cocaine trade. For the PCC, it became the cornerstone of Marcola's expansionist vision.

Colombia has been the headwaters of the global cocaine trade for more than three decades, with an estimated 61 percent of all coca-leaf cultivation and manufacture of refined cocaine concentrated within its national borders.[41] In the few years preceding the Colombian peace accords, the PCC slowly but steadily ventured into cocaine production by establishing field operations in Peru and Bolivia. However, for as long as the FARC remained mobilized, the epicenter of cocaine production would remain beyond the PCC's control. And while the FARC (and other armed groups in Colombia) had maintained a working relationship with the PCC for years, they tended to prioritize trade relations with criminal networks in Venezuela and the Caribbean to export cocaine to Europe.

Yet in the immediate aftermath of the FARC's demobilization, the ability of any trafficking organization in Colombia to provide international buyers with consistent and large quantities of cocaine was drastically limited. Consequently, those few transnational criminal groups endowed with the organizational wherewithal to establish permanent bases of operation in Colombia began to do so. Mexican cartel groups were among the first to jump in, securing supply for markets in North America, still the largest consumer market for the white powder. The PCC followed suit, and in doing so secured its own domination of the cocaine supply chain linking South America to the world's second-largest market for cocaine, that of western Europe.[42]

Consequent to these developments, a monumental shift in transatlantic cocaine smuggling has occurred since 2016. Prior to this date, most Europe-bound cocaine left South America through Venezuela and the Caribbean via light aircraft or small seafaring vessels before finally being deposited from speedboats along the Iberian coastline. At that time, only 15 to 25 percent of Europe-bound cocaine departed from Brazilian ports,[43] a minority share, if still substantial. More recent estimates, however, put this number at over half,[44] and some media agencies have claimed that Brazilian crime syndicates control the export of as much as 80 percent.[45] Efforts to track trends in illegal smuggling are necessarily imprecise, of course, and are given to exceedingly wide margins of error. Nonetheless, there is little doubt that, since 2016, the gravitational center of the global cocaine train has shifted southward to Brazil.

This shift has led to other significant changes as well. As the PCC secured control of its cocaine supply in the Andean region, it had also begun infiltrating the regulatory bureaucracies of several Brazilian seaports, including Latin America's largest seaport, the Porto de Santos on the coast of São Paulo. Ultimately, this allowed the PCC to pioneer a new method of transatlantic cocaine smuggling: the use of modular shipping containers within which large quantities of processed cocaine could be effectively hidden among legally traded goods shipped around the world. For Europe, this meant that the geographical hotspot for cocaine imports would move from the Iberian coastline to northern Europe, where today high-quantity loads float into the ports of Antwerp and Rotterdam atop massive transoceanic vessels, right under the noses of the European Union's customs authorities.

But as the story of the PCC also indicates, Brazilian crime syndicates have not limited their ambitions to the cocaine markets of western Europe. Recognizing cocaine's potential in emerging markets elsewhere, the PCC has spent much of the past decade establishing working relationships with criminal groups along both the east and west coasts of Africa as well as across Europe. To illustrate, an international police investigation in 2019, dubbed Operation Spaghetti Connection, uncovered a trade network that linked the PCC to several Italian mafia groups, including the 'Ndrangheta, the Camorra, and the Calabrian mafia, which had succeeded in smuggling multiple tons of cocaine from the Porto de Santos to Europe via Côte d'Ivoire in West Africa.[46] The following year, a top-ranking PCC leader (and reportedly Marcola's "right-hand man") was arrested in Mozambique, where he was allegedly working with local criminal groups to establish a new trading hub that might serve emerging cocaine markets in eastern Africa, eastern Europe, and even Asia.[47]

Recent UNODC reports show that cocaine consumption in all of these regions is indeed on the rise,[48] a trend that Brazilian criminal groups like the PCC seem poised to take advantage of. And while the PCC's expansion into new consumer markets is more decentralized and more reliant on independent service providers than its efforts to control cocaine production at its source, it nevertheless represents a significant increase in the group's global reach and power. As they move in this direction, they continue to put Brazil on the map as the emerging epicenter of the global cocaine trade.

Conclusion

The past decade has seen a major transformation in the global cocaine trade. During this time, a handful of Brazilian crime syndicates rooted in the country's overcrowded prisons succeeded in transforming themselves into highly complex transnational criminal organizations that fundamentally changed the ways and means of cocaine trafficking worldwide, placing Brazil at the center of this illicit global market.

The consequences of these changes are likely to be profound and multifaceted, if difficult to predict. With respect to the criminal organizations themselves, particularly the PCC, it is likely they will continue to grow and become more powerful as they expand their operations and trade networks into new markets internationally. In this case, they will probably wiggle (or buy) their way into the Brazilian state apparatus itself, corrupting its institutions from within and making the problem of organized crime more intractable still.

But such expansion is also likely to generate tensions within these organizations that national and international law enforcement agencies will be keen to exploit, which may ultimately lead to their fragmentation and weakening. Crime syndicates like the PCC, then, may well end up like many of their predecessors, the large cartels and guerrilla groups of Colombia and Mexico. Of course, this scenario might not be much better for Brazil because, like Colombia and Mexico, the fragmentation of criminal organizations at this advanced stage of their development could easily result in a deep and violent territorialization—and even politicization—of criminal conflict. At that point, studies of Mexico's cartel wars may become uncomfortably familiar to a Brazilian audience.

Whatever the future holds for Brazil's now infamous criminal groups, Brazil itself is likely to remain at the center of global cocaine trafficking for some time to come. This is partly because of its extremely high levels of domestic consumption (Brazilians consume nearly 18 percent of the world's cocaine, according to the UNODC), which all but guarantee the country's continued predominance, independent of other factors. But it is also due to the nature and complexity of transnational trade networks and trafficking systems, which tend to be far more impervious to state intervention than the criminal organizations themselves. Now that they are firmly established throughout Brazil and abroad, these networks and systems will almost certainly continue to be useful for getting cocaine out of South America and out into rest of the world, no matter who is behind it.

Notes

1. "Over 500 kg of Cocaine Found in Coffee Delivery for Nespresso," Reuters, May 6, 2022, https://www.reuters.com/business/over-500-kg-of-cocaine-found-coffee-delivery-nespresso-2022-05-05/.

2. United Nations Office on Drugs and Crime, *Global Report on Cocaine 2023: Local Dynamics, Global Challenges* (Vienna: United Nations, 2023).

3. United Nations Office on Drugs and Crime, *Global Report on Cocaine 2023*.

4. United Nations Office on Drugs and Crime, *Cocaine Insights 4: Brazil in the Regional and Transnational Cocaine Supply Chain; The Impact of COVID-19* (Vienna: United Nations, 2023).

5. Paul Gootenberg, "The 'Pre-Colombian' Era of Drug Trafficking in the Americas: Cocaine, 1945–1965," *The Americas* 64, no. 2 (October 2007): 133–76.

6. Alba Zaluar, "Brazilian Drug Worlds and the Fate of Democracy," *Interventions* 7, no. 3 (2005): 338–41.

7. Brodwyn Fischer, *A Poverty of Rights: Citizenship and Inequality in Twentieth-Century Rio de Janeiro* (Stanford, CA: Stanford University Press, 2008).

8. Zaluar, "Brazilian Drug Worlds and the Fate of Democracy."

9. Carlos Amorim, *Comando Vermelho: A história secreta do crime organizado* (Rio de Janeiro: Editora Record, 2003).

10. William da Silva Lima, *Quatrocentos contra um: Uma história do Comando Vermelho* (Rio de Janeiro: ISER, 1991).

11. Robert Gay, *Bruno: Conversations with a Brazilian Drug Dealer* (Durham, NC: Duke University Press, 2015).

12. Caco Barcellos, *Abusado: O Dono do Morro Dona Marta* (Rio de Janeiro: Editora Record, 2003).

13. Enrique Desmond Arias, *Drugs and Democracy in Rio de Janeiro: Trafficking, Social Networks, and Public Security* (Chapel Hill: University of North Carolina Press, 2006).

14. Ben Penglase, "The Bastard Child of the Dictatorship: The Comando Vermelho and the Birth of 'Narco-Culture' in Rio de Janeiro," *Luso-Brazilian Review* 45, no. 1 (June 2008): 118–45.

15. Michael Jerome Wolff, "Building Criminal Authority: A Comparative Analysis of Drug Gangs in Rio de Janeiro and Recife," *Latin American Politics and Society* 57, no. 2 (2015): 21–40.

16. João Apolinário da Silva, "Sistema prisional e segurança pública: Analise sobre a contenção da criminalidade a partir do sistema prisional," Observatório de Segurança Pública, Universidade Salvador, Brazil, 2017.

17. Evan Williams, "Death to Undesirables: Brazil's Murder Capital," *The Independent*, May 5, 2009, https://www.independent.co.uk/news/world/americas/death-to-undesirables-brazil-s-murder-capital-1685214.html.

18. Josmar Jozino, *Cobras e lagartos: A verdadeira história do PCC* (São Paulo: Editora Via Leitura, 2017).

19. Karina Biondi, *Sharing This Walk: An Ethnography of Prison Life and the PCC in Brazil*, trans. John F. Collins (Chapel Hill: University of North Carolina Press, 2016).

20. Today (in 2024), Brazil has the world's third-largest incarcerated population.

21. Benjamin Lessing, "Counterproductive Punishment: How Prison Gangs Undermine State Authority," *Rationality and Society* 29, no. 3 (2017): 257–97.

22. David Skarbek, "Governance and Prison Gangs," *American Political Science Review* 105, no. 4 (November 2011): 702–16.

23. Jozino, *Cobras e lagartos*.

24. Graham Denyer Willis, "Deadly Symbiosis? The PCC, the State, and the Institutionalization of Violence in São Paulo, Brazil," in *Youth Violence in Latin America: Gangs and Juvenile Justice in Perspective*, ed. Gareth A. Jones and Dennis Rodgers (New York: Palgrave Macmillan, 2009), 167–81.

25. Marcos Alan Ferreira, "Brazilian Criminal Organizations as Transnational Violent Non-State Actors: A Case Study of the Primeiro Comando da Capital (PCC)," *Trends in Organized Crime* 22, no. 61 (June 2019): 148-65.

26. Amnesty International, "Brazil: Killers of Law-Enforcement Officers Must Be Brought to Justice," Public Statement, May 15, 2006, https://www.amnesty.org/fr/wp-content/uploads/2021/08/amr190232006en.pdf.

27. Biondi, *Sharing This Walk*.

28. Jozino, *Cobras e lagartos*.

29. Ferreira, "Brazilian Criminal Organizations"; and Biondi, *Sharing this Walk*.

30. Ciro Biderman, Renato Sergio de Lima, and João Manoel Pinho de Mello, "Pax Monopolista and Crime: The Case of the Emergence of the Primeiro Comando da Capital in São Paulo," CAF Working Paper no. 2014/03, Development Bank of Latin America, 2014, https://cep.lse.ac.uk/conference_papers/01_10_2015/deMello.pdf.

31. Amnesty International, "Brazil: Killers of Law-Enforcement Officers Must be Brought to Justice."

32. Stephanie G. Stahlberg, "From Prison Gangs to Transnational Mafia: The Expansion of Organized Crime in Brazil," *Trends in Organized Crime* 25, no. 2 (April 2022): 443–65.

33. Approximately 92 percent of the PCC's revenue comes from taxing the crack trade.

34. Benjamin Lessing and Graham Denyer Willis, "Legitimacy in Criminal Governance: Managing a Drug Empire from Behind Bars," *American Political Science Review* 113, no. 2 (May 2019): 584–606.

35. Ferreira, "Brazilian Criminal Organizations."

36. "The Rise of the PCC: How South America's Most Powerful Prison Gang Is Spreading in Brazil and Beyond," Center for Latin American and Latino Studies Working Paper no. 30, December 2020, https://insightcrime.org/wp-content/uploads/2020/12/InSight-Crime_The-Rise-of-the-PCC-1.pdf.

37. Natalie Southwick, "Bolivia Reports Spread of Cocaine Factories," InSight Crime, October 14, 2013, https://insightcrime.org/news/brief/bolivia-reports-spread-of-cocaine-factories/.

38. Chris Feliciano Arnold, "Brazil Has Become a Gangland," *Foreign Policy*, June 6, 2017, https://foreignpolicy.com/2017/06/06/brazil-has-become-a-gangland-prison-riot/.

39. Ryan C. Berg, "Tussle for the Amazon: New Frontiers in Brazil's Organized Crime Landscape," Research Publications 45, Florida International University Digital Commons, 2021, https://digitalcommons.fiu.edu/jgi_research/45.

40. United Nations Office on Drugs and Crime, *Global Report on Cocaine 2023*.

41. European Union Drugs Agency, "Coca and Cocaine Production," May 6, 2022, https://www.emcdda.europa.eu/publications/eu-drug-markets/cocaine/production_en.

42. United Nations Office on Drugs and Crime, *Global Report on Cocaine 2023*.

43. Ross Eventon and David R. Bewley-Taylor, "An Overview of Recent Changes in Cocaine Trafficking Routes into Europe," European Union Drugs Agency, April 4, 2016, https://www.emcdda.europa.eu/drugs-library/overview-recent-changes-cocaine-trafficking-routes-europe_en.

44. United Nations Office on Drugs and Crime, *Global Report on Cocaine 2023*.

45. Vice News, "Inside Brazil's Deadliest Drug Gangs," YouTube, August 21, 2022, https://www.youtube.com/watch?v=1mSqo_SKjMk.

46. Cecilia Anesi, Margherita Bettoni, and Giulio Rubino, "'Armed and Dangerous': Inside the 'Ndrangheta's Intercontinental Cocaine Pipeline," Organized Crime and Corruption Reporting Project, August 5, 2021, https://www.occrp.org/en/ndrangheta/armed-and-dangerous-inside-the-ndranghetas-intercontinental-cocaine-pipeline.

47. Gabriel Stargardter and Manuel Mucari, "Brazil Cocaine Kingpin Nabbed in Mozambique as Gang Expands," Reuters, April 15, 2020, https://www.reuters.com/article/world/brazil-cocaine-kingpin-nabbed-in-mozambique-as-gang-expands-idUSKCN21W2Q9/.

48. United Nations Office on Drugs and Crime, *Global Report on Cocaine 2023*.

CHAPTER 5

Cocaine Trafficking in Ecuador and Its Crossroads

Daniel Pontón C.

Ecuador has been in the "eye of the hurricane" of international drug trafficking in recent years. The United Nations Office on Drugs and Crime (UNODC), in its 2023 *Global Report on Cocaine*, identifies Ecuador as the main port of departure in Latin America for cocaine to Europe, displacing Colombia.[1] Moreover, Ecuador has the third-highest number of annual cocaine seizures of countries worldwide. The evidence shows that in 2021 and 2022, seizures exceeded 350 metric tons (figure 5.1). This is far higher than the level registered in the 1990s and early 2000s, when Ecuador played a marginal role in the dynamics of international trafficking. Bloody feuds between criminal gangs, high levels of street violence, and prison massacres have been associated with the pervasive influence of international cocaine trafficking. Although the impact of illegal economies in Ecuador is varied, the proliferation of cocaine trafficking is the basis on which a complex, powerful, and globally connected criminal platform is sustained, with enormous repercussions on national life. It should be noted that cocaine is still considered to generate one of the largest criminal economies in the world, and the most conflictive and violent.[2]

What has brought Ecuador to this point? What is the reality, and how can we understand it? Who are the actors, and what are the trends behind it? This chapter will argue that drug trafficking is a complex and long-term process that has currently led Ecuador to hyper-specialization as a transit country in the cocaine supply chain. The objective of this chapter, therefore, is to elucidate the process of specialization in the cocaine supply chain that has placed Ecuador at a complex crossroads.

This chapter draws on scholarship in political economy, which conceives of economic factors as the cause or consequence of relevant events in society and the world.[3] In this dynamic, there is an intimate connection between analyses of the domestic and international levels in understanding social phenomena, and they

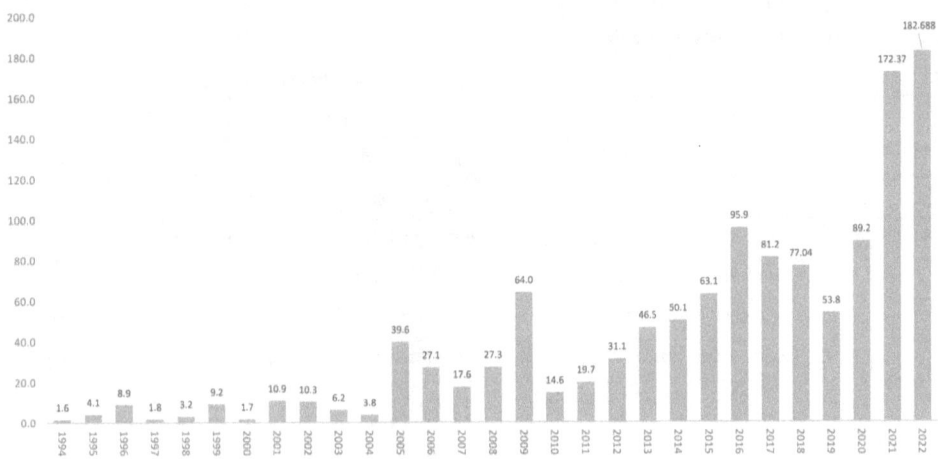

Figure 5.1. Cocaine seizures in Ecuador, 1994–2022, indicating numbers of tons. Source: Created by the author with data from the Ministry of the Interior of Ecuador (2023).

cannot be separated from each other.[4] This same theoretical framework can be applied to analyzing cocaine trafficking and other activities related to organized crime. Following this approach, a series of globally connected submerged economies can be said to converge in the different value chains of cocaine trafficking.[5] Cocaine, therefore, is a catalyst for organized crime on a local and global level. The conflicts caused by this economy subject states to complex "crossroads" in terms of their actions. In the same way, I will utilize the approach of the British theory of "comparative advantages" of international trade formulated by David Ricardo at the beginning of the nineteenth century, which alludes to the fact that when a country produces products or services with relatively low prices, that country tends to specialize in the production of those goods or services, having an advantage over other countries.[6] These two perspectives are presented as the explanatory framework in understanding the growth of cocaine trafficking in Ecuador, since this activity creates a temporal and spatial interconnection of social phenomena and the consequent local specialization in the cocaine supply chain.

The chapter will first examine the geopolitical role of Ecuador in the cocaine supply chain. It then will explore the global and local factors that led Ecuador to this aggressive proliferation of cocaine trafficking. Subsequently, I will analyze the exogenous and endogenous criminal dynamics that feed on this illegal economy and its relations with violence.

From a Transit Country to a Producing Country?

Ecuador has historically played a passive role in the global "war on drugs" due to the absence of coca-leaf crops in its territory. This has led the country to play a secondary role in international antidrug cooperation efforts despite its shared borders and close commercial, political, and social relationships with the two largest cocaine-producing countries worldwide since the 1980s, namely Colombia and Peru.[7] Until now, the production of coca leaf in Ecuador has been extremely marginal, which has not favored its strategic insertion in the cocaine supply chain. Opium poppies and marijuana crops are also a dispersed practice, as these crops grow wild and are not linked to the commercial logic of the international drug market.[8]

Ecuador has similar or even better geographical conditions than Peru and Colombia for cultivating coca. The reasons why coca plantations have not proliferated there are still uncertain, but history can offer some clues. In the first place, some scholars maintain that the cultivation and consumption of coca leaf was lost as an ancient practice, unlike in other Andean countries such as Peru and Bolivia, due to structural reasons of the colonial economy.[9] Others maintain that a peasant economy linked to the commercial production of coca leaf could never arise due to the absence of agronomic knowledge to develop the sustained production of the leaf.[10] Finally, the hypothesis that the absence of cultivation is the consequence of a particular form of colonization of Ecuadorian territory by military forces who were reluctant to develop this activity during the period of oil extraction in the 1970s is also convincing.[11] All these hypotheses explain the absence of a cultural tradition of coca production in Ecuador, thus making it difficult for the country to enter the international production circuit.

In this context, Ecuador has traditionally been considered a transit point for cocaine to international markets.[12] This role has been maintained to this day despite the fact that since around 2010 the international community has made nominal attempts to label Ecuador as a "connection center," "collection" country, and "drug hub," as indicated by the systemic growth of drug seizures and the capture of certain dangerous Colombian and European criminal actors in the country.[13]

After the implementation of Plan Colombia in 2000 and because of the systematic increase of coca-leaf cultivation in Colombia's southern border region (the departments of Putumayo and Nariño), Ecuador became recognized as a source of chemical precursors for drug trafficking. Several clandestine locations and fluvial and maritime ports were evidenced in Ecuador's northern border provinces. Ecuador's geographical proximity to the main centers of harvesting and manufacture of illegal drugs such as cocaine, as well as the jungle environment of its northern border region, give Ecuador some strategic advantages in providing the precursors for the manufacture of illicit drugs in Colombia.

As a result, Ecuador's role has remained practically unchanged in the international narrative since the turn of the twenty-first century. In fact, the annual reports of the International Narcotics Control Strategy issued by the US Department of State show no major changes in Ecuador's classification since 2005. Consequently, Ecuador has been characterized with descriptive terms such as "transit country," "drug routes," "porous borders," "institutional weakness," and "money laundering" in documentation related to the "war on drugs" initiated by the United States in the Andean region.[14]

Yet in recent years, a debate on Ecuador's systematic rise in cocaine refining has surfaced. Numerous journalistic accounts have tried to alert Ecuadorian government authorities about the imminent growth of this activity, which would clearly change Ecuador's status to that of a "producing country."[15] Added to this situation in Ecuador is the reportage in the UN's 2022 *World Drug Report* revealing the systematic growth of refining laboratories in different countries in the Andean region and even in Europe.[16] However, the statistical evidence reported by the Ecuadorian National Police does not show significant changes in terms of the country's refining capacity. The presence of refining laboratories has been frequently reported by authorities since around 2000, but in very marginal numbers. Since 2020, for example, fifteen laboratories have been destroyed (primarily in the country's northern border provinces).[17] This amount is dramatically lower than the almost 680 laboratories destroyed in Colombia during this same time period.[18] This would not make Ecuador a country of refinement in itself, as even the United States recognizes it as only a marginal producer. Yet it is always necessary to remain alert about a possibly developing scenario.

Given that Ecuador's status as a drug "transit country" remains unchanged, there is no doubt that what has proliferated in recent years is the volume of drugs passing through the country. This trend has favored the development of an economy of criminal services, exacerbating various conflicts between criminal organizations. Under this premise, what seems to have happened in recent years in Ecuador is that its territorial specialization as a center for the collection and shipment of drugs abroad through maritime and air routes has been consolidated. But what factors have generated this growth?

Table 5.1.

2005	2022
Sharing porous borders and a contiguous seacoast with Colombia and Peru, Ecuador is a major transit country for illicit drugs and chemicals. The violent conflict in Colombia complicates drug interdiction on Ecuador's northern border, but drug seizures in the northern border area increased in 2004 thanks to improved police and military activity. Most drugs leave Ecuador by sea. Ecuadorian authorities are seeking to improve port cargo inspections.... Ecuador is a party to and has enacted legislation to implement the provisions of the 1988 UN Drug Convention.... Weak public institutions, widespread corruption, and a poorly regulated financial system make Ecuador vulnerable to organized crime. Border controls of persons and goods are undependable. Much of the population lives in poverty. Scanty government presence in a large portion of the country contributes to lawlessness. The National Police (ENP) and military forces are inadequately equipped and trained.	Situated between the world's two largest cocaine-producing countries, Colombia and Peru, Ecuador is a major transit country for illicit drugs. Ecuador is not a major drug-producing country, though authorities have discovered some clandestine cocaine-processing facilities in the jungle along the Colombian border. Porous land borders and a largely unprotected coastline enable transnational criminal organizations to traffic cocaine from Colombia and Peru for distribution to the United States and Europe. Ecuador is also a major transit country for chemical precursors to process illicit drugs. Ecuador's government is committed to efforts to address drug trafficking, and authorities seized a record quantity of narcotics in 2021. While the government has increasingly turned to the United States as its security partner of choice, the police, military, and justice sector lack sufficient resources to effectively confront transnational crime.

Source: Created by the author with data from the US Department of State: left column (2005), US Department of State, International Narcotics Control Strategy Report, vol. 1, Drug and Chemical Control (Washington, DC: Bureau of International Narcotics and Law Enforcement Affairs, 2005), https://2009-2017.state.gov/j/inl/rls/nrcrpt/2005/index.htm; and right column (2022), US Department of State, International Narcotics Control Strategy Report, vol. 1, Drug and Chemical Control (Washington, DC: Bureau of International Narcotics and Law Enforcement Affairs, 2022), https://www.state.gov/2022-international-narcotics-control-strategy-report-2/.

Opportunity Costs:
Exogenous and Endogenous Factors

The political economy approach and a consideration of comparative advantages offer an explanatory framework for understanding the reality of Ecuador today. Ecuador presents some opportunity costs that have enabled the country to favorably host logistics services for the collection and international trafficking of cocaine. Yet this specialization has not occurred overnight; rather, it has resulted from a systematic process that began around the year 2000. The factors that have contributed to generating this problem can be divided into those that are exogenous, and those that are endogenous.

Exogenous Factors

The exogenous sphere refers to structural factors in an international context over which Ecuador has had very little control. In particular, the geopolitical preponderance of drug trafficking in Ecuador was systematically affected by the relevance of the Pacific Ocean as a trafficking route. In the 1970s and 1980s, the development of the Caribbean route marked an important milestone in the growth of drug trafficking in Colombia.[19] Currently, the main exit ports for cocaine bound for North America are on the Pacific, and these routes are currently controlled by powerful Mexican cartels.[20]

Because Colombia has no major Pacific ports, drug traffickers have systematically increased the flow of container-borne cocaine through Guayaquil and other Ecuadorian ports to the United States and, currently, even to Europe. Similarly, the transfer of drug cargo from small boats to large vessels on the sea is very common, using the vast and unprotected Ecuadorian maritime space in the Galápagos Islands. Speedboats can deliver large shipments of cocaine from Ecuador to the Central American and Mexican coasts in one day.[21] The use of foreign planes and submersibles as a cocaine trafficking strategy is also part of this trend.

Another structural factor is associated with the effects of Plan Colombia. This aspect is known as the "balloon effect" and involves the spatial displacement of drug production when state authorities focus on combating drugs in a certain conflictive area. This was a primary characteristic of the old "war on drugs," which had partial success but often simply spread the problem to other territories.[22] As a result of the intensification of the campaign against narcoguerrillas in Colombia in 2000, cocaine crops and production withdrew to the Ecuadorian border region, thus generating new conflicts for that country. The same cannot be said of Peru, since its production centers are still very far from the Ecuadorian border.

According to the Observatorio de Drogas de Colombia, between 2017 and 2023 almost 40 percent of Colombia's total coca crop and 23 percent of the total number of cocaine laboratories were concentrated near the border with Ecuador. Nariño Department by itself harbored almost 30 percent of the crop.[23] Tumaco is an administrative territory in Nariño Department of around three thousand square kilometers, contiguous with the border with Ecuador and with direct access to the Pacific. In 2021, this territory had almost 10 percent of the coca crop in all of Colombia and almost 10 percent of all destroyed laboratories. The flow of drugs from this territory found an important and natural exit point in ports on the Ecuadorian coastline. Colombian cocaine continues to be the most in demand internationally (80 percent of the cocaine seized in the United States and Europe is of Colombian origin).[24] In other words, Ecuador borders the world's largest producer of cocaine, which feeds the bulk of world demand.

The balloon effect, however, is not the only factor. As of 2012, Colombia began to experience an abrupt escalation of coca cultivation and cocaine production in its territory, with enormous repercussions on its southern border (figure 5.2).[25] It is estimated that by 2022, Colombia was producing more than 1,500 tons of cocaine at its highest purity annually, an unprecedented figure.[26] Among the reasons for this growth are the relaxation of Colombian state control since the beginning of the peace negotiations between the government and the Fuerzas Armadas Revolucionarias de Colombia (FARC), the elimination of the use of glyphosate for the eradication of coca-leaf crops and the low effectiveness of the subsequent manual and forced eradication strategy in Colombia, the ultimate failure to implement the peace accords in Colombia, and other socioeconomic factors.

Consequently, this greater flow of cocaine production in Colombia likely motivated the sudden growth of drug trafficking in Ecuador. As shown in figure 5.3, cocaine seizures in Ecuador have increased in proportion to seizures in Colombia. It is estimated that, in 2022, of all cocaine seizures in Ecuador and Colombia together, Ecuador's share had risen to 20 to 30 percent of the total. According to the UNODC's 2023 *Global Report on Cocaine*, global drug seizures

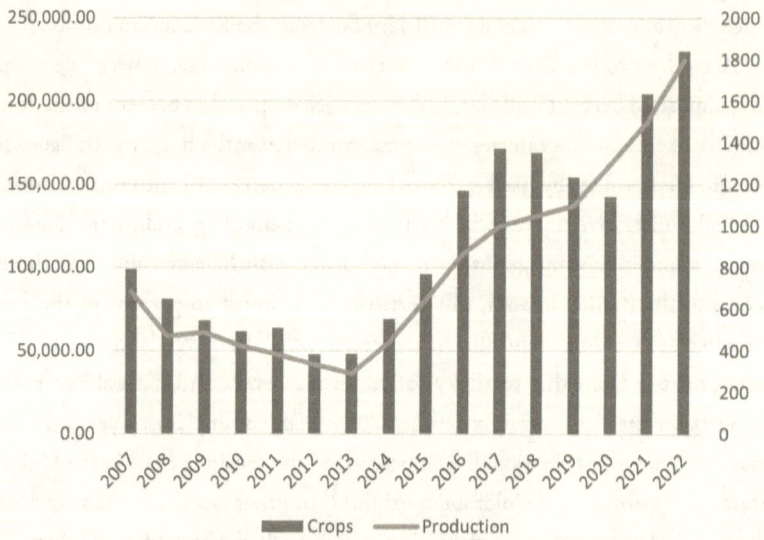

Figure 5.2. Coca-leaf crops vs. estimated cocaine production in Colombia, 2007–2022. The numbers on the left-hand side of the graph indicate coca-leaf crops in hectares, and on the right-hand side production in tons of pure cocaine. Source: Created by the author with data from the Ministerio de Justicia de Colombia, Observatorio de Drogas del Colombia (2023); and the United Nations Office on Drugs and Crime, *World Drug Report* (2022). *Estimated figure.

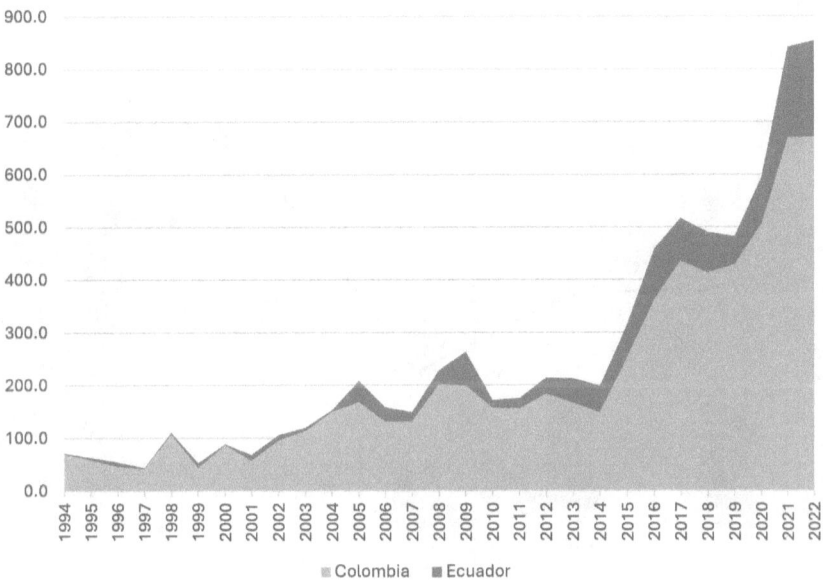

Figure 5.3. Cocaine seizures in Ecuador and Colombia, 1994–2022, indicating number of tons. Source: Created by the author with data from the Ministerio de Justicia de Colombia, Observatorio de Drogas del Colombia (2023); and the Ministry of the Interior of Ecuador (2023).

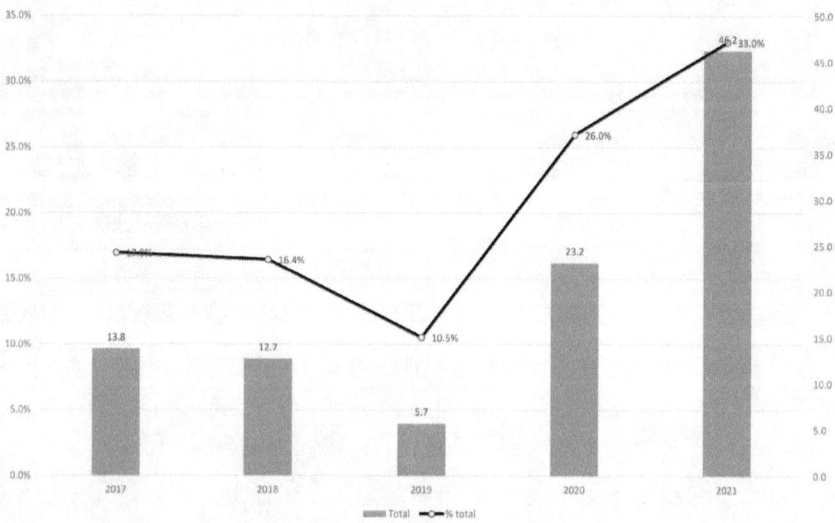

Figure 5.4. Cocaine seizures in Ecuadorian seaports, 2017–2021. The numbers on the left-hand side of the graph indicate percentage of all cocaine seized in Ecuador that is seized in seaports, and on the right-hand side tons of cocaine seized in seaports. Source: Created by the author with data from the Ministry of the Interior of Ecuador (2022).

have been growing systematically year by year since around 2015, and this seems to be associated, in part, to a growth in production. In other words, the increasing number of seizures is convincing evidence of a greater flow of drugs, which in Ecuador has forged a highly specialized criminal economy.

Notwithstanding the upward trend, the sudden growth in the number of seizures cannot be explained without factoring in the COVID-19 pandemic. Ecuadorian authorities have made a concentrated effort to explain this phenomenon, finding that it is associated with the logistical problems in commercial maritime transport evidenced during the pandemic period.[27] These logistical problems have created a substantial backlog in drugs awaiting export through Ecuadorian ports. As can be seen in figure 5.4, based on the number of seizures, there has been a marked growth in cocaine exports through Ecuadorian ports. Since 2020, it has been common in Ecuador to have cocaine seizures of more than ten metric tons in a single incident.[28] In 2021, more than one hundred tons of the alkaloid were seized in one operation in Colombia.[29] These cases illustrate an explosive rise in cocaine exports after the stagnation in the supply chain because of the coronavirus.

In this structural panorama, the substantial increase in world demand for cocaine cannot be ruled out. According to the 2023 *Global Report on Cocaine*, there has been constant growth in the number of cocaine users, especially habitual users, since 2010. This increase is largely due to the global diversification of markets (European and Asian, among others) that has offset the stagnation in the demand for cocaine in the United States. A large part of these new markets and their supply routes have found an opportunity niche for sourcing in Ecuador. The trade agreement between Ecuador and the European Union has contributed to a growth in trade between the two partners. Antwerp in Belgium is the main port of entry for cocaine into Europe, and most of this cocaine, originating in Colombia, is shipped out of Ecuador.[30] Similarly, the volume of drugs trafficked from Ecuador to other European ports has begun to grow significantly.[31] This increased trade has been nourished by a growing demand.

The increase in the flow of drugs over Ecuadorian territory can also be analyzed in an inverse way. In this sense, in addition to the increase in the volume of cocaine production in Colombia, this growth could also be the product of an increase in global seizures. The logic is that the more drugs seized, the less drugs on the market, and given that international demand continues to grow, this forces producers to supply more drugs. Since, in the cocaine supply chain, criminal organizations largely impose the price on producers, a natural propensity for agricultural innovation in rural coca growing can be expected; as a result, the harvest cycle has increased from three to six times per year, and farmers have achieved a better yield of coca-leaf production per hectare. These improvements also point to a better performance in the cocaine-refining process. The greater the seizure, the greater the production for replacement.[32]

This contradiction in global drug control strategy has also affected Ecuador, since bigger seizures in Ecuador and Colombia may be the cause of greater production in those countries' common border areas. Thus, innovations on the part of law enforcement authorities in locating and seizing drug shipments have fostered greater production. The global seizure average is 30 to 50 percent of total production, which is significantly higher than the 15 to 20 percent average during the 1990s.[33] The logic suggests that being more efficient in controlling the drug trade de facto drives higher production.

Endogenous Factors

Among the endogenous factors (those that specifically apply to Ecuador) that explain this systematic onslaught of drug trafficking and territorial specialization is the issue of money laundering. Ecuador adopted the US dollar as its own currency in 2000, which has gradually configured a new scenario for the country's economic, commercial, and financial relations internally and externally. There is much speculation about how this situation is linked to drug trafficking. Estimates indicate that, in Ecuador, $3.5 billion a year could be laundered as a result of drug trafficking (2 to 3 percent of the national GDP),[34] an amount that reflects the growth and importance of this illegal economy in the national and international financial and economic structure.

The sectors of the Ecuadorian economy most affected by this activity are the banking system, real estate, vehicles, and the informal economy. Money laundering also serves as a platform for drug-trafficking operations such as bribery; the purchase of services, property, and vehicles for drug-trafficking operations; and other things. Many of these activities are carried out through shell companies.[35] The operating scheme of dollarization based on the elimination of exchange controls has been classified as a risk factor for the proliferation of this type of submerged economy. This has sparked extensive debate about the effectiveness and efficiency of Ecuador's internal control system among the ever-vigilant international community.[36]

Another endogenous factor is the failure of Ecuador's state control system, especially with respect to its air space and maritime territory. Drug trafficking in Ecuador has gone from being a border issue to becoming a problem that affects the vast majority of the coastal territory. The increasing use of private and public ports (especially Guayaquil), the departure of drugs by sea and air routes in provinces such as Manabí and Santa Elena, and the use of collection centers in the provinces of Los Ríos, El Oro, and Santo Domingo de los Tsáchilas are some examples of this intensive penetration. In other words, beyond the structural issue, the lack of a sustained dissuasive policy on air and maritime control by the state has contributed to this escalation.

Consequently, the debate on the closure of the US government's Manta base in 2009 has stood out in recent years.[37] Ecuador has not been able to sustain an effective governance scheme of control over strategic areas since 2010. For example, there is still no coordinated policy for the use of scanners for monitoring and controlling commercial maritime traffic. Port control is still manually done, which makes the monitoring process extremely difficult. There are also problems associated with the use of radar systems and other proprietary technologies for maritime and air interdiction.[38]

Analogous problems are witnessed in Ecuador's aerial control. In 2017, after almost a decade of debate, the government announced the purchase and installation of aerial radar systems. In 2021, one radar system was relocated under strong military backing.[39] A week later, this radar system was boycotted and disabled, arousing enormous suspicions of corruption and mafia infiltration within the military institution.[40] Frequently, local authorities as well as foreign observers denounce such acts of corruption in the police and judicial ranks. In 2022, for example, the US ambassador to Ecuador denounced the presence of narcogenerals in the armed forces and national police.[41]

The Crime Agency

In 2017, drug lord Édison Washington Prado Álava (alias "Gerald") was captured in Colombia. In February 2018, he was extradited to the United States, tried, and sentenced to nineteen years in prison for crimes associated with cocaine trafficking. Gerald was an Ecuadorian fisherman accused of sending more than 250 tons of cocaine to Central America and the United States from 2015 to 2017. His excellent knowledge of navigation in the Pacific Ocean and the establishment of marine "gas stations"—vessels that supplied speedboats with illicit cargoes—allowed him to quickly ascend in the hierarchy of international drug trafficking.[42]

The Gerald case should not be analyzed purely for the shocking amounts of cocaine trafficked to the United States but also because, for the first time, a local drug trafficker had acquired such a level of power to the point of being considered the "Ecuadorian Pablo Escobar." This case also stands out for the legacy of skills and capacities Gerald transferred to other criminals, installing a new dynasty that has marked a milestone in the development of Ecuador as a center for the collection and transit of drugs. Indeed, in February 2023, Wilder Emilio Sánchez Farfán (alias "El Gato"), a drug trafficker who acted as an emissary for the powerful Jalisco Nueva Generación cartel (CJNG; Jalisco New Generation cartel) and the Sinaloa cartel, was also captured in Colombia. El Gato was as efficient as Gerald in collecting and transporting drugs by air and sea, though he did so more silently and away from propaganda. These are examples of the progressive facet of territorial specialization of Ecuador in the cocaine supply chain.[43]

Connections with Colombian and Mexican Cartels

The cases of Gerald and Farfán were not a matter of chance. As noted, in the 1980s and 1990s Ecuador was a marginal player in international cocaine trafficking. The country's underworld at that time was composed of small traffickers who participated in the weakest links of the cocaine supply chain (e.g., mules). The Ecuadorian routes began to gain prominence at the end of the 1990s as Colombian cartels began to make use of Ecuador's territory and port infrastructure for international traffic. The most emblematic case was the Cartel del Norte del Valle (North Valley Cartel)'s interest in Ecuador's tuna industry, which they used to transport quantities of cocaine abroad. With the implementation of Plan Colombia, Ecuador was also affected by the criminal diaspora resulting from the Colombian government's prosecution of guerrilla cells of the FARC and certain paramilitary groups in the border area with Ecuador.

After the decrease in coca cultivation in Colombia's southern border area, Ecuadorian territory began to gain prominence for many criminal organizations. Those organizations began to vie for control of Ecuadorian border crossings in the early 2000s. The goal was to maintain in situ control of cocaine production in Colombia and dominate the coveted and nascent Pacific route. One group that increased their power during this period was Los Rastrojos, a criminal band that evolved out of the paramilitary demobilization. They were the heirs of the dismantled Cartel del Norte del Valle.[44] Ecuador also attracted the interest of the increasingly powerful Mexican cartels, who sought out Colombian allies to control drug-smuggling routes. The partnership between Mexican and Colombian cartels in Ecuador required an alliance with local criminal networks, which were specializing in the provision of logistics and protection services for transnational organized crime. A clear example of this is the emergence of Los Choneros, currently the most dangerous and powerful criminal group in Ecuador. This gang was operational in the early 2000s and became powerful due to drug trafficking.

In 2009, Juan Salcedo (alias "Juan Kili"), a well-known international drug trafficker wanted by the US Drug Enforcement Administration (DEA) and Interpol, was arrested in Colombia. In 2010, Ramón Quintero, a member of Los Rastrojos and one of the most wanted drug lords in the world, was also imprisoned. In 2012 and 2013, respectively, Juan Carlos Serna and Jorge Domínguez, top leaders of Los Rastrojos, were arrested in Ecuador.[45] In the late 2000s, the presence of the Sinaloa cartel in Ecuador was already a reality, and the most notorious example was the presence of Captain Telmo Castro, a member of the Ecuadorian armed forces accused of being the tentacle in Ecuador for the operations of the Sinaloa cartel, then led by Joaquín "El Chapo" Guzmán and "El Mayo" Zambada. Castro's capture in 2013 and subsequent murder in 2019 inside a prison facility in Ecuador revealed a series of international contacts, an alliance with local groups and networks of corruption, and institutional protection that facilitated the collection and transport of drugs abroad.[46]

Links with European Organizations

In 2010, DEA agent Jay Bergman declared Ecuador to be "the united nations of organized crime."[47] That statement alluded to the increasing number of cases evidencing the penetration of the Mexican and Colombian cartels, and the recurring complaints of the presence of Russian and Italian mafias, in the territory of Ecuador. The role of these mafias has been crucial in the logistical management of the entry of cocaine into Europe to satisfy a growing demand.[48] Since 2014, Ecuadorian authorities have made significant captures of Albanian citizens, who under the guise of "businessmen" had been able to take advantage of the local business infrastructure to establish a network of bribery and corruption with the aim of managing the port of Guayaquil.[49] This activity, operated by the Albanian network, has gained strength since the trade agreement between Ecuador and the European Union in 2017.

It should be noted that the operation of this international trafficking network has been key in positioning Ecuador as the main site of South American cocaine exports to Europe in recent years. This has occurred in collaboration with local criminal networks and with the complicity of high-level authorities.[50] The US ambassador's announcement of the presence of "narcogenerals" alluded to this complex association with European mafias. In particular, the evidence suggests that the Albanian network has extended its tentacles to high government spheres in Ecuador since 2021.[51]

Criminal Violence

Another factor in the proliferation of foreign criminal networks in Ecuador is the leading role of FARC dissidents after the beginning of that organization's peace process with the Colombian government in 2012. These dissidents sought to take control of the activities of the now extinct organization in cocaine production. Collection and transport, therefore, had to be operated by the growing local drug-trafficking groups of Ecuador. For example, the leader of the FARC dissidents was accused of having close ties with the Gerald group.[52] The penetration of the FARC dissidents peaked in 2018, when a series of terrorist acts took place on the northern border of Ecuador during which three kidnapped journalists were murdered. All these acts, according to the official discourse, were reprisals for the large amounts of cocaine seized by the Ecuadorian government.[53]

Ecuador has also been facing a dramatic change in terms of security. From 2009 to 2018, Ecuador witnessed a progressive decrease in its homicide rate, at fewer than six homicides annually per one hundred thousand inhabitants. Since 2019, a sustained increase in the homicide rate has occurred: in 2023, it was close to forty-seven per one hundred thousand people. Ecuador is currently the most violent country in all of South America and the fifth most violent country in Latin America and the Caribbean.[54]

This increase is not only quantitative but also qualitative. Since 2019, Ecuador has been experiencing a bloody prison crisis whose effects are directly related to the expansion of the country's prison capacity and the consequent explosive growth of its prison population. From 2010 to 2020, the incarcerated population in Ecuador practically quadrupled, and the government has subsequently lost total control of the prisons.[55] This has led to more than four hundred deaths as a result of disputes between criminal gangs linked to illicit drug trafficking.[56] Although similar crises have existed in other Latin American countries (e.g., Brazil and Colombia), the Ecuadorian prison crisis has been one of the most violent due to both the number of deaths and their cruelty.

Starting in 2021, these prison disputes have manifested in the streets, which has led the country to witness a series of terrorist events. Emulating the violence in other Latin American countries, explosions at police facilities, gas stations, and homes, massacres of civilians, and mutilated and hanging corpses, among other things, have become daily events in Ecuador. Under these circumstances, in April 2023, the government of Ecuador declared criminal gangs linked to street drug trafficking as a "terrorist threat."[57]

Disputes between these criminal gangs have led to some splitting off from Los Choneros, which, under the leadership of Jorge Luis Zambrano (alias Rasquiña), emerged as the most powerful gang in the country. Zambrano's murder at the end of 2020 led to the appearance of various prison groups such as the Wolves, the Chone Killers, the Tiguerones, and others, who all claim a criminal monopoly over the cocaine retail market and other illicit activities such as extortion, assassination, and kidnapping. The operations of these groups currently extend over a large part of Ecuador's coastal territory, subjecting the country to one of the worst security crises in its history. Some suggest that the Tiguerones group already has a territorial presence in Peru and possibly across other countries in the region and Europe due to Ecuador's high number of migrants.[58]

There is a relationship between criminal disputes over drug trafficking and the pandemic growth of violence in Ecuador. According to the Ecuadorian police, about 40 percent of these deaths are related to microtrafficking (table 5.2). What is not clear is the complicity of transnational crime organizations in this dynamic. The violence derived from international drug trafficking, according to the National Police, is marginal compared to deaths from microtrafficking. Due to the size of its territory as well as its population and income, Ecuador is not such an important market to justify such high levels of violence based on the economic interests of transnational crime. In other words, the Ecuadorian domestic market for drugs does not seem large enough to motivate the interest of transnational criminal organizations such that it would generate this wave of street and prison violence. In this context, it is possible that the reason for the violence boils down to disputes between local gangs for the control of drug-trafficking routes as well as to a local pedagogical adaptation of the violent practices of the Mexican cartels.

Indeed, the Ecuadorian trafficking routes are highly coveted by transnational criminal organizations. Yet the relationship between the operation of these local criminal gangs and the global dynamics of cocaine is not entirely clear. Some journalistic sources suggest the presence of relations between Los Choneros, Los Lobos, and the Tiguerones (three of Ecuador's most violent active criminal groups, with the largest number of members) on the one hand, and the Sinaloa cartel and the CJNG on the other.[59] This relationship is articulated to the provision of logistical and protection services. In fact, there are rumors of a connection between El Gato, Farfán, the CJNG, and the Tiguerones, who are responsible for several prison massacres.[60] However, as with gangs in Central America, some experts maintain that these local groups are too anarchic, violent (therefore striking), and unpredictable to be at the strict service of the complex international machinery of cocaine trafficking.

What is certain is that the operation of these local criminal gangs has been functional to organized crime in an indirect manner. Consequently, this has

Table 5.2. Number of murders in Ecuador related to large-scale drug trafficking and street sales of drugs.

	2020	2021	2022
Large-scale drug trafficking	8	59	69
Street sales of drugs	304	793	1853
Total deaths from drug trafficking	312	852	1922

Source: Created by the author with data from the Ministry of Interior of Ecuador (2022).

generated a wave of panic among the Ecuadorian population and undermined the institutional morale and political credibility of the current government. In fact, confronting the wave of violence in Ecuador is seen as one of the main demands of the citizenry, and the government itself has identified drug trafficking and organized crime as the cause of the violence. In 2022, more than 50 percent of Ecuadorians said that insecurity and crime were their main concern.[61] Although the problems of violence and drug trafficking should be treated as separate issues (with different causes and solutions), a weak state with limited capacity for territorial control and a frightened population are the perfect breeding ground for organized crime. Therefore, this complex dynamic between local and international criminal elements is part of Ecuador's systematic process of territorial specialization in the cocaine supply chain.

Conclusion

Cocaine trafficking occurs in a global market where each territory, country, or region marks an important milestone in the supply chain of this illicit commodity. For this reason, it is important to explore the Ecuadorian case from a political economy perspective, since it allows us to analyze how global dynamics are connected with local ones. In this sense, the global cocaine supply chain has fueled an unprecedented criminal industry, the effects of which have generated Ecuador's worst insecurity crisis in its history. This is a demonstration of the effects of drug trafficking on various territorial realities and a clear example of the contradictions of the "war on drugs" and its direct and indirect effects on the reality of a country.

Within the framework of the political economy of cocaine, Ecuador has historically been considered a transit country. This status has not really changed in recent years, and attempts to turn Ecuador into a producing country have not proliferated. However, Ecuador has experienced a systematic territorial specialization in drug collection and transit services that has forged important quantitative and qualitative changes. This specialization process—although it is part of an adaptive dynamic to the global process—has the capacity to give a new shape and identity to the problem.

The volumes of cocaine passing through Ecuador are considerably higher now than in the past. This has forged a dangerous criminal economy with far-reaching repercussions on the political and social life of the country. Ecuador is currently one of the main strategic outlets for cocaine worldwide and is the drug's main port of departure to Europe. This has led Ecuador to be considered a strategic site of interest for transnational criminal organizations, which have forged a vast network of alliances with local gangs. This scenario has prevailed within a framework of a spectacular wave of local crime and violence unprecedented in the history of Ecuador.

Reversing this situation does not seem to be an easy task, since this specialization, which gives Ecuador broad comparative advantages in the cocaine supply chain, has been generated by a historical process in which exogenous and endogenous factors converge. In other words, exporting cocaine from Ecuador has beneficial comparative opportunity costs. This expansive dynamic of drug trafficking in Ecuador accounts for the complex situation that the country is experiencing with respect to organized crime, a situation that has placed the country at a complex crossroads with as yet undetermined local, regional, and global projections.

Notes

1. United Nations Office on Drugs and Crime, *Global Report on Cocaine 2023: Local Dynamics, Global Challenges* (Vienna: United Nations, 2023), https://www.unodc.org/documents/data-and-analysis/cocaine/Global_cocaine_report_2023.pdf.

2. United Nations Office on Drugs and Crime, *World Drug Report 2023: Executive Summary* (Vienna: United Nations, 2023), https://www.unodc.org/res/WDR-2023/WDR23_Exsum_fin_SP.pdf.

3. Pablo Bustelo Gómez, "Enfoque de la regulación y economía política internacional: ¿Paradigmas convergentes?," *Revista de Economía Mundial*, no. 8 (January 2003): 143–73.

4. Anthony Payne, "The Study of Governance in a Global Political Economy," in *Globalizing International Political Economy*, ed. Nicola Phillips (Basingstoke, Hants., England: Palgrave Macmillan, 2005), 55–81.

5. Katharina Hofmann, "The Impact of Organized Crime on Democratic Governance: Focus on Latin America the Caribbean," Dialogue on Globalization, Briefing Paper no. 13, Friedrich Ebert Stiftung, Berlin, September 2009, http://library.fes.de/pdf-files/iez/global/06697.pdf.

6. Raquel González Blanco, "Diferentes teorías del comercio internacional," *ICE: Revista de Economía*, no. 858 (January–February 2011): 103–17, https://www.guao.org/sites/default/files/biblioteca/Diferentes%20teor%C3%ADas%20del%20comercio%20intenacional.pdf.

7. Francisco E. Thoumi, *Illegal Drugs, Economy, and Society in the Andes* (Washington, DC: Woodrow Wilson Center Press; Baltimore: Johns Hopkins University Press, 2003); Paul Gootenberg, *Andean Cocaine: The Making of a Global Drug* (Chapel Hill: University of North Carolina Press, 2008); Bruce Michael Bagley, "Colombia and the War on Drugs," *Foreign Affairs* 67, no. 1 (Fall 1988): 70–92; Bruce Michael Bagley, "Globalisation and Latin American and Caribbean Organised Crime," *Global Crime* 6, no. 1 (2004): 32–53; and Francisco E. Thoumi, "Illegal Drugs in Colombia: From Illegal Economic Boom to Social Crisis," *Annals of the American Academy of Political and Social Science* 582, no. 1 (July 2002): 102–16.

8. United Nations Office on Drugs and Crime, *Ecuador: Indicadores de cultivos ilícitos en el Ecuador, 2013* (Vienna: United Nations, 2014), https://www.unodc.org/documents/peruandecuador/Informes/ECUADOR/Ecuador_web_OPT.pdf.

9. Adrián Bonilla, *Las sorprendentes virtudes de lo perverso: Ecuador y narcotráfico en los 90* (Quito: Editorial FLACSO, 1993); and Adrián Bonilla and Alexei Páez, "Estados Unidos y la región andina: Distancia y diversidad," *Nueva Sociedad*, no. 206 (November–December 2006): 126–39.

10. Fredy Rivera Vélez, "Las formas de una guerra amorfa: Drogas, democracia y derechos humanos en Ecuador," Íconos: Revista de Ciencias Sociales, no. 20 (September 2004): 14–24.

11. Jorge Núñez Vega, *Cacería de brujas: Drogas "ilegales" y sistema de cárceles en Ecuador* (Quito: Editorial FLACSO, 2016).

12. Fredy Rivera Vélez and Fernando Torres Gorena, "Ecuador, ¿país de tránsito o país productor de drogas?" Programa de Cooperación en Seguridad Regional, Friedrich Ebert Stiftung, Berlin, July 2011, https://library.fes.de/pdf-files/bueros/la-seguridad/08331.pdf.

13. Fernando Carrión Mena, "El Ecuador, un HUB del narcotráfico," *Diario Hoy* (Quito), 2012, https://works.bepress.com/fernando_carrion/519/.

14. Juan Gabriel Tokatlian, ed., *Drogas y prohibición: Una vieja guerra, un nuevo debate* (Buenos Aires: Libros del Zorzal, 2010).

15. Maria Jose Pesantez, "Ecuador: De país de tránsito a país productor y distribuidor de droga," Geopol 21, October 14, 2022, https://geopol21.com/ecuador-de-pais-de-transito-a-pais-productor-y-distribuidor-de-droga/.

16. United Nations Office on Drugs and Crime, *World Drug Report 2022: Global Overview* (Vienna: United Nations, 2022), https://www.unodc.org/res/wdr2022/MS/WDR22_Booklet_2.pdf.

17. Observatorio Ecuatoriano del Crimen Organizado, "Laboratorios de drogas destruidos y su ubicación," 2023, https://oeco.padf.org/visualizador-de-datos-total-de-laboratorios-de-drogas-destruidos-y-ubicacion/.

18. Ministerio de Justicia de Colombia, Observatorio de Drogas del Colombia, "Sistema de información de drogas de Colombia," 2023, https://www.minjusticia.gov.co/programas-co/ODC/Paginas/SIDCO.aspx.

19. Lilian Bobea, "Seeking Out the State: Organized Crime, Violence, and Statetropism in the Caribbean," In *Drug Trafficking, Organized Crime, and Violence in the Americas Today*, ed. Bruce Michael Bagley and Jonathan D. Rosen (Gainesville: University Press of Florida, 2015), 293–322; and Ivelaw L. Griffith, "Narcotics Arms Trafficking, Corruption and Governance in the Caribbean," *Journal of Money Laundering Control* 1, no. 2 (1997): 138–47.

20. Laura Sánchez Ley, "Con narcosubmarinos, cárteles mexicanos controlan trasiego de droga en el Pacífico," *Milenio*, February 24, 2022, https://www.milenio.com/policia/carteles-mexicanos-controlan-trasiego-droga-pacifico.

21. James Bargent, "Ecuador: Autopista de la cocaína hacia Estados Unidos y Europa," InSight Crime, October 30, 2019, https://es.insightcrime.org/investigaciones/ecuador-autopista-de-la-cocaina-hacia-estados-unidos-y-europa/.

22. Bruce Michael Bagley, "Drug Trafficking and Organized Crime in the Americas: Major Trends in the Twenty-First Century," Woodrow Wilson Center, August 2012, https://www.wilsoncenter.org/sites/default/files/media/documents/publication/BB%20Final.pdf.

23. Ministerio de Justicia de Colombia, Observatorio de Drogas del Colombia, "Sistema de información de drogas de Colombia."

24. Since Peru also shares a border with Ecuador, cocaine from that country also has enormous potential to exit the region through Ecuadorian ports. However, given international market preferences, Peruvian cocaine has destinations apart from the coveted routes along the northern Pacific coastline. Therefore, the export of Colombian cocaine plays a fundamental role in the geopolitics of control in the countries with the highest consumption and world income. See Cynthia McClintock, "The War on Drugs: The Peruvian Case," *Journal of Interamerican Studies and World Affairs* 30, nos. 2–3 (Summer-Autumn 1988): 127–42; Olga Marcela Cubides Salazar, "La violencia del narcotráfico en los países de mayor producción de coca: Los casos de Perú y Colombia," *Papel Político* 19, no. 2 (2014): 657–90; Bruce Michael Bagley, "The Evolution of Drug Trafficking and Organized Crime in Latin America," *Sociologia, problemas e práticas*, no. 71 (2013): 99–123; and Bárbara Grease Merino Villadoma, "Operaciones de erradicación e interdicción y la reducción de cultivos de coca en Perú, 2011–2016," *Revista Gobierno y Gestión Pública* 6, no. 1 (2019): 58–82.

25. From these circumstances, numerous criminal organizations began to compete for control of the drug trade in Colombia, including the Mexican cartels. In 2018, Colombia produced more than two hundred thousand hectares of coca leaf, which generated pressure from the US government to start aerial spraying again. Aerial spraying had been prohibited in Colombia in 2015 by the country's Constitutional Court, due to the environmental consequences of the chemicals used in aerial fumigation, and the public health of the local population.

26. United Nations Office on Drugs and Crime, *Global Report on Cocaine 2023*.

27. Renato Rivera-Rhon and Carlos Bravo-Grijalva, "Crimen organizado y cadenas de valor: El ascenso estratégico del Ecuador en la economía del narcotráfico," *URVIO: Revista Latinoamericana de Estudios de Seguridad*, no. 28 (September–December 2020): 8–29, https://revistas.flacsoandes.edu.ec/urvio/article/view/4410/3475.

28. Julieta Pelcastre, "Ecuador incauta casi 10 toneladas de cocaína," *Diálogo Américas*, August 6, 2021, https://dialogo-americas.com/es/articles/ecuador-incauta-casi-10-toneladas-de-cocaina/.

29. Sean Doherty and Douwe den Held, "Balance de InSight Crime de las incautaciones de cocaína en 2022," InSight Crime, March 8, 2022, https://es.insightcrime.org/noticias/balance-insight-crime-incautaciones-cocaina-2022/.

30. "La mayor parte de cocaína en Bélgica llega desde Ecuador," *Primicias*, February 7, 2023, https://www.primicias.ec/noticias/sucesos/cocaina-belgica-procede-ecuador/.

31. Yalilé Loaiza, "El puerto de Guayaquil es el 'hub logístico' para el envío de cocaína a Estados Unidos y Europa," Infobae, May 2, 2022, https://www.infobae.com/america/america-latina/2022/05/03/el-puerto-de-guayaquil-es-el-hub-logistico-para-el-envio-de-cocaina-a-estados-unidos-y-europa/.

32. Tom Wainwright, *Narconomics: Cómo administrar un cártel de drogas* (Madrid: Editorial Debate, 2018).

33. United Nations Office on Drugs and Crime, *Informe mundial sobre las drogas, 2017: Resumen, conclusiones y consecuencias en materia de políticas* (Vienna: United Nations, 2017), https://www.unodc.org/wdr2017/field/WDR_Booklet1_Exsum_Spanish.pdf.

34. "Cuánto dinero se lava en el sistema financiero ecuatoriano: Una aproximación desde las cifras macroeconómicas," Centro Estratégico Latinoamericano de Geopolítica, January 14, 2023, https://www.celag.org/cuanto-dinero-se-lava-en-el-sistema-financiero-ecuatoriano-una-aproximacion-desde-las-cifras-macroeconomicas/.

35. "Narcodinero de 'El Chapo' se movió en empresas que creó en Ecuador," *El Telégrafo* (Quito), February 18, 2019, https://www.eltelegrafo.com.ec/noticias/judicial/12/narcodinero-elchapo-empresas-ecuador.

36. Jessica Andrade, "Lavado de dinero en el Ecuador: El caso Prada," master's thesis, Facultad Latinoamericana de Ciencias Sociales, 2009.

37. The Manta base was a "Forward Operating Location" of the US government, one of a series of airbases on foreign soil for US aircraft that were on antinarcotics detection and monitoring missions; the bases housed members of the US military, the DEA, the Coast Guard, and customs personnel to support and coordinate the communications and intelligence gathered by these flights. In Ecuador, the Base de Manta was granted a concession in 1999 for a period of ten years. In September 2009, once the agreement had expired, the base had to close down due to a constitutional mandate approved in 2008 that prohibited foreign military bases.

38. Alexander García, "Guayaquil concentra el 68% de decomisos de drogas en puertos," *Primicias*, May 8, 2023, https://www.primicias.ec/noticias/sucesos/narcotrafico-guayaquil-droga-puertos-antinarcoticos/.

39. Presidencia, República del Ecuador, "Presentación del sistema integrado de radares de Ecuador," March 30, 2017, https://www.presidencia.gob.ec/wp-content/uploads/downloads/2017/04/2017.03.30-PRESENTACI%C3%93N-DEL-SISTEMA-DE-RADARES.pdf.

40. Fermín Vaca Santacruz, "La accidentada historia de los radares en Ecuador," *Plan V*, November 15, 2021, https://www.planv.com.ec/historias/politica/la-accidentada-historia-radares-ecuador.

41. Karina Sotalín, "Caso narcogenerales: Informes señalan responsabilidad penal contra 3 oficiales de la policía," *El Comercio* (Quito), August 5, 2022, https://www.elcomercio.com/actualidad/seguridad/caso-narcogenerales-contraloria-responsabilidad-penal-policias.html.

42. "Gerald según Gerald: Este fue el testimonio inédito en EE.UU. del mayor capo ecuatoriano," *Plan V*, January 3, 2023, https://www.planv.com.ec/historias/crimen-organizado/gerald-segun-gerald-este-fue-el-testimonio-inedito-eeuu-del-mayor-capo.

43. "¿Quién es El Gato Farfán, el narcotraficante ecuatoriano?," *GK*, May 24, 2023, https://gk.city/2023/02/13/quien-es-el-gato-farfan/.

44. "Los Rastrojos," InSight Crime, July 20, 2022, https://es.insightcrime.org/noticias-crimen-organizado-colombia/rastrojos-perfil/; Natalia López López, "Las bacrim: ¿Actores del conflicto armado colombiano?," *Derecho Público*, no. 34 (2015): 26; and Javier Osorio, Mohamed Mohamed, Viveca Pavon, and Susan Brewer-Osorio, "Mapping Violent Presence of Armed Actors in Colombia," *Advances in Cartography and GIScience of the ICA* 1 (July 2019): 16.

45. James Bargent, "Líder de los Rastrojos es arrestado en Ecuador," InSight Crime, August 21, 2013, https://es.insightcrime.org/noticias/noticias-del-dia/lider-de-los-rastrojos-es-arrestado-en-ecuador/.

46. "Los últimos pasos de Telmo Castro," *Plan V*, December 9, 2019, https://www.planv.com.ec/investigacion/investigacion/ultimos-pasos-telmo-castro.

47. "Ecuador se convierte en 'Naciones Unidas' del crimen organizado, según la DEA," *El Universo* (Guayaquil), May 10, 2011, https://www.eluniverso.com/2011/05/10/1/1355/cocaina-colombiana-peruana-pasa-traves-ecuador-segun-dea.html/.

48. "Esta es la relación de Ecuador con las mafias italiana y albanesa," *Primicias*, May 4, 2023, https://www.primicias.ec/noticias/en-exclusiva/narcotrafico-mafias-italia-albania-ecuador/.

49. "La mafia albanesa evade silenciosamente el control en Ecuador," *El Comercio* (Quito), March 1, 2023, https://www.elcomercio.com/actualidad/mafia-albanesa-evade-control-ecuador.html.

50. "15 aspectos desconocidos de las operaciones de la mafia albanesa en Ecuador," *Plan V*, February 23, 2023, https://www.planv.com.ec/historias/crimen-organizado/15-aspectos-desconocidos-operaciones-la-mafia-albanesa-ecuador.

51. "La relación de Rubén Cherres con el narcotráfico tendría unos 24 años," *Primicias*, March 30, 2023, https://www.primicias.ec/noticias/politica/rubencherres-narcotrafico-mafia-albanesa-danilocarrera/.

52. "'Guacho,' una pieza clave de la agrupación criminal de 'Gerald,'" *Plan V*, April 10, 2018, https://www.planv.com.ec/investigacion/investigacion/guacho-una-pieza-clave-la-agrupacion-criminal-gerald.

53. "'El primer atentado terrorista en Ecuador': El presidente Lenín Moreno decreta estado de excepción por explosión que dejó 14 policías heridos," BBC News, January 28, 2018, https://www.bbc.com/mundo/noticias-america-latina-42851034.

54. Juliana Manjarrés and Christopher Newton, "Balance de InSight Crime de los homicidios en 2023," InSight Crime, February 21, 2024, https://insightcrime.org/es/noticias/balance-insight-crime-homicidios-2023/.

55. Daniel Pontón Cevallos, "Las nuevas cárceles en Ecuador: Un ecosistema para la reproducción del crimen complejo," *Universitas XXI: Revista de Ciencias Sociales y Humanas*, no. 37 (August 2020): 173–99, https://universitas.ups.edu.ec/index.php/universitas/article/view/6247.

56. "Once masacres carcelarias y 413 presos asesinados en 21 meses," *Primicias*, November 18, 2022, https://www.primicias.ec/noticias/en-exclusiva/carceles-nueve-masacres-victimas-ecuador/.

57. "Ecuador declara terroristas a las organizaciones criminales," Deutsche Welle, April 28, 2023, https://www.dw.com/es/ecuador-declara-terroristas-a-las-organizaciones-criminales/a-65458050.

58. Chris Dalby and Henry Shuldiner, "Asesinato de líder de los Choneros fragmentará más la banda en Ecuador," InSight Crime, May 10, 2023, https://es.insightcrime.org/noticias/asesinato-lider-choneros-fragmentara-banda-ecuador/.

59. "Los rastros del Cartel Jalisco Nueva Generación aparecen en Ecuador," *Primicias*, February 16, 2022, https://www.primicias.ec/noticias/en-exclusiva/huellas-cartel-jalisco-nueva-generacion-ecuador/.

60. "¿Quién es El Gato Farfán, el narcotraficante ecuatoriano?"

61. Eduardo Varas, "La inseguridad es lo que más preocupa a los ecuatorianos, según encuesta de Ipsos," *GK*, September 7, 2022, https://gk.city/2022/09/07/inseguridad-preocupa-ecuatorianos-encuesta-ipsos/.

CHAPTER 6

Changing Dynamics of Cocaine Trafficking

The Caribbean in the Global Matrix

Ivelaw Lloyd Griffith

> The global supply of cocaine is at record levels. Cultivation doubled between 2013 and 2017, peaked in 2018 and rose sharply again in 2021. The process from coca bush cultivation to cocaine hydrochloride has also become more efficient, contributing even further to the global supply of cocaine. . . . Cocaine use is on the rise at the global level. The number of people who use cocaine has been increasing at a faster rate than population growth. The main markets for cocaine worldwide are North America, Western and Central Europe, followed by South and Central America and the Caribbean.
>
> —*Global Report on Cocaine 2023*

Close observers of the global narcotics landscape are aware of several important modifications in the production–trafficking–consumption–money laundering matrix of these substances, which are proscribed across the global commons. Indeed, in relation to cocaine, as reflected in the epigraph of this chapter, the United Nations Office on Drugs and Crime's *Global Report on Cocaine 2023* provides abundant evidence of some of the sharp increases in production and consumption, among other changing dynamics. Thus, given that trafficking is a key factor in the link between production and consumption, it is understandable that trafficking would also warrant significant scrutiny. The Caribbean region, therefore, becomes an important unit of analysis, as the region has long played a crucial role in the movement of cocaine—and other drugs—from South America to North America, Europe, Africa, and Asia, sometimes circuitously.[1]

This chapter examines some of the changing dynamics of this substance, which has a multiplicity of public health, economic, public security, and social consequences, focusing on the Caribbean as an integer in the global narcotics matrix. First, it is important to place the narcotics phenomenon writ large in conceptual context. This is followed by an appreciation of the geography of drug trafficking, which explains the role and utility of the Caribbean in illicit commerce. The global community has witnessed increased smuggling to Europe since the dawn of the 2020s. Accordingly, probing some of the elements of this new reality is essential. Individual nation-states and a variety of international organizations have been active combatants in the battle against drugs. Thus, we end with an appreciation of some of the cooperation that underlines trafficking countermeasures and some of the gains secured in recent years.

Conceptual Context

The Geonarcotics Framework provides one set of conceptual lenses to help decipher the multiple dimensions of the drugs business. It was first outlined in *International Journal*[2] and then applied empirically in a study of the Caribbean.[3] Although the framework has been used to examine a range of drugs, it will be applied here, perhaps for the first time, to probe the dynamics in relation to just one substance: cocaine. The framework posits the dynamic interaction of four factors: narcotics, geography, power, and politics; that the narcotics phenomenon is multidimensional, with four main problem areas (drug production, consumption-abuse, trafficking, and money laundering); that these problem areas give rise to actual and potential threats to the security of states; and that drug operations and the activities they spawn precipitate both conflict and cooperation among various state and nonstate actors. Moreover, the four problem areas give rise to other challenges such as violent crime, corruption, and arms trafficking, as shown in figure 6.1.

Geography is a factor in this schema because certain physical, social, and political geography features of countries facilitate drug operations. Power involves the ability of individuals and groups to secure compliant action. This power is both state and nonstate in origin, and in some cases nonstate power holders command relatively more power than state power holders. Politics entails the ability of power brokers to determine who gets what, how, and when through the allocation of resources. Since power in this milieu is not only state power, resource allocation is also correspondingly not exclusively a function of state power holders. Moreover, politics becomes perverted, and even more perverted in situations where there are preexisting conditions that facilitate such.

There is no uniformity in drug operations or in their impact on individuals and societies anywhere. Some countries are affected by several or all operations, while others are impacted by just a few. However, because the narcotics phenomenon is multidimensional, a meaningful understanding of any single drug operation or security implication requires an appreciation of the complete narcotics package. A comprehensive approach offers the best possible prospect for meaningful understanding of both the phenomenon as a whole and the dynamics of its individual parts, although comprehensive analysis is not always necessary. The geonarcotics milieu involves a variety of actors, state as well as nonstate, and actors vary in the way they are affected by the various problem areas. Some initiate and maintain counternarcotics regimes; others strive to circumvent or eliminate them. Actors are proactive as well as reactive, and both proactive and reactive behaviors are possible from the same actor. For example, cartels are proactive in relation to production and trafficking but reactive when states, international nongovernmental organizations (INGOs), and nongovernmental organizations (NGOs) introduce countermeasures.

Drug operations generate two basic kinds of interactions—conflict and cooperation—among different actors and at different levels. Relationships are bilateral and multilateral, symmetrical and asymmetrical, and involve both vertical and horizontal flows. Not all interactions involve force or military capabilities. Some involve nonmilitary pressures, such as the application of economic and political sanctions by the United States against countries that, in its estimation, are not proactive enough in fighting drugs. The range of sanctions includes loss of tariff benefits, a 50 percent withholding of bilateral aid, suspension of air services, cancellation of visas, and the denial of support for aid requested from multilateral funding institutions.

Conflict interactions include protests, complaints, warnings, threats, seizures, blockades, and armed attacks. Many of these conflict types exist in the geonarcotics milieu. Some actors are engaged simultaneously in both cooperation and conflict.

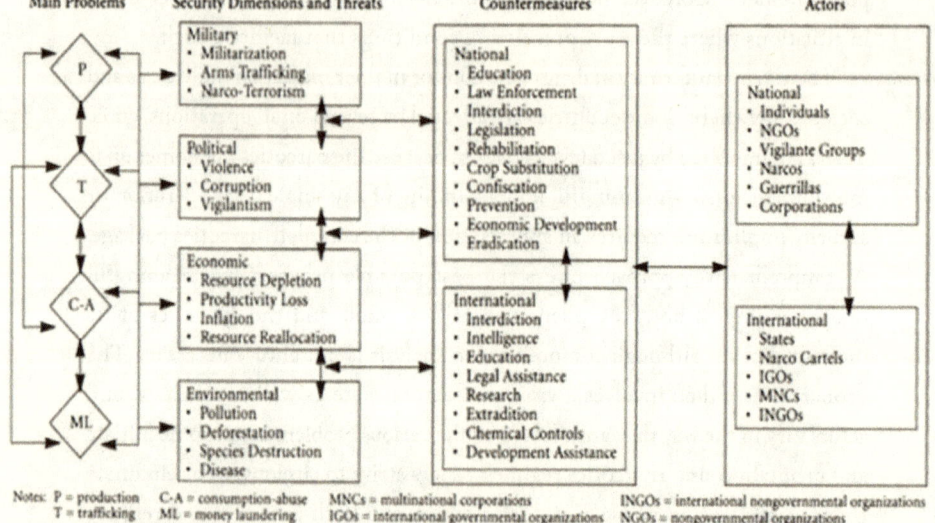

Figure 6.1. Geonarcotics Framework. Source: Ivelaw L. Griffith, "From Cold War Geopolitics to Post–Cold War Geonarcotics," *International Journal* (Canada) 49, no. 1 (Winter 1993–1994): 32.

Over the years, the relationships between the United States and Colombia, the United States and Afghanistan, and the United States and Cuba provide evidence of this. As well, conflict interactions exist both nationally and internationally. The nature and source of drug threats could be external, internal, or both, depending on the actors and problem areas involved. For states, while some problems create threats within one area, the multidimensional and transnational nature of drug operations precludes strict internal-external distinctions between threats or implications. Whether the state faces one problem (e.g., production) or several (e.g., production, abuse, and trafficking), the security implications generally have both internal and external ramifications. As such, the real issue is not whether there are internal or external implications but the nature and extent of both sets of implications.

International countermeasures offer the best prospect for dealing with the transnational drug phenomenon, especially since all state and nonstate actors battling the dilemma face resource limitations. However, collaboration among states also results in conflict, often because of domestic factors, including party rivalry, leadership changes, composition and control of the military, and budgetary and economic conditions. Some of these factors help explain a second reason for conflict: perceptual differences among ruling elites, which cause disparate definitions of the nature and severity of threats and, therefore, varied policies and measures to deal with them. The multiple dynamics of the geonarcotics milieu presented above have considerable implications for the issue of sovereignty. The challenge to sovereignty at the international level is not restricted to relationships among states. It is also a function of interaction between states and narcos, between states and international governmental organizations (IGOs), and between states and INGOs. Some IGOs are able to challenge and often subordinate small states to their interests because they possess relatively greater economic, political, military, or other resources than some small states around the world are able to mobilize. Further, the sovereignty challenge does not arise only from conflict relations; it also results from efforts at cooperation.[4]

The Geography of Drug Trafficking

Although production, consumption-abuse, trafficking, and money laundering are all present in the Caribbean, it is trafficking that dramatizes the importance of geography as a geonarcotics factor. The question is: Why? The Caribbean Sea is the most dominant geographical feature of the region. The islands in the Caribbean Sea form a chain almost 2,500 miles long but never more than 160 miles wide, creating a bridge between North and South America. Both the region's physical and social geography make it conducive to drug trafficking. Aspects of the former are more important than the latter, and in the physical geography area the key elements are island character and location.

Except for mainland Belize, French Guiana, Guyana, and Suriname, Caribbean countries are all island territories. This island character permits entry into and use of Caribbean territories from scores, sometimes hundreds, of different places from the surrounding sea. For the mainland states, access is from various places in the Atlantic Ocean in the case of Guyana, Suriname, and French Guiana, and from the Caribbean coast in the case of Belize. And when one adds to the matrix the inability of Caribbean countries to provide adequate territorial policing, their vulnerability to trafficking is more readily appreciated. The most important location feature of the region's physical geography is proximity. This proximity has two aspects: to South America, a major drug supply source, and to North America, a major drug consumer. There is not much distance between the Caribbean and South America, or between the Caribbean and the United States, especially the southern and northeastern parts of the United States. Some countries, like the Bahamas, Cuba, Haiti, Jamaica, and the Cayman Islands, are practically just "a stone's throw" away from Miami. Except for French Guiana and Suriname, all Caribbean countries are less than two thousand miles from Miami.

As for distances between the Caribbean and some main South American drug centers, twenty-four Caribbean territories are less than one thousand miles from Caracas, and all except Belize (in relation to Caracas), French Guiana (in relation to Cali and Medellín), and Suriname (in relation to Medellín) are less than 1,500 miles away from Bogotá, Cali, Caracas, and Medellín. For some trafficking purposes the distances are often shorter, given the fact that there are places in some Caribbean territories, outside of the capitals, that are closer to US or Latin American territory, and traffickers use this greater proximity. For example, Nassau is only 183 miles away from Miami, but Bimini is even closer—40 miles from the Florida Keys. The distance between Port of Spain and Caracas is 371 miles, but a mere seven miles separate La Brea in southwestern Trinidad and Pedernales in northeastern Venezuela, a point called Serpent's Mouth.[5]

Interdiction and surveillance show that a variety of private go-fast speedboats, pleasure craft, and fishing vessels are used in transshipment operations. Semisubmersibles and aircraft have been used, and drugs are also hidden in legitimate, containerized cargo. Understandably, trafficking patterns vary over time. One report commissioned by the US Senate found three maritime pathways for trafficking mainly cocaine, heroin, and synthetic drugs from South America to North America. They are reflected in figure 6.2, and are:

» The "Central Corridor," used mostly for cocaine leaving South America and flowing through Jamaica, Haiti, the Dominican Republic, and the Bahamas into the United States.
» The "Eastern Corridor," comprising the eastern Caribbean and Trinidad and Tobago. Often, cocaine and heroin make their way to Puerto Rico for onward passage to the United States.
» The "ABC Corridor" of Aruba, Bonaire, and Curaçao, which is used for cocaine shipment and, to a lesser extent, for synthetic drugs.[6]

One modus operandi is to ship the drugs from South America to Europe or Africa, and back to the Caribbean for onward movement to the United States. Nigerians once cornered the circuitous trafficking market, moving drugs from South America to Africa to Europe—or to Europe and then Africa—and then to the Caribbean for onward shipment to the United States, or from South America to Europe and directly to the Caribbean and thence to North America.[7] As a matter of fact, the *Global Report on Cocaine 2023* notes: "Seizure data suggest that the role of Africa, especially West and Central Africa, as a transit zone for cocaine on its way to markets in Europe has picked up substantially since 2019. Both the total quantity seized in Africa and the number of large seizures appear to have reached record levels during 2021."[8] Consequently, trafficking suspicions have been raised in parts of Latin America whenever foreigners of African descent are seen at airports or seaports, or in remote parts of the country. Elsewhere,

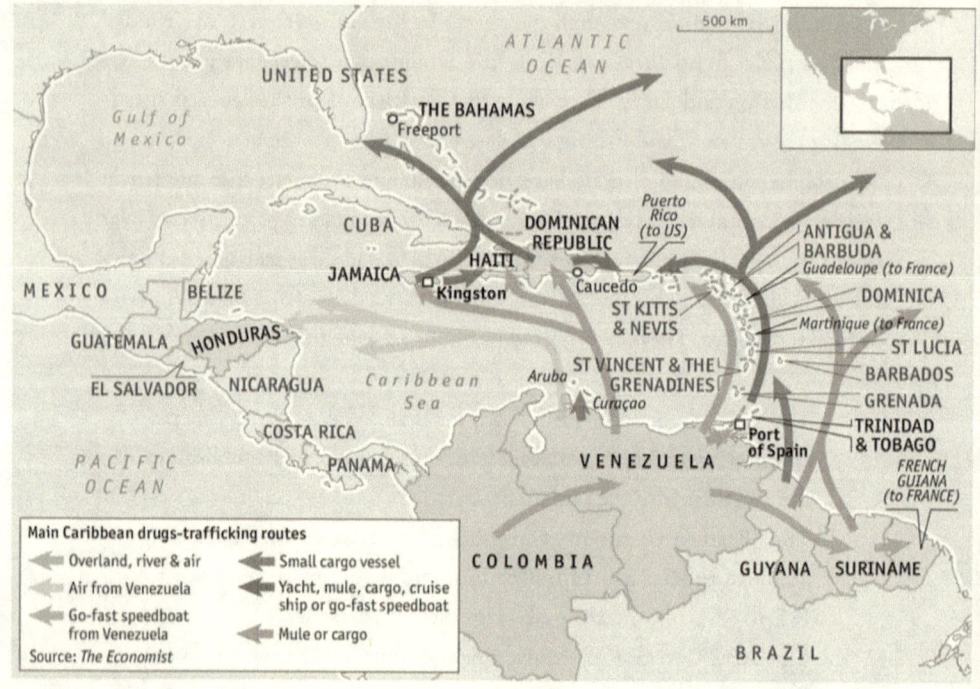

Figure 6.2. Main North American maritime trafficking routes. Source: "Drug Trafficking in the Caribbean: Full Circle," *The Economist*, May 24, 2014, https://www.economist.com/the-americas/2014/05/24/full-circle.

this writer recounted the full details of his experience in this regard in Ecuador in the mid-1990s.[9] Here is a summary of the experience.

I had gone to Quito for a European Union–Rio Group conference on security in November 1996 and was heading back to the United States the day before Thanksgiving. After checking in at the American Airlines ticket counter at Mariscal Sucre International Airport, I headed toward the immigration control area. Two undercover narcotics police officers then approached me. They discreetly flashed their badges, introduced themselves, asked for my passport, and then "invited" me for an "inspection" in the airport's police outpost. They took possession of my luggage and led me to the police outpost, which was ensconced in the mezzanine of the building. I was "handed over" to the commanding officer on duty, a boyish but courteous individual who appeared to be in his mid- to late twenties. He took my passport and examined it. There was a distinct facial expression of relief when he saw that it was a US passport. (There was an additional expression of relief later when he saw my official conference invitation letter.)

The officer in charge posed five questions: Where did I live? How long had I been in Ecuador? Did I go outside of Quito? Where had I stayed in the city? Was I there as a tourist, or for business? My response was: Miami! Three days! No, only Quito! Hotel Oro Verde! Business! Next, they conducted a body search, thankfully not a strip search. This was followed by the luggage search. I had only two pieces of luggage: a flight attendant's bag and a briefcase. Two of the officers started examining the two items simultaneously. However, I objected, and insisted on the right to observe the inspection of each piece one at a time. I was not prepared to risk having any drugs "found" in my luggage. The commanding officer readily agreed, and the search proceeded uneventfully. Afterward, I asked the commanding officer why I had been singled out for the inspection. He was diplomatic in explaining some of the then fairly new realities of circuitous drug smuggling through Ecuador. It was obvious to me that smuggler profiling was in play; I am of African descent, was traveling lightly, and was taking the first flight of the day to Miami. Thus, my presence sent a red flag up their counternarcotics flagpole.

Yet as suggested earlier, the Caribbean plays a role in relation to trafficking to Europe. As such, a comment on transatlantic drug movement is warranted. In this respect, the authoritative United Nations Office on Drugs and Crime (UNODC) explains that trafficking groups use a growing variety of vessels including yachts, speedboats, ferries, and fishing boats to move their illicit product to destination. Figure 6.3 provides a portrait of some of the staging areas and maritime routings. Importantly,

> traffickers frequently offload cocaine from the mother ship before reaching land. Ship-to-ship transfers occur at rendezvous points using small and medium-sized vessels, like speedboats and fishing boats. This method is widely used around West and North Africa, in Central America and the Caribbean, and in the Pacific islands. Container ships are also known to have dropped off cocaine to be picked up by speedboats. This is a known tactic for vessels bound for the Netherlands and Belgium.[10]

While traffickers of cocaine (and other illegal substances) have long taken advantage of shipping containers, as noted above, intelligence reports and seizures suggest that use of this smuggling method has been increasing over recent years. It is important to know that cocaine trafficked in container ships can be introduced at various stages—away from the port or in transit to the port as well as at sea. Smugglers use creative ways to camouflage their operations, sometimes stuffing the drugs in fruit, passing it off as sugar or flour, mixing it with soya, and even hiding it in the structure of the container, among other things.

More Powder Across the Global Commons

Over recent years, some of the changing dynamics involving cocaine have been increased trafficking and use of the substance in Australia and Europe. Although the focus here is on Europe, it is worth noting in relation to Australia that as "[a]n exceptionally lucrative destination, average prices per kilogram have climbed in recent years with the Australian Criminal Intelligence Commission reporting numbers as high as AU$278,000 in 2021, more than tripling figures seen in European markets."[11] According to Australian criminal justice authorities, the high cost helps to offset the costs incurred by sheer distance and logistical expertise required to ship cocaine to the Land Down Under. It is felt that "such undertakings require not only efforts from powerful organizations like the

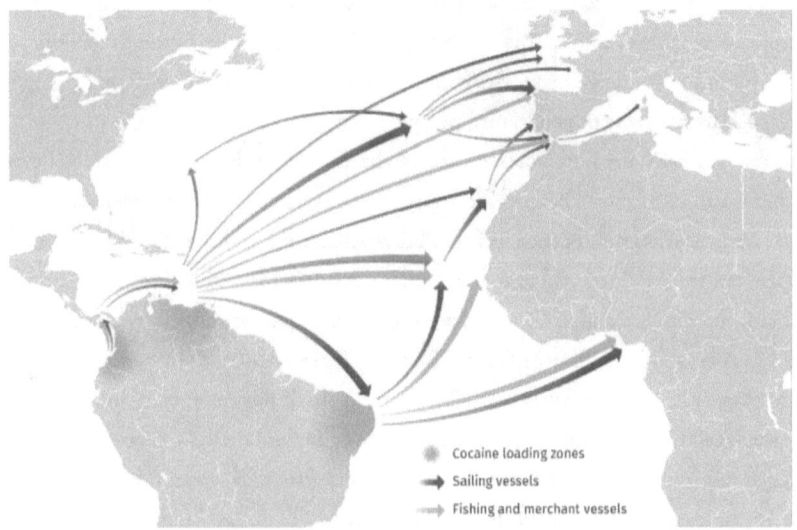

Figure 6.3. Transatlantic cocaine trafficking routes, 2022. Source: United Nations Office on Drugs and Crime, *Global Report on Cocaine 2023: Local Dynamics, Global Challenges*, March 2023, 28.

Sinaloa Cartel and Colombia's Urabeños, but also a collaborative relationship with local organized crime to receive, house and distribute the drug in retail markets."[12] Indeed, Australia witnessed its largest-ever drug haul in March 2023 when an undercover operation led to the seizure in Western Australia of 2.4 tons of cocaine worth about AU$1 billion.[13]

Europe has long been a huge drug-consuming area, with some of the cocaine (and other substances) trafficked through the Caribbean. In geonarcotics terms, several reasons explain this. Although space limitations preclude extensive examination of the geonarcotics connection between the Caribbean and Europe, especially in terms of geography, politics, communications, and transportation, a few realities are noteworthy. One is the proximity between the Caribbean and South America, the cocaine source area. A second relates to commercial, communications, and other linkages between Europe and the Caribbean, which provide the institutional and other infrastructure for trafficking. In addition, because French Guiana, Guadeloupe, and Martinique are *départements d'outré-mer* of France; Anguilla, Bermuda, the British Virgin Islands, the Cayman Islands, Montserrat, and the Turks and Caicos are British dependencies; and Bonaire and Saba are integral parts of the Kingdom of the Netherlands, there are certain customs, immigration, and transportation connections between these territories and their respective European "owners" that are exploited by traffickers. Some of the arrangements are similar to those involving the United States and Puerto Rico and the US Virgin Islands, which also facilitate traffickers aiming for destinations in the continental United States.

A brief appreciation of a few of the Caribbean-Europe interrelationships might be helpful. Citing the French Ministry of the Interior, one 2023 study by the respected Center for Strategic and International Studies explains that over the past ten years, cocaine seizures in France have increased fivefold. While the seizures in 2021 amounted to 27.7 tons valued at 1.8 billion euros, in 2012 the amount was 5.6 tons. Notable, too, is that in 2022, 55 percent of cocaine seizures entering mainland France, which was 14 tons, came from the French Antilles and French Guiana.[14] Pointing to the multidimensionality involved, the observation was made that:

Drug trafficking cases have become so endemic in French Guiana—especially on commercial aircraft—that they are affecting broad sectors of society. In 2021, officials seized 1.3 tons of cocaine at Félix Eboué airport from travelers going to mainland France carrying drugs on or in their person or their luggage—a huge amount for individuals to be carrying. In fact, departures from the airport to the mainland had an average of 10 to 30 individual mules on each flight, overwhelming police and customs officials. In response, authorities instituted a new policy of searching 100 percent of all passengers and luggage as of October 21, 2022, relying on extensive search powers granted under a 1946 law on the customs service. However, France's Constitutional Court declared in September 2022 that the provision was too broad and ordered its repeal beginning September 1, 2023. French legislators are now rushing to provide an alternative rewrite, as the current, now unconstitutional provision is the cornerstone of illicit-narcotics enforcement.[15]

With respect to the Netherlands, the Dutch Ministry of Defense reported that in 2022, the HMS *Groningen* made eighteen drug seizures, ranging in size from 2.3 to 300 kilos and totaling 21,230 metric tons. The same year, the HMS *Friesland* seized 3.9 metric tons of drugs and the HMS *Holland* seized 15.6 metric tons. Altogether, the three ships seized a total of 40.7 metric tons, the largest-ever seizures by the Dutch navy in the Caribbean. And, in a reflection of transcontinental connectivity, it was noted that "[t]hese seizures resulted from intercepting go-fast boats and occasionally fishing boats from Venezuela headed to Aruba. In waters off Curaçao or Aruba, Dutch and Colombian authorities have interdicted even large commercial ships such as the Russian-flagged bulk carrier *Aressa*, detained in 2020 on its way to Thessaloniki, Greece, after leaving Puerto Guaranao, Venezuela. The ship was carrying 5 metric tons of cocaine believed to be destined for Europe."[16]

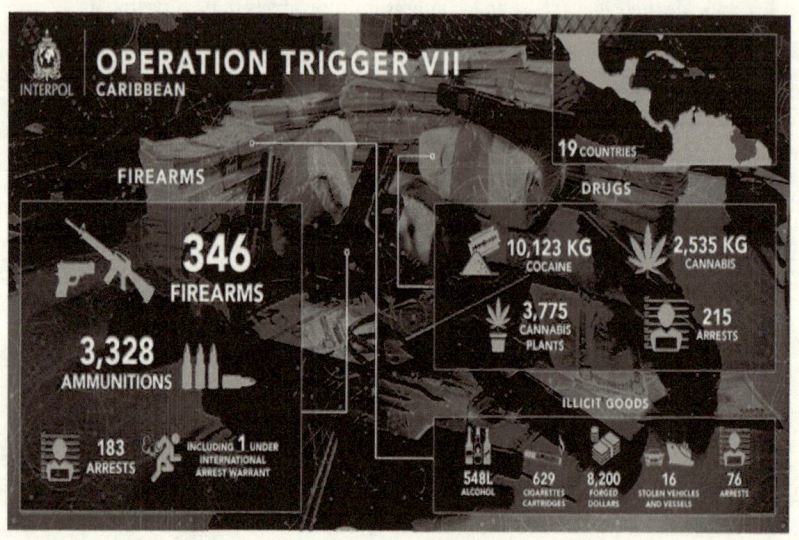

Figure 6.4. INTERPOL operation in the Caribbean, 2022. Source: INTERPOL, "Hundreds of Firearms and 12.6 Tonnes of Drugs Seized in Caribbean Operation," October 13, 2022, https://www.interpol.int/en/News-and-Events/News/2022/Hundreds-of-firearms-and-12.6-tonnes-of-drugs-seized-in-Caribbean-operation.

Cooperation and Countermeasures

From a geonarcotics perspective, the multidimensional and transnational character of cocaine trafficking, along with the resource limitations of state and international governmental actors, have necessitated commensurate multidimensional and transnational cooperation in battling the phenomenon. Cooperation generally occurs in the context of Multilateral Security Engagement Zones (MSEZ), which are geographic spaces for policy and operational collaboration and cooperation by state and nonstate actors in relation to defense and security matters. The zones exist at the subregional, regional, hemispheric, and international systemic levels, and they involve states, international governmental organizations, and nonstate actors such as businesses, with treaties, protocols, conventions, and memorandums of understanding guiding the various forms of engagement.[17]

Understandably, because of the transnationality involved, cooperation often involves engagement across zones. One relatively recent example of this involved the regional, hemispheric, and international systemic zones. During the week of September 24–30, 2022, the International Criminal Police Organization (INTERPOL) (international systemic zone) and the CARICOM Implementation Agency for Crime and Security (IMPACS) (regional zone) conducted a joint operation that produced considerable results, which are shown in figure 6.4. Known as Operation Trigger VII, it led to the seizure of 350 weapons, 3,300 rounds of ammunition, 10 tons of cocaine, and 2.5 tons of marijuana. A total of 510 arrests were also made. Germany funded the multinational operation, in which the United States—hemispheric zone—played a crucial role. The operation involved the following countries: Antigua and Barbuda, the Bahamas, Barbados, Belize, Bonaire, Curaçao, Dominica, the Dominican Republic, France (Guadeloupe and Martinique), Grenada, Guyana, Haiti, Jamaica, Trinidad and Tobago, Saint Lucia, Saint Kitts and Nevis, the Turks and Caicos, Saint Vincent and the Grenadines, and Suriname.[18]

Understandably, the cross-zone cooperation reflected in the INTEROL operation is but one of many pursued over the years. To help deal with the containerizing of drugs at multiple points between origin and destination locations, the UNODC and the World Customs Organization (WCO) created the UNODC-WCO Container Control Program in 2004. The program aims to strengthen the security and management of ports by establishing Port Control

Units (PCUs) in order to minimize access to maritime containers for drug trafficking and other criminality. As of 2022, there were twenty-two PCUs in Latin America and the Caribbean, although only six in the Caribbean—in the Bahamas, Cuba, the Dominican Republic, French Guiana, Jamaica, and Suriname.

CARICOM IMPACS is the main counternarcotics and countercrime cooperation mechanism in the regional MSEZ. Formed in 2006, part of the agency's architecture includes a Joint Regional Communications Centre and a Regional Intelligence Fusion Centre. Capability limitations and skepticism within the region constrain the extent of the possible gains. In this regard, two observers observe rightly that "the progress that CARICOM IMPACS has achieved has been stunted by the lack of cooperation and buy-in from reluctant Caribbean states. For example, just two out of the 15 member states—Trinidad and Tobago and Jamaica—cover most of the organization's funding, and the IMPACS budget was reduced from an initial [US]$14 million to $7 million by 2022. Furthermore, the lack of trust regarding asset sharing, along with demonstrated reluctance to share intelligence, present immediate challenges to the success of the organization."[19] Predating the IMPACS by several decades is the Regional Security System (RSS), which dates to 1982 and comprises Antigua and Barbuda, Barbados, Dominica, Grenada, Guyana, Saint Kitts and Nevis, Saint Lucia, and Saint Vincent and the Grenadines, Guyana being the most recent addition to the group, having joined in 2022.[20]

Noteworthy, too, is Europe's Maritime Analysis and Operations Centre-Narcotics (MAOC-N), which focuses on "multilateral cooperation to tackle illicit drug trafficking by sea and air." The MAOC-N pools naval and air assets from partner nations and shares intelligence relevant to drug-trafficking operations. MAOC-N partnership nations include France, Ireland, Italy, Spain, the Netherlands, Portugal, and the United Kingdom. However, Belgium, which reportedly accounts for 40 percent of all cocaine delivered to Europe, is uninvolved. In addition to CARICOM IMPACS and the MAOC-N, the US Southern Command's Joint Interagency Task Force South (JIATF-S), along with the Royal Netherlands Navy and the Royal Canadian Navy, also play crucial counternarcotics roles in terms of intelligence, interdiction, and training of Caribbean operatives.[21]

Criminal Movers and Shakers

As suggested earlier, the engagement space of the geonarcotics milieu is occupied by both state and nonstate actors. Although some of the criminal movers and shakers often are corrupt police, or army, customs, and other state officials, the trafficking operators are generally nonstate actors, both individuals and organized groups. A few examples will suffice.

In November 2011, José Figueroa Agosto, aka "Junior Capsula," reputedly then head of the largest drug-trafficking organization in the Caribbean, pleaded guilty to drug-trafficking charges before Judge Juan Manuel Pérez-Giménez of the US District Court for the District of Puerto Rico following an investigation by US Immigration and Customs Enforcement's Homeland Security Investigations. Figueroa had been charged earlier with a twelve-count indictment with conspiracy to import narcotics into the United States, conspiracy to possess with intent to distribute controlled substances, and money laundering. Other leaders in the Figueroa organization were also arrested. They included José Miguel Marrero Martell (aka "Pito Nariz"), Jorge Luis Figueroa Agosto, and Eddy Brito. According to the indictment, the Figueroa organization had imported multiple kilos of cocaine into Puerto Rico mainly from the Dominican Republic, the drugs having been smuggled earlier from Colombia.[22]

Cuban Americans Augusto Guillermo Falcón and Salvador Magluta, considered by some analysts as perhaps the most prolific of the early Caribbean traffickers, reputedly smuggled about sixty-eight metric tons of cocaine through the Caribbean to the United States between 1975 and 1991. Also notable has been Nankissoon Boodram, alias "Dole Chadee," from Trinidad and Tobago, who built a criminal enterprise of trafficking, corruption, and murder. His criminal reign ended in 1994 when he was awarded the death penalty on conviction for murder. César Peralta from the Dominican Republic, known as "the Abuser," used his homeland as the base of operations to smuggle large quantities of cocaine from South America to European and US markets. By 2015, he was one of the region's main traffickers. Indeed, authorities in the Dominican Republic compared him to Mexico's infamous operative Joaquín Guzmán Loera, alias "El Chapo." As other movers and shakers did, Peralta used legitimate businesses to launder drug proceeds and gain access to business and political elites in the region. Indeed, he once was linked to former Dominican Republic president Danilo Medina

Sánchez, who admitted to having accepted campaign contributions from Peralta but denied knowing they came from illicit activities.

A discussion of movers and shakers in the Caribbean would be incomplete without reference to Christopher "Dudus" Coke, criminal entrepreneur and leader of the Shower Posse and of Tivoli Gardens, a geographic-criminal-political zone in Jamaica. There are differing explanations of the origin of the name "Shower." One is that it derived from the reputation of the gang for spraying—showering—opponents with bullets. Another is that it came from the promises of politicians associated with it to "shower" supporters with gifts. Father of four children, Coke assumed control of the Shower Posse at age twenty-two following the death of his father and elder brother. Coke's infamy is related to a political volcano that erupted in Jamaica over attempts to arrest and extradite him to the United States in May 2010 that led to clashes between his supporters and security forces, resulting in more than one hundred fatalities, 4,614 arrests, and the destruction of billions of dollars' worth of property.

The saga began in August 2009, when an indictment was unsealed in New York against Coke for conspiracy to distribute guns and illegal drugs. That same month, the United States requested extradition. Between August 2009 and April 2010, both the Jamaican government and the Jamaica Labour Party made efforts to forestall the extradition. In March 2010, the opposition People's National Party raised the matter in Parliament, causing the prime minister to reverse himself and order Coke's arrest and extradition in May 2010. The months May through July of that year saw the declaration of a state of emergency for major parts of the island; Coke was detained on June 22, which prompted his supporters to battle security forces for several days. Coke was eventually flown to New York. Two years later he was found guilty and sentenced to twenty-three years in prison. He is expected to be released on July 4, 2030.

However, cocaine (and marijuana) movers and shakers did not hail just from the larger island nations; they also came from small ones, such as Saint Kitts and Nevis, as was the case of Charles Miller, who allegedly masterminded the movement of tons of Colombian cocaine into the United States, significantly using the cargo airline Amerijet. Following several failed extradition efforts, one of which prompted a threat by Miller to kill American students at Ross University School of Veterinary Medicine in Saint Kitts, he was eventually extradited in 2000, convicted, and sentenced to life in prison for trafficking, murder, and other felonies. In the Dutch Caribbean there was Shurendy "Tyson"

Quant, the leader of the No Limit Soldiers (NLS) gang in Curaçao, whose group operated smuggling operations into Europe in the 2000s. He was allegedly part of the smuggling network of infamous Brazilian trafficker Sérgio Roberto de Carvalho, who is suspected of having moved as much as forty-five tons of cocaine to Europe. Quant was arrested in Dubai in November 2020 and later charged with ordering several murders, kidnapping, leading a criminal organization, and money laundering.[23]

Conclusion

Sadly, the saying *plus ça change, plus c'est la même chose* (the more things change, the more they remain the same) seems not to apply to the global cocaine business; in so many respects, circumstances are worse in terms of global production and consumption-abuse in 2023 than they were a decade ago. This is not for want of engagement efforts by state and international governmental actors at subregional, regional, hemispheric, and international systemic levels. The geonarcotics milieu, both globally and regionally, continues to be complex, the complexity elements all the grimmer when one adds to the matrix the collateral and consequential crime, violence, and arms trafficking, and the accompanying corruption and impunity.

Although the Caribbean is not a significant cocaine consumption area, it plays outsize roles in relation to trafficking and money laundering and is a significant victim area insofar as crime and arms trafficking are concerned.[24] One gets a sense of the multidimensionality and severity of the circumstances from the sober reflection of the Caribbean prime minister who has portfolio responsibility for crime and security within the CARICOM quasi-cabinet when he spoke in April 2023 at the crime summit held in Trinidad and Tobago: "During the last 15 years, using the Trinidad and Tobago example, in the growing quest for safety and security we have seen a significant increase in the allocation in the national budget for National Security. In 2008 policing alone represented 32 percent of the TT$4 billion National Security budget. By 2017 this rose to 38 percent. Even in the tighter budgetary environment of 2023 policing still accounted for 43 percent of the National Security allocation."[25] For all this, the leaders and citizens of the Caribbean and the world at large do not have the luxury of being fatalistic; they are obligated to sustain efforts to combat the cocaine scourge.

Notes

1. Of course, the role and implications of the Caribbean in the global drugs business extend beyond trafficking. Political economy dynamics are very much involved, as has been shown in Ivelaw L. Griffith, ed., *The Political Economy of Drugs in the Caribbean* (Basingstoke, Hants., England: Macmillan, 2000); and Menno Vellinga, ed., *The Political Economy of the Drug Industry: Latin America and the International System* (Gainesville: University Press of Florida, 2004).

2. Ivelaw L. Griffith, "From Cold War Geopolitics to Post–Cold War Geonarcotics," *International Journal* (Canada) 49, no. 1 (Winter 1993–1994): 1–36.

3. See Ivelaw Lloyd Griffith, *Drugs and Security in the Caribbean: Sovereignty Under Siege* (University Park: Pennsylvania State University Press, 1997).

4. Griffith, "From Cold War Geopolitics to Post–Cold War Geonarcotics," 32–35.

5. Griffith, *Drugs and Security in the Caribbean*, 54–62.

6. See US Senate, *Preventing a Security Crisis in the Caribbean: A Report by the United States Senate Caucus on International Narcotics Control*, 112th Cong., 2nd Sess., September 2012, 11–14, https://www.feinstein.senate.gov/public/_cache/files/9/0/90bb66bc-3371-4898-8415-fbfc31c0ed24/82FE9908E85FB144D84F73F217DAC7A6.caribbean-drug-report.pdf. Understandably, the role of the Caribbean as a transshipment area has changed over the years.

7. Circuitous trafficking is intended to throw off law enforcement in their counter-narcotics efforts and capitalize on weak capabilities and institutional corruption in parts of the Global South. However, it adds to product cost, which is passed on to clients.

8. United Nations Office on Drugs and Crime, *Global Report on Cocaine 2023: Local Dynamics, Global Challenges* (Vienna: United Nations, 2023), 22, https://www.unodc.org/documents/data-and-analysis/cocaine/Global_cocaine_report_2023.pdf. See also Gavin Voss, "Nigerian Couriers Central to Brazil–West Africa Cocaine Route," InSight Crime, September 28, 2023, https://insightcrime.org/news/nigerian-couriers-key-brazil-west-africa-cocaine-route/.

9. Griffith, *Drugs and Security in the Caribbean*, 90–91.

10. United Nations Office on Drugs and Crime, *Global Report on Cocaine 2023*, 28.

11. Scott Mistler-Ferguson, "Crafty Trafficking: How Cocaine Is Flowing Between LatAm and Australia," InSight Crime, May 17, 2022, https://insightcrime.org/news/crafty-trafficking-how-cocaine-is-flowing-between-latam-and-australia/.

12. Mistler-Ferguson, "Crafty Trafficking."

13. Rebecca Peppiatt, "Biggest Drug Bust in Australian History: Cocaine Worth $1 Billion Seized in WA Sting," *WAToday* (Perth), March 4, 2023, https://www.watoday.

com.au/national/western-australia/biggest drug bust-in-australian-history-cocaine-worth-1-billion-seized-in-wa-police-sting-20230304-p5cpdi.html. The Western Australia police commissioner revealed how the combined action of local and international law enforcement officials outsmarted cartel operators who had attempted to bring the country's biggest-ever stash of drugs onshore via Perth beaches, replacing the cocaine with plaster of paris before arresting the alleged smugglers. For more about trafficking and consumption-abuse in Australia, see United Nations Office on Drugs and Crime, *Global Report on Cocaine 2023*, 92–97.

14. Christopher Hernandez-Roy and Rubi Bledsoe, "Building Barriers and Bridges: The Need for International Cooperation to Counter the Caribbean-Europe Drug Trade," Center for Strategic and International Studies Special Report, July 14, 2023, https://www.csis.org/analysis/building-barriers-and-bridges-need-international-cooperation-counter-caribbean-europe-drug.

15. Hernandez-Roy and Bledsoe, "Building Barriers and Bridges," 4.

16. Hernandez-Roy and Bledsoe, "Building Barriers and Bridges," 4–5. For a sobering portrait of the increased scope of trafficking in Europe, see Chris Dalby, "France Dealing with Influx of Cocaine from Caribbean Territories," InSight Crime, September 26, 2022, https://insightcrime.org/news/france-dealing-influx-cocaine-caribbean-territories/; Théo Bourgery-Gonse, "France Seizes 'Historic' 157 Tons of Drugs in 2022," Euractiv, March 2, 2023, https://www.euractiv.com/section/politics/news/france-seizes-historic-157-tons-of-drugs/; and Yago Rosado, "Europe: Cocaine's Ever-Expanding Market," InSight Crime, August 17, 2023, https://insightcrime.org/news/europe-cocaines-ever-expanding-market/.

17. Ivelaw Lloyd Griffith, "The Caribbean Security Scenario at the Dawn of the 21st Century: Continuity, Change, Challenge," Agenda Paper no. 65, University of Miami North-South Center, September 2003, 18–19.

18. INTERPOL, "Hundreds of Firearms and 12.6 Tonnes of Drugs Seized in Caribbean Operation," October 13, 2022, https://www.interpol.int/en/News-and-Events/News/2022/Hundreds-of-firearms-and-12.6-tonnes-of-drugs-seized-in-Caribbean-operation.

19. Hernandez-Roy and Bledsoe, "Building Barriers and Bridges," 8. For more on CARICOM IMPACS, see the agency's website at https://www.caricomimpacs.org/. As I have explained in *The Quest for Security in the Caribbean: Problems and Promises in Subordinate States* (New York: M. E. Sharpe, 1993), "The Caribbean Security Scenario at the Dawn of the 21st Century," and elsewhere, the funding imbalance reflects the deep financial limitations of most member states within the group and is one of the manifestations of the challenged sovereignty of these and other subordinate states in the region. For an exposition on challenged sovereignty, see my *Challenged Sovereignty: The Impact of*

Drugs, Crime, Terrorism, and Cyber Threats in the Caribbean (Urbana: University of Illinois Press, 2024).

20. For a discussion of the RSS, see Ivelaw L. Griffith, "The RSS: A Decade of Collective Security in the Caribbean," *The Round Table* 81, no. 324 (October 1992): 465–75; and Dion E. Phillips, *The Military of the Caribbean: A Look at the Defence Forces of the Anglo Caribbean, 1958–2022* (Bridgetown, Barbados: Caribbean Chapters Publishing, 2022), 463–85.

21. Hernandez-Roy and Bledsoe, "Building Barriers and Bridges," 8–9.

22. US Immigration and Customs Enforcement, "Puerto Rican Drug Lord and Leader of Largest Caribbean Drug Trafficking Organization Pleads Guilty," March 27, 2012, https://www.ice.gov/news/releases/puerto-rican-drug-lord-and-leader-largest-caribbean-drug-trafficking-organization.

23. Milko, "From the Caribbean to Dubai and Europe: Profile of International Drug Boss Shurendy 'Tyson' Quant," Gangsters Inc., January 28, 2021, https://gangstersinc.org/profiles/blogs/from-the-caribbean-to-dubai-and-europe-profile-of-international-d.; and Douwe den Held and Gavin Voss, "A History of the Caribbean's Most Powerful Drug Kingpins," InSight Crime, May 12, 2023, https://insightcrime.org/news/history-caribbean-most-powerful-drug-kingpins/. The discussion on Coke draws on chapter 6 of this writer's *Challenged Sovereignty*.

24. For a troubling assessment of the arms-trafficking challenge in a study conducted by Small Arms Survey and CARICOM IMPACS, see Anne-Séverine Fabre, Nicolas Florquin, Aaron Karp, and Matt Schroeder, *Weapons Compass: The Caribbean Firearms Study*, Small Arms Survey, April 2023, https://www.smallarmssurvey.org/resource/weapons-compass-caribbean-firearms-study.

25. "Opening Remarks by Dr. the Hon. Keith Rowley, Prime Minister of the Republic of Trinidad and Tobago to the Regional Symposium: Violence as a Public Health Issue—The Crime Challenge, April 17, 2023," https://caricom.org/opening-remarks-by-dr-the-hon-keith-rowley-prime-minister-of-the-republic-of-trinidad-and-tobago-to-the-regional-symposium-violence-as-a-public-health-issue-the-caricom-challenge-april-1/.

CHAPTER 7

Central America's *Maras*

A Negative Case of DTO Evolution

Michael Ahn Paarlberg

The gangs of the Northern Triangle of Central America—particularly Mara Salvatrucha (MS-13) and Barrio 18 (18th Street)[1]—present a unique negative case in the evolution of drug-trafficking organizations—particularly in El Salvador, historically the country of their greatest presence. Their trajectory contradicts what is generally presumed to be that of transnational organized crime: an evolution toward increasing sophistication, greater profit, diversification of activities, and eventual semi-legitimacy in both the economic and political realms. Since their founding in the United States and spread to Central America, MS-13 and Barrio 18 have indeed grown and transnationalized; they have become entrenched in poor communities and present dire problems for citizen security in multiple countries.

Yet they have not, as might be expected, transformed into more sophisticated cartel-like enterprises. Nor have they developed cross-border contraband operations like Guatemala's and Honduras's *transportistas*—independent, family-run smuggling networks that expanded from livestock and car theft to drug transport.[2] Their activities have remained largely confined to the street level. And regarding the cocaine trade, their involvement has been limited, centering more on microtrafficking than transnational smuggling. While exact trafficking figures are impossible to ascertain, law enforcement records, studies, and news reports paint a picture of the *maras* as minor players in international cocaine markets, playing at best an ancillary role as subcontractors to the larger cartels, primarily in Mexico.

Several anecdotal cases show frustrated attempts by the largest mara, MS-13, to enter the narcotics trade.[3] In the early 2000s, MS-13's US leader, Nelson

Comandari, reportedly approached the Mexican Mafia—an established gang based in the California prison system—through a family connection, to offer MS-13 as a drug distribution network. He was later arrested, turned state's evidence, and went into witness protection.[4] A decade later, an attempt by MS-13 member Luis Gerardo Vega to broker a methamphetamine trafficking arrangement with La Familia Michoacana in Mexico and the Mexican Mafia in the United States also resulted in his arrest and the breakup of this network by federal law enforcement. Yet another attempt, in 2015, by incarcerated MS-13 member Jesus Navarete to partner with existing methamphetamine distributors in Arkansas and Oklahoma also resulted in detection and Navarete's arrest.[5]

While survivorship bias limits any conclusions drawn only from successful law enforcement busts, patterns emerge among foiled attempts by the maras to engage in cocaine or other narcotics trafficking. First, these attempts always place the gang in a supporting role for another gang or cartel already established in the cocaine trade. Second, such connections are always brokered with contacts outside of the maras—through personal relationships with members of said gangs or cartels, rather than being set up by mara leadership—suggesting that these deals are ad hoc and opportunistic in nature, and not a deliberate strategy implemented by the maras themselves. Third, these established drug-trafficking organizations (DTOs) regard the maras as unreliable partners due to them being outside the DTOs, their high public profiles, and their reputation for volatility. One analysis thus concludes that "MS13, it appears, is still far from constituting a drug cartel or anything like it."[6]

In Central America, the maras have gained more of a toehold in the cocaine trade by operating in a support capacity for DTOs, whose activities mostly involve cocaine trafficking and money laundering (in El Salvador, the Perrones and Texis cartels) or migrant smuggling (various Mexican coyote networks); the maras provide muscle but do not operate at the center of DTO activities, as they are generally not trusted with drug transport or handling money. Within Central America, the maras do run their own microtrafficking networks, and in some areas such as San Pedro Sula in Honduras, MS-13 has succeeded in dominating the street trade.[7] However, this monopoly relies on the gangs' control of these territories through their mostly autonomous constituent franchises. Even in areas where they control territory outright, they have failed to control the drug trade above the street level, at best working as intermediaries or distributors for other cartels.

Within the maras' universe of criminal activities, drug trafficking at any level takes a distant second position to extortion, which continues to be their main activity and source of revenue. As a business model, this is far from lucrative; while profits from illicit activity cannot be independently verified and estimates vary, evidence from law enforcement and independent analysts suggests that they are low. Police confiscations of extortion proceeds from the gangs totaled just under US$35,000 over three years in El Salvador. In 2015, the peak year of gang homicides in El Salvador, MS-13's estimated annual revenue was reported to be just over $31 million.[8] It is questionable even how accurately the terms "DTO" and "transnational organized crime" (TOC) should apply to what are essentially neighborhood street gangs running protection rackets, albeit in multiple countries.

Why do we fail to see an evolution of the maras into larger and more profitable cartels? Why do they continue to concentrate their illicit activities in relatively unprofitable areas: extorting informal businesses and individuals, and selling drugs in poor neighborhoods? Central America's maras are as much a social phenomenon as they are criminal enterprises, more akin to a youth subculture than a cartel. As such, their activities cannot be explained by profit motive alone. This chapter addresses this question of their lack of evolution, or, from a DTO perspective, squandered opportunity. It can be explained by three factors: their histories, organizational structures, and memberships. And while their future trajectory may yet lead to either consolidation or fragmentation and "disarticulation"—in the words of reporters for *El Faro*[9]—this future depends on state responses, which will also be examined, both private accommodation and public repression: policies that are often simultaneous.

Gangs and the Taxonomy of DTOs

Questions of taxonomy have important policy implications when it comes to state response to criminal actors. In the context of the US drug war, the tendency of public officials has been to inflate the threat of (what are perceived to be) foreign criminal actors, often in conjunction with broader waves of xenophobia: fears of Chinese triads coinciding with the Chinese Exclusion Act; Irish and Italian gangsters during their respective migration waves; Japanese yakuza during Japan's investment and export boom. This serves both to justify budget outlays to law enforcement and to ignite public safety fears with which to mobilize voters. The perception of all-powerful transnational drug cartels operating in multiple criminal underworlds (e.g., migrant, sex, and drug trafficking) can distract from problems closer to home (e.g., opioid abuse and local crime). It can also be reinforced by depictions in popular culture (e.g., films and series such as *Narcos*, *Sicario*, and *Sin Nombre*). It is worth interrogating whether popular perceptions of criminal organizations such as cartels are applicable to all DTOs such as the maras.

It is an open question whether this model is applicable even to cartels themselves; Oswaldo Zavala asks whether what are essentially supply chains made up of several autonomous, small-scale, and localized groups operating in specialized areas of illicit activity (production, trafficking, distribution, security, etc.) can reasonably be described as a single unitary criminal organization.[10] To be sure, it is in the interest of those operating such organizations to project a sense of power and control on potential rivals and security forces; it is also in the interest of politicians to project the same for reasons stated above. And it is arguable that the projection of unified control applies to many areas of legitimate business as well; in the words of fictional television character Logan Roy from the series *Succession*, "the Ford Motor Company barely exists"; indeed, any corporate brand is ultimately "a time-saving expression for a collection of financial interests."

Among criminal enterprises typically referred to as cartels, there are differences in level of coordination that vary by leadership, area of business, and generation. The first-generation model of a unitary cartel answering entirely to a dictatorial CEO figure, popularized by Pablo Escobar's Medellín cartel and Miguel Ángel Félix Gallardo's Guadalajara cartel, does not apply today to their more decentralized successors in both Colombia and Mexico. It is due to criminal learning, in response to various government campaigns including Plan Colombia and the Mérida Initiative, militarized policing, "decapitation" strategies, and threats of US extraditions, that new-generation cartels have evolved away from centralized models dependent on single leaders.

For self-interested reasons, both government and criminal actors are motivated to conflate illicit organizations with different structures, geographies, profit-making activities, and methods. An illustration can be seen in a statement by the US attorney general under the first Donald Trump administration, Jeff Sessions, naming the top criminal threats to the United States to be MS-13, the Sinaloa cartel, and Hezbollah.[11] However, this tendency is not unique to the United States: although the Trump administration considered naming Mexican cartels terrorist organizations but ultimately did not—due to the likely side effect of strengthening the cases of asylum seekers from Mexico—the Supreme Court of El Salvador has designated maras as terrorists, facilitating suspensions of civil liberties amid antigang crackdowns.

Taxonomy presents challenges within the context of broader civil conflict. In Colombia, the fluidity of the drug trade between organizations with different origins and ostensible political aims, but often with the same involvement in illicit activities, has led to shifting and dubious official designations. As the cocaine trade shifted from "classic" personalist cartels in Medellín and Cali to guerrilla and paramilitary armies to fractured criminal organizations descended from those armies, and as the government has pursued varying policies of counterinsurgency, secret cooperation, negotiation, and amnesty, those organizations' reactions to the carrots and sticks of successive Colombian administrations has informed their designations. The term BACRIM—*bandas criminales*, or criminal gangs—is the official term for DTOs that descended from the Autodefensas Unidas de Colombia (AUC; United Self-Defense Forces of Colombia) umbrella group of paramilitaries. As the AUC was given amnesty in exchange for demobilization and was subsequently banned, those AUC constituent paramilitaries that refused to demobilize were subsequently deemed BACRIM—a semantic sleight of hand to allow the government to declare that the AUC, and the much older phenomenon of paramilitarism, no longer exist in Colombia. In Central America, histories of civil war and the legacy of governments designating their guerrilla enemies as terrorists inform the present-day designation of gangs as such, while both justifying and legally facilitating measures (*mano dura* policing and vigilante death squads) with clear wartime origins.

The common background in civil conflict for Colombia and Central America raises an additional question of comparison. Perhaps, rather than asking why the maras did not become cartels, we should ask why they did not become BACRIM-style narco-paramilitaries. The distinction is partly semantic—both cartels and BACRIM engage in a variety of criminal activities, operate transnational trafficking networks, and maintain large standing armies, sometimes with military training. But given the legacy of decades-long civil wars in El Salvador and Guatemala and postwar societies marked by weak institutions, political corruption, economic underdevelopment, social immobility, and availability of small arms, to some degree it is remarkable that a greater number of former combatants did not put their training to use for higher-level organized crime. Indeed, the makeup of the maras has consistently skewed young: teenagers with no personal experience in the civil conflict. This profile, as will be discussed below, has had a detrimental effect on the professionalization and institutionalization of Central America's maras.

In the following sections of this chapter, I will elaborate on the factors that limit the maras' activity in the international cocaine supply chain: their unique transnational origins, their decentralized and localized structure, and their juvenile membership. I will then discuss policing responses by the government of El Salvador over different periods of time and assess the government's success, including with regard to (as of 2025) the ongoing "State of Exception" of the Nayib Bukele administration.

Origins, Evolution, and Transnationalization

The origins of Central America's maras are shrouded in street folklore and self-mythologization, as detailed by several journalistic accounts, ethnographies, and memoirs.[12] Key to the type of transnational criminal organization the maras became are the related facts that they began not in Central America but in the United States, and that they transnationalized through the actions of the US government, specifically through the deportation system. As I have theorized elsewhere, assessing transnational organized crime requires locating the actor with agency in the process of their evolution, both within and across borders.[13] Popular conceptions of mafias and cartels imagine TOC enterprises to be in control and deliberate in their spread from one country to others, as part of a strategic business model. In contrast, MS-13 and Barrio 18 have been subject to processes directed by government authorities at every stage of their evolution. The maras were exported to Central America by the United States and have been continually shaped by law enforcement policies in both regions. As such, they adapted their activities to new environments—California to Central America, streets to prisons, urban to rural—on a more ad hoc basis.

Rivals MS-13 and Barrio 18—the latter now since split into two rival factions itself—share their origins in Los Angeles within the Salvadoran diaspora community. This diaspora was itself the product of violence from El Salvador's 1980–1992 civil war, which pushed thousands to flee for safety to the United States, with the community augmented by later periods of economic instability and natural disaster, as well as family-based migration. The first-generation US *mareros* initially settled in the largely Chicano neighborhoods of Los Angeles and, according to the folklore, faced the challenge of standing out as newcomers and as a minority in terms of national identity in contrast to their more established Mexican American neighbors.[14] They faced an additional challenge of navigating an environment where micro street gangs controlled territory demarcated by neighborhood and street; the name in English for Barrio 18, 18th Street, derives from a street in the Pico-Union district of Los Angeles. Barrio 18 had existed long before the arrival of Salvadoran migrants, tracing back to the 1960s, but was unique among the Chicano gangs in accepting the new migrants as members. The gang that came to be its rival, and known eventually as MS-13, was at the time called the Mara Salvatrucha Stoners. Made up more exclusively of Salvadoran teenagers, they distinguished themselves from Chicano gangs by their appearance (long hair and tight, dark clothing) and musical preference (metal bands such as Judas Priest), which reflected other groupings of juvenile gangs in 1980s southern California around favorite bands.

Both gangs were, in effect, social groupings providing a sense of belonging to recently arrived adolescents navigating a new and hostile environment by getting high and getting in fights with other adolescents.[15] As threats to public safety, they were seen as a minor risk and one of dozens of similar groupings of teenagers defined by neighborhood, attracted to petty vandalism and punk and metal concerts. Even after the point at which MSS evolved into MS-13, in 1989, the Los Angeles Police Department estimated its membership to be fewer than five hundred.[16] It was in fact the LAPD that catalyzed this evolution in 1984, through mass arrests of alleged gang members as part of a citywide clean-up-the-streets campaign ahead of the Los Angeles Summer Olympics.

These arrests heralded the first transformation of the maras from juvenile street gangs to prison gangs, as the first generation of Barrio 18 and MSS members were socialized into the California penal system and its attendant prison gang culture, which included affiliating with and paying tribute to other, more established gangs. It was in this period that MS dropped the "Stoners" moniker and added the "13," as a tribute to the Mexican Mafia,[17] a largely Chicano gang dating back to 1957.

The second transformation of the maras, their transnationalization, came about in 1996 through two pieces of legislation at the federal level signed by President Bill Clinton: the Illegal Immigration Reform and Immigrant Responsibility Act and the Antiterrorism and Effective Death Penalty Act. The new laws, meant to address then-peaking levels of violence from both street crime and domestic terrorism,[18] facilitated deportations by expanding the list of crimes for which an undocumented immigrant would be prioritized for deportation.[19] These laws thus inaugurated the current era of mass deportations; from 1994 to 2014, deportations from the United States to the Northern Triangle of Central America went from five thousand to one hundred thousand annually.[20] Such deportations continued unabated under subsequent Republican and Democratic administrations, peaking during the Barack Obama administration. The Trump administration made MS-13 in particular a public bogeyman, with Trump and his cabinet members citing the supposed threat posed by the gang—including in one State of the Union address—as a justification for their envisioned border wall and harsh anti-immigration measures more broadly. The fact that the gang did not come from Central America but originated in the United States was an inconvenient detail left unmentioned.

For El Salvador, Guatemala, and Honduras, the result of the twentyfold surge of deportations from the United States created a sudden and sustained dilemma. The receiving countries did not have the resources to absorb tens of thousands of jobless return migrants arriving each year. Some had gang ties, others did not, but the rhetoric from the United States of expelling "gangbangers" stoked fears among the general public of an inundation of hardened criminals. Social stigmas and assumptions of criminality were attached to them, correctly or not. Many were poorly socialized, having lived for most of their lives in the United States; many did not speak Spanish well. Facing few job prospects in the face of such suspicions, those with gang connections reconstituted the maras in El Salvador first, and their membership soon multiplied with subsequent planeloads of deportees, spreading to other parts of the country and the Northern Triangle a whole.

The response by the governments to this new, if exaggerated, threat to public safety was a zero-tolerance policing policy called *mano dura*. As discussed in greater detail below, the effect of mano dura policing only further expanded the gang's reach by chasing them first from the city of San Salvador to the countryside, then from El Salvador to neighboring countries, and eventually to the prison system, over which the gangs came to exert hegemonic control. The evolution of the maras in Central America thus mirrored their evolution in the United States, from street gangs to prison gangs, but with greater ties from prisons to the streets, with neighborhood-level cliques ostensibly answering to incarcerated gang leaders who controlled the prisons where street members expect to end up one day.

In short, the different stages of evolution of the maras have always been subject to state policy: whether policing policy or deportation policy, whether in the United States or Central America. This unintentional geographic spread, including transnationalization, stands in contrast to the cartel model of transnationalization, a proactive process of setting up supply chains, trafficking routes, and distribution networks with a profit motive in mind. Although these evolutions have expanded the maras' membership and geographic reach, the reactive and nearly accidental nature of this spread has inhibited longer-term strategic planning and involvement in more lucrative transnational criminal enterprises, including cocaine trafficking much beyond the street level.[21]

Localized Structures

The second factor limiting the maras' activities is their decentralized and localized structure. Far from a single unitary criminal organization, the maras exist as a loose network of *clicas*, or cliques, operating at the neighborhood level. These cliques are founded on a franchise model, paying tribute to the gang—and its incarcerated leadership—for the right to use its name, a tributary system reflective of both gangs' historical relationship with the Mexican Mafia in California. Although they have a common organizational form with defined roles, rituals, and lines of promotion, cliques are largely self-directed: those who lead them, the *palabreros* or shot callers, are afforded more autonomy than most middle management. Shot callers will direct their cliques' activities on the ground, within the defined boundaries they claim as their territory. Their activities are hyperlocal in scope, involving whatever profits can be made from the populations in the neighborhoods they control. These are primarily protection rackets, imposed on local businesses and residents who are forced to pay what is euphemistically called *renta*, or rent. The significance of this term situates the clique as the de facto landlord of the neighborhood, as well as the local governing authority. Gangs justify extortion payments as effective taxes for security they allegedly provide, not only from themselves but from rival gangs in neighboring territory. Such invisible boundaries have historically severely restricted the movement of people within these territories, with a gang demanding they not cross into other gangs' territory—even to visit family or go to work—for fear that they will cooperate with that gang's rivals. Entire communities are thus effectively conscripted into the cliques' activities, and members can treat civilians in neighboring areas as valid targets for violence simply based on where they live.[22]

In some cases, cliques can be grouped together as *programas*, programs (in MS-13) or *tribus*, tribes (in Barrio 18), an organizational reform initiated by the incarcerated leadership in the early 2000s, overseen by *corredores*, or runners. Some of these programs/tribes are themselves transnational, such as the Sailors program, a collection of MS cliques based in both El Salvador and the Washington, DC, area; and the Los Angeles program, anchored to the Normandie Locos, one of the oldest MS cliques, since expanding to El Salvador and the East Coast of the United States. Nevertheless, members assert that their primary loyalty remains with the clique, thus frustrating efforts to coordinate criminal activities transnationally through programs.[23]

Cliques and programs that have attempted such higher-level coordination have faced swift responses by law enforcement. An early case in Los Angeles in 2005 tested the application of the Racketeer Influenced and Corrupt Organizations (RICO) Act—a prosecutorial tool used mostly against the Italian American Mafia—by bringing conspiracy charges against twenty-four MS-13 members.[24] In 2016, a Los Angeles MS-13 clique leader seeking to establish a "National Program" for drug trafficking in conjunction with the Mexican Mafia was arrested. In a later case, a meeting of various cliques in Richmond, Virginia, that had been monitored resulted in another successful RICO case by the US Justice Department and multiple arrests, breaking up what might have been a trafficking network operating throughout the East Coast of the United States.[25] The vulnerability of programs to federal investigation and prosecution, particularly through RICO given their interstate nature, underscores the relative safety of concentrating activity at the local level, primarily extortion.

Ambitions for greater sophistication have been thwarted in Central America as well. In 2007, El Salvador's National Civil Police (Policía Nacional Civil) intercepted an MS-13 strategy plan dubbed "Plan 503" to expand the group's criminal operations. According to alleged conversations among incarcerated MS leaders, the gang's leadership, collectively known as the *ranfla*, proposed to shift activities away from the extortion business and develop into a true drug-trafficking organization. Changes proposed included calling a truce with Barrio 18, acquiring military-grade weapons and training, developing elite units to directly confront government security forces, and building greater ties to political parties.[26] Some of these changes were implemented to a limited degree: the maras consolidated ties to politicians and elected officials of all parties at all levels of government through both bribery and displays of violence. And at certain moments they have directly targeted security personnel, notably MS-13's Plan Bitter Tears and Plan Orphan Children during the Salvador Sánchez Cerén administration, in response to that administration's targeting of gang members and their families with paramilitary units (the now-disbanded Fuerza Especializada de Reacción [FES]) in an undeclared "dirty war." Nevertheless, such reforms were never fully realized, nor was the ranfla's expressed dreams to, according to the National Civil Police, "unify MS-13 across the globe to carry out large-scale operations," "cease the war with Barrio 18 to carry out joint operations against the state," gain "formal recognition" by political parties, or fully "develop and consolidate relationships with Mexican cartels."[27]

While it is impossible to independently verify such reporting by US and Salvadoran law enforcement, and both have self-interested reasons to report grand plans by gang leadership, should such plans be true, the continued concentration of criminal activities in extortion rackets at the neighborhood level is evidence of the maras' inability to expand from the street to national or international levels. The apparent ease by which such plans have been intercepted and foiled by law enforcement points to coordination challenges among the cliques and programs/tribes, and more generally to collective action problems inherent in decentralized systems of semiautonomous local chapters.

Localized organizational structures are not a mark of weakness, however. As Sarah Zukerman Daly shows in the case of Colombia, localized criminal groups are more likely to maintain their networks and capacity over time than nonlocalized groups.[28] The challenge for a growing DTO is to maintain those localized networks while coordinating activity at the national and transnational level. Lack of coordination does not speak to lack of public threat: the maras succeeded in driving homicide rates in the Northern Triangle of Central America to the highest in the world in the mid-2010s. But the spectacular—and often performative—acts of violence have betrayed problems for the gangs in projecting their power. In contrast to the archetypal cartels conducting their business efficiently in the shadows, with the cooperation of authorities, the maras' reliance on public violence indicates their inability to force official cooperation through other means. In some cases, they have extracted concessions: a 2010 transportation strike by gang-controlled bus systems led eventually to the first gang truce brokered secretly by the government of Mauricio Funes. But violent means are not entirely effective, often sparking crackdowns—such as the Bukele government's State of Exception, which was imposed following a spate of gang killings in March 2022.

Membership Profile

A third factor limiting the maras' establishment in higher-level activity is the age profile of their membership. Since their founding in the United States, the identity of both maras has continued to be as juvenile street (and later prison) gangs.

Made members are called *homeboys* or *homies*, reflecting their roots in California gang culture, those who have been formally initiated into the gang through a 13- (for MS-13) or 18- (for Barrio 18) second beating called a *brinco*. Beneath the made members are probationary members: *paros*, later *observaciones*, and eventually *chequeos*. Those who advance from probationary to full status are understood to be in the gang for life, with their understood final destination to be death or prison. Teen and preteen boys make up the bulk of gang membership, particularly in the cliques; while imprisoned members can be much older, they are not the members engaging in the gang's profit-making enterprises on the street.

While no comprehensive transnational membership survey exists, estimates of the average age of members range from thirteen to sixteen in the United States. New members have, over time, grown younger still, as the gangs have shifted recruitment targets from high school to middle school or even elementary school age. In El Salvador, the National Civil Police has reported the traditional age for new recruits to be between ages seven and twelve.[29] Maras have various motives for recruiting ever younger prospects: children's impressionability and vulnerability to peer pressure, their ability to avoid detection, and the fact that they cannot be tried as adults, thus avoiding harsher penalties.

The maras' cohesion thus revolves less around the maximization of profit than around the social benefit of belonging that the cliques promise to prospective members. Adolescents do not join the maras expecting to get rich. Journalistic accounts of their activities in El Salvador estimate that members earn on average US$16 per week, just half of the minimum wage.[30] Members and leaders live in the same poor neighborhoods that they extort, in modest homes, without flashy possessions such as luxury cars. Many are still in school, or have dropped out and work day jobs, with gang activity supplementing their incomes.

Instead, the maras seek to provide their members with a surrogate family, often substituting for the lack of parental or sibling support within their members' own homes. Multiple ethnographies emphasize the social appeal of the maras over the monetary. Much of this motivation to join is related to the gang's protection rackets: boys in poor neighborhoods feel victimized and alienated growing up in a threatening environment; seeking protection, they join the very gangs that contribute to that environment. Members who have provided testimonies report finding "courage" and "self-respect" in joining.[31] Other reports point to members' desire for social status as well as sex, most perniciously encapsulated in the "gang girlfriend" phenomenon of sexual slavery of girls and women who attract the attention of mareros.

Given gangs' memberships, conflicts have often revolved around interpersonal rather than business disputes, including the original break between MS-13 and Barrio 18, which gang lore attributes to a shooting at a Los Angeles house party in 1988 and, according to one account, arising from a wife cheating on her partner with a rival gang member.[32] The territorial delineations of the maras' protection rackets inevitably precipitate disputes over turf—who has the right to extort which bus lines or to sell marijuana on which block—which mirror the teenage neighborhood rivalries from which the maras originated. These disputes are no less deadly than disputes with greater monetary value. Bus line extortion fights have resulted in some of the most gruesome acts of violence directed at civilians: shootings and burnings of buses killing dozens of passengers, in both El Salvador and Honduras.[33]

The degree of violence of such acts, it should be noted, is disproportionate to the money that can be earned from these rackets: from estimates and police raids, in the tens of thousands, not multi-millions, of dollars. As noted above, the maras have long relied on spectacular acts of violence to intimidate their sometimes more powerful rivals, in ways that are not the most strategic, symbolized by their early adoption of machetes as weapons of choice—which are less effective than guns but intended to strike fear into their enemies. It can be surmised that such practices—emphasizing confrontation, shock tactics, and violence for its own sake, deemphasizing profit and cooperation—stem in part from being carried out by mostly teenage boys, not adult career criminals.

This lack of a profit motive also inhibits the maras' ability to partner with other DTOs. Mara leaders view members who are motivated by money with suspicion, considering them to be self-interested and liable to betray the gang if they do not buy into the "family" aspect of the clique. However, larger cartels that are profit minded can similarly view the maras' lack of interest or experience in profitable enterprises as a liability.

State Responses:
Mano Dura and the State of Exception

The combination of decentralized structure, juvenile membership, and an extortion-based business model make the maras at once vulnerable to and a challenge for state enforcement. Successive governments in Central America have attempted, without success, to eliminate the gangs with overwhelming force, in law enforcement strategies dubbed mano dura, hardhanded or ironfisted policing. When they fail, these policies have been rebranded as super mano dura, territorial control plans, and Régimen de Excepción or State of Exception—because what they seek to combat is not a single criminal organization but a social phenomenon more akin to a youth subculture.

At the same time, the maras themselves are too disorganized to effectively confront the state. The maras do wield power, but only in recent years have they learned to deploy it politically. Although at certain moments the maras have announced plans to directly target police officers, assassinations have been limited and precipitated harsh crackdowns, in comparison to attacks on other gang members or even civilians. Gangs have learned to use violence to pressure governments indirectly, with more successful results: as homicide rates have become highly politically salient for politicians in Central America, maras have threatened to drop bodies to pressure governments for concessions, threats demonstrated to be real by periodic murder sprees during negotiations with government officials. In the past, these concessions were entirely motivated by self-interest on the part of imprisoned gang leaders and have included prison perks, visitation privileges for ranfleros, and control over entire prisons historically segregated by gang. Under the Bukele administration, all evidence suggests that the maras have grown more sophisticated in their demands, insofar as El Salvador's government has blocked the extradition of several MS-13 leaders wanted by the United States. In one notorious incident, a member of the Bukele cabinet personally escorted a gang leader out of El Salvador so as to avoid extradition.[34] The unacknowledged no-extradition concession—which has held throughout the Bukele government's much-heralded antigang crackdown—indicates that gang leaders have come to understand a vulnerability of the government and have tested their ability to make significant demands, the importance of which is evident in the government's willingness to jeopardize diplomatic relations with the United States in order to maintain compliance.

Such Faustian bargains are politically risky and thus vociferously denied by governments, even in the face of overwhelming evidence, reporting, and testimony of gang members, and in the case of the Bukele government, police document leaks. The earlier administration of Mauricio Funes negotiated a truce between MS-13 and Barrio 18, brokered by the Catholic Church in 2012, which the government long denied even while celebrating the drop in homicides, which paved the way for the election of Funes's vice president, Salvador Sánchez Cerén, as his successor. Yet revelations of the negotiations made the truce unpopular and politically infeasible to maintain, precipitating another mano dura crackdown and rise in homicide rates, reaching their historical zenith in 2015. The subsequent drop in homicides under President Bukele—who as mayor of San Salvador had previously negotiated with Barrio 18 to facilitate the rehabilitation of a downtown shopping area—coincided with another secret pact, later revealed through reporting, video evidence, and leaked documents. More alarmingly, the drop in homicides coincided as well with a rise in disappearances and the discovery of multiple mass graves, reflecting testimony by a Barrio 18 leader to El Faro of an agreement between the two parties to hide bodies and not to investigate them.[35]

However, these deals only reflect the "carrot" side of the government's approach to the maras, which has historically leaned heavily on the stick in the form of mano dura. Breakdowns in negotiations precipitate harsh measures, mass incarcerations, and in the present situation (in 2025), the deployment of the military and suspension of civil liberties. The maras have always survived these crackdowns, but they have never been in control of the circumstances. Previous mano dura campaigns have precipitated the jailing of thousands of alleged gang members in overcrowded prisons at between 200 and 400 percent capacity, thus effectively relocating and concentrating the maras within the prison system, which they subsequently took over. This development, prior to the 2012 truce, empowered the ranflas by giving them control over a larger population, a base of operations, and the ability to direct violent acts on the streets, giving them bargaining leverage in future government negotiations.

The latest gang crackdown by the Bukele government, and subsequent suspension of civil liberties under an ongoing State of Exception, was precipitated by a breakdown in the last negotiated truce, which lasted from the start of the Bukele administration in June 2019 until March 2022. The breakdown was reportedly over nonpayment of an agreed sum by the government to MS-13, which sparked a murder spree in which eighty-seven people were killed from March 25 to 27, 2022. In response, the government broke off talks, deployed the army to occupy gang neighborhoods, and initiated mass arrests on a scale not seen before in El Salvador: as of this writing (2025), more than eighty-five thousand have been arrested, swelling the prison population to 2 percent of the country's adult population and giving El Salvador the highest incarceration rate in the world. Many detainees have not been told of their charges or allowed to see their lawyers or families, and many have suffered harsh treatment. A very large number likely have no gang ties at all, according to an assessment by a former inspector general of the national police, who estimated that 70 percent of those arrested under the State of Exception are non-gang-affiliated civilians.[36] Around three hundred people are confirmed to have died in custody since the beginning of the State of Exception, although human rights advocates believe the number to be much higher. A report by El Salvador's Cristosal, based on interviews with released detainees, cites widespread use of torture and the deaths of detainees by beatings and strangulation.[37] The Bukele government has paraded prisoners before cameras to demonstrate their success; these prisoners, mostly middle aged and thus arrested years ago by previous governments, are clearly not the (mostly adolescent) recently arrested, but given their tattooed visages—a practice that has been largely phased out by the gangs and not seen on the streets for at least a decade—they have provided shock value propaganda for a government presenting itself as the toughest on crime in history.

Yet such harsh measures are targeted on a specific population: the lowest level of gang membership, or those suspected of such. At the highest level, the ranfla leaders have maintained their privileges, have remained protected from extradition, and have even been released from prison and allowed to leave the country. Public officials corrupted by the maras have similarly been left untouched. As the maras soon learned, far more effective than direct confrontation with security officials is co-optation, whether through bribes or intimidation. Thus, entire police forces and municipal governments have come to be in the pay of MS-13 or Barrio 18; this degree of cooperation reached a peak in Honduras under the administration of Juan Orlando Hernández, which directed its antigang measures exclusively at Barrio 18 at the behest of MS-13. In both countries, the phenomenon of "narco mayors" has underscored the degree to which organized crime—gangs and cartels alike—has infiltrated local government. At the national level in El Salvador, the Bukele government includes cabinet ministers who have worked for the maras and the Texis cartel,[38] or have been linked to coyote rings.[39] One top diplomat—the consul general of El Salvador in Long Island, New York—is an admitted "former" member of MS-13. Several Salvadoran government officials have been named and sanctioned by the US government for criminal ties, including the social fabric director, who escorted an MS-13 leader out of the country, and the director of prisons, who brokered negotiations with the maras and embezzled prison funds. None have faced prosecution under the State of Exception.

Despite human rights abuses, ongoing protection of both criminals and corrupt officials, and misrepresentation of fact, the latest mano dura campaign in the form of the State of Exception has been effective in suppressing violence and gang activity. Certainly, as a political measure, it has been very successful for the Bukele government in driving up approval ratings. Although presented to the public as a repression-only measure, it employs the same carrot-and-stick approach of previous governments, with each directed at different levels of the maras, both leadership and rank-and-file. The impact for the maras has been transformative if not quite decimating: reporting suggests that in many (but not all) parts of El Salvador, protection rackets have been dormant, and members who have not been arrested have largely gone into hiding or fled the country.[40]

A Future Gang State?

It is unlikely that the maras have been eliminated, as the government alleges. Instead, they are likely lying low, assessing the latest crackdown, and reorganizing. This is in line with reactions by maras to previous mano dura campaigns, which precipitated their relocations and entrenchments in new areas. At each stage, the maras adapted to new environments and found new ways to carry out their criminal activities and put pressure on the government. It is more likely that they will reemerge, possibly with new names under a new structure, or possibly fractured into many mini-gangs.

A likelier scenario is a co-optation of the gangs by the government. The Bukele government's divide-and-conquer approach has reportedly found success in alienating gang membership from the leadership. The Bukele government, for its part, has built ties to illicit business elsewhere, notably money laundering—including the Texis cartel and Venezuela's state oil company, Petróleos de Venezuela (PDVSA).[41] It has also, to much fanfare but with little economic success, introduced Bitcoin as legal tender and sought to use the cryptocurrency to attract investment and financing in the face of falling bond ratings and contentious negotiations over a billion-dollar loan from the International Monetary Fund. The Bukele administration has also built closer ties to the Chinese government as relations under the Biden administration soured, with Bukele's brother Karim—who has business interests with China—acting as the unofficial foreign minister. These developments together point to deepening criminal ties and activities by the Bukele government itself, specifically around money laundering. Bukele's high popularity, purging of the judiciary and Supreme Court, supermajority in the legislature, personal control of the military,[42] lack of transparency in public budgets, and unofficial delegation of power to his family together make him unaccountable to any checks or balances. These factors make possible the development in El Salvador of what has been described in Honduras as a narco-state,[43] albeit one that is even more unified under a single figure. As the largest criminal networks in the country, the maras have a useful role to offer such a government. But it would be one that would be subordinate to the interests of the state—and in its current form, the interests of Bukele and his family. These interests do not currently align: it is far more probable that any illicit state activity will revolve around money laundering rather than neighborhood-level extortion. For the maras to survive, they will have to adapt to the business model set by the state.

Yet this gang-state scenario is perilous and requires coordination between both gang and state; as José Miguel Cruz and Angélica Durán-Martínez note, the success of any such negotiation depends on internal cohesion and is complicated by the fragmentation and multiplicity of veto players—a significant risk under the decentralized franchise model.[44] Despite their numbers, fearsome reputation, and capacity for violence, Central America's maras have never been in control of the circumstances that have shaped their forms and activities. They have been pushed from the United States to Central America, and within Central America, by government efforts to expel or eliminate them. These efforts were never successful, but they have compelled the gangs to spread, decentralize, and concentrate their activities at the neighborhood level. As juvenile street gangs, they have been sustained more by social than by financial capital. They have learned from the crucibles of gangland LA, the prison system, and mano dura. In some ways they have grown more sophisticated, particularly in dealing with the government. They have managed to co-opt officials and also to be co-opted by them. Insofar as they present to politicians a threat through their capacity for violence, and an opportunity through their large membership, they will remain relevant political actors.

Yet unlike cartels, the opportunity they offer state officials is not proceeds from lucrative businesses they control. As of now, it has been their membership itself, and the territory they control: successive ruling parties have negotiated with them for exclusive access to their neighborhoods for political campaigns, or for their members to campaign for the ruling party directly. The Bukele government arranged for gang members to impose COVID pandemic quarantines and helped the director of prisons steal and resell pandemic food relief packages.[45] As corrupt practices, these are relatively minor. But they speak to ongoing interest by multiple governments in the maras as useful tools, despite officially branding them as terrorists. Should the maras continue to thrive, it will not be as consolidated cartels trafficking cocaine but as junior partners to other criminal actors, including those in government.

Notes

1. Barrio 18 has split into two factions, the Revolucionarios (Revolutionaries) and the Sureños (Southerners), which act as rival gangs.

2. Steven Dudley, "Central America's 'Transportistas,'" InSight Crime, November 22, 2010, https://insightcrime.org/investigations/insight-brief-central-americas-transportistas/.

3. Drawn from Douglas Farah and Kathryn Babineau, "The Evolution of MS 13 in El Salvador and Honduras," *PRISM* 7, no. 1 (2017): 58–73; Tom Diaz, *No Boundaries: Transnational Latino Gangs and American Law Enforcement* (Ann Arbor: University of Michigan Press, 2009); and Steven Dudley and Héctor Silva Ávalos, "MS13 in the Americas: Major Findings," InSight Crime, February 16, 2018, https://insightcrime.org/investigations/ms13_major_findings/.

4. Diaz, *No Boundaries*.

5. Dudley and Silva Ávalos, "MS13 in the Americas."

6. Dudley and Silva Ávalos, "MS13 in the Americas," 66.

7. Farah and Babineau, "The Evolution of MS 13."

8. Óscar Martínez, Efren Lemus, Carlos Martínez, and Deborah Sontag, "Killers on a Shoestring: Inside the Gangs of El Salvador," *New York Times*, November 20, 2016, https://www.nytimes.com/2016/11/21/world/americas/el-salvador-drugs-gang-ms-13.html.

9. Carlos Martínez, Efren Lemus, and Óscar Martínez, "Régimen de Bukele desarticula a las pandillas en El Salvador," *El Faro*, February 3, 2023, https://elfaro.net/es/202302/el_salvador/26691/R%C3%A9gimen-de-Bukele-desarticula-a-las-pandillas-en-El-Salvador.htm.

10. Oswaldo Zavala, *Drug Cartels Do Not Exist: Narcotrafficking in US and Mexican Culture*, trans. William Savinar (Nashville: Vanderbilt University Press, 2022).

11. Michael Balsamo, "Sessions Creates Task Force Targeting MS-13 Gangs, Drug Cartels," Associated Press, October 15, 2018, https://www.pbs.org/newshour/politics/sessions-creates-task-force-targeting-ms-13-gangs-drug-cartels.

12. See José Manuel Valenzuela Arce, Alfredo Nateras Domínguez, and Rossana Reguillo Cruz, eds., *Las maras: Identidades juveniles al límite* (Tijuana, Mexico: El Colegio de la Frontera Norte, 2007); Samuel Logan, *This Is for the Mara Salvatrucha: Inside the MS-13, America's Most Violent Gang* (New York: Hachette Books, 2009); Thomas W. Ward, *Gangsters Without Borders: An Ethnography of a Salvadoran Street Gang* (New York: Oxford University Press, 2013); Óscar Martínez, *A History of Violence: Living and Dying in Central America*, trans. John B. Washington and Daniela Ugaz (London: Verso, 2016); Sonja Wolf, *Mano Dura: The Politics of Gang Control in El Salvador* (Austin: University of Texas Press, 2017); Juan

José Martínez D'Aubuisson, *A Year Inside MS-13: See, Hear, and Shut Up*, trans. Natascha Elena Uhlmann (New York: OR Books, 2019); William Wheeler, *State of War: MS-13 and El Salvador's World of Violence* (New York: Columbia Global Reports, 2020); Steven Dudley, *MS-13: The Making of America's Most Notorious Gang* (New York: Hanover Square Press, 2020); and Roberto Lovato, *Unforgetting: A Memoir of Family, Migration, Gangs, and Revolution in the Americas* (New York: HarperCollins, 2020).

13. Michael Ahn Paarlberg, "Transnational Gangs and Criminal Remittances: A Conceptual Framework," *Comparative Migration Studies* 10, no. 1 (December 2022): 24.

14. Ward, *Gangsters Without Borders*.

15. Valenzuela Arce, Nateras Domínguez, and Reguillo Cruz, *Las maras: Identidades juveniles al límite*.

16. Diaz, *No Boundaries*, 35.

17. The letter *M* being the thirteenth letter of the alphabet, gangs thus paying tribute to the Mexican Mafia were and are affiliated with the broad umbrella group of Sureños, or Southerners, referring to southern California. Some gangs within this grouping add "13" to their names. Both MS-13 and Barrio 18 are affiliated with this larger umbrella group within the California prison system, but they are rivals. As mentioned earlier, Barrio 18's two factions are the Revolucionarios and the Sureños, the latter also reflecting the early ties to the Mexican Mafia.

18. The latter law was passed in response to the Oklahoma City bombing, the perpetrators of which were US-born citizens.

19. Undocumented immigrants can be detained for deportation proceedings at any time, but in practice they are not a priority for immigration enforcement unless they have committed a crime. Prior to 1996, such crimes were more often serious felonies. After, they could include petty crimes such as DUI, public intoxication, and drug possession.

20. Rodrigo Dominguez-Villegas and Victoria Rietig, "Migrants Deported from the United States and Mexico to the Northern Triangle," Migration Policy Institute, September 2015, https://www.migrationpolicy.org/research/migrants-deported-united-states-and-mexico-northern-triangle-statistical-and-socioeconomic.

21. This is particularly true in El Salvador. As the maras have spread to Guatemala, Honduras, and southern Mexico, they have come to be involved with transnational trafficking networks, but more in a support role. And this is more human trafficking of migrants than drug trafficking, which remains concentrated in more established Mexican cartels. Within Central America, the gangs' primary business remains extortion at the neighborhood level.

22. Michael Ahn Paarlberg, "Gang Membership in Central America: More Complex than Meets the Eye," Migration Policy Institute, August 26, 2021, https://www.migrationpolicy.org/article/complexities-gang-membership-central-america.

23. José Miguel Cruz, Jonathan D. Rosen, Luis Enrique Amaya, and Yulia Vorobyeva, *The New Face of Street Gangs: The Gang Phenomenon in El Salvador*, Florida International University and Fundación Nacional para el Desarrollo, 2017, https://lacc.fiu.edu/research/the-street-gangs-in-central-america-research-initiative-scrain/the-new-face-of-street-gangs-the-gang-phenomenon-in-el-salvador-eng.pdf.

24. Dudley, *MS-13: The Making of America's Most Notorious Gang*, 149–59.

25. Parker Asmann, "MS13 East Coast Violence Fails to Consolidate Gang's US Presence," InSight Crime, August 27, 2020, https://insightcrime.org/news/analysis/ms13-violence-east-coast-presence/.

26. David E. Spencer, Herard von Santos, and Juan Carlos Morales, *Adversarial System Analysis of the Salvadoran Gangs* (Washington, DC: William J. Perry Center for Hemispheric Defense Studies, National Defense University, 2022), https://www.govinfo.gov/content/pkg/GOVPUB-D5_400-PURL-gpo185675/pdf/GOVPUB-D5_400-PURL-gpo185675.pdf.

27. Spencer, Von Santos, and Morales, *Adversarial System Analysis of the Salvadoran Gangs*, 31–32.

28. Sarah Zukerman Daly, *Organized Violence After Civil War: The Geography of Recruitment in Latin America* (Cambridge: Cambridge University Press, 2016).

29. Federal Bureau of Investigation, "Mara Salvatrucha (MS-13): An International Perspective," National Gang Center, 2005, 12, https://nationalgangcenter.ojp.gov/library/publications/mara-salvatrucha-ms-13-international-perspective.

30. Ó. Martínez et al., "Killers on a Shoestring."

31. Ward, *Gangsters Without Borders*, 98.

32. Martínez D'Aubuisson, *A Year Inside MS-13*, 6.

33. In 2004, MS-13 members in San Pedro Sula, Honduras, raked a city bus with automatic gunfire, killing twenty-eight passengers. In 2010, Barrio 18 members shot at a bus in Mejicanos, El Salvador, doused it in gasoline, and set it on fire with passengers inside, killing seventeen. Governments in Honduras and El Salvador have at different times reported between thirty and fifty bus burnings per year in wars between MS-13 and Barrio 18 over control of the bus lines.

34. Michael Ahn Paarlberg, "The Emerging Gang State in El Salvador," Global Americans, February 15, 2022, https://theglobalamericans.org/2022/02/the-emerging-gang-state-in-el-salvador/.

35. Paarlberg, "The Emerging Gang State in El Salvador."

36. Gabriel Labrador and Óscar Martínez, "One Year Under a Police State in El Salvador," *El Faro*, March 31, 2023, https://elfaro.net/en/202303/el_salvador/26793/one-year-under-a-police-state-in-el-salvador.

37. "Un año bajo el régimen de excepción: Una medida permanente de represión y de violaciones a los derechos humanos," Cristosal, May 29, 2023, https://cristosal.org/ES/informe-un-ano-bajo-el-regimen-de-excepcion-una-medida-permanente-de-represion-y-de-violaciones-a-los-derechos-humanos/.

38. The Texis cartel is the name of a constellation of illicit businesses controlled by Herbert Saca, cousin of former president Antonio Saca, who was jailed for corruption but is a close ally of Bukele. Many top Bukele officials have backgrounds in the Saca administration. The current attorney general and minister of security worked for Herbert Saca and have ties to the cartel.

39. "PNC vinculó a Michelle Sol con red de coyotes," *La Prensa Gráfica* (San Salvador), February 8, 2015, https://www.laprensagrafica.com/elsalvador/PNC-vinculo-a-Michelle-Sol-con--red-de-coyotes-20150208-0047.html.

40. C. Martínez, Lemus, and Ó. Martínez, "Régimen de Bukele desarticula a las pandillas en El Salvador."

41. Alba, a conglomerate of retail businesses financed by Venezuela's PDVSA, has served as an offshore money laundering network for the Venezuelan government, which is beset by sanctions by the United States. Proceeds from this operation have profited previous Salvadoran governments of the Left, those of Funes and Sánchez Cerén. Although Bukele has sought to prosecute both former presidents for their own gang negotiations, he has inherited the ties to Alba through its chief intermediary in El Salvador, José Luis Merino, a former communist guerrilla who has since allied with Bukele.

42. Like many authoritarian leaders, Bukele has used the military for political and nonmilitary roles, including sending soldiers to occupy the Legislative Assembly to intimidate lawmakers to pass a bill, and deploying the army to neighborhoods to carry out policing functions under the State of Exception. In return, the Bukele government has protected top military officials from investigation, including by blocking the opening of military archives for ongoing trials about the massacre at El Mozote by an army battalion during the 1980–1992 civil war.

43. Dana Frank, *The Long Honduran Night: Resistance, Terror, and the United States in the Aftermath of the Coup* (Chicago: Haymarket Books, 2018).

44. José Miguel Cruz and Angélica Durán-Martínez, "Hiding Violence to Deal with the State: Criminal Pacts in El Salvador and Medellin," *Journal of Peace Research* 53, no. 2 (March 2016): 197–210.

45. Seth Robbins, "US Blacklists El Salvador Officials, Bolstering Accusations of Gang Pacts," InSight Crime, December 9, 2021, https://insightcrime.org/news/us-blacklists-el-salvador-officials-bolstering-accusations-gang-pacts/.

CHAPTER 8

Cocaine in Mexico

The Forgotten Drug and Its Implications

Nathan P. Jones and Gary Hale

Today, nearly all US attention is focused on the rise of synthetic drugs such as fentanyl and methamphetamines, flowing through Mexico into the United States. This is understandable given the role of synthetic drugs in the US overdose epidemic. However, cocaine has long been an important market and source of profit for Mexican organized crime groups (OCGs). This chapter assesses cocaine in Mexico, the drug that turned small bands of Mexican traffickers into the transnational criminal organizations (TCOs) they are today in the cases of the Sinaloa cartel and the Cártel de Jalisco Nueva Generación (CJNG; Jalisco New Generation cartel). This chapter will elucidate the history of cocaine flows in Mexico, the role the drug has played in the rise of Mexican cartels, Mexican cartel precursors, cocaine's continued role in illicit profits, the expansion of Mexican OCG cocaine trafficking to new markets, and the role of cocaine price volatility in organized crime violence in Mexico.

During the 2022–2023 period, the price of cocaine in Mexico dropped dramatically. This is not unique to Mexico, as the overall price of cocaine in the Andean region has also dropped, leading to fears of food instability in the Andean region among coca growers who depend on the profits of the coca crop to survive.[1] This has had less of an impact in Mexico, where Mexican cartels have long been polycrime organizations. While they have been some of the leading traffickers of cocaine and have even achieved international illicit market penetration in South America, the Caribbean, Central America, and other regions, the fact that Mexican cartels have moved increasingly into highly diverse criminal portfolios that include extortion, oil theft, prostitution, water theft, and synthetic drugs such as methamphetamines and more recently fentanyl means that the historic drop in cocaine prices is likely to have a limited impact on Mexican cartels.

The cocaine supply chain vis-à-vis Mexico is inherently transnational given that most of the supply begins in the Andean region. Mexican traffickers emerged in the 1980s and 1990s as what some have described as the "FedEx" or delivery service for Colombian traffickers, who faced significant pressures as the US government targeted the Medellín and Cali cartels.[2]

Mexican cartels have become preeminent players in international drug markets in part due to large cocaine profits and their role in the cocaine market.[3] Mexican OCGs have achieved market penetration and direct on-the-ground operations in countries such as Colombia, Ecuador, Guatemala, El Salvador, Honduras, and Belize, and they increasingly operate in international markets in Europe, Australia, New Zealand, and other places.[4] These same transnational criminal organizations also source synthetic drug precursors from East Asia, specifically China, and India, as evidenced in US Drug Enforcement Administration (DEA) reports.[5] Yet it was cocaine and various changes resulting from globalization that supercharged these cartels into the dominant position in the 1990s. They were able to take advantage of the cocaine "flows," their unique position on the US-Mexico border, and the structure of the cocaine supply chain, which had many cultivators in the Andean region and many retail sellers in the domestic market, but a narrow "funnel" position for traffickers.[6]

Understanding Cocaine Supply Chains

The US government has long measured drug markets, in particular cocaine, in terms of price, purity, and availability. It is important to know that cocaine as it travels from the Andean region through Central America, Mexico, and into the United States changes hands many times and at each point can be contaminated and adulterated to increase its volume and reduce its purity. This allows those involved in sales at the street level to increase their profits by mixing in contaminants to increase the volume of their cocaine. Mexican cartels no doubt engage in this process of contamination and adulteration for the purpose of increasing the volume of the cocaine, leading to different wholesale and retail prices as depicted in figure 8.1.[7] But this is more likely to happen within the US wholesale and retail markets.

Figure 8.2 shows cocaine wholesale prices in the United States in US dollars per kilogram. The figure shows both real prices and inflation-adjusted prices. We can see that since 1990 there has been a significant drop in cocaine prices when adjusting for inflation. Without adjusting for inflation over the thirty-year period, we see surprising price stability. We further see incredible price stability over the past twenty years, suggesting that demand and supply have been relatively stable despite extensive interdiction efforts during the period when Mexican cartels dominated cocaine flows. It should be noted that this chart does not include recent massive drops in cocaine prices (2022–2023), which are likely a temporary result of a glut of supply due to many factors that arose in the Andean region. Nor does this chart show the 1980s, which, given the high prices during that decade, would serve to further highlight the massive price drops later.

Mexican Organized Crime and Cocaine

Understanding cocaine in Mexico requires first understanding the OCGs that have been empowered by cocaine trafficking in that country. These OCGs, sometimes referred to as drug cartels and self-proclaiming as such in the case of the Sinaloa cartel and the CJNG, also traffic other drugs, having gotten their start with marijuana and opium for heroin in the nineteenth century. As previous research has shown, the state of Sinaloa, with its fertile agricultural land and mountainous regions, has long been the heart of Mexican drug trafficking.[8] The father of Joaquín "El Chapo" Guzmán Loera, for example, was known as a *gomero* or opium grower.[9] Famous DEA agent Enrique Camarena was killed in 1985 by Mexican drug traffickers in part because of the Buffalo ranch seizure: a massive seizure of vast marijuana fields in 1984 controlled by Caro Quintero of the Guadalajara cartel.[10] Before we can discuss the rise to dominance of Mexican cartels in the cocaine market, we must first explore their antecedents and how they wrested control of the North American cocaine market and increasingly the global market.

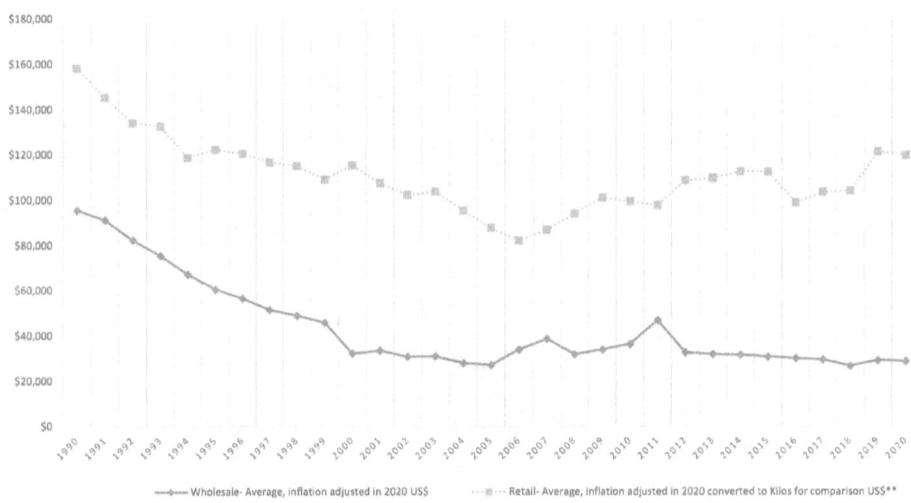

Figure 8.1. US wholesale and retail cocaine prices, 1990–2020. Source: Created by the authors with data from the United Nations Office on Drugs and Crime.

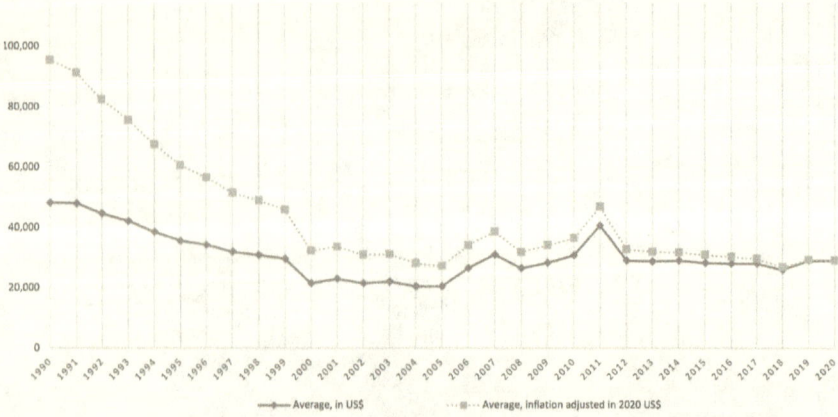

Figure 8.2. Raw and inflation-adjusted US wholesale cocaine prices. Source: Created by the authors with data from the United Nations Office on Drugs and Crime Annual Report Questionnaire. The inflation adjustment is based on historical Bureau of Labor Statistics data.

The Precursors to the Mexican Traffickers: Bolivians, Colombians, and the Andes

The earliest major cocaine producers were not Colombian, but Bolivian. This was in some ways natural, as cocaine has a long, endemic history in the region as a stimulant among Incan soldiers and other traditional uses that continue today.[11]

Roberto Suárez Gómez was the "King of Cocaine" and the grandfather of cocaine trafficking in Bolivia in the 1980s. He was ultimately brought down in a DEA kingpin operation that involved technically sophisticated radio tracking and was most notable for its logistical sophistication and organization.[12]

Early sources of cocaine in the Andean region were Peru, Ecuador, and Bolivia. The Colombians were the most sophisticated traffickers and ultimately moved into the market, bringing increased coca cultivation and processing to Colombia but also organizing it throughout the broader Andean region. Colombian actors then trafficked that refined cocaine to the United States.

Two dominant cartels emerged: the Medellín cartel led by Pablo Escobar and the Cali cartel led by the Rodríguez Orejuela brothers. Both were based in their respective major Colombian cities. On a much larger scale than in the Bolivian case, the US government moved against Escobar in part because of the severe violence he was inflicting on Colombian society, and because of the fact that he was the largest cocaine trafficker in the world. The famous manhunt, chronicled by journalist Mark Bowden in his seminal book *Killing Pablo*, involved a scenario wherein with significant US government pressure and assistance, Colombian forces systematically destroyed Escobar's logistical support apparatus with paramilitary support by vigilantes known as Los Pepes. Colombian law enforcement ultimately put Escobar on the run and killed him with the help of US intelligence.[13]

Upon Escobar's death in 1993, the US government began to exert pressure on the Colombians to shift their attention to the Cali cartel and the Orejuela brothers. The Colombian government was reticent in part because the Cali cartel was not as violent as the Medellín cartel. But the government ultimately acquiesced and by 1995 had effectively dismantled the Cali cartel by working with high-level informants inside the organization to extradite the leadership figures.[14] Mexican cartels at this time had effectively been transporting cocaine on behalf of the Colombians, often for a set fee.

South American Precursors

In the mid- to late 1970s, most drugs were imported to the United States from Latin America and the Caribbean, primarily from Colombia, Mexico, and Jamaica (mainly marijuana). In the early 1980s, the Medellín and Cali cartels in Colombia began producing cocaine. Initially, they focused on producing primarily in Colombia. However, as they found success in marketing their product and as demand increased, they started reaching out to other countries such as Bolivia and Peru to obtain cocaine base, produced from cocaine paste as will be described below.

Cocaine is derived from the coca leaf. While this can be cultivated at lower or higher altitudes, the best altitude for growth is between 1,650 and 4,950 feet, according to DEA reports.[15] Therefore, the coca leaf is primarily cultivated on the slopes of the Andean Ridge, stretching from Colombia to Peru along the western side of South America.[16] The Indigenous peoples of these nations have been cultivating coca for centuries, using it for various purposes, including chewing it for energy and as a cultural tradition.[17] However, the Colombians successfully converted the leaf into cocaine hydrochloride, with steady source of coca plants being provided by growers in Ecuador, Peru, Bolivia, and, of course, Colombia.

When we mention cocaine, we usually refer to cocaine hydrochloride, which is the finished white powder product. However, several steps are required to reach this final product. It starts with the coca leaf, which needs to be cultivated, harvested, and then converted into cocaine paste. The process involves digging trenches and putting about six hundred pounds of leaves in each trench. This amount of leaves yields roughly a kilo of cocaine. Gasoline and other products are used to break down the leaves and extract the alkaloid—the active ingredient—from the leaves into a liquid solution. Substances like cement (or a similar material) are added to absorb the liquid from the solution, resulting in a gooey substance known as cocaine paste. The paste is then cleaned, washed, and filtered to produce cocaine base, which is similar to crack but in this process is produced in larger, wholesale quantities. The base has a dough-like appearance, resembling pizza dough. Imagine a ton of this substance, two thousand pounds, containing roughly one thousand of these base units (a base unit is 1 kilo, or 2.2 pounds).[18]

The Bolivians and Peruvians were not as proficient as the Colombians in converting the base into the final product, cocaine hydrochloride. While some conversion took place in Bolivia and Peru, most cocaine remained in the base form. To facilitate the conversion, the Colombians developed what was known as an "airbridge." Single- or twin-engine private aircraft would fly back and forth between the jungles of Bolivia and Peru and the jungles of Colombia, delivering cocaine base. Colombian laboratories, which grew larger and became megalabs, would then convert the base into cocaine hydrochloride, often producing large quantities of the drug weekly. This streamlined process allowed cocaine to go from the coca-leaf farms all the way to the streets of New York following a linear market model known as the "source to the street" model. Following this model, Colombians procured the base from Bolivia and Peru, converted it to hydrochloride in Colombia, transferred it to Mexico (or the Caribbean, in the early 1980s), and then smuggled it into the United States. From there, they would distribute the drug to various cities such as Atlanta, New York, Chicago, and Detroit, using their own contacts to sell the product on the streets.

In the 1990s, the US Department of Justice and other government agencies successfully targeted the cartels' money-laundering operations, seizing assets and properties. This forced the Colombians to divest themselves of operations outside of Colombia. At the same time, increased pressure on Caribbean trafficking routes by the US government also led to changes in trafficking routes, an example of the balloon effect analogy (see below). Consequently, the Mexicans took over the transportation and distribution aspects of the drug trade. They arranged transportation through the transit zone, moving the drug from Colombia to Panama to northern Mexico by various means, including boats and planes. With control of illicit flows across the US-Mexico border, the Mexicans then distributed the drug on the streets of the United States, and they have continued using this model to the present day.[19]

However, as discussed above, the Medellín and Cali cartels began expanding their operations to obtain cocaine base from Bolivia and Peru. This shift occurred around the mid-1980s, and the DEA identified the highly efficient airbridge facilitating the cartels' activities.

The DEA in Bolivia determined that the airbridge of the cocaine supply chain was composed of two legs: one was internal to Bolivia, from the Chapare region to Beni Department, the country's Amazon region. The Chapare is the area where Bolivian coca leaf is cultivated, on the eastern slopes of the Bolivian Andes. Coca would then be turned into paste or base, which would then be flown from the Chapare to Beni Department. On this first leg of the airbridge, small aircraft would take the paste or the base to laboratories in Beni. There, this would be converted into hydrochloride. The product was then flown to Colombia on the second leg of the airbridge. Traffickers in Colombia would purify it, clean it, and synthesize it even more to provide a higher yield in terms of purity. DEA agents in Bolivia, for their part, initiated Operation Screaming Eagle to target and dismantle the airbridge operating internally in Bolivia, and within a year the Bolivian government had seized three to four hundred single-engine aircraft. Many had been stolen from neighboring countries, flown to Bolivia, and had their registrations or tail numbers painted over.[20]

During Operation Screaming Eagle, the DEA provided technical equipment to the Bolivian police, who vacuumed suspect aircraft to look for cocaine crystals trapped in the vacuum filters. If such crystals were found, this gave Bolivian police the probable cause needed to seize the airplane, because under the Napoleonic Code of law, Bolivian officers could arrest someone or seize something and hold them for an undetermined amount of time while further evidence was gathered. The difference here is that in the Bolivian jurisdiction, if any cocaine crystals are found, the aircraft is automatically forfeited to the Bolivian government without further proceedings.[21]

In 1989, the DEA conducted Operation Tandem, which was the biggest binational counterdrug operation at the time; it involved moving some three hundred people, including Bolivian police officers from the Unidad Móvil de Patrullaje Rural (UMOPAR; Mobile Rural Patrol Unit). The operation employed three C-130 transport aircraft, ten helicopters, and two DEA airplanes to move the officers into the jungle to raid a village called San Ramón, which was being used as a staging area for the airbridge.[22]

The Early Economics of Cocaine

During that time, the DEA collected intelligence on the prices of coca leaves, cocaine paste, base, and hydrochloride as well as on the price of cocaine, including wholesale prices at the laboratories and prices in the transit zone and in Mexico, Texas, and most big cities in the US market such as Atlanta, Chicago, Houston, and New York. For instance, at the wholesale level, if traffickers purchased a ton of cocaine hydrochloride at a laboratory, the price would be around US$2,000 per kilo. However, once the Colombians had stepped back from the market and the Mexicans took over, they would go to Colombia to purchase cocaine directly from the laboratories.[23] In those cases, Mexican traffickers might purchase significant quantities like five or ten tons per month and then incur transportation costs to get it to Mexico, across the border, and on to New York and other major US cities. Factoring in those additional costs, a kilo that cost approximately US$2,000 at the source might be sold for $30,000 wholesale in New York, generating a significant profit margin (see figure 8.2).

At the retail level, the dynamics were different. A kilo of cocaine, which is about 2.2 pounds in weight, would be broken down into individual dosage units, resembling clear sugar packets but filled with cocaine. Each of these packets, thousands of which could be obtained from a single kilo, would be sold individually on the street. The profit margin became exceptional, considering the original purchase price of US$2,000 per kilo of hydrochloride and the price of US$30,000 per kilo at the wholesale level. Sales prices were even higher if made outside of an established distribution chain, for example to other US distributors such as Jamaicans, Italians, or the US-based Italian Mafia, known to the FBI as traditional organized crime. This situation led to exceptional profits in the cocaine supply chain in the 1980s and 1990s.

Cash to Cocaine

In 1989, the US government seized 21.5 tons of cocaine at a warehouse in southern California. The "Sylmar seizure" (after the suburban Los Angeles neighborhood where the raid occurred) was the result of a dispute between Mexican traffickers who had transported the cocaine for Colombian traffickers. The Mexicans held the cocaine in the warehouse and continued to deliver more to that location but refused to release it. This led to a massive seizure, and it changed the way Colombians compensated their Mexican counterparts.[24] Thus, in the 1990s, Mexican traffickers such as Osiel Cárdenas Guillén of the Gulf cartel and others began to renegotiate their relationship with the Colombian traffickers, and with the cocaine markets themselves. They did this by demanding that they be paid in cocaine, not in cash. They would keep 50 percent of every load of cocaine they transported into the United States on behalf of the Colombians.[25] The Mexicans' success in this renegotiation may have been prompted by the implied threat that they would simply buy from Bolivian, Peruvian, and other sources.[26]

The new arrangement allowed Mexican traffickers to enter the domestic US wholesale and retail cocaine markets. This increased potential profits, but also potential exposure to US law enforcement. It also fundamentally renegotiated the relationship between Mexican and Colombian traffickers. This marked the moment when Mexican traffickers began to increase their power both in Mexico, as they were supercharged by cocaine profits, and throughout the world.[27]

The US Drug War and Mexican Cocaine Flows

The following section will describe the US drug war as it relates to cocaine flow through Mexico. Numerous factors led to Mexican groups becoming some of the world's preeminent drug-trafficking organizations in the 1990s. First and foremost, Mexico shares a border with the world's largest drug consumer market and one of the world's largest economies, the United States. Second, increased pressure on Caribbean routes by the US government and the drug war would push greater drug flow through Mexico.[28] Third, in the 1990s, free trade agreements like the

North American Free Trade Agreement (NAFTA), which will be described below, increased opportunities for Mexican drug-trafficking organizations to move product into the United States and beyond.[29]

In the 1980s, a new variant of cocaine known as "crack" emerged. During that decade, the majority of cocaine flowed from the Andean region along Caribbean routes through countries like the Dominican Republic, and into Florida and the US Gulf Coast. The Ronald Reagan administration and that of his successor, George H. W. Bush, applied incredible pressure on the Caribbean trafficking zone by utilizing US naval and Coast Guard assets via the US Southern Command. In a quintessential example of the balloon effect analogy, the pressure on the Caribbean zone simply caused the balloon to bulge into Mexico.[30] This was ultimately a boon to Mexican traffickers, who took an increasingly dominant role in the cocaine market.

A couple of trends are worth noting here. First, the United States, Mexico, and Canada negotiated and in 1994 implemented a major free trade agreement, NAFTA. This trade agreement greatly increased trade between the three countries. While NAFTA has been replaced by another, updated, yet similar free trade agreement (the United States–Mexico–Canada Agreement, or USMCA), in the first quarter of 2023 it led Mexico into becoming the United States' top trading partner. But the increased trade in the 1990s allowed traffickers to hide greater amounts of drugs, including cocaine, within legal trade flows (thousands of cars and trucks crossing the land border each day).[31]

Second, cocaine profits supercharged Mexican organized crime in the 1990s. It was during this period that Mexican traffickers began taking payment from their Colombian counterparts—weakened by the fall of the Medellín and Cali cartels—in cocaine instead of cash. This led to Mexican OCGs entering the US wholesale and retail drug markets. They increasingly had more direct involvement in drug distribution in the United States, though they maintained a lower profile than they did in Mexico.[32]

In Mexico, traffickers were able to corrupt government officials through a strategy of *plata o plomo* (take my silver or take my lead).[33] There were incredibly high levels of corruption in Mexico, infiltrating even the Mexican drug czar General Jesús Héctor Gutiérrez Rebollo, who was found to be on the payroll of the Juárez cartel in the 1990s, a major embarrassment for both the United States and Mexico.[34]

Mexico was also going through a democratic transition at this time. Opposition parties had won state elections in Baja California in the late 1980s and 1990s, breaking the monopoly of power held by the Partido Revolucionario Institucional (PRI; Institutional Revolutionary Party) for more than seventy years. This was a process that progressed throughout the 1990s and culminated in the election of Vicente Fox, of the conservative Partido Acción Nacional (PAN; National Action Party), as president in 2000. This democratic transition meant that there was a decentralization of power, and, as scholars have demonstrated, without long-term horizons, politicians could no longer make credible promises to drug traffickers who could buy them off.[35] In short, the corrupt PRI regime had kept a lid on violence by negotiating with and controlling traffickers. The end of the PRI regime prompted drug traffickers to buy their own protection and build their own paramilitary apparatuses.[36] It also meant, as Guillermo Trejo and Sandra Ley point out, that these criminal actors now engaged in significant violence against local mayors to create subnational opportunities for criminal governance.[37] They further argue that cartels have taken on political ambitions.[38] This new violence and political ambition was aided by loose gun laws in the United States, which allowed and continue to allow Mexican criminal organizations to arm themselves and build their own security forces outside the purview of the state.[39]

The Militarization of the Drug War

While Mexican homicides had been declining in the 1990s and early 2000s, the election of a new president in 2006, Felipe Calderón, also of the PAN, marked a dramatic shift in the Mexican view of the drug war. President Calderón effectively declared war on organized crime in Mexico and used the military to target it.[40]

While the military had been used to target organized crime in the drug war in Mexico before, what Calderón did was a dramatic break in that it was on a much larger scale. The effects of this have been intensively debated. What is not debatable is that 2007 saw a dramatic increase in violence in the drug war in Mexico. Many blamed Calderón for this, but his administration pointed out that violence had been starting to tick up before they came into office, and that the more-trusted and better-trained military was the only standing force in Mexico capable of confronting large OCGs.[41] Unfortunately for Mexico, law enforcement was simply too corrupt and infiltrated, and Calderón's *sexenio* or six-year term (2006–2012) ended with one hundred thousand deaths in the drug war.[42]

At a meeting in Mérida, Yucatan, with US president George W. Bush, President Calderón proposed what would become the Mérida Initiative.[43] This program, inaugurated in 2007, would be a major partnership between the United States and Mexico that would provide the latter with training and equipment to combat organized crime. Additionally, the United States promised to do something about the flow of chemical precursors and guns into Mexico. In its initial days, the Mérida Initiative was focused on military equipment, but that shifted to increased capacity building as the years moved on. During the Calderón administration, there were high levels of cooperation between US and Mexican security forces. In historical hindsight, the head of the federal police at that time, who also later occupied a cabinet-level security position, Genaro García Luna, was on the payroll of the Sinaloa cartel.[44] He was put on trial in early 2023 and convicted in a Brooklyn, New York, courtroom, and later sentenced to thirty-eight years in prison.[45]

How Does Cocaine Flow Through Mexico?

Mexican cartels utilize three dominant conveyance mechanisms for moving cocaine from the Andean region, often through Mexico, and into the United States; these include air, land, and maritime routes. In the 2000s, Mexican cartels often flew small planes from the Andean region to landing strips in Central America, then used land routes north to the US-Mexico border. Today, Honduras is a major hotspot for such flights. They also used maritime routes from the Andean region toward Central America or Mexico. Most narcotics headed for Europe, including cocaine flowing through the Caribbean, was sent via maritime routes; countries such as the Netherlands, with its strong maritime transportation critical infrastructure, became major transshipment points for cocaine flowing into Europe.[46]

Figure 8.3, based on US Coast Guard data from 2013, demonstrates that the primary flow of cocaine from the Andean region into the United States—the world's largest drug market—was via land routes through Mexico. Caribbean aerial and maritime routes were the primary conveyance methods for entering the European market. As Mexican drug cartels became more dominant in the

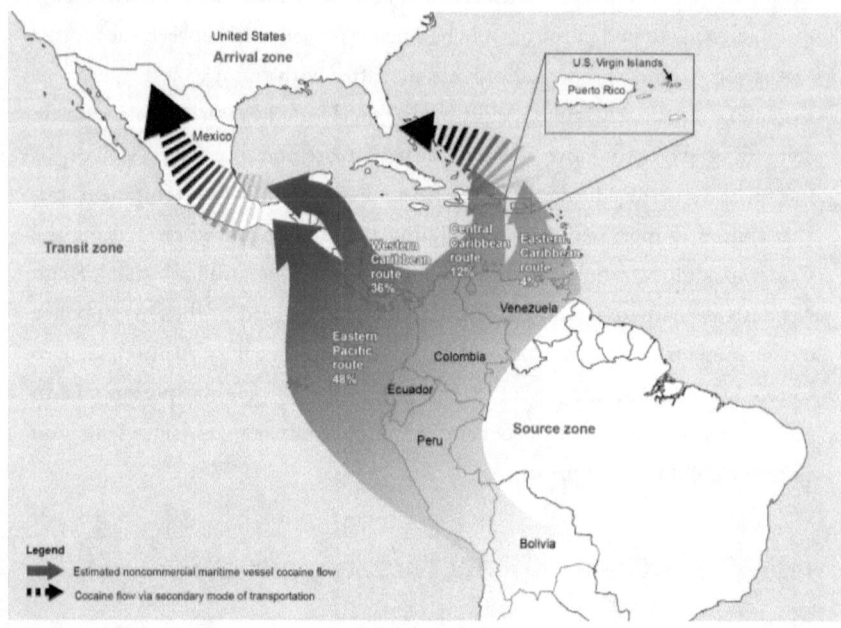

Figure 8.3. The source, transit, and arrival zones and the percentage of estimated noncommercial maritime vessel flows of cocaine in fiscal year 2013, by smuggling route. Source: public domain. Reproduced from "Coast Guard: Resources Provided for Drug Interdiction Operations in the Transit Zone, Puerto Rico, and the U.S. Virgin Islands," Government Accountability Office, Washington, DC, GAO-14-527, June 16, 2014, https://www.gao.gov/products/gao-14-527.

1990s and the US government put pressure on land and aerial routes in Central America and Mexico following the Mérida Initiative, Mexican cartels worked with Caribbean criminal partners to move the product directly into Europe and the United States through weak countries like the Dominican Republic (2010s).[47] This is another example of the balloon effect, by which cocaine supply chains respond to government pressure. Unintentionally, this pressure pushed flows back to their 1980s routes.

In the 1990s, Amado Carrillo Fuentes, the head of the Juárez cartel, became famous for arranging flights of large aircraft loaded with cocaine. In some cases, these traveled all the way from the Andean region directly into Mexico; the cocaine would then be hidden in vehicular compartments and trafficked via land borders directly through ports of entry into the United States. These large 737s with the seats ripped out to make space for more cocaine, and often on one-way trips given the high profits, earned Carrillo Fuentes the nickname Señor de los Cielos or Lord of the Skies.[48]

Kingpin Strategy

The "kingpin strategy," targeting high-value leadership figures of the Mexican cartels, began under President Felipe Calderón. These kingpin arrests led to media "perp walks," which the government claimed was a demonstration of success in the drug war. But over the years, it became clear to many academics and the public that the "hydra effect" was at play.[49] The kingpin strategy, or "cutting off the head of the snake," was only leading to more heads of snakes emerging. With more cartels, there was more bloodshed in Mexico. Today in Mexico we see many organized crime groups at all levels, be they designated as cartels, mafias, *bandas criminales*, or *pandillas* (local street gangs). This new ecosystem of organized crime is far more difficult to control without strong state institutions with great resilience, because while these criminal groups are smaller, they are able to network with each other in alliances, as documented by recent scholarship showing hundreds of organized crime groups in Mexico.[50] These new, smaller, and more violent groups diversified their criminal portfolios into predatory and novel crimes like oil theft (*huachicol*) and water theft (*aguachicol*).[51]

A Bipolar Networked Structure: The Sinaloa Cartel and the CJNG

Today in Mexico we see a generally bipolar structure, with the two dominant cartels being the CJNG and the Sinaloa cartel.[52] These OCGs are worthy of note, given that they are the most transnationalized of the organized crime groups operating in Mexico.[53] According to recent DEA statements, the Jalisco and Sinaloa cartels have operations in all fifty US states and one hundred countries around the world.[54] Recent academic work by scholars Rafael Prieto-Curiel, Gian Maria Campedelli, and Alejandro Hope has suggested that Mexican cartels as a whole are the fifth-largest employer in Mexico.[55] The next section will give a brief history of the Sinaloa cartel and the CJNG, the two largest organized crime groups in Mexico.

The Sinaloa Cartel

The Sinaloa cartel as we know it today is best thought of as a federation of traffickers, as previous scholars have pointed out.[56] It traces its roots back to the Guadalajara cartel led by Miguel Ángel Félix Gallardo, better known as "El Padrino" or "the Godfather."[57] Traffickers like Chapo Guzmán worked under El Padrino. After the 1985 killing of Enrique Camarena, an American DEA agent, the US and Mexican governments put incredible pressure on the Guadalajara cartel and dismantled it. As the cartels split, they came into conflict. Chapo Guzmán was arrested in Guatemala after the Tijuana cartel attempted to kill him in 1993 at Guadalajara International Airport but instead killed the archbishop of Guadalajara.[58]

From behind bars, Chapo Guzmán built an empire that would later become the Sinaloa cartel. He was famous for the rapid delivery of cocaine shipments from Colombia to the United States. His cartel specialized in corrupting Mexico's federal police, as described by the intrepid reporter Anabel Hernández. In 2001, Guzmán escaped from prison and built the modern Sinaloa cartel.[59]

Authorities arrested Guzmán in 2014, only for him to escape again in 2015. Guzmán was never alone in building his drug empire. He worked with fellow traffickers like Ismael "El Mayo" Zambada, who had never previously spent a day in jail; the Beltrán Leyva brothers; his brother "El Guano"; and, in later years, his sons, known collectively as "Los Chapitos."[60] Since his 2016 recapture followed by his 2017 extradition and subsequent conviction in a US court, Guzmán's sons have become an increasingly important faction within the Sinaloa cartel.

In October 2019, the Mexican government attempted to arrest one of Chapo's sons, Ovidio Guzmán.[61] The Sinaloa cartel, led by the Chapitos, responded viciously and violently with an urban siege.[62] They released prisoners from a correctional facility to sow chaos, used .50 caliber sniper rifles and .50 caliber machine guns mounted on the backs of trucks, burned vehicles at strategic chokepoints, and went to military barracks to threaten the families of soldiers. Ultimately, the Mexican government decided to release Ovidio Guzmán to stop the bloodshed. This became a major embarrassment for the Mexican government and proved that the Chapitos were now willing to directly confront the state.[63] The old-school Sinaloa cartel had been known for corrupting the state. Indeed, the former head of the federal police in the era when Chapo Guzmán was most powerful was convicted in February 2023 of being on the Sinaloa cartel's payroll in the 2000s and early 2010s.[64] The US put pressure on the Mexican government because the sons of Chapo Guzmán were pioneers of the fentanyl trade, which was killing seventy thousand Americans per year as of 2022.[65] The Sinaloa cartel was acting like another violent cartel, the CJNG.

Cártel de Jalisco Nueva Generación

The CJNG has its roots in the Sinaloa cartel and an earlier iteration, the Milenio cartel (1990s), based in the Jalisco region and including surrounding states such as Michoacán. In 2010, Mexican authorities killed a Sinaloa cartel lieutenant, Nacho Coronel, who had controlled the remnants of the Milenio cartel as a subsidiary. The traffickers who had worked for him fell into a civil war. The winning faction would become known as the Cártel de Jalisco Nueva Generación. Nemesio Rubén Oseguera Cervantes, better known as "El Mencho," led the CJNG. El Mencho's wife, Rosalinda González Valencia, is of the Valencia family, who had been key leaders of the old Milenio cartel. Rosalinda was known for her money-laundering capacity, and El Mencho was known for his ruthlessness and street smarts.[66] Together they built an empire that would focus on synthetic drugs like fentanyl and methamphetamines, rapidly expanding across the country during the 2010s. The CJNG took advantage of the fragmentation of other cartels like the violent Zetas, which had been splintered by Mexican government kingpin strikes supported by the United States. As Héctor de Mauleón points out, the CJNG was particularly good at adopting orphan cells that had been isolated as larger groups were decapitated.[67]

The CJNG developed a reputation for incredible violence and paramilitarization, like the Zetas before them.[68] In 2015, they made their presence known by downing a Mexican military helicopter in a direct confrontation with the state and ambushing dozens of state and federal police officers.[69]

The CJNG fought brutally for control of ports so that they could import chemical precursors for synthetic drugs like fentanyl and methamphetamines and no doubt also plant-based drugs such as cocaine.[70] It is important to note that fentanyl is often cut into cocaine, increasing cocaine's likelihood of leading to overdoses. This will be discussed in greater detail below.

In 2021, the US Office of Foreign Assets Control (OFAC) sanctioned members of the CJNG. These economic sanctions make it so that targeted entities cannot do business with entities in the United States. In the sanctions press release, the Treasury Department, which oversees the OFAC, described how the port of Manzanillo, a major port in Colima State, Mexico, was critical to the CJNG's strategy of controlling ports for the purpose of importing increased amounts of synthetic chemicals from Asia for the manufacture of synthetic drugs, in addition to importing cocaine from Colombia.[71] Indeed, port cities like Manzanillo and Lázaro Cárdenas have become hotly contested cartel battlegrounds as the Sinaloa cartel and the CJNG battle each other directly and through allies. Both these cartels have taken on greater international roles, establishing relationships with local criminal groups in other countries and establishing direct presence in places like Colombia to enter the cocaine supply chain and even earlier stages including processing and production.[72]

Mexico: A Transit Nation?

Mexico is thought of as a transit country for cocaine. But there has been increased domestic drug consumption within Mexico. Further and of particular interest here, there has also been domestic cocaine production. These are typically isolated cultivation operations in southern states such as Chiapas and Guerrero.[73] They do not represent a significant portion of the overall cocaine market but do demonstrate the adaptive role of Mexican trafficking networks.

Recent Mexican Cocaine Prices

While cocaine prices have generally been fairly stable since around 2000, there have been more recent surges and drops in price in Mexico. According to Mark Wilson of InSight Crime, 2022 saw an increase in cocaine seizures in Mexico; Wilson argues that this may have been due to the use of the navy at ports, as the US government has pressured Mexico for more drug controls to stop fentanyl flows into the United States.[74] More recent reporting from 2023 demonstrates a dramatic drop in Mexican cocaine prices in border cities in the northeastern part of the country.[75] Many have pointed to a glut of supply in the Andean region, leading to food insecurity for Andean farmers dependent on the crop.[76] There are many potential theses for why there has been a sudden global drop in the price of cocaine. Some have speculated on the role of the rising synthetic drug market cutting into the cocaine market.

Cocaine: Cutting In the Fentanyl

There are an increasing number of examples of cocaine in the US market contaminated with fentanyl.[77] Many academics have speculated that this might result in a shift in cocaine markets away from cocaine, a stimulant, and toward the much more dangerous fentanyl (a painkiller and depressant). Some, as well as some DEA agents, have speculated that this shift is a ploy by drug traffickers or dealers to make the product more addictive or to change the nature of the market toward the cheaper and easier to obtain fentanyl.[78] We are agnostic on these arguments but only wish to introduce them here. It should be noted that the overdose rates of synthetic fentanyl are incredibly high in the United States, which now sees seventy to eighty thousand overdose deaths per year attributed exclusively to fentanyl.

In figure 8.4, we see that cocaine overdose deaths have been stable since 1999. However, we can also see that overdose deaths from cocaine cut with fentanyl are now more than double the overdose deaths from cocaine alone. We can also see that the driver of total overdose deaths in the United States is fentanyl alone. For this reason, some Republican congresspeople have proposed using US special forces inside of Mexican sovereign territory to target fentanyl labs. This proposition is problematic given the decentralized nature of fentanyl production in Mexico and the fact that it would destroy all bilateral cooperation on other security issues important to the United States such as immigration, border enforcement, and the broader fight against organized crime. It is important to recognize that legislators making such proposals are political entrepreneurs responding to the demands of their constituents, who for their part are appalled by the genuinely high number of overdose deaths stemming from a drug that has become the most dangerous on the market.

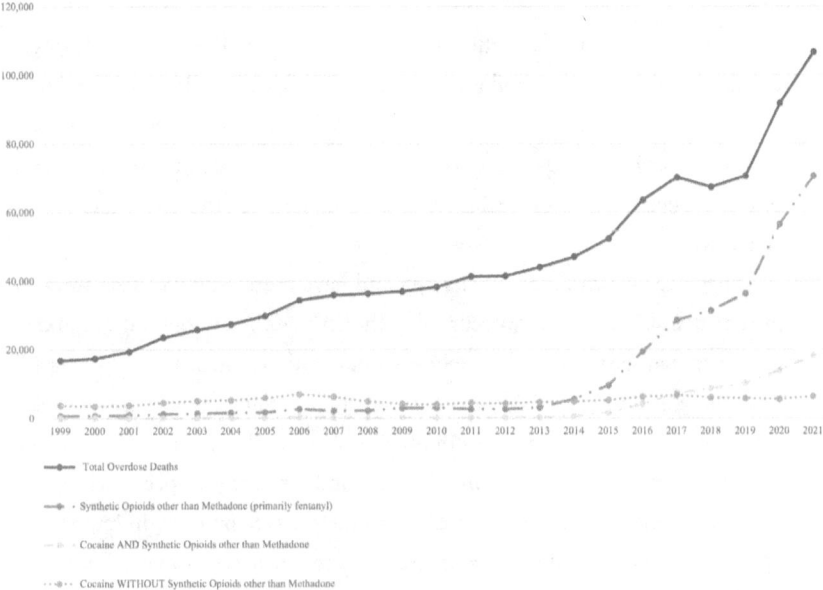

Figure 8.4. US overdose deaths by drug type. Source: Created by authors with data from the Centers for Disease Control and Prevention, National Center on Health Statistics, CDC Wonder.

Conclusion

Cocaine played a major role in the rise of what are popularly known as Mexican drug cartels, or large, organized crime groups. Today, the Sinaloa cartel and the Cártel de Jalisco Nueva Generación are widely considered preeminent global transnational criminal organizations with operations in more than one hundred countries, much of it involving cocaine.[79] But what is the future of cocaine flow through Mexico?

Mexican cartels and global drug demand have increasingly shifted toward synthetic drugs. This initially occurred with methamphetamines but has taken on a more potent position in the public discourse with fentanyl. The public alarm over fentanyl is understandable given its deadly consequences and the fact that synthetic opiates are so dangerous in causing accidental overdoses, which have increased dramatically in the United States and are likely to occur wherever fentanyl has penetrated the market. Mexican cartels were pioneers in importing fentanyl and the chemical precursors necessary to synthesize it from China and India.[80] Recent indictments show that the Chapitos faction of the Sinaloa cartel (the sons of Chapo Guzmán) had moved into fentanyl by 2014. That is not to say that plant-based drugs will not continue to have significant markets. These plant-based drugs include cocaine derived from coca leaf, heroin derived from opium poppies, and marijuana derived from the cannabis leaf. Mexican cartels have been highly diversified, and one indication of this is the fact that there are polydrug and polychrome organizations. As if to recognize that cocaine will continue to play a major role in drug markets, since 2016 both the Sinaloa cartel and the CJNG have increased their presence in Colombia and elsewhere in South America.[81] This suggests that the preeminent Mexican OCGs, with their diversified criminal portfolios, will continue to traffic cocaine, a drug that helped them achieve a preeminent status in world drug markets and the global criminal underworld.

Acknowledgments

The authors would like to thank research assistant Christian Pamfile of Sam Houston State University for research and assistance with transcription. The authors would also like to thank editors Jonathan D. Rosen and Sebastián A. Cutrona for their comments and edits.

Notes

1. Adam Isacson, "Crisis and Opportunity: Unraveling Colombia's Collapsing Coca Markets," Washington Office on Latin America, August 24, 2023, https://www.wola.org/analysis/crisis-opportunity-unraveling-colombias-collapsing-coca-markets/; Joshua Collins, "Plunging Coca Prices Create 'Humanitarian Emergency' in Colombia," *Al Jazeera*, March 31, 2023, https://www.aljazeera.com/news/2023/3/31/plunging-coca-prices-create-humanitarian-emergency-in-colombia; and Luke Taylor, "Fentanyl, Cartels or Simple Market Glut: What's Behind Collapse of Colombia's Coca Market?," *Guardian*, September 13, 2023, https://www.theguardian.com/world/2023/sep/13/colombian-coca-market-collapsed-cocaine-precursor.

2. George W. Grayson, *The Cartels: The Story of Mexico's Most Dangerous Criminal Organizations and Their Impact on U.S. Security* (Santa Barbara, CA: Praeger, 2014); and George W. Grayson, *Mexico: Narco-Violence and a Failed State?* (New Brunswick, NJ: Transaction Publishers, 2009).

3. The term "cartel" is hotly debated and often derided by scholars. Many scholars dislike the term because, in a strictly economic definition, cartels are suppliers with sufficient market control to manipulate price. With rare exception, Mexican cartels have not been able to do that. There has been recent scholarship on the origin of the term "cartel." However, we often use the term here because it is a proper noun in the sense that many of the Mexican cartels self-identify as such; e.g., the Sinaloa cartel, the Gulf cartel, and the Cártel de Jalisco Nueva Generación. We will also use the terms "transnational criminal organizations" (TCOs) and "organized crime groups" (OCGs) in part to depict their international linkages and their diversified income streams. For more on this subject, see the following sources: Marc Lacey, "Drug Wars: When a 'Cartel' Really Isn't," *New York Times*, September 21, 2009, http://economix.blogs.nytimes.com/2009/09/21/drug-wars-when-a-cartel-really-isnt/?scp=1&sq=merida%20initiative&st=cseID-526; Tom

Wainwright, *Narconomics: How to Run a Drug Cartel* (New York: PublicAffairs, 2016); and Michael Kenney, *From Pablo to Osama: Trafficking and Terrorist Networks, Government Bureaucracies, and Competitive Adaptation* (University Park: Pennsylvania State University Press, 2007).

4. United Nations Office on Drugs and Crime, *Global Cocaine Report 2023: Local Dynamics, Global Challenges* (Vienna: United Nations, 2023), https://www.unodc.org/documents/data-and-analysis/cocaine/Global_cocaine_report_2023.pdf.

5. US Drug Enforcement Administration, "2017 National Drug Threat Assessment," October 2017, https://www.dea.gov/sites/default/files/2018-07/DIR-040-17_2017-NDTA.pdf.

6. Willem van Schendel and Itty Abraham, eds., *Illicit Flows and Criminal Things: States, Borders, and the Other Side of Globalization* (Bloomington: Indiana University Press, 2005); and Patricia A. Adler, *Wheeling and Dealing: An Ethnography of an Upper-Level Drug Dealing and Smuggling Community* (New York: Columbia University Press, 1993).

7. Juan Diego Posada and Yago Rosado, "5 Takeaways from UN Global Report on Cocaine 2023," InSight Crime, March 17, 2023, https://insightcrime.org/news/5-takeaways-from-un-global-report-on-cocaine-2023/.

8. Anabel Hernández, *Narcoland: The Mexican Drug Lords and Their Godfathers*, trans. Iain Bruce (London: Verso, 2013); Luis Astorga, *El siglo de las drogas: El narcotráfico, del Porfiriato al nuevo milenio* (Mexico City: Plaza y Janés, 2005); and Luis Astorga and David A. Shirk, "Drug Trafficking Organizations and Counter-Drug Strategies in the U.S.-Mexican Context," Center for U.S.-Mexican Studies, University of California San Diego, 2010, https://escholarship.org/uc/item/8j647429.

9. Malcolm Beith, *The Last Narco: Inside the Hunt for El Chapo, the World's Most Wanted Drug Lord* (New York: Grove Press, 2010).

10. James H. Creechan, *Drug Wars and Covert Netherworlds: The Transformations of Mexico's Narco Cartels* (Tucson: University of Arizona Press, 2021), 48.

11. Peter Andreas, *Killer High: A History of War in Six Drugs* (New York: Oxford University Press, 2019).

12. Paul Flahive, "Catching 'The King of Cocaine' with Gary Hale," Texas Public Radio, September 9, 2016, http://tpr.org/post/catching-king-cocaine-gary-hale.

13. Mark Bowden, *Killing Pablo: The Hunt for the World's Greatest Outlaw* (New York: Atlantic Monthly Press, 2001).

14. William C. Rempel, *At the Devil's Table: The Untold Story of the Insider Who Brought Down the Cali Cartel* (New York: Random House, 2011).

15. "Coca Cultivation and Cocaine Processing: An Overview," US Drug Enforcement Administration, Office of Intelligence, Strategic Intelligence Section, Latin America Unit, February 1991, https://www.ojp.gov/pdffiles1/Digitization/132907NCJRS.pdf.

16. "Coca Cultivation and Cocaine Processing."

17. Andreas, *Killer High*.

18. "Coca," Drug Enforcement Administration Museum, 2021, https://museum.dea.gov/exhibits/online-exhibits/cannabis-coca-and-poppy-natures-addictive-plants/coca.

19. Douglas Farah and Molly Moore, "Mexican Drug Traffickers Eclipse Colombian Cartels," *Washington Post*, March 29, 1997, https://www.washingtonpost.com/archive/politics/1997/03/30/mexican-drug-traffickers-eclipse-colombian-cartels/021e4b6d-b949-4e49-9ce1-0cfa1741558b/.

20. M. G. Angulo, "Texas House District 28 Candidate Gary J. Hale: Soldier, Statesman and Scholar," *Absolutely! Katy Community Magazine*, October 1, 2019, http://absolutelykaty.com/texas-house-district-28-candidate-gary-j-hale-soldier-statesman-and-scholar/.

21. In US jurisdiction, there are two steps. The first is a seizure, and then there is a forfeiture, proceeding to determine if the government keeps the property or returns it to its owner even if cocaine has been found in the aircraft based on a search warrant. Gary Hale, "Gary J. Hale: U.S.-Mexico National Security and Intelligence Policy Expert," Voir Dire International, April 2019, https://voirdireinternational.com/wp-content/uploads/2020/07/GHale-Mexico-SME-12APR19.pdf.

22. James Painter, *Bolivia and Coca: A Study in Dependency* (Boulder, CO: Lynne Rienner, 1994), p.32.

23. Farah and Moore, "Mexican Drug Traffickers Eclipse Colombian Cartels."

24. US Drug Enforcement Administration, "History (1985–1990)," 65, https://www.dea.gov/sites/default/files/2021-04/1985-1990_p_58-67.pdf.

25. Andreas, *Killer High*, chap. 6.

26. Farah and Moore, "Mexican Drug Traffickers Eclipse Colombian Cartels."

27. Paul Gootenberg, "Cocaine's Blowback North: A Pre-History of Mexican Drug Violence," *LASA Forum* 42, no. 2 (Spring 2011): 9.

28. Bruce Michael Bagley, "Drug Trafficking and Organized Crime in the Americas: Major Trends in the Twenty-First Century," Woodrow Wilson International Center for Scholars, Latin American Program, August 2012, https://www.wilsoncenter.org/sites/default/files/media/documents/publication/BB%20Final.pdf.

29. Peter Andreas, *Border Games: Policing the U.S.-Mexico Divide*, 2nd ed. (Ithaca, NY: Cornell University Press, 2009).

30. Tony Payan, *The Three U.S.-Mexico Border Wars: Drugs, Immigration, and Homeland Security*, 2nd ed. (Santa Barbara, CA: Praeger Security International, 2016), 32.

31. Peter Andreas, *Border Games: The Politics of Policing the U.S.-Mexico Divide*, 3rd ed. (Ithaca, NY: Cornell University Press, 2022); and Andreas, *Border Games*, 2nd ed. (2009).

32. US Drug Enforcement Administration, "2017 National Drug Threat Assessment."

33. William Finnegan, "Silver or Lead," *New Yorker*, May 24, 2010, http://www.newyorker.com/reporting/2010/05/31/100531fa_fact_finnegan.

34. Tracy Wilkinson, "Jose de Jesus Gutierrez Rebollo Dies at 79; Disgraced Mexican General," *Los Angeles Times*, December 20, 2013, http://articles.latimes.com/2013/dec/20/local/la-me-jose-gutierrez-rebollo-20131221.

35. Richard Snyder and Angélica Durán-Martínez, "Does Illegality Breed Violence? Drug Trafficking and State-Sponsored Protection Rackets," *Crime, Law and Social Change* 52, no. 3 (September 2009): 253–73; Angélica Durán-Martínez, *The Politics of Drug Violence: Criminals, Cops, and Politicians in Colombia and Mexico* (New York: Oxford University Press, 2018); and Nathan P. Jones, "Transnational Crime," in *Contemporary Security Studies*, ed. Alan Collins, 6th ed. (Oxford: Oxford University Press, 2022), 404–21.

36. Guadalupe Correa-Cabrera, "Violence on the 'Forgotten' Border: Mexico's Drug War, the State, and the Paramilitarization of Organized Crime in Tamaulipas in a 'New Democratic Era,'" *Journal of Borderlands Studies* 29, no. 4 (2014): 419–33; and Guadalupe Correa-Cabrera, *Los Zetas Inc.: Criminal Corporations, Energy, and Civil War in Mexico* (Austin: University of Texas Press, 2017).

37. Guillermo Trejo and Sandra Ley, *Votes, Drugs, and Violence: The Political Logic of Criminal Wars in Mexico* (Cambridge: Cambridge University Press, 2020), 250.

38. Guillermo Trejo and Sandra Ley, "High-Profile Criminal Violence: Why Drug Cartels Murder Government Officials and Party Candidates in Mexico," *British Journal of Political Science* 51, no. 1 (January 2021): 203–29; and Trejo and Ley, *Votes, Drugs, and Violence*, 250.

39. Nathan P. Jones, "El flujo ilegal de armas de Estados Unidos a México," *Foreign Affairs Latinoamérica* 23, no. 2 (April 2023), https://revistafal.com/fal-23-2/; Nathan P. Jones, "Appendix A: Goat Horns, Blackbirds, and Cop Killers; U.S. Guns in Mexico's Drug Violence," in *Cooperative Mexican-U.S. Antinarcotics Efforts*, by Sidney Weintraub and Duncan Wood (Washington, DC: Center for Strategic and International Studies, November 2010), 52–73; and Jessica Farb, "Firearms Trafficking: U.S. Efforts to Combat Firearms Trafficking to Mexico Have Improved, but Some Collaboration Challenges Remain," US Government Accountability Office, January 2016, https://www.gao.gov/products/gao-16-223.

40. Grayson, *Mexico: Narco-Violence and a Failed State?*; and Nathan P. Jones, *Mexico's Illicit Drug Networks and the State Reaction* (Washington, DC: Georgetown University Press, 2016).

41. Kevin Sabet and Viridiana Rios, "Why Violence Has Increased in Mexico and What We Can Do About It," Working Paper, Department of Government, Harvard University, November 28, 2009, https://scholar.google.com/

citations?view_op=view_citation&hl=en&user=FmoE8H0AAAAJ&cstart=20&pagesize=80&sortby=pubdate&citation_for_view=FmoE8H0AAAAJ:YopCki6q_DkC; and Viridiana Rios Contreras, "How Government Structure Encourages Criminal Violence: The Causes of Mexico's Drug War," PhD diss., Harvard University, 2013, https://scholar.harvard.edu/files/vrios/files/rioscontreras_gsas.harvard_0084l_10752.pdf.

42. Daniel Hernandez, "Calderon's War on Drug Cartels: A Legacy of Blood and Tragedy," *Los Angeles Times*, December 1, 2012, https://www.latimes.com/world/la-xpm-2012-dec-01-la-fg-wn-mexico-calderon-cartels-20121130-story.html.

43. Sabrina Abu-Hamdeh, "The Merida Initiative: An Effective Way of Reducing Violence in Mexico?," *Pepperdine Policy Review* 4, no. 5 (Spring 2011): 37–54; Colleen W. Cook, Rebecca G. Rush, and Clare Ribando Seelke, "Merida Initiative: Proposed U.S. Anticrime and Counterdrug Assistance for Mexico and Central America," Defense Technical Information Center, 2008, https://apps.dtic.mil/sti/citations/ADA485861; and Clare Ribando Seelke and Kristin Finklea, "U.S.-Mexican Security Cooperation: The Mérida Initiative and Beyond," Congressional Research Service, June 29, 2017, https://sgp.fas.org/crs/row/R41349.pdf.

44. Francisco Sollano Jr., "A Social Network Analysis of Genaro García Luna and His Alleged Ties to the Sinaloa Cartel," *Small Wars Journal*, January 11, 2022, https://smallwarsjournal.com/jrnl/art/social-network-analysis-genaro-garcia-luna-and-his-alleged-ties-sinaloa-cartel; and Justice in Mexico, "The Garcia Luna Trial: Implications for U.S.-Mexico Relations," Vimeo, March 7, 2023, https://vimeo.com/805262266.

45. US Department of Justice, "Ex-Mexican Secretary of Public Security Genaro Garcia Luna Sentenced to Over 38 Years' Imprisonment," Press Release, US Attorney's Office, Eastern District of New York, October 16, 2024, https://www.justice.gov/usao-edny/pr/ex-mexican-secretary-public-security-genaro-garcia-luna-sentenced-over-38-years.

46. Cara Tabachnick, "Record-Breaking 17,600 Pounds of Cocaine Seized in the Netherlands," CBS News, August 10, 2023, https://www.cbsnews.com/news/rotterdam-netherlands-17600-pounds-of-cocaine-seized/.

47. Ezra Fieser, "Sinaloa Cartel Carves Drug Routes in the Caribbean," The World, May 13, 2017, https://theworld.org/stories/2012-02-18/sinaloa-cartel-carves-drug-routes-caribbean; and Lilian Bobea, "Organized and Disorganized Crime: Muertos Legales and Ilegales in the Caribbean," *ReVista: Harvard Review of Latin America* 11, no. 3 (Spring 2012), https://revista.drclas.harvard.edu/organized-and-disorganized-crime/.

48. Jones, *Mexico's Illicit Drug Networks*; and "Juárez Cartel," InSight Crime, July 10, 2020, https://insightcrime.org/mexico-organized-crime-news/juarez-cartel-profile/.

49. Falko Ernst, "Mexico's Hydra-Headed Crime War," International Crisis Group, June 3, 2019, https://www.crisisgroup.org/latin-america-caribbean/mexico/mexicos-hydra-headed-crime-war; and H. Richard Friman and Peter Andreas, eds., *The Illicit Global Economy and State Power* (Lanham, MD: Rowman and Littlefield, 1999).

50. Oscar Contreras Velasco, Nathan P. Jones, Daniel Weisz Argomedo, John P. Sullivan, and Chris Callaghan, "The Use of Similarity-Based Algorithms to Predict Links in Mexican Criminal Networks," Research Paper, Baker Institute for Public Policy, Rice University, August 30, 2023, https://www.bakerinstitute.org/research/use-similarity-based-algorithms-predict-links-mexican-criminal-networks; Oscar Contreras Velasco, "Unintended Consequences of State Action: How the Kingpin Strategy Transformed the Structure of Violence in Mexico's Organized Crime," *Trends in Organized Crime*, July 10, 2023, https://doi.org/10.1007/s12117-023-09498-x; and Nathan P. Jones, Irina A. Chindea, Daniel Weisz Argomedo, and John P. Sullivan, "Mexico's 2021 Dark Network Alliance Structure: An Exploratory Social Network Analysis of Lantia Consultores' Illicit Network Alliance and Subgroup Data," Research Paper, Baker Institute for Public Policy, Rice University, April 11, 2022, https://www.bakerinstitute.org/research/mexicos-2021-dark-network-alliance-structure-an-exploratory-social-network-analysis-of-lantia-consul.

51. Nathan P. Jones and John P. Sullivan, "Huachicoleros: Criminal Cartels, Fuel Theft, and Violence in Mexico," *Journal of Strategic Security* 12, no. 4 (2019): 1–24, https://digitalcommons.usf.edu/jss/vol12/iss4/1/; and María Elena Morera, "Aguachicol, la guerra por el agua," *El Universal* (Mexico City), June 18, 2022, https://www.eluniversal.com.mx/opinion/maria-elena-morera/aguachicol-la-guerra-por-el-agua.

52. Nathan P. Jones, Irina A. Chindea, Daniel Weisz Argomedo, and John P. Sullivan, "A Social Network Analysis of Mexico's Dark Network Alliance Structure," *Journal of Strategic Security* 15, no. 4 (2022), https://digitalcommons.usf.edu/jss/vol15/iss4/5/.

53. Vanda Felbab-Brown, "The Foreign Policies of the Sinaloa Cartel and CJNG, Part 1: In the Americas," Brookings Institution, July 22, 2022, https://www.brookings.edu/articles/the-foreign-policies-of-the-sinaloa-cartel-and-cjng-part-i-in-the-americas/.

54. US Department of Justice, "Statement of Anne Milgram, Administrator, Drug Enforcement Administration," July 27, 2023, https://www.justice.gov/d9/2023-07/administrator_written_sfr_july_2023_final.pdf.

55. Rafael Prieto-Curiel, Gian Maria Campedelli, and Alejandro Hope, "Reducing Cartel Recruitment Is the Only Way to Lower Violence in Mexico," *Science* 381, no. 6664 (September 22, 2023): 1312–16, https://www.science.org/doi/10.1126/science.adh2888.

56. Astorga and Shirk, "Drug Trafficking Organizations and Counter-Drug Strategies"; and Hernández, *Narcoland*.

57. Jones, *Mexico's Illicit Drug Networks*.

58. Hernández, *Narcoland*; and Jones, *Mexico's Illicit Drug Networks*.

59. Hernández, *Narcoland*.

60. June S. Beittel, "Mexico: Organized Crime and Drug Trafficking Organizations," Congressional Research Service, June 7, 2022, https://sgp.fas.org/crs/row/R41576.pdf.

61. Azam Ahmed, "The Stunning Escape of El Chapo's Son: It's Like 'a Bad Netflix Show,'" *New York Times*, October 18, 2019, https://www.nytimes.com/2019/10/18/world/americas/mexico-cartel-chapo-son-guzman.html.

62. Daniel Weisz Argomedo, Nathan P. Jones, and John P. Sullivan, "Virtual Urban Siege: Modern Urban Siege and Swarming in Culiacán, 2019 and 2023," *Journal of Strategic Security* 16, no. 3 (2023): 30–52, https://digitalcommons.usf.edu/jss/vol16/iss3/4/.

63. John P. Sullivan, Nathan P. Jones, and Daniel Weisz Argomedo, "Urban Security: From High-Intensity Crime to Large-Scale Combat Operations and Everything in Between," *Journal of Strategic Security* 16, no. 3 (2023): i–x, https://digitalcommons.usf.edu/jss/vol16/iss3/1/.

64. Justice in Mexico, "The Garcia Luna Trial."

65. US Department of Justice, "Statement of Anne Milgram."

66. Josh Eells, "The Brutal Rise of El Mencho," *Rolling Stone*, July 11, 2017, http://www.rollingstone.com/culture/features/the-brutal-rise-of-el-mencho-w491405.

67. Héctor de Mauleón, "CJNG: La sombra que nadie vio," *Nexos*, June 1, 2015, https://www.nexos.com.mx/?p=25113.

68. Correa-Cabrera, "Violence on the 'Forgotten' Border."

69. Nathan P. Jones, "The Strategic Implications of the Cártel de Jalisco Nueva Generación," *Journal of Strategic Security* 11, no. 1 (2018): 19–42, https://digitalcommons.usf.edu/jss/vol11/iss1/3/.

70. Carlos Flores Pérez, "Cártel Jalisco Nueva Generación: Elementos a considerar sobre la reconfiguración de las organizaciones del tráfico de drogas en México," in *Atlas de la seguridad y la defensa de México (2016)*, ed. Raúl Benítez Manaut and Sergio Aguayo Quezada (Mexico City: Instituto Belisario Domínguez del Senado de la República; Colectivo de Análisis de la Seguridad con Democracia, 2017), 221–30; and Raúl Benítez Manaut and Josué González, "The Cártel de Jalisco Nueva Generación: The Most Significant Security Challenge in the Mexico–United States Relationship," *Small Wars Journal*, October 1, 2023, https://smallwarsjournal.com/jrnl/art/cartel-de-jalisco-nueva-generacion-most-significant-security-challenge-mexico-united.

71. Mark Wilson, "US Sanctions Reveal How Mexico's Powerful Jalisco Cartel Is Seizing Control at a Major Pacific Port," Business Insider, October 22, 2021, https://www.businessinsider.com/us-sanctions-show-mexicos-powerful-jalisco-cartel-controls-major-port-2021-10; Benítez Manaut and González, "The Cártel de Jalisco Nueva Generación: The Most Significant Security Challenge"; and Flores Pérez, "Cártel Jalisco Nueva Generación: Elementos a considerar."

72. Felbab-Brown, "The Foreign Policies of the Sinaloa Cartel and CJNG."

73. Henry Shuldiner, "Coca Cultivation Grows in Guerrero, Mexico, but Scalability Remains Doubtful," InSight Crime, December 16, 2022, https://insightcrime.org/news/coca-cultivation-grows-guerrero-though-scalability-remains-doubtful/; and Luis Chaparro, "Mexico's Cartels Are Experimenting with Control of Another Part of the Cocaine Trade," Business Insider, May 7, 2021, https://www.businessinsider.com/mexican-cartels-are-experimenting-with-cocaine-production-in-mexico-2021-5.

74. Wilson, "US Sanctions Reveal How Mexico's Powerful Jalisco Cartel Is Seizing Control."

75. Parker Asmann and Steven Dudley, "Is Mexico's CJNG Pushing the Gulf Cartel from Tamaulipas?," InSight Crime, May 17, 2023, https://insightcrime.org/news/mexico-cjng-gulf-cartel-tamaulipas/.

76. Isacson, "Crisis and Opportunity"; and Taylor, "Fentanyl, Cartels or Simple Market Glut?"

77. Sam Quinones, *Dreamland: The True Tale of America's Opiate Epidemic* (New York: Bloomsbury Publishing, 2015); and Sam Quinones, *The Least of Us: True Tales of America and Hope in the Time of Fentanyl and Meth* (New York: Bloomsbury Publishing, 2021).

78. "Deadly Contaminated Cocaine Widespread in Florida," Drug Enforcement Administration Bulletin, DEA-MIA-BUL-039-18, February 2018, https://www.dea.gov/sites/default/files/2018-07/BUL-039-18.pdf.

79. "AMLO Disputes DEA Claims About Mexican Cartels' Worldwide Reach," *Mexico News Daily*, July 28, 2023, https://mexiconewsdaily.com/politics/amlo-disputes-dea-claims-about-mexican-cartels-worldwide-reach/.

80. Audrey Travère and Jules Giraudat, "Revealed: How Mexico's Sinaloa Cartel Has Created a Global Network to Rule the Fentanyl Trade," *Guardian*, December 8, 2020, https://www.theguardian.com/world/2020/dec/08/mexico-cartel-project-synthetic-opioid-fentanyl-drugs.

81. Felbab-Brown, "The Foreign Policies of the Sinaloa Cartel and CJNG."

CHAPTER 9

Cocaine in the United States

A Brief History

Marten Brienen

Cocaine is the alkaloid found in the leaves of the *Erythroxylum coca* bush, which grows in the central Andes. Cultivation of the bush goes back several thousand years at least, and the leaves of the plant are masticated by Indigenous peoples of the Peruvian and Bolivian highlands. The plant has a long history in this part of the world. Indeed, coca leaf and its consumption—by brewing tea, mastication, or candies, and so on—has been both legal and largely uncontroversial in Bolivia and the Peruvian highlands.[1]

Disregarding alcohol, cocaine remains the second drug of choice among Americans,[2] after marijuana, but this was not always so. Indeed, cocaine's history in the United States is a somewhat peculiar one, with two periods of tremendous popularity bookending a long period of forgetting. That said, cocaine as a substance of true consequence is a relatively recent phenomenon, starting quite abruptly in the mid-1980s as crack cocaine exploded onto the scene and produced a kind of mass hysteria or moral panic that briefly allowed it to dominate public debate and policymaking decisions, both in domestic and international affairs.[3]

In this chapter, I will briefly outline that history, starting with the slow spread of the substance's popularity in the late nineteenth century, the ensuing efforts to suppress it in the early twentieth century in the era of the temperance movement and its virtual disappearance from the American marketplace from the 1920s onward, to its slow resurgence beginning in the 1960s.[4] Then, I will discuss how cocaine made its comeback first in the shadow of Richard Nixon's "war on drugs," and then exploding into public consciousness in late 1984, precipitating an ever more punitive atmosphere in American politics and reorienting US foreign policy objectives in the aftermath of the Cold War.[5]

New Habits of the Modern Era

The initial popularity of cocaine has been well documented. Isolated in 1860 by Albert Niemann, production was taken over by the Merck pharmaceutical company in Germany, which produced small amounts of the drug over the next few decades as it rather slowly gained traction with the European and North American public. Key moments in launching cocaine as a popular product included the invention of a cocaine-wine tonic, first concocted in 1868 by Angelo Mariani, marketed as Vin Mariani in 1870 and becoming hugely popular first in France and then in Great Britain and the United States. It was in the latter that Mariani encountered the toughest competition, which mainly consisted of producers who included 35–50 percent more cocaine in their bottles of wine.[6]

Another such moment came in 1884, when Karl Koller demonstrated to the world his (re)discovery of the effectiveness of cocaine as a local anesthetic useful in eye surgery. In fact, this application had first been discovered in 1855 by Friedrich Gaedcke, who named the substance erythroxyline, but it had effectively been forgotten until Koller's 1884 demonstration, which cemented the position of cocaine as a modern topical anesthetic.[7] The utility of cocaine was further cemented by Sigmund Freud's enthusiastic embrace of the product in his essay "Über Coca," in which he extolled the virtues of this product in combating depression and a host of other psychological ailments.[8]

In the aftermath of these revelations, the alkaloid quickly gained prominence in the European and North American markets, prompting an explosion in the production of cocaine, which in turn helped to greatly reduce its price and therefore increase its availability and accessibility. From an average price of US$280 per ounce around 1885, prices dropped to about US$3 per ounce by 1914.[9] From an exclusively Peruvian export, coca became a major cash crop in the Dutch East Indies as well as in Japanese Formosa (Taiwan), while the manufacture of cocaine hydrochloride was centered around factories in the Netherlands, Japan, Germany, and the United States.

In the United States, public opinion shifted against cocaine at the start of the twentieth century. The drug had proliferated throughout American society, having popularized well-known products such as Coca-Cola (which eliminated the cocaine alkaloid from its formulation in 1903) and becoming a focus of increasingly suspicious attitudes toward a variety of "tonics" with outlandish claims regarding their medicinal abilities—heroin being similarly affected—in the face of increasing anxiety with regard to the impact of the unchecked availability of these drugs to the American public. This concern was not limited to the United States, as British observers grew alarmed at the effects of these "tonics" on British combat readiness, especially because of the wide availability of both cocaine and heroin during the early years of the First World War.[10]

In the United States, these concerns reflected the importance of the temperance movement—which objected to intoxicants in general, not just alcohol. Of course, the campaign against cocaine should also be viewed against the backdrop of early twentieth-century racist backlash against Reconstruction, as obvious anti-Black fearmongering grew to a fever pitch with claims of cocaine's nefarious effects, especially on African Americans.[11] While the cause of the rapid turn of US sentiment against cocaine is debated,[12] the reality is that the United States was becoming a global leader in the fight against the recreational use of cocaine, a turn that Paul Gootenberg describes as "anticocainism."[13]

In response to this change in sentiment, lawmakers embarked on several successive efforts that would severely curtail the availability of cocaine in US markets outside the offices of ear, nose, and throat (ENT) doctors—where they remain to this day under the brand names Goprelto and Numbrino. The first effort resulted in the 1906 Pure Food and Drug Act, which required the labeling of ingredients by the Bureau of Chemistry in the Department of Agriculture—which became the Food and Drug Administration (FDA) in 1930—and declared cocaine to be a dangerous substance. This had the effect of significantly reducing the amount of cocaine consumed in the United States.[14]

This effort was followed by the 1914 Harrison Narcotics Tax Act, which regulated and taxed the importation and distribution of opioids as well as coca and its salts. Moreover, the act has been regarded as the starting point in the criminalization of drug addiction in the United States in that it has been interpreted by the courts as establishing that drugs cannot be prescribed to addicts, as addiction is not considered to constitute a medical condition.

That effort was followed by the 1922 Jones-Miller Act (or Narcotic Drugs Import and Export Act, as it is less commonly referred to), which created the Federal Narcotics Control Board to oversee the importation and export of primarily opiates but also the coca necessary for the production of cocaine, and to effectively prohibit the recreational use of medical substances as well as the importation of psychoactive substances for any purpose other than medical ones.

Perhaps the final nail in the coffin was the 1927 discovery of the stimulant effects of amphetamines and the emergence of a variety of amphetamines and methamphetamines around the globe. American Benzedrine, German Pervitin, and Japanese Philopon exploded with the drug-fueled Second World War, during which both Axis and Allied commanders supplied their troops with copious amounts of these drugs, without which neither Blitzkrieg nor extended bomber runs would have been possible.[15] In the United States, the use of Benzedrine and later Dexedrine continued through the Korean and Vietnam Wars, and indeed in the air force it continued until 2012.[16] The widespread use of these drugs and their popularity as weight-loss (Obetrol) and energy (pep) pills effectively displaced any continued need for cocaine in the American marketplace,[17] to the extent that by the 1920s cocaine had become a scarcity, and by the 1930s it had become largely absent from US markets.

Finally, 1930 saw the creation of the Federal Bureau of Narcotics (FBN), which was to be Harry J. Anslinger's private antidrug fiefdom for the next thirty-two years, primarily to battle against "reefer" (marijuana) but also to continue pushing for international prohibitions against the recreational use of cocaine.[18]

Re(dis)covery

One might well argue that these early efforts in the antidrug effort should be counted as a success, given that in the postwar period, cocaine remained little more than a curiosity that one might encounter in the office of an ENT doctor or in major port cities such as Los Angeles and New York, especially while ocean liners remained a key mode of transportation. Ships coming through the port of Callao (Peru) and later Arica (Chile) might take on some of the substance, still produced in the Upper Huallaga Valley in Peru, and make it available at their destination cities. Thus, while the FBN could report on the occasional seizure, for much of the immediate postwar period this amounted to little more than a few ounces here and there. Then again, as I argued above, one should see this relative success in the context of the continued availability of a number of stimulants that were regarded as appropriate treatments for a wide variety of ailments.

This notwithstanding, the FBN continued to pressure Peru to end the remaining production of illicit cocaine in the Upper Huallaga Valley, and ultimately they got the Peruvian government to crack down, effectively pushing production into neighboring postrevolutionary Bolivia, where coca cultivation was an accepted historical practice but where there had been no history of cocaine manufacture. The environment in Bolivia lent itself especially well to a small but thriving cocaine manufacturing and distribution network that emerged in the mid-1950s and peaked in the early 1960s, just in time for the rise of the counterculture in the United States. The pressure exerted on Peru to eliminate its cocaine business, while succeeding temporarily, thus produced the conditions for an increase in production and an attendant decrease in price. The uptick in yearly seizures was notable.[19] Likewise, while Havana had been a hotspot for cocaine in the 1950s, the Cuban Revolution pushed those networks into the United States, thus helping to establish Miami as a hub for cocaine distribution.

The stage was thus set for cocaine's comeback during the 1960s, initially as a drug of choice for cultural and economic elites on the coasts—where the drug had the greatest availability. Due to its relative scarcity, cocaine was expensive and thus the exclusive province of Hollywood elites and Wall Street bankers, with a smattering of musicians and literati thrown into the mix. Not surprisingly, in this era of experimentation, this did result in the very slow but sure spread of renewed interest in the substance. Likewise, changed sociopolitical circumstances in Peru allowed the peasants of the Huallaga Valley to slowly return to what they had been doing before: cultivating coca to help satisfy growing demand overseas. Now, in part as a direct result of Anslinger's success in the 1950s, there were two countries actively cultivating coca leaf and producing cocaine, enhancing the supply. By the mid-1960s, what had been the occasional capture of an ounce here and an ounce there had become increasingly frequent captures of tens of kilograms at once.[20]

Meanwhile, cultural and sociopolitical forces combined toward the end of the 1960s to position cocaine for a truly remarkable transformative period. As antiwar protesters and hippies alike challenged the established order and assailed the ongoing war in Vietnam, President Richard Nixon (1969–1974) revitalized old efforts to combat the scourge of drugs—especially marijuana and heroin. His reasons for doing so have been hotly debated, with some arguing that they constituted a targeted campaign to eliminate antiwar protesters and African American activists,[21] while others have argued that the privately drug-hating Nixon had legitimate concerns about the impact of the proliferation of heroin in the US military and in other sectors of society,[22] as illustrated by the rather progressive inclusion of treatment options in Nixon's antidrug vision. Nixon famously—infamously, depending on whom you ask—launched the renewed "war on drugs" in June 1971, declaring that drugs constituted America's public enemy number one, and followed up his rhetoric with the creation of the Drug Enforcement Administration (DEA), the successor agency to Anslinger's FBN, in 1973.

Nixon's focus was on hippies and other ne'er-do-wells who had the gall to question authority amid the Vietnam War with their free love and their liberal use of drugs, and thus he was interested primarily in heroin and marijuana, which he regarded as undermining the very fabric of society. Later, in 1977, President Jimmy Carter's "drug czar" Peter Bourne was describing cocaine as "not physically addicting, and acutely pleasurable,"[23] indicating that this particular substance was not considered of importance by the drug warlords of the time. Indeed, this perception would remain throughout the 1970s and into the early 1980s.

It was a set of contemporaneous policy choices that helped create the conditions for cocaine's eventual meteoric rise to the forefront of the American imagination. The Nixon administration was exceedingly anxious about the growing influence of the Left in Latin America, and hence he was supportive of those regimes that would pursue leftists of any bent vigorously. This included supporting the overthrow of the Salvador Allende presidency in Chile in 1973 and replacing it with General Augusto Pinochet's dictatorship.[24] Pinochet cracked down heavily on drug traffickers, who had established routes to North America from Bolivia through the ports of Arica and Iquique, thereby necessitating that Bolivian producers find new routes north for their product, which they found in troubled Colombia. This country provided several strategic advantages: ongoing armed conflict, which ensured that the national government did not possess actual control over its entire territory, leaving parts of it to rebel groups; a long history of smuggling necessitated by high import and export tariffs typical of the region; and the presence of a handful of entrepreneurs who were very good at moving goods from one place to another.[25] From the mind-1970s onward, Colombians began by transporting raw coca and *pasta* base via small airplanes from Bolivia and Peru across the unpatrolled vastness of the Amazon rainforest to Colombia, where they could process these substances into cocaine, but they soon discovered that Colombian farmers were perfectly capable of producing the shrub locally. Now, a third country producing coca and cocaine had been added, one that would prove more consequential than either Peru or Bolivia.

Moreover, the drug war launched in the United States against primarily marijuana and heroin was successful insofar as it succeeded in suppressing the Mexican marijuana industry that had long been the source of "reefer" in the

United States, necessitating the location of new sources for the substance, as demand had hardly died down. Colombian growers were more than happy to step in to replenish dwindling supplies, requiring the services of precisely the kind of entrepreneurs who had long managed to move goods across borders without subjecting them to taxation.[26] The rerouting of Bolivian cocaine through Colombia combined with the need to move Colombian marijuana to the United States in the context of a war on drugs that did not concern itself (yet) with cocaine, effectively gave rise to a new era in US drug markets: the Era of Cocaine.

The Era of Cocaine

By the late 1970s and early 1980s, the stage was set for the rise of cocaine. With Colombian producers coming online with entirely in-house cocaine production and a Colombian government that neither controlled the national territory nor was all that interested in what petty criminals were up to, the supply of cocaine grew exponentially and was largely flown in via Caribbean air routes and delivered to Miami, which soon became a major hub for cocaine and its enthusiasts. Still relatively pricy, it retained its somewhat glamorous image as a drug for trendsetters, musicians, bankers, and movie producers through the very early 1980s. Moreover, as a result of the victories achieved in the war on drugs, namely the eradication of Mexican weed fields and the crackdown on heroin suppliers, shortage of these more traditional drugs helped to invigorate demand for the one substance that that continued to be regarded as low priority by law enforcement.[27]

It was in the mid-1980s that cocaine's status as an upmarket drug was truly transformed, as a new form of cocaine entered the American marketplace. Indeed, cocaine's true march to prominence began in reality in 1984, as crack cocaine first arrived on the scene in major urban areas. While freebasing had been practiced before, crack cocaine as a readymade product was new and proved immediately popular among consumers. Before long, news reports proliferated about the arrival of this "new" drug. In essence, crack cocaine is the product of a chemical reaction involving cocaine hydrochloride, sodium bicarbonate, water, and heat, which produces a solid form of cocaine that has the benefit of vaporizing at 90 degrees Celsius (194 Fahrenheit) rather than at 190 degrees

Celsius (374 Fahrenheit), making it suitable for inhalation by smoking, producing a very fast high compared to powder cocaine.[28] Pharmacologically identical to powder cocaine, crack cocaine can be smoked, which constitutes a more efficient delivery vehicle for the alkaloid into the bloodstream; this increased efficiency translates into lower cost to the consumer per dose, and as such crack obtained a reputation for being a cheaper alternative to powder cocaine.[29]

With the appearance of crack cocaine, the drug was suddenly introduced to people on the lower rungs of society, and it spread rapidly to inner cities across the country—while powder cocaine remained a more elite product. The fear brought on by extensive press coverage of this demon drug swept the nation faster than the drug itself could spread. Tales of death and destruction brought on by this drug were broadcast at an ever-increasing crescendo, while dictionaries expanded with the attendant neologisms—from crack baby to crack whore[30]—inspiring a widespread fear that drugs were undoing the moral fabric of the nation. Combined with images of crumbling inner cities, which were home to many of the victims of this plague, such reportage made for a bleak view of the future of the nation, demanding drastic measures to counteract this phenomenon. Indeed, public pressure was enormous, as fear of the "crack epidemic" dominated public debate during the second half of the 1980s.[31]

Now, it is important to note that the specter of drugs as the enemy of the nation had been wielded by the Reagan administration (1981–1989) before crack cocaine came on the scene. It was in 1982 that Ronald Reagan declared war on the "drug racketeers" whom he held responsible for the nation's moral decline.[32] Indeed, leaders of both the Republican and Democratic Parties spent much of the 1980s and 1990s falling all over themselves attempting to prove to the American public just how willing they were to mete out stiffer and stiffer penalties for the mere possession of at times negligible quantities of drugs—which, we should remind ourselves, had only years earlier been deemed largely harmless—piling on the mandatory minimum sentences and three-strikes laws, resulting in a veritable explosion of the national prison population. This was no time for sympathy, and the treatment options that still typified Nixon's approach were soon replaced with more sentencing.[33] Drug dealers were demonized as "pushers" who accosted schoolchildren with offers of free drugs in public service announcements throughout the 1980s and 1990s, while nary a child escaped the important lessons of Project D.A.R.E. and its analogues throughout the United States.[34]

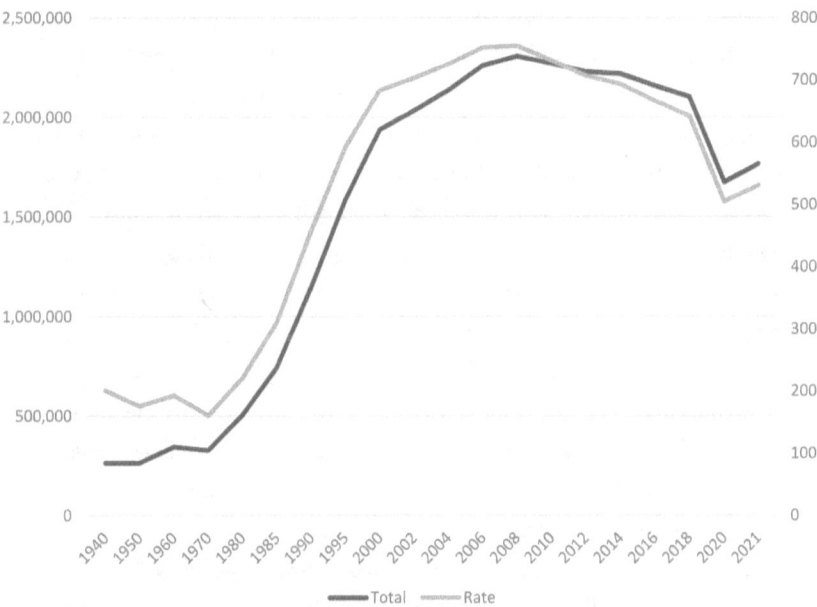

Figure 9.1. Incarceration in the United States, 1940–2021. The numbers on the left-hand side of the graph indicate number of persons incarcerated, and on the right-hand side number of incarcerations per 100,000 people. Source: Created by the author with data from World Prison Brief, https://www.prisonstudies.org/country/united-states-america.

One of the results of this moral panic has been well documented and is presented in figure 9.1: through a series of justice reforms aimed at drug users and traffickers alike, the prison population in the United States exploded from just over 500,000 in 1980 to over 2.3 million by 2008. Mandatory minimum sentences, three-strikes laws, and other draconian measures were introduced throughout the 1980s and 1990s, impacting especially those communities that used crack as opposed to cocaine: the disparity in sentencing between the two reached a factor of 1:100,[35] a disparity that was reduced, but not eliminated, by the 2010 Fair Sentencing Act.[36] Indeed, beyond draconian sentencing laws and exploding prison populations with their attendant issues on the most affected communities,[37] the antidrug war relaunched by President Reagan also started the process of the reorientation of American law enforcement through the strengthening of civil forfeiture and profit-sharing arrangements, as well as the slow militarization of American law enforcement.[38]

Not only did the advent of the crack cocaine epidemic—whether moral panic or not—affect domestic politics, causing leaders of both parties to embrace tough-on-crime approaches, but it also had a significant effect on the nation's international outlook. The emergence of highly visible criminal organizations with an outsize media profile—especially Pablo Escobar's Medellín cartel—effectively demanded action on the part of the federal government with regard to foreign policy as well. As cocaine, in any of its variants, boomed in the 1980s, the profits generated by Colombian drug cartels—by the mid-1980s responsible for the production of about 80 percent of the world's supply of cocaine[39]—were in the billions of dollars, although estimates have been unreliable, predictably so for illicit goods.[40]

Détente with the Soviet Union, combined with public pressure to do something about the "crack epidemic" at the source, and the sheer notoriety of Escobar, encouraged the United States to involve itself directly in the fight against the cocaine cartels—mainly the Medellín and Cali cartels, together responsible for the vast majority of exports to the United States—by sending DEA agents to Colombia with ample funding to support the effort to behead the cartels in what is known as the "kingpin strategy."[41] Massively increased law enforcement and antidrug budgets, beginning with the Comprehensive Crime Control Act of 1984,[42] enabled a reinvigorated DEA to take the fight to the cartels, scoring its greatest victory with the death of Escobar in 1993.[43] Meanwhile, US drug enforcement, with the assistance of the Coast Guard, was busily destabilizing the trafficking routes from Colombia to the United States through the Caribbean that had been established in the 1970s, compelling the cartels to reorient their business model by engaging middlemen in the form of Mexican criminal organizations with a history of smuggling illicit goods (such as marijuana and heroin) across the border into the United States.[44] Here again, US antidrug policy had serious unintended consequences by rerouting the Colombian drug trade through Mexico, thereby vastly enriching the traditional Mexican drug cartels and giving them new business in the aftermath of the destruction of their marijuana industry.

While the initial panic of the 1980s had passed by the early 1990s and cooler heads prevailed with regard to the exceptionally dire cultural outlook that had been popularized in the press,[45] the end of the Cold War meant that the US military—initially not too excited about participating in the antidrug effort[46]—needed a mission to pivot toward, now that history was at an end and old enemies, it was hoped, would soon become reliable allies. An expansion of the role of the US military in the struggle against transnational criminal organizations and against dope fiends quickly became a very welcome addition to the mission and a pillar of US foreign policy until the events of September 11, 2001.

This meant a multipronged approach to the problem of cocaine in the United States: first, there was the domestic approach, which saw, as we have seen, millions of people incarcerated on drug charges, and many of them given very long sentences;[47] and second, there was the supply-side approach, which called for a variety of ways to combat the scourge of drugs at the point of origin, which in turn meant putting pressure on the countries producing the drugs to help to eradicate them.

In Bolivia, enthusiasm for this effort was quite limited, especially in the 1980s and 1990s. The Bolivian government in the 1980s did cooperate in the creation of a new legal framework, the 1988 Ley 1008, which was exceedingly harsh with regard to those caught up in the production of cocaine—in part due to the very severe economic crisis that the country found itself in in the aftermath of democratization—but there was relatively little enthusiasm to enforce it consistently, or indeed to combat the cultivation of coca.[48] Indeed, given the economic importance of coca in the Bolivian economy, it seemed not in Bolivia's best interest to suppress this activity.[49] Perhaps the greatest obstacle to Bolivian involvement in the antidrug war was that coca itself has been a traditional crop for at least several thousand years and has been a legal crop to cultivate and sell throughout colonial and republican history. To criminalize this activity has been consistently very unpopular among Bolivians.[50]

Indeed, it was not until the very end of the twentieth century that the United States gained any real traction in Bolivia under the administration of Hugo Bánzer Suárez (1997-2001), who enthusiastically embraced the "Zero Coca" banner and promised the eradication of all *coca excedentaria*—coca grown outside of the two specially designated regions that were legally permitted to produce coca for the domestic market only—with the help of US-trained Fuerza Especial de Lucha Contra el Narcotráfico (FELCN) forces assisted by the DEA.[51] While the effort, launched in 1998 as Plan Dignidad (Plan Dignity), was successful in reducing the acreage dedicated to coca in Bolivia to historical lows, this apparent success came at a cost:[52] although the effort to eradicate significant acreage of smallholder coca did succeed, the effects were (a) only temporary, as Bolivian *cocaleros* (coca farmers) adapted and replanted; (b) unforeseen, as the effort proved enormously unpopular and propelled the leader of the cocalero movement—Juan Evo Morales Ayma—to the forefront of Bolivian politics, eventually allowing him to win the 2005 presidential elections and to become the longest-serving president in Bolivian history as a staunch member of the "pink tide," all the while promoting the virtues of coca at every turn; and (c) predictable in that in the absence of a reduction in demand for cocaine, the reduction in Bolivian production merely resulted in an expansion of in-house Colombian coca production in what is commonly known as the "balloon effect."[53]

In Peru, the story was both different and similar in that due to the terror campaign waged by the Sendero Luminoso (Shining Path) movement during the late 1970s and 1980s, the Peruvian government was far more interested in undermining the ability of that movement to generate income through the taxation of coca and cocaine in the Andean highlands, where the movement was strongest.[54] Especially after the election of Alberto Fujimori to the Peruvian presidency in 1990, the United States was able to pursue a vigorous anticocaine campaign in Peru with the enthusiastic support of the Fujimori administration (1990-2000), so long as this was accompanied by material support for the anti-Sendero campaign being waged by the Peruvians. For the United States, this entailed success in their efforts to combat the flights that transported coca and pasta base to Colombia, while also working actively to eradicate coca from the Peruvian highlands. For the Peruvians, it meant success in bringing Sendero to heel. However, while the United States considered this effort as much a success as the effort in neighboring Bolivia, it mostly resulted in the massive expansion of coca cultivation in Colombia, where ongoing civil war made it much more difficult for the United States to operate.[55]

Ultimately, and certainly in part because of the approaches taken in Peru and Bolivia, over the course of the 1990s Colombia grew from being mainly a producer of cocaine on the basis of raw materials produced in Peru and Bolivia to becoming the largest producer of both.[56] Given that the country had been in a state of civil war since the late 1960s, this posed a serious challenge for the antidrug warriors of the era: during the 1980s, the emerging cartels were an additional complication for the Colombian government, whose power had been under threat for decades already. Just as it did not have the capacity to halt the cartels, it also lacked the capacity to curtail the activities of the armed movements that controlled parts of the national territory—primarily the Ejército de Liberación Nacional (ELN; National Liberation Army) and the Fuerzas Armadas Revolucionarias de Colombia (FARC; Revolutionary Armed Forces of Colombia).[57]

The great push came in the form of Plan Colombia, which had been envisioned by President Andrés Pastrana Arango (1998-2002) as a kind of Marshall Plan for Colombia in which the provision of resources would allow the state to rebuild its institutions, and by improving the state and the quality of life of its citizens, the plan would partially render obsolete the tired guerrilla movements agitating for social and political change.[58] For this, Plan Colombia sought major contributions from a host of donors, but it was the United States that proved most willing to work with Colombians on the plan, so long as it fit US policy needs. Thus, the plan was rather quickly transformed into a tool in the war on drugs, through the promise of substantial financial contributions dedicated largely to the fight against drug cartels. In fact, the project bore the American stamp to such an extent that most other potential donors no longer felt comfortable contributing in any meaningful manner to this now rather militaristic effort.[59]

Combining billions of dollars and US personnel and matériel, Plan Colombia became a major push against the production of coca and cocaine in Colombia after its signing in 1999 during the tenure of President Bill Clinton (1993-2001). It provided for the aerial spraying of coca fields throughout national territory, as well as specially trained troops who could swoop in and torch fields of planted coca. Of course, there were provisions for alternative crops, but these have not proven especially lucrative. For the Colombians, a major sticking point—the inability to use the military provisions and available funding to go after FARC rebels, who posed a constant threat to the Colombian state—was largely resolved in the aftermath of the September 11, 2001, terror attacks against the World Trade Center in New York City and other targets, as then president Álvaro Uribe Vélez

(2002–2010) was able to convince the George W. Bush administration to view the rebel group as "narco-terrorists" who should qualify as a legitimate target for Plan Colombia funding.[60]

Just as with the successes booked around 1999–2001 in Bolivia, while the US government has been able to claim success in the eradication of coca fields in Colombia, this has not translated into a change in the availability or purity of cocaine in the American marketplace. Indeed, since the mid-1990s, the retail price of powder cocaine has remained remarkably stable.[61] Of course, since Plan Colombia ended in 2015, the attention of the American public has shifted to the next demon drug: in the 1990s and early 2000s, it was methamphetamines that took center stage, while as of 2023 we find ourselves in the midst of an opioid epidemic with a special focus on the role of fentanyl, leaving cocaine still the second-most popular drug after marijuana, but not much of a topic of discussion in the current climate.

This puts the United States in rather a strange position with regard to this particular "demon drug." It is understandable that the opioid epidemic has taken center stage, given the staggering impact of the proliferation of especially fentanyl: for 2022, the Centers for Disease Control reported 109,753 fatal overdoses of fentanyl,[62] while many Americans have become familiar with the phenomenon of addicts "nodding off" in the streets of major urban centers like Philadelphia.[63] Inhabitants of major urban areas are daily confronted with a crisis of addiction masquerading as a homelessness crisis. It is no wonder, given the circumstances, that the focus has been redirected toward this latest drug crisis, but in the meantime, cocaine—whether powder or crack—has not diminished in popularity since the panic of the late 1980s and early 1990s.[64] As such, the threat that cocaine poses to the American public is not diminished, and it has been observed that in recent years—primarily as a result of comorbidities, that is the combined use of cocaine with much more dangerous opioids—the number of cocaine-involved fatal overdoses is on the rise.[65] The panic of the late 1980s effectively blew over, and cocaine's place as the second drug of choice among Americans has been firmly cemented.

Meanwhile, of course, the criminal actors involved are essentially the same as they have been since the mid-1980s: for the United States, this is primarily a collection of Colombian and Mexican transnational criminal organizations that undergo constant evolution as Mexican and Colombian authorities, with a heavy dose of US support, combat them. Effectively, as authorities continue their "kingpin strategy" of going after the leadership of these organizations, they splinter and produce an ever-increasing number of cartels and *cartelitos* (little cartels), which seem to become increasingly violent with each iteration.[66] The much-touted and heavily publicized capture (2016), trial, and conviction (2019) of Joaquín "El Chapo" Guzmán had no effect on the availability or pricing of cocaine in the United States, but will predictably result in further fragmentation.[67]

Meanwhile, cocaine consumption patterns in the United States have in many ways remained stable. Unlike opioids, there is no real medical pathway toward addiction to this drug—even for its legitimate medical uses—leaving it effectively a strictly recreational drug. While there is always an ebb and flow in usage rates for such drugs, the overall number of users in the United States has remained remarkably stable, between 6.8 million users in 1990 and 6.1 million users by 2016.[68] Prices for cocaine, as has been well documented, have consistently fallen over the course of the war on drugs, from $320/gram in 1990 to $61/gram by 2015 (in 2015 US dollars).[69] One important and worrisome change has been a fairly sharp increase in the number of cocaine-related poisonings and overdoses, especially since 2011, with the cocaine-related overdose death rate rising from 1.5 per 100,000 in 2011 to 7.3 per 100,000 by 2021.[70] It has, however, been observed that this is a by-product of the fentanyl crisis that has gripped the country; cocaine-related overdoses without the involvement of opioids had a substantially lower death rate of 1.5 per 100,000 in 2021.[71]

Conclusion

There is no escaping the fact that the history of cocaine in the United States, and especially in the era of the so-called war on drugs, is a testament to the self-defeating nature of that exercise. This is an economic problem at its root: assuming that success in the war on drugs is understood to mean a reduction in the availability thereof—preferably a significant reduction at that—then such success, in the context of relatively inflexible demand, necessarily results in increased prices and therewith increased profit margins, thereby making participation in the trafficking of these substances more economically attractive. There cannot be better evidence than that in those countries where drug trafficking is punished by death—the ultimate deterrent, one should think—people are still put to death for that crime.[72] The reality has been that our efforts to stamp out the production of cocaine in the Upper Huallaga Valley of highland Peru moved that production next door to Bolivia. Similarly, our efforts to stamp out production in *that* country resulted in a move of production to Colombia, where efforts to pressure the Colombian government necessarily fell on deaf ears since that government did not exercise sovereignty in the areas where the cocaine was produced. Now, instead of one cocaine-producing Andean country, there are three.

Likewise, while the defeat of the Medellín and Cali cartels was touted as resounding successes of US antidrug efforts, it did not result in a decrease in the availability of the drug itself in the American marketplace;[73] nor indeed did the "successes" of the Zero Coca campaign in Bolivia, or the equally successful antidrug efforts under the Fujimori presidency in Peru, bring about any true disruption in the availability or pricing of powder cocaine across the United States.

It is in many ways remarkable how cocaine—in either of its predominant forms in the US marketplace—came to as much prominence as it did in the 1980s and 1990s. The era of the crack epidemic, which was commonly depicted at the time as a state of almost complete moral and societal decay,[74] saw the rise of mass incarceration and a complete pivot of US foreign policy to embark on a full-scale war on the criminal organizations that shipped cocaine to our shores. Effectively, no expense was spared. What makes this so very remarkable in one way is the fact that the period of cocaine primacy happens also to be a period in US history with some of the lowest overdose death rates. Whereas in the 1970s, when heroin was an important cause of overdose death, the overdose death rate steadily remained above 3.0 per 100,000, in the 1980s it remained between 1.1 (1980) and 2.0 (1989).[75]

Indeed, as the United States embarked on its historical collaboration with Plan Colombia to finally tackle the drug-trafficking organizations that were hauling cocaine to the United States, ultimately spending billions of dollars on that effort, other important changes were taking place in US drug markets. Most important among these, of course, was the transition to prescription opioids and the subsequent outbreak of the most severe drug crisis the country has ever witnessed: the opioid crisis that the country is currently struggling with. Driven primarily by Purdue Pharma, the late 1990s and early 2000s saw an explosive increase in the number of opioid prescriptions, in part due to that company's highly aggressive marketing tactics that hinged on the supposed nonaddictive nature of its product OxyContin (oxycodone). The impact of this is very clearly visible in the overdose death rates, which nearly tripled in five years from 3.6 per 100,000 in 1998 to 8.9 per 100,000 by 2003.[76] This first wave of prescription-related overdoses was followed by a brief second wave in which increased restrictions of opioid prescriptions drove individuals to heroin as a substitute, which was followed by a third and even deadlier wave in which heroin and other opioids were increasingly adulterated with fentanyl and fentanyl analogues, resulting in an unprecedented number of fatal overdoses for a rate that exceeded 28.3 per 100,000 by 2020 and killed an estimated 645,000 people between 1999 and 2021.[77]

Never before has the United States gone through a crisis of addiction such as the current one, and it is difficult not to come to the conclusion that the dogged fight against cocaine in fact laid the groundwork in many ways for this current crisis, given that it was this earlier effort that ultimately connected what had been dispersed centers of production into decentralized criminal networks with tentacles that span the globe. The Mexican cartels as we know them today—responsible now for the movement of fentanyl into the US marketplace—are very much the result of pressure on Colombian cartels in the 1980s and 1990s. In the same vein, the Colombian *bandas criminales* and transnational criminal organizations are themselves the result of antidrug efforts of the 1980s and 1990s, while the big cartels of that era arose as a result of pressure placed on first Peru and then Bolivia to curtail their very limited production in the decades prior to that.

Perhaps, in light of the current crisis, in which more than 100,000 people die each year of fatal overdoses of all illicit substances combined, it is difficult to understand the urgency with which federal and local authorities started to pursue a particular drug—cocaine—when fatal overdoses at the height of *that* crisis hovered around 4,000 per year (peaking at 5,035 in 1989).

Notes

1. Steven B. Karch, *A Brief History of Cocaine*, 2nd ed. (Boca Raton, FL: CRC Press, 2006).
2. Megan E. Patrick, Richard A. Miech, Lloyd D. Johnston, and Patrick M. O'Malley, "Monitoring the Future: Panel Study Annual Report; National Data on Substance Use Among Adults Ages 19 to 60, 1976–2022," Institute for Social Research, University of Michigan, 2023, https://monitoringthefuture.org/wp-content/uploads/2023/07/mtfpanel2023.pdf.
3. Erich Goode and Nachman Ben-Yehuda, *Moral Panics: The Social Construction of Deviance*, 2nd ed. (Malden, MA: John Wiley and Sons, 2009).
4. Paul Gootenberg, *Andean Cocaine: The Making of a Global Drug* (Chapel Hill: University of North Carolina Press, 2008).
5. Roland G. Fryer Jr., Paul S. Heaton, Steven D. Levitt, and Kevin M. Murphy, "Measuring Crack Cocaine and Its Impact," Harvard University Society of Fellows, April 2006, https://scholar.harvard.edu/files/fryer/files/fhlm_crack_cocaine_0.pdf.
6. Karch, *A Brief History of Cocaine*.
7. Howard Markel, "Über Coca: Sigmund Freud, Carl Koller, and Cocaine," *Journal of the American Medical Association* 305, no. 13 (2011): 1360–61; and Friedrich Gaedcke, "Ueber das Erythroxylin, dargestellt aus den Blättern des in Südamerika cultivirten Strauches Erythroxylon Coca Lam," *Archiv der Pharmazie* 132, no. 2 (1855): 141–50.
8. Markel, "Über Coca," 1360–61.
9. Peter Andreas, *Killer High: A History of War in Six Drugs* (New York: Oxford University Press, 2020).
10. Andreas, *Killer High*.
11. Gootenberg, *Andean Cocaine: The Making of a Global Drug*.
12. Joseph F. Spillane, *Cocaine: From Medical Marvel to Modern Menace in the United States, 1884–1920* (Baltimore: Johns Hopkins University Press, 2000).
13. Gootenberg, *Andean Cocaine: The Making of a Global Drug*.
14. Gootenberg, *Andean Cocaine: The Making of a Global Drug*.
15. Andreas, *Killer High*.
16. US Air Force Aeromedical Special Operations, Air Force Special Operations Command Instruction 48-101, November 30, 2012, https://static.e-publishing.af.mil/production/1/af_sg/publication/afi48-101/afi48-101.pdf.
17. Andreas, *Killer High*.

18. John C. McWilliams, *The Protectors: Harry J. Anslinger and the Federal Bureau of Narcotics, 1930–1962* (Newark: University of Delaware Press, 1990).

19. Gootenberg, *Andean Cocaine: The Making of a Global Drug.*

20. Gootenberg, *Andean Cocaine: The Making of a Global Drug.*

21. André Douglas Pond Cummings, "'All Eyez on Me': America's War on Drugs and the Prison-Industrial Complex," *Journal of Gender, Race and Justice* 15 (2012): 417-48.

22. Michael Massing, *The Fix* (Berkeley: University of California Press, 2000).

23. Karch, *A Brief History of Cocaine.*

24. Gootenberg, *Andean Cocaine: The Making of a Global Drug.*

25. Francisco E. Thoumi, "Illegal Drugs in Colombia: From Illegal Economic Boom to Social Crisis," *Annals of the American Academy of Political and Social Science* 582, no. 1 (July 2002): 102-16.

26. Thoumi, "Illegal Drugs in Colombia."

27. Gootenberg, *Andean Cocaine: The Making of a Global Drug.*

28. Dorothy K. Hatsukami and Marian W. Fischman, "Crack Cocaine and Cocaine Hydrochloride: Are the Differences Myth or Reality?" *Journal of the American Medical Association* 276, no. 19 (1996): 1580-88.

29. Hatsukami and Fischman, "Crack Cocaine and Cocaine Hydrochloride."

30. Kristen W. Springer, "The Race and Class Privilege of Motherhood: The *New York Times* Presentations of Pregnant Drug-Using Women," *Sociological Forum* 25, no. 3 (September 2010): 476-99.

31. Craig Reinarman and Harry G. Levine, "Crack in the Rearview Mirror: Deconstructing Drug War Mythology," *Social Justice* 31, nos. 1-2 (2004): 182-99.

32. Hatsukami and Fischman, "Crack Cocaine and Cocaine Hydrochloride."

33. Michelle Alexander, *The New Jim Crow: Mass Incarceration in the Age of Colorblindness* (New York: New Press, 2010).

34. Steven L. West and Keri K. O'Neal, "Project D.A.R.E. Outcome Effectiveness Revisited," *American Journal of Public Health* 94, no. 6 (2004): 1027-29.

35. Richard D. Hartley and J. Mitchell Miller, "Crack-ing the Media Myth: Reconsidering Sentencing Severity for Cocaine Offenders by Drug Type," *Criminal Justice Review* 35, no. 1 (2010): 67-89.

36. Kyle Graham, "Sorry Seems to Be the Hardest Word: The Fair Sentencing Act of 2010, Crack, and Methamphetamine," *University of Richmond Law Review* 45, no. 3 (2011): 765-99.

37. Alexander, *The New Jim Crow.*

38. Jefferson E. Holcomb, Tomislav Victor Kovandzic, and Marian R. Williams, "Civil Asset Forfeiture, Equitable Sharing, and Policing for Profit in the United States," *Journal of Criminal Justice* 39, no. 3 (2011): 273–85.

39. Bruce Michael Bagley, "Colombia and the War on Drugs," *Foreign Affairs* 67, no. 1 (Fall 1988): 70.

40. Francisco E. Thoumi, "The Numbers Game: Let's All Guess the Size of the Illegal Drug Industry!," *Journal of Drug Issues* 35, no. 1 (Winter 2005): 185–200.

41. Robert J. Nieves, "Colombian Cocaine Cartels: Lessons from the Front," *Trends in Organized Crime* 3, no. 3 (Spring 1998): 13–29.

42. Shawn Everett Kantor, Carl Kitchens, and Steven Pawlowski, "Civil Asset Forfeiture, Crime, and Police Incentives: Evidence from the Comprehensive Crime Control Act of 1984," Working Paper no. 23873, National Bureau of Economic Research, Cambridge, Massachusetts, September 2017, https://www.nber.org/system/files/working_papers/w23873/w23873.pdf.

43. Jon Lee Anderson, "The Afterlife of Pablo Escobar," *New Yorker*, March 5, 2018.

44. Paul Gootenberg, "Blowback: The Mexican Drug Crisis," *NACLA Report on the Americas* 43, no. 6 (November 2010): 7–12.

45. Washington Estellano, "From Populism to the Coca Economy in Bolivia," trans. Kathryn Nava-Ragazzi, *Latin American Perspectives* 21, no. 4 (Autumn 1994): 34–45.

46. Peter Zirnite, Martin Jelsma, and Coletta Youngers, "Reluctant Recruits: The US Military and the War on Drugs," Washington Office on Latin America, 1997.

47. Alexander, *The New Jim Crow*.

48. Linda Farthing, "Social Impacts Associated with Antidrug Law 1008," in *Coca, Cocaine, and the Bolivian Reality*, ed. Madeline Barbara Léons and Harry Sanabria (Albany: State University of New York Press, 1997), 253–70.

49. Estellano, "From Populism to the Coca Economy in Bolivia."

50. Will Reisinger, "The Unintended Revolution: U.S. Anti-Drug Policy and the Socialist Movement in Bolivia," *California Western International Law Journal* 39, no. 2 (2008): 237.

51. Kathryn Ledebur, "Bolivia: Clear Consequences," in *Drugs and Democracy in Latin America: The Impact of U.S. Policy*, ed. Coletta A. Youngers and Eileen Rosin (Boulder, CO: Lynne Rienner, 2005), 143–84.

52. Bettina Schorr, "Von nützlichen Feinden und verfehlter Politik: Der Drogenkrieg der USA in Bolivien," in *Bolivien: Staatszerfall als Kollateralschaden*, ed. Thomas Jäger (Wiesbaden, Germany: Springer Verlag für Sozialwissenschaften, 2009), 175–204.

53. Schorr, "Von nützlichen Feinden und verfehlter Politik"; and Reisinger, "The Unintended Revolution," 237.

54. Bruce Michael Bagley and Jonathan D. Rosen, eds., *Drug Trafficking, Organized Crime, and Violence in the Americas Today* (Gainesville: University Press of Florida, 2015).

55. Bagley and Rosen, *Drug Trafficking, Organized Crime, and Violence*.

56. Jonathan D. Rosen, "The War on Drugs in Colombia: A History of Failure," in *New Approaches to Drug Policies: A Time for Change*, ed. Marten W. Brienen and Jonathan D. Rosen (New York: Palgrave Macmillan, 2015), 59–60.

57. Eduardo Pizarro and Pilar Gaitán, "Plan Colombia and the Andean Regional Initiative: Lights and Shadows," in *Addicted to Failure: U.S. Security Policy in Latin America and the Andean Region*, ed. Brian Loveman (Lanham, MD: Rowman and Littlefield, 2006), 53–79.

58. Rosen, "The War on Drugs in Colombia," 61.

59. Thoumi, "Illegal Drugs in Colombia"; and Jonathan D. Rosen, *The Losing War: Plan Colombia and Beyond* (Albany: State University of New York Press, 2014).

60. Thoumi, "Illegal Drugs in Colombia."

61. Daniel Mejía and Carlos Esteban Posada, "Cocaine Production and Trafficking: What Do We Know?," World Bank Policy Research Working Paper no. 4618, May 1, 2008, https://papers.ssrn.com/sol3/papers.cfm?abstract_id=1149121; and United Nations Office on Drugs and Crime, *World Drug Report 2022*, vol. 4, *Drug Market Trends: Cocaine, Amphetamine-Type Stimulants, New Psychoactive Substances*, 38, https://www.unodc.org/unodc/en/data-and-analysis/world-drug-report-2022.html.

62. Centers for Disease Control and Prevention, National Center for Health Statistics, "Provisional Drug Overdose Death Counts," https://www.cdc.gov/nchs/nvss/vsrr/drug-overdose-data.htm.

63. This practice puts users at risk of being robbed or otherwise victimized, which has caused some addicts to combine their opioid use with methamphetamine use to maintain alertness. Andrew Ivsins, Taylor Fleming, Allison Barker, Manal Mansoor, Kinna Thakarar, Kimberly Sue, and Ryan McNeil, "The Practice and Embodiment of 'Goofballs': A Qualitative Study Exploring the Co-Injection of Methamphetamines and Opioids," *International Journal of Drug Policy* 107 (September 2022).

64. Manuel Cano, Sehun Oh, Christopher P. Salas-Wright, and Michael G. Vaughn, "Cocaine Use and Overdose Mortality in the United States: Evidence from Two National Data Sources, 2002–2018," *Drug and Alcohol Dependence* 214 (July 2020).

65. Cano et al., "Cocaine Use and Overdose Mortality in the United States."

66. Laura H. Atuesta and Yocelyn Samantha Pérez-Dávila, "Fragmentation and Cooperation: The Evolution of Organized Crime in Mexico," *Trends in Organized Crime* 21, no. 3 (September 2018): 235–61.

67. Parker Asmann, "Fragmentation: The Violent Tailspin of Mexico's Dominant Cartels," InSight Crime, January 16, 2019, https://insightcrime.org/news/analysis/violence-spikes-criminal-groups-fragmment-mexico/.

68. Humberto Bernal, "Demand and Supply in the Cocaine Market: An Empirical Study," *Journal of Globalization and Development* 11, no. 1 (July 2020): 1–39.

69. Bernal, "Demand and Supply in the Cocaine Market," 18–19.

70. Merianne Rose Spencer, Arialdi M. Miniño, and Margaret Warner, "Drug Overdose Deaths in the United States, 2001–2021," NCHS Data Brief no. 457, Centers for Disease Control and Prevention, National Center for Health Statistics, December 2022, 5, https://www.cdc.gov/nchs/data/databriefs/db457.pdf.

71. Merianne Rose Spencer, Arialdi M. Miniño, and Matthew F. Garnett, "Co-Involvement of Opioids in Drug Overdose Deaths Involving Cocaine and Psychostimulants, 2011–2021," NCHS Data Brief no. 474, Centers for Disease Control and Prevention, National Center for Health Statistics, July 2023, 2, https://www.cdc.gov/nchs/products/databriefs/db474.htm.

72. Yingyos Leechaianan and Dennis R. Longmire, "The Use of the Death Penalty for Drug Trafficking in the United States, Singapore, Malaysia, Indonesia and Thailand: A Comparative Legal Analysis," *Laws* 2, no. 2 (2013): 115–49.

73. Siddharth Chandra, Samuel Peters, and Nathaniel Zimmer, "How Powdered Cocaine Flows Across the United States: Evidence from Open-Source Price Data," *Journal of Drug Issues* 44, no. 4 (September 2014): 344–61.

74. Donna M. Hartman and Andrew Golub, "The Social Construction of the Crack Epidemic in the Print Media," *Journal of Psychoactive Drugs* 31, no. 4 (1999): 423–33.

75. Centers for Disease Control and Prevention, National Center for Health Statistics, Mortality Data on CDC WONDER, "Mortality for 1979–1998 with ICD 9 Codes," https://wonder.cdc.gov/mortsql.html, compiled from Compressed Mortality Files CMF 1968–1988, Series 20, no. 2A, 2000, and CMF 1989–1998, Series 20, no. 2E, 2003; and Centers for Disease Control and Prevention, National Center for Health Statistics, Mortality Data on CDC WONDER, "Mortality for 1968–1978 with ICD 8 Codes," https://wonder.cdc.gov/mortsql.html, compiled from Compressed Mortality File CMF 1968–1988, Series 20, no. 2A, 2000.

76. Centers for Disease Control and Prevention, National Center for Health Statistics, Mortality Data on CDC WONDER, "1999–2020: Underlying Cause of Death by Bridged-Race Categories," https://wonder.cdc.gov/Deaths-by-Underlying-Cause.html. Data are from the Multiple Cause of Death Files, 1999–2020, as compiled from data provided by the fifty-seven vital statistics jurisdictions through the Vital Statistics Cooperative Program.

77. Spencer, Miniño, and Warner, "Drug Overdose Deaths in the United States, 2001–2021."

CHAPTER 10

Cocaine Trafficking in Europe

Alberto Aziani

The cocaine market occupies a prominent position as one of the most profitable illegal markets in Europe. This is attributed to the high value of cocaine and the widespread presence of large markets across the region. The economic appeal of the market drives profitable trafficking operations, facilitated by diverse networks of individuals and groups that connect European countries with production areas in South America and transit nations situated along major trafficking routes.

While the impact of cocaine trafficking in European societies may not reach the severity observed in the Americas, it nonetheless has noteworthy consequences that extend beyond the immediate economic considerations. In Europe, cocaine trafficking and distribution are associated with the perpetration of violence, the distortion of competition through money-laundering schemes, and the spread of corruption.[1] These consequences have profound implications for societal well-being and stability.

Despite the growing literature on cocaine trafficking in Europe, it still falls short of academic production in the United States. This is because cocaine markets have historically been more prominent in the United States, research funding is more generous, and empirical culture is more deeply rooted.[2] At the same time, the availability of empirical research on cocaine trafficking is not homogeneous across Europe. Studies published in English, in particular, disproportionately focus on the United Kingdom, the Netherlands, and to a lesser extent Spain and Italy.[3] The prominence of the United Kingdom and the Netherlands in research on cocaine trafficking reflects their strong tradition of academic work on crime more broadly. Attention on Spain and Italy is explained by Spain's role as a transit point for cocaine trafficking, and in the participation of mafia groups in cocaine trafficking in Italy. Much less is known about cocaine trafficking in central and eastern Europe. While seizures and estimates of consumption suggest that cocaine trafficking is less prominent in these areas than in western Europe, this knowledge gap remains relevant, since European subregions differ in many respects.[4] Assuming that patterns observed in the United Kingdom, the Netherlands, Spain, or Italy apply to the entire continent can be misleading.

Therefore, considering the heterogeneity of Europe in terms of prices, consumption habits, prevalence, violence levels, presence of criminal organizations, and other factors related to cocaine trafficking, this chapter provides an introductory overview of cocaine trafficking in the region. The first section will focus on the political economy of cocaine trafficking, examining the role of European countries as final destination markets and transit points in global cocaine flows, along with the relationship between enforcement efforts and the dynamics of cocaine prices. The second section will discuss the role of Europe as the second-largest market for cocaine in the world after North America and explore the main differences in terms of cocaine consumption within the region. The third section will illustrate the primary trafficking routes through which cocaine is transported from South America to European markets, emphasizing the transformative nature of these routes over time in response to enforcement pressures. The fourth section will concentrate on the role of large seaports as major hubs for cocaine trafficking to and within Europe. Finally, the fifth section will examine the actors involved in cocaine trafficking in Europe, highlighting the heterogeneity of organizational forms and dispelling myths surrounding so-called organized crime monopolies. It will also explore the main types of groups participating in this illegal market and their connections beyond Europe.

Political Economy

The cultivation of coca, the only source of raw material for cocaine production, is not prevalent in Europe. Coca plants, which contain the cocaine alkaloid, are indigenous to the Andean region of South America, where the climate and altitude conditions are conducive to their growth. On the contrary, the combination of climate, temperature, and altitude in Europe is generally unsuitable for the successful cultivation of coca. Furthermore, the remote Andean valleys are hard for national authorities to patrol. Contrarily, legal institutions exert strong territorial control in European countries, posing challenges to the cultivation of coca there. These factors make it more convenient to produce coca in distant countries where land and labor costs are lower and where governments impose fewer costs through eradication and seizures than cultivating coca in the European destination markets.[5] As a result, Europe does not engage in any significant coca cultivation for cocaine manufacturing, relying instead on the importation of processed cocaine originating from Colombia, Peru, and Bolivia for its consumption.

Colombia, Peru, and to a lesser extent Bolivia are the primary regions for coca cultivation, and they also serve as the main sites for cocaine manufacturing. The first phases of the processing of coca leaves typically take place near the cultivation areas, and the entire manufacturing process is usually conducted in the Andean Ridge.[6]

Since the 2020s, the detection of significant quantities of cocaine paste, *pasta* base in Spain, and chemical precursors during seizures conducted by Spanish, Dutch, and other European law enforcement agencies suggests that European countries have begun to host stages of the cocaine manufacturing process.[7] However, transcontinental shipments still primarily involve highly refined cocaine, as the economic value lies in the cocaine alkaloid, the active principle sought by users, rather than the organic components of the leaves. This strategic approach ensures that the valuable cocaine remains intact during transportation, minimizing both transportation costs and the risk of detection by border authorities.

The cocaine supply chain connecting manufacturing to consumption can be modeled around three primary activities, whose boundaries have become more blurred over the years: transnational trafficking, domestic distribution linking imports to street or retail sales, and retailing.[8] All three phases of the supply chain occur within each European country.

Indeed, Europe has a significant concentration of cocaine consumption, while coca cultivation does not occur on the continent. Consequently, European markets are entirely reliant on transnational trafficking to import cocaine and meet internal demand. Moreover, most European countries, despite being primarily destination markets for cocaine, also act as transit spots, as cocaine is both imported and exported to other European destinations as well as to the Middle East and Australia.[9]

Overall, the transnational trafficking, domestic distribution, and retailing of cocaine generate large revenues and economic opportunities. Indeed, cocaine supply is arguably one of the most lucrative illegal markets in Europe. A kilo of cocaine, which can be bought in a production area in South America for few thousand euros, can easily be sold at the wholesale level in Europe for ten times that price. Upon reaching its destination market, one consignment of cocaine can undergo as many as half a dozen transactions, which collectively drive up the price per gram.[10] Depending on the country, quality, and specific circumstances, the final retail price can range from less than 40 euros to over 170 euros per gram. Consequently, a kilogram of cocaine can ultimately command a retail price in Europe of between 40,000 and 170,000 euros, in certain cases even higher.[11]

Adulterants are often added to cocaine, either directly during the cocaine manufacturing process, at higher levels in the distribution chain in South America, or closer to the final consumer. Adulteration can make consumption easier, enhance the overall experience for the user, or increase revenues by inflating the volume of the drug with cheaper substances. With this in mind, there is very little processing between export and retail sale.[12] Price increases are primarily the result of enforcement, which is the principal mechanism driving the high retail prices under prohibition. Additionally, rivalries between criminal organizations contribute to price hikes by escalating operational risks and costs, which are ultimately passed on to consumers.[13]

Law enforcement efforts can increase the price of illegal drugs in several ways. First, such efforts can increase the risks and costs associated with drug trafficking. For example, if drug dealers are caught, they may face fines, legal fees, and imprisonment. To compensate for these risks and costs, dealers may charge higher prices for their products.[14] Additionally, when law enforcement agencies crack down on drug trafficking, that can disrupt the supply chain, making it more difficult for dealers to obtain and distribute their products. This can create a temporary shortage of drugs, which can drive up prices as buyers compete for a limited supply.

The biggest increase in the value of cocaine, in terms of percentage, occurs during the transnational trafficking phase as traffickers purchase cocaine in bulk and then seek compensation for the relatively high risks intrinsic in crossing national borders. The biggest increases in cost per unit weight occur instead in Europe, during the retail phase. Retailers, indeed, purchase cocaine, which is already much more expensive than it was in South America, but they also seek their profit and compensation for their risk.[15] As such, as posited by world-systems theory,[16] greater added values are concentrated in European countries, and thus at the core of the world economy in the Global North.[17]

While the economic dynamics of the cocaine trade drive its profitability and global reach, these same factors also foster competitive tensions and systemic violence. The inability of criminals operating within the cocaine industry to access legal institutions, and the lack of resources available to legitimate enterprises to adapt to these changes, exacerbate their reliance on violence.[18] Drug-related lethal violence in Europe is notably less prevalent than in Latin America or the United States, with western and southern European countries displaying average homicide rates five times lower than the global average. However, in the context of relatively low levels of lethal violence, concerns remain regarding systemic violence associated with illegal market operations in Europe. For instance, in Italy approximately one in every five homicides, and more than half of homicides lacking intimate or expressive motives, can be attributed to systemic violence within drug markets.[19] Similarly, in Sweden, gun violence is heavily concentrated in vulnerable neighborhoods where open drug markets operate.[20] While comprehensive studies on systemic violence in Europe are absent and specific data on the contribution of the cocaine market to overall systemic violence in European countries is unavailable, it is believed to be significant.[21]

Markets for Consumption

Europe is a large market for cocaine, and cocaine is the main type of stimulant drug consumed in most European countries. As of 2022, the prevalence of cocaine use among adults on the entire continent was estimated at about 1 percent, which is more than double the global average but much lower than in North America (almost 2 percent) and Australia (above 2.5 percent). As in the rest of the world, the prevalence of cocaine use is even more significant among young adults in Europe. Surveys conducted within the European Union reveal that nearly 2.2 million individuals aged fifteen to thirty-four (equivalent to 2.2 percent of this age group) reported cocaine use within the past year.[22]

At the same time, cocaine consumption varies significantly between European countries. Western and central Europe boast the highest levels of cocaine consumption, making them the second-largest cocaine market globally. Approximately five million individuals within western and central Europe reported using cocaine in the past year (2024), resulting in an estimated prevalence of 1.5 percent of the population.[23] Wastewater analyses, a method used to estimate drug consumption in communities, confirm a significant geographical disparity. Cocaine use remains highest in western European cities, particularly in Belgium, the Netherlands, Spain, and Portugal, and lowest in eastern Europe. These countries hold strategic locations as gateways for drug trafficking from South America.[24] For instance, the Netherlands, with its well-established transport infrastructure and bustling ports, emerged as a key hub for transit crimes.[25] The transit of cocaine then fueled local consumption. Similarly, high levels of cocaine consumption in Belgium, Portugal, and Spain are partly driven by their position as major entry points for cocaine trafficking into Europe.[26]

The United Kingdom, France, and Italy are also notable destinations for cocaine due to their large populations and relatively high prevalence of use, as shown by survey results based on representative probabilistic samples of the entire population provided by the European Monitoring Centre for Drugs and Drug Addiction (EMCDDA). Furthermore, the developed economies of these countries contribute to the ability of individuals to afford and access drugs like cocaine.

Like in many other parts of central and western Europe, the emergence of these markets is a recent development, reflecting two periods of rapid expansion in the early 2000s and in the mid-2010s. For instance, in England and Wales, people who said they had used cocaine in the previous year rose from less than 1 percent to 2 percent between 1995 and 2000.[27] Between 2000 and 2008, the lifetime prevalence of cocaine use among seventeen-year-olds in France rose from 0.9 percent to 3.3 percent.[28]

Knowledge of the supply and prevalence of cocaine in eastern Europe is less comprehensive than in western Europe. Existing studies have indicated recent rising trends in cocaine consumption in eastern countries. Nonetheless, in the majority of eastern European cities, where methamphetamines are frequently the most prevalent stimulant recreational drugs, cocaine consumption remains comparatively lower than in western Europe.[29] During the Soviet era in the USSR, stringent and often repressive measures were implemented to control the production, distribution, and use of illicit substances.[30] Additionally, the limited commercial ties between countries in the former Soviet bloc and western capitalist economies likely contributed to a reduced flow of cocaine into eastern Europe, as the Soviet bloc did not cultivate coca plants.

More generally, a combination of indicators suggests that cocaine availability and use are expanding in Europe, and the rest of the world. The growth in both cocaine availability and use has been consistently observed since 2015, with a minor and temporary interruption in 2020 due to COVID-19 restrictions, as suggested by slight changes in the results of wastewater analyses.[31] The growth in both cocaine availability and use was marked by distinct trends including an escalation in purity levels, higher rates of seizures, and an increase in cocaine-related offenses and treatment cases linked to cocaine use disorders, as well as relatively stable prices.[32] This recent increase in cocaine availability in Europe is likely connected to increases in the areas under coca cultivation in Latin America as well as to improvements in the efficiency of cocaine manufacturing.[33]

In terms of types of products, powder cocaine consumption through intranasal insufflation remains the most widespread method among European cocaine users in all countries. Since the mid-2010s, there has been an increase in the use of crack cocaine in several European countries, particularly among marginalized populations.[34] However, crack cocaine still accounts for a small fraction of the overall market, with the United Kingdom and the Netherlands being notable exceptions.[35] An official inquiry conducted in the United Kingdom identified increased availability, affordability, and social acceptability of crack as possible explanations for its rise in consumption.[36] Crack cocaine is rarely trafficked across borders or over long distances, at least in Europe. This is because crack tends to be manufactured from cocaine hydrochloride close to its retail and use locations. Across Europe, no other forms of cocaine, such as coca paste or freebase, play any significant role in the market, where powder cocaine and crack dominate consumption patterns.

Transcontinental Routes

Despite theoretically having numerous viable routes for moving their product, drug traffickers tend to operate along specific pathways due to the heterogeneous levels of policing in different countries and the limited number of possible trading partners typically involved in such activities.[37]

The absence of any legal institution that enforces contracts in illegal markets, combined with pressure from state authorities and competition with other traffickers, incentivizes traffickers to collaborate preferentially with trusted partners who share the same language and common cultural and social norms.[38] This type of cooperation helps reduce uncertainty and information asymmetries. The reliance of these trusted partnerships on social and cultural proximity often shapes trafficking routes.[39] For example, Portugal is predominantly connected to Brazil, which was a Portuguese colony until 1822, while Spain has closer ties to Colombia, which received independence from Spain in 1810. Transnational networks of compatriots coordinate their activities along these trafficking routes.[40]

More generally, maritime trafficking especially via shipping containers, facilitated by evading authorities or corrupting security checkpoints, allows for a direct connection between Latin America and the European market.[41] From 2018 to 2021, approximately 90 percent of the cocaine seized in Europe was transported by sea, surpassing any other region in the world in terms of the share of cocaine seized at sea.[42] For reference, in the same period, the share of legal goods imported into Europe via sea freight was about 70 percent of total legal imports, in quantity terms. Accordingly, a significant route for such shipments involves direct transportation across the Atlantic Ocean, especially from Brazil, Colombia, Ecuador, and Venezuela, to destination ports in Europe, particularly via ports in the Netherlands and Belgium on the North Sea or via the ports of Portugal and Spain. Finally, within Europe, overland smuggling is prevalent, especially along the border between Spain and France as well as between the Netherlands and Germany.[43]

On the other hand, the routes by which cocaine moves across countries from place of production to final consumer markets may change over time due to displacement effects triggered by interdiction efforts on land, in the air, and at sea.[44] For example, since December 2006, when newly elected president Felipe Calderón sent 6,500 Mexican army soldiers to the state of Michoacán to end drug violence there, the escalation and militarization of the drug war have led to the fragmentation of organized crime in Mexico and caused trafficking routes to shift toward other regions in Latin America, with consequences for Europe as well.

The Southern Cone has emerged as a crucial transshipment hub for cocaine trafficking toward Europe and West Africa, prioritizing nontraditional ports and exploiting their lack of reputation for trafficking cocaine.[45] Consequently, criminal organizations in countries like Brazil, and to a lesser extent Argentina, have become increasingly involved in the profitable cocaine trade.[46]

Among departure countries, Brazil in particular has seen a significant increase in its role as a hub for cocaine transportation to Europe. Cocaine departing from Brazil reaches Europe either directly via the Atlantic or by transiting through West and North Africa, or through other Portuguese-speaking countries like Mozambique and Cape Verde.[47] Brazil's geography provides numerous advantages. As a significant industrial and agricultural nation with extensive trade ties to Europe, Brazil offers ample opportunities for concealing and trafficking illegal cargo within the context of legitimate trade.[48]

In the early 2000s, West Africa and the neighboring islands of Cape Verde, Madeira, and the Canaries emerged as a significant corridor connecting Latin America, primarily Brazil, to the markets in western and central Europe. Since then, the relevance of this route has fluctuated, experiencing periods of expansion and contraction.[49] While there is no conclusive agreement on why the West African trafficking route first emerged, several concurring factors can be identified. As a push factor, the increased effectiveness of interdictions along the Caribbean smuggling routes created a displacement effect, diverting shipments toward new routes where enforcement was less severe.[50] Simultaneously, as a pull factor, the presence of the African diaspora and improved international travel services attracted cocaine flows toward West Africa, which emerged as a convenient stopover for cocaine directed to Europe.[51]

Part of the cocaine transiting through Nigeria, Benin, Ghana, and other countries in West Africa moves via land and sea routes to North Africa, where Morocco serves as a key hub.[52] Morocco's strategic location, positioned between the Atlantic and the Mediterranean and just a few kilometers from Spain, combined with its well-established hashish-smuggling networks, place it as a key transshipment point for cocaine from South America to Europe.[53] Apart from Spain, the Netherlands, Belgium, the United Kingdom, and France are notable destinations for seized cocaine transiting through Africa.[54]

Although on a smaller scale, another notable example of geographic displacement in cocaine trafficking directed toward Europe is the diversion of cocaine shipments from South America to Europe through the United States. In this scenario, flows originating in the United States are often deemed less suspicious, so traffickers exploit legitimate trade routes and major American ports.[55]

Trafficking Hubs

In the domain of cocaine trafficking, transshipment hubs assume a critical role as strategic points where the drug is stored, repackaged, or transported to other locations. Europe hosts several significant maritime transshipment hubs that facilitate the movement of cocaine within the continent and beyond. Extensive research has demonstrated the central role of the port of Rotterdam in transnational drug trafficking, including cocaine, with organized criminal groups taking advantage of its favorable geographical and functional infrastructures.[56] From 1962 to 2004, Rotterdam held the title of the world's busiest port in terms of annual cargo tonnage. Even today, it remains the largest seaport in Europe and the world's largest seaport outside of East Asia. With such prominence in legal trade, it is unsurprising that Rotterdam also plays a significant role in illegal activities. Seizure data reveals that other primary hubs for cocaine importation into Europe are Antwerp in Belgium and Hamburg in Germany. Their renowned infrastructures, efficient logistics, accessibility, well-connected transport networks, and proximity to major European markets, along with their integration in legitimate trade flows, make these ports critical spaces for cocaine trafficking.[57]

Various seaports in Spain and, to a lesser extent, Italy are other significant hubs in the cocaine transshipment network. The ports of Valencia, Algeciras, and Barcelona in Spain play vital roles as entry points for cocaine shipments from South America.[58] In addition to their well-developed facilities and strategic geographical positioning, these ports' close ties with Latin American countries make them attractive targets for drug traffickers seeking to access the European market. Similarly, the ports of Gioia Tauro and Genoa in Italy have gained prominence as transshipment hubs due to their strategic location in the Mediterranean region and the high volume of vessels passing through. Moreover, the influence exerted by 'ndrangheta groups in the areas surrounding these ports further enhances their significance.[59] However, nearly all major European seaports can serve as gateways to the region's consumer markets.

While cargo ships are the primary means of transport for cocaine, traffickers are known to use a variety of types of craft and to adapt and diversify their transportation methods to elude detection. These include sailing yachts, small and fast boats, and fishing boats; and transporting cocaine in packages affixed to the bulbous bow of vessels, below the waterline.[60] Even artisanal submarines, once used exclusively along the coasts of the Americas and able to go undetected by law enforcement and pirates, are now reaching European shores, too, as certified by recent seizures along the coast of Spain.[61] However, utilizing containers remains advantageous for traffickers, as this method incurs minimal costs.

Cocaine traffickers can exploit commercial shipping lines instead of investing in their own ships, which allows them to avoid the expenses associated with owning vessels, and the risk that they might be seized. Although traffickers might have to provide compensation to the individuals who deal with the containers carrying cocaine, these costs are generally not significant. By collaborating with port coordinators, drug traffickers can ensure a seamless passage, making the process safer for them.[62] Additionally, the use of containers allows traffickers to minimize the expected costs of enforcement interventions, as transportation by aware or unaware third parties reduces the risk that a trafficker might be arrested.

On the other side, enforcing the law and maintaining security in transshipment hubs, particularly ports, pose formidable challenges to the authorities due to a combination of factors.[63] Policing these areas proves arduous as they are in a constant state of flux, with a myriad of activities taking place simultaneously. The presence of diverse infrastructure, owned by various stakeholders with differing interests, further complicates the task. Transshipment hubs such as ports experience a continuous flow of ships, cargo, personnel, and vehicles, creating a dynamic environment that requires constant surveillance and intervention. The complexity deepens as different entities, including port authorities, shipping companies, terminal operators, and customs agencies each have their own protocols and security measures and operate within the port premises. Balancing the need for smooth operations while ensuring effective law enforcement and security becomes a delicate endeavor. Finally, the sheer scale of these hubs, often handling substantial volumes of cargo and serving as crucial links in global trade, makes it challenging to monitor and detect illicit activities amid the legitimate flow of goods.[64]

In addition to seaports, airports also play a role in cocaine transshipment. The airports of Madrid and Barcelona, situated in Spain, are notable hubs in the movement of illegal drugs. During the period prior to the COVID-19 pandemic, relatively small amounts of cocaine were smuggled into Europe via commercial passenger flights. Couriers would travel from airports located in South and Central America as well as the Caribbean to prominent European airports. This journey often involved direct flights, or there were layovers in countries like Morocco, Nigeria, and the United Arab Emirates.[65] After the COVID-19 pandemic, anecdotal evidence suggests a shift toward using unaccompanied baggage to transport larger quantities of cocaine on commercial flights. Additionally, there has been more frequent use of cargo flights, with no commercial passengers, for this purpose. However, it is unclear whether this shift is directly related to the pandemic, or if it is independent of it.[66]

Actors

In recent years, academic studies have made strides in enhancing our understanding of drug-trafficking organizations operating in Europe. Scholars have researched the organizational aspects of people participating in cocaine trafficking,[67] of their financial management,[68] of their international connections along the supply chain,[69] and of their recourse to the use of violence.[70] Despite these contributions, our comprehension of the organizational dynamics of traffickers acting in the region remains limited, especially with respect to high-level profiles involved in trafficking cocaine from South America to Europe. The degree of overlap and interconnection between organized crime and drug trafficking itself remains uncertain, and it is often contingent upon the definitions adopted for both organized crime and drug trafficking. If we define organized crime as solely mafia-type criminal groups and cocaine trafficking as any activity occurring between drug production and consumption, then it is safe to say that the role of organized crime in cocaine trafficking is marginal. On the other hand, if we define organized crime more generically as the planned commission of criminal offenses to acquire profit and cocaine trafficking as activities that allow the drug to be moved across borders, then the role of organized crime is prominent.[71]

The available theories and evidence support the understanding that individual actors and criminal organizations involved in the cocaine trade do not have a unique typical form but vary significantly across countries and distribution levels in terms of their size, durability, and relationship to other criminal activities.[72] At the same time, these organizations are numerous. For instance, starting with the estimates on cocaine consumption by Federico Sallusti,[73] Jonathan P. Caulkins and colleagues estimate that, around 2010, Italy may have had between 400 and 800 operations involved in trafficking multi-kilo quantities of cocaine at the domestic level, between 2,500 and 7,500 wholesale cocaine dealers, and between 12,500 and 27,500 professional operations engaged in the retail sale of cocaine.[74]

Somehow, in contradiction to this "disorganized" interpretation of cocaine trafficking, in some countries, there is a tendency among law enforcement and policymakers to depict drug-trafficking activities in Europe as highly centralized. This centralized depiction may be driven by a desire to reinforce a narrative that justifies more robust measures and expanded powers to combat these phenomena, portraying them as highly organized threats and thus warranting additional funding, technology, and legislative authority. This fuels assumptions of quasi-monopolistic market structures. For example, in 2008 and then again in 2018, the Italian parliamentary anti-mafia commission released reports suggesting that the 'Ndrangheta, a powerful Calabrian mafia organization, controlled the bulk of transatlantic cocaine trafficking to Europe, claiming the pivotal influence of this single criminal entity in the illicit drug trade.[75] Then, this "mythical idea" of quasi-monopolistic control of cocaine trafficking into Europe by Italian criminal organizations gained popularity among law enforcement agencies and even researchers.[76] Similarly, in 2021, supranational and international institutions made reference to the 'Ndrangheta's supposed monopoly in the transatlantic cocaine trade up to the moment of the dissolution of the United Self-Defense Forces of Colombia (AUC), which caused a shift in the dynamics of drug trafficking.[77]

Currently, there is no substantial evidence to suggest that any group has the ability to exert monopolistic power over a large national market for cocaine, let alone across all of Europe. In this regard, Peter Reuter presents a compelling argument that the continuous decline in cocaine purity-adjusted prices over the past decades is a strong indication that monopolistic forces are not at play.[78] Since we observe prices going down in almost all European countries, the absence of a monopoly seems to apply to all countries, including Italy.

The lack of evidence for monopolistic power in transatlantic cocaine trafficking does not mean that structured groups, including mafia-type organizations, are not significant players in the market. The trafficking of large amounts of drugs over long distances requires organization. Therefore, while it is possible for individuals to purchase cocaine in South America and resell it in Europe, cocaine trafficking is mostly an organized activity. It is carried out by both unstructured, loose networks of individuals and more structured criminal organizations.[79] These groups do not exert control over the entire complex chain of cocaine transportation from South America to destination markets. Rather, various stages of the chain involve different actors who engage in mutually beneficial partnerships.[80] While it is not accurate to describe cocaine markets as homogeneous entities, in Europe, the groups responsible for importing and distributing locally tend to be based in Europe, with only a smaller proportion coming from departure and transit countries.[81]

Due to the strategic location and operational efficiency of seaports like Rotterdam and Antwerp, Belgian and especially Dutch nationals have been found to play a significant role in cocaine trafficking into Europe. Similarly, Spanish groups are active in cocaine importing and distribution due to Spain also serving as key entry point for cocaine shipments. Notably, investigations have identified individuals connected to the Brazilian criminal organization Primeiro Comando da Capital (PCC), who are actively involved in the distribution of cocaine in Portugal. The presence of PCC members in Portugal is likely due to the fact that the PCC has been engaged in transshipments of cocaine to Europe since before 2020.[82]

Other Latin American groups, particularly those based in Colombia, have historically played a role in cocaine trafficking to Europe.[83] These groups operate networks that involve multiple layers of individuals, ranging from low-level "mules" responsible for drug transportation to higher-level financiers, facilitators, and brokers who handle the logistical aspects of the trade. Yet visibility is a limitation for these organizations. As Damián Zaitch has shown with respect to the Netherlands, the number of Colombian firms engaged in import-export in the country is small. This makes it more difficult to conceal fake companies, and as a result, new, small Colombian companies associated with illegal operations can easily become targets for authorities.[84]

By the early 1980s, Ghanaians and Nigerians had become involved in cocaine trafficking; since the 2000s, their role had grown in relevance.[85] Criminal entrepreneurialism often taps into the same drivers of creativity and energy that fuel legitimate businesses, and Nigerians in particular have a rich and significant entrepreneurial tradition that extends throughout history.[86] Corrupt governance, a significant diaspora, a weak civil society, and low domestic wages collectively create favorable conditions for securing protection for illegal transactions within Nigeria and facilitate valuable connections outside the country.[87] Data on foreign nationals arrested in Europe in connection with cocaine seizures also reveal the relevant involvement of Moroccan citizens in mid-level distribution operations.[88]

The involvement of Latin American and African nationals in cocaine trafficking in Europe is further explained by social embeddedness theory. Drug traffickers operate within a context where trust is scarce among the individuals involved. Consequently, they rely on interpersonal networks that develop around kinship, personal connections, and shared national identities. Social embeddedness theory explains how personal relationships and other commonalities among offenders in origin and transit countries, and along major trafficking routes, provide them with competitive advantages through shared networks of contacts and a deeper understanding of each other facilitated by common language, social codes, and habits. These factors contribute to their increased effectiveness in navigating the cocaine trafficking trade.[89]

Finally, while Italian mafia organizations have no quasi-monopolistic influences on the import of cocaine into Europe, groups that are part of the Sicilian mafia, 'Ndrangheta, and Camorra are active in cocaine trafficking. 'Ndrangheta groups in particular have established extensive distribution networks in Italy and other European countries, often collaborating with Latin American criminal organizations to ensure a consistent supply of cocaine.[90] Clans belonging to the 'Ndrangheta are successful in cocaine trafficking thanks to their ability to operate secretly and raise capital to fund large purchases. Their participation in drug trafficking has led these groups to establish connections outside their territories of origin in southern Italy. While the 'Ndrangheta's major connections seem to be with traffickers operating in major European trafficking hubs such as the Netherlands and Spain, recent reports indicate that they have expanded their operations to places such as Australia, Canada, the United States, and Latin America, all of which have had substantial historical Italian migration.[91] In these contexts, these groups leverage their family ties and other personal connections to benefit cocaine trafficking.

Conclusion

This chapter provides a snapshot of the current understanding of cocaine trafficking in Europe. It is evident that western and central Europe are now key destination markets for cocaine, whose availability in Europe is increasing and whose purity-adjusted prices are declining. Cocaine flows toward Europe along multiple sea routes, which are in partial and constant adaptation due to enforcement pressure. Large European seaports are key hubs of these routes, thanks to their facilities and infrastructure. A wide range of actors, from individual brokers to mafia-type criminal groups, are involved in these trafficking activities. Yet, most frequently, trafficking operations are conducted by ephemeral organizations with no capacity to influence the dynamics of price in the market.

There is still ample scope for further research to enhance our understanding in this knowledge framework. Studies focusing on cocaine trafficking within specific European subregions that have received limited attention thus far would make valuable contributions to the existing literature. Exploring variations in prices, the presence of criminal organizations, consumption patterns, prevalence rates, and levels of violence across Europe would provide a solid basis for such investigations. Moreover, more comprehensive studies delving into the interactions among different categories of actors involved in cocaine trafficking would be highly informative. Additionally, while it is known that trafficking routes readapt to evade enforcement efforts, the decision-making processes and modus operandi of actual traffickers in relation to these adaptations remain largely unexplored. In general, the mechanisms driving change and evolution in the organization of cocaine trafficking in Europe remain predominantly speculative at this stage. A greater understanding of the mechanisms behind modifications in illegal markets would be beneficial for policymakers and law enforcement agencies. This knowledge would equip them with tools to better assess the potential impact of their strategies.

Notes

1. Alberto Aziani, "Violent Disequilibrium: The Influence of Instability in the Economic Value of Cocaine Markets on Homicides," *Crime, Law and Social Change* 74, no. 4 (October 2020): 245–72; Jonathan P. Caulkins and Peter H. Reuter, "How Much Demand for Money Laundering Services Does Drug Selling Create? Identifying the Key Parameters," *International Journal of Drug Policy* 103 (May 2022): 103652; and Jo-Anne Kramer, Arjan A. J. Blokland, Edward R. Kleemans, and Melvin R. J. Soudijn, "Money Laundering as a Service: Investigating Business-Like Behavior in Money Laundering Networks in the Netherlands," *Trends in Organized Crime* 27, no. 3 (2023): 314–41.

2. Peter H. Reuter, "Drug Markets and Organized Crime," in *The Oxford Handbook of Organized Crime*, ed. Letizia Paoli (New York: Oxford University Press, 2014), 359–80.

3. For instance, see Laura Baika and Paolo Campana, "Centrality, Mobility, and Specialization: A Study of Drug Markets in a Non-Metropolitan Area in the United Kingdom," *Journal of Drug Issues* 50, no. 2 (2020): 107–26; Francesco Calderoni, "The Structure of Drug Trafficking Mafias: The 'Ndrangheta and Cocaine," *Crime, Law and Social Change* 58, no. 3 (December 2012): 321–49; Jonathan P. Caulkins, Emma Disley, Marina Tzvetkova, Mafalda Pardal, Hemali Shah, and Xiaoke Zhang, "Modeling the Structure and Operation of Drug Supply Chains: The Case of Cocaine and Heroin in Italy and Slovenia," *International Journal of Drug Policy* 31 (May 2016): 64–73; Andrea Giménez-Salinas Framis, "Illegal Networks or Criminal Organizations: Structure, Power, and Facilitators in Cocaine Trafficking Structures," in *Crime and Networks*, ed. Carlo Morselli (New York: Routledge, 2014), 131–47; Geoffrey Pearson and Dick Hobbs, "Middle Market Drug Distribution," Home Office, London, November 2001; and Damián Zaitch, "Recent Trends in Cocaine Trafficking in the Netherlands and Spain," in *Global Organized Crime: Trends and Developments*, ed. Dina Siegel, Henk van de Bunt, and Damián Zaitch (Dordrecht: Kluwer Academic Publishers, 2003), 7–17.

4. United Nations Office on Drugs and Crime, *World Drug Report 2022*, 5 vols. (Vienna: United Nations, 2022), https://www.unodc.org/unodc/en/data-and-analysis/world-drug-report-2022.html.

5. Letizia Paoli, Victoria A. Greenfield, and Peter H. Reuter, *The World Heroin Market: Can Supply Be Cut?* (New York: Oxford University Press, 2009).

6. Francisco E. Thoumi, "Illegal Drugs in Colombia: From Illegal Economic Boom to Social Crisis," *Annals of the American Academy of Political and Social Science* 582, no. 1 (July 2002): 102–16.

7. See Sebastián A. Cutrona and Jonathan D. Rosen's introduction to this volume.

8. Caulkins et al., "Modeling the Structure and Operation of Drug Supply Chains."

9. Luca Giommoni, Giulia Berlusconi, and Alberto Aziani, "Interdicting International Drug Trafficking: A Network Approach for Coordinated and Targeted Interventions," *European Journal on Criminal Policy and Research* 28, no. 4 (2022): 545–72; and United Nations Office on Drugs and Crime, *World Drug Report 2022*.

10. Mark A. R. Kleiman, Jonathan P. Caulkins, and Angela Hawken, *Drugs and Drug Policy: What Everyone Needs to Know* (Oxford: Oxford University Press, 2011).

11. Alberto Aziani, *Illicit Financial Flows: An Innovative Approach to Estimation* (Cham, Switzerland: Springer, 2018); Jonathan P. Caulkins, "Effects of Prohibition, Enforcement and Interdiction on Drug Use," in *Ending the Drug Wars: Report of the LSE Expert Group on the Economics of Drug Policy*, ed. John F. Collins (London: London School of Economics and Political Science, 2014), https://www.lse.ac.uk/ideas/Assets/Documents/reports/LSE-IDEAS-Ending-the-Drug-Wars.pdf; Reuter, "Drug Markets and Organized Crime"; and United Nations Office on Drugs and Crime, *World Drug Report 2022*.

12. Julian Broséus, Natacha Gentile, and Pierre Esseiva, "The Cutting of Cocaine and Heroin: A Critical Review," *Forensic Science International* 262 (May 2016): 73-83; Caulkins, "Effects of Prohibition, Enforcement and Interdiction on Drug Use," 20; and Oliver Kudlacek, Tina Hofmaier, Anton Luf, Felix P. Mayer, Thomas Stockner, Constanze Nagy, Marion Holy, Michael Freissmuth, Rainer Schmid, and Harald H. Sitte, "Cocaine Adulteration," *Journal of Chemical Neuroanatomy* 83-84 (October 2017): 75-81.

13. Peter H. Reuter and Mark A. R. Kleiman, "Risks and Prices: An Economic Analysis of Drug Enforcement," *Crime and Justice* 7 (January 1986): 289–340; and Jonathan P. Caulkins and Peter H. Reuter, "How Drug Enforcement Affects Drug Prices," *Crime and Justice* 39, no. 1 (August 2010): 213–271.

14. Reuter and Kleiman, "Risks and Prices."

15. Caulkins, "Effects of Prohibition, Enforcement and Interdiction on Drug Use"; and Reuter and Kleiman, "Risks and Prices."

16. World-systems theory, developed by Immanuel Wallerstein, explains global inequalities through a hierarchical structure of nations: the core, which dominates through political influence, technological control, and the ability to set global economic rules; the periphery, which is exploited for raw materials and cheap labor; and the semiperiphery, which serves as an intermediary between the two. Fully emerging in the sixteenth and seventeenth centuries with the rise of capitalism and colonialism, this system perpetuates global disparities, although shifts within the hierarchy are possible. The theory challenges traditional development models by highlighting the structural barriers to economic equality. Immanuel Wallerstein, *The Modern World-System I: Capitalist Agriculture and the Origins of the European World-Economy in the Sixteenth Century* (New York: Academic Press, 1974).

17. Nicholas R. Magliocca, Kendra McSweeney, Steven E. Sesnie, Elizabeth Tellman, Jennifer A. Devine, Erik A. Nielsen, Zoe Pearson, and David J. Wrathall, "Modeling Cocaine Traffickers and Counterdrug Interdiction Forces as a Complex Adaptive System," *Proceedings of the National Academy of Sciences* 116, no. 16 (2019): 7784–92.

18. Peter H. Reuter, *Disorganized Crime: The Economics of the Visible Hand* (Cambridge, MA: MIT Press, 1983); and Peter H. Reuter, "Systemic Violence in Drug Markets," *Crime, Law and Social Change* 52, no. 3 (September 2009): 275–84.

19. Alberto Aziani, *Violenza e mercati illegali: Teorie ed analisi della realtà italiana* (Violence and Illegal Markets: Theories and Analysis of the Italian Reality) (Milan: Vita e Pensiero, 2022).

20. Manne Gerell, Joakim Sturup, Mia-Maria Magnusson, Kim Nilvall, Ardavan Khoshnood, and Amir Rostami, "Open Drug Markets, Vulnerable Neighbourhoods and Gun Violence in Two Swedish Cities," *Journal of Policing, Intelligence and Counter Terrorism* 16, no. 3 (2021): 223–44.

21. Roel de Bont, Teodora Groshkova, Andrew Cunningham, and Marieke C. A. Liem, "Drug-Related Homicide in Europe: First Review of Data and Sources," *International Journal of Drug Policy* 56 (April 2018): 137–43; and Paul R. Smit, Rinke R. de Jong, and Catrien C. J. H. Bijleveld, "Homicide Data in Europe: Definitions, Sources, and Statistics," in *Handbook of European Homicide Research: Patterns, Explanations, and Country Studies*, ed. Marieke C. A. Liem and William Alex Pridemore (New York: Springer, 2012), 5–23.

22. United Nations Office on Drugs and Crime, *World Drug Report 2022*.

23. The data comes from the United Nations Office on Drugs and Crime's *World Drug Report 2024*. In this report, when referring to western and central Europe, the UNODC refers to Andorra, Austria, Belgium, Cyprus, Czechia, Denmark, Estonia, Finland, France, Germany, Greece, Hungary, Iceland, Ireland, Italy, Latvia, Liechtenstein, Lithuania, Luxembourg, Malta, Monaco, the Netherlands, Norway, Poland, Portugal, San Marino, Slovakia, Slovenia, Spain, Sweden, Switzerland, the United Kingdom of Great Britain and Northern Ireland, the Faroe Islands, Gibraltar, and the Holy See.

24. Tim Boekhout van Solinge, "Global Cocaine Flows, Geographical Displacement, and Crime Convergence," in *The Evolution of Illicit Flows: Displacement and Convergence Among Transnational Crime*, ed. Ernesto U. Savona, Rob T. Guerette, and Alberto Aziani (Cham, Switzerland: Springer, 2022), 57–81; and Giommoni, Berlusconi, and Aziani, "Interdicting International Drug Trafficking."

25. Henk van de Bunt, Dina Siegel, and Damián Zaitch, "The Social Embeddedness of Organized Crime," in *The Oxford Handbook of Organized Crime*, ed. Letizia Paoli (New York: Oxford University Press, 2014), 321–38.

26. Ross Eventon and Dave Bewley-Taylor, "An Overview of Recent Changes in Cocaine Trafficking Routes into Europe," Background Paper, European Monitoring Centre for Drugs and Drug Addiction, Lisbon, 2016.

27. Office for National Statistics, "Drug Misuse in England and Wales. Year Ending June 2022," London, 2022, https://www.ons.gov.uk/peoplepopulationandcommunity/crimeandjustice/articles/drugmisuseinenglandandwales/yearendingjune2022.

28. Stéphane Legleye, Stanislas Spilka, Olivier Le Nézet, and Cécile Laffiteau, "Les drogues à 17 ans: Résultats de l'enquête ESCAPAD 2008 (Drug Use of Seventeen-Year-Olds: Results of the 2008 ESCAPAD Survey)," *Tendances*, no. 66 (June 2009): 1–6.

29. Agnieszka Klupczynska, Paweł Dereziński, Janusz Krysztofiak, and Zenon J. Kokot, "Estimation of Drug Abuse in 9 Polish Cities by Wastewater Analysis," *Forensic Science International* 260 (2016): 14–21; Tomáš Mackuľak, Igor Bodík, Jamal Hasan, Roman Grabic, Oksana Golovko, Andrea Vojs-Staňová, Miroslav Gál, Monika Naumowicz, Jozef Tichý, Paula Brandeburová, and Ján Híveš, "Dominant Psychoactive Drugs in the Central European Region: A Wastewater Study," *Forensic Science International* 267 (2016): 42–51; and United Nations Office on Drugs and Crime, *World Drug Report 2022*.

30. Natalya Aleksandrovna Mileshina, Lyudmila Aleksandrovna Potapova, and Tatyana Sergeevna Kil'myashkina, "Противодействие Наркомании в Советской России и СССР (1917–1920-е Гг.) (Countering Drug Addiction in Soviet Russia and the USSR [1917–1920s])," Манускрипт (Manuscript) 12, no. 2 (2019): 32–35.

31. See, e.g., Tim Boogaerts, Maarten Quireyns, Maarten De Prins, Bram Pussig, Hans De Loof, Catharina Matheï, Bert Aertgeerts, Virginie Van Coppenolle, Erik Fransen, Adrian Covaci, and Alexander L. N. van Nuijs, "Temporal Monitoring of Stimulants During the COVID-19 Pandemic in Belgium Through the Analysis of Influent Wastewater," *International Journal of Drug Policy* 104 (June 2022): 103679; Andrea Estévez-Danta, Lubertus Bijlsma, Ricardo Capela, Rafael Cela, Alberto Celma, Félix Hernández, Unax Lertxundi, João Matias, Rosa Montes, Gorka Orive, Ailette Prieto, Miguel M. Santos, Rosario Rodil, and José Benito Quintana, "Use of Illicit Drugs, Alcohol and Tobacco in Spain and Portugal During the COVID-19 Crisis in 2020 as Measured by Wastewater-Based Epidemiology," *Science of the Total Environment* 836 (August 2022): 155697; and Reinhard Oertel, Sara Schubert, Björn Helm, and Robin Mayer, "Drug Consumption in German Cities and Municipalities During the COVID-19 Lockdown: A Wastewater Analysis," *Naunyn-Schmiedeberg's Archives of Pharmacology* 396, no. 5 (May 2023): 1061–74.

32. European Monitoring Centre for Drugs and Drug Addiction, *European Drug Report 2022: Trends and Developments* (Luxembourg: Publications Office of the European Union, 2022).

33. United Nations Office on Drugs and Crime, *World Drug Report 2022*.

34. Ruud Steenbeek, Erik Emke, Dennis Vughs, João Matias, Tim Boogaerts, Sara Castiglioni, Marina Campos-Mañas, Adrian Covaci, Pim de Voogt, Thomas Ter Laak, Félix Hernández, Noelia Salgueiro-González, Wim G. Meijer, Mario J. Dias, Susana Simões, Alexander L. N. van Nuijs, Lubertus Bijlsma, Frederic Béen. "Spatial and Temporal Assessment of Crack Cocaine Use in 13 European Cities Through Wastewater-Based Epidemiology," *Science of the Total Environment* 847, no. 6 (2022): 157222.

35. Gabriella Conti, Stephen E. Pudney, Mark L. Bryan, Celia Badillo, Jonathan Burton, and Maria Iacovou, "Estimating the Size of the UK Illicit Drug Market," in *Measuring Different Aspects of Problem Drug Use: Methodological Developments*, Home Office, London, November 2006; Malcolm J. Reid, Katherine H. Langford, Merete Grung, Hallvard Gjerde, Ellen J. Amundsen, Jorg Morland, and Kevin V. Thomas, "Estimation of Cocaine Consumption in the Community: A Critical Comparison of the Results from Three Complimentary Techniques," *BMJ Open* 2, no. 6 (2012); and Tom Frijns and Margriet van Laar, "Amphetamine, Ecstasy and Cocaine: Typology of Users, Availability and Consumption Estimates," in *Further Insights into Aspects of the Illicit EU Drugs Market*, ed. Franz Trautmann, Beau Kilmer, and Paul Turnbull (Luxembourg: Publications Office of the European Union, 2013), 183–242, https://home-affairs.ec.europa.eu/system/files/2020-09/eu_market_full.pdf.

36. Magdalena Harris, "An Urgent Impetus for Action: Safe Inhalation Interventions to Reduce COVID-19 Transmission and Fatality Risk Among People Who Smoke Crack Cocaine in the United Kingdom," *International Journal of Drug Policy* 83 (2020): 102829.

37. Rémi Boivin, "Drug Trafficking Networks in the World Economy," in *Crime and Networks*, ed. Carlo Morselli (New York: Routledge, 2014), 182–94; Rémi Boivin, "Risks, Prices, and Positions: A Social Network Analysis of Illegal Drug Trafficking in the World-Economy," *International Journal of Drug Policy* 25, no. 2 (March 2014): 235–43; and Rob T. Guerette and Alberto Aziani, "The Displacement and Convergence of Transnational Crime Flows," in *The Evolution of Illicit Flows: Displacement and Convergence Among Transnational Crime*, ed. Ernesto U. Savona, Rob T. Guerette, and Alberto Aziani (Cham, Switzerland: Springer, 2022), 9–25.

38. Van de Bunt, Siegel, and Zaitch, "The Social Embeddedness of Organized Crime."

39. Alberto Aziani, Giulia Berlusconi, and Luca Giommoni, "A Quantitative Application of Enterprise and Social Embeddedness Theories to the Transnational Trafficking of Cocaine in Europe," *Deviant Behavior* 42, no. 2 (2021): 245–67.

40. Eventon and Bewley-Taylor, "An Overview of Recent Changes in Cocaine Trafficking Routes."

41. Marleen Easton, "Policing Flows of Drugs in the Harbor of Antwerp: A Nodal-Network Analysis," in *Maritime Supply Chains*, ed. Thierry Vanelslander and Christa Sys (Amsterdam: Elsevier, 2020), 115–34; Yarin Eski and Romano Buijt, "Dockers in Drugs: Policing the Illegal Drug Trade and Port Employee Corruption in the Port of Rotterdam," *Policing: A Journal of Policy and Practice* 11, no. 4 (December 2017): 371–86; and Damián Zaitch, "From Cali to Rotterdam: Perceptions of Colombian Cocaine Traffickers on the Dutch Port," *Crime, Law and Social Change* 38, no. 3 (2002): 239–66.

42. United Nations Office on Drugs and Crime, *Global Report on Cocaine 2023: Local Dynamics, Global Challenges* (Vienna: United Nations, 2023).

43. United Nations Office on Drugs and Crime, *Global Report on Cocaine 2023*.

44. Jonathan P. Caulkins, Gordon Crawford, and Peter H. Reuter, "Simulation of Adaptive Response: A Model of Drug Interdiction," *Mathematical and Computer Modelling* 17, no. 2 (January 1993): 37-52; Guerette and Aziani, "The Displacement and Convergence of Transnational Crime Flows"; and Peter H. Reuter, "The Mobility of Drug Trafficking," in *Ending the Drug Wars: Report of the LSE Expert Group on the Economics of Drug Policy*, ed. John F. Collins (London: London School of Economics and Political Science, 2014), 33-40.

45. Carolina Sampó and Valeska Troncoso, "Cocaine Trafficking from Non-Traditional Ports: Examining the Cases of Argentina, Chile and Uruguay," *Trends in Organized Crime* 26, no. 1 (January 2022): 235-57.

46. Frank O. Mora, "Victims of the Balloon Effect: Drug Trafficking and U.S. Policy in Brazil and the Southern Cone of Latin America," *Journal of Social, Political, and Economic Studies* 21, no. 2 (Summer 1996): 115.

47. Eventon and Bewley-Taylor, "An Overview of Recent Changes in Cocaine Trafficking Routes"; Mora, "Victims of the Balloon Effect"; and United Nations Office on Drugs and Crime, *Global Report on Cocaine 2023*.

48. Boekhout van Solinge, "Global Cocaine Flows."

49. Boekhout van Solinge, "Global Cocaine Flows"; and Eventon and Bewley-Taylor, "An Overview of Recent Changes in Cocaine Trafficking Routes."

50. Reuter, "The Mobility of Drug Trafficking."

51. Emmanuel Akyeampong, "Diaspora and Drug Trafficking in West Africa: A Case Study of Ghana," *African Affairs* 104, no. 416 (July 2005): 429-47.

52. United Nations Office on Drugs and Crime, *Global Report on Cocaine 2023*.

53. Boekhout van Solinge, "Global Cocaine Flows."

54. Cecilia Meneghini, "Structure and Evolution of Drug Trafficking Networks in North Africa: The Impact of Rule of Law and Corruption," in *The Evolution of Illicit Flows: Displacement and Convergence Among Transnational Crime*, ed. Ernesto U. Savona, Rob T. Guerette, and Alberto Aziani (Cham, Switzerland: Springer, 2022), 173-92; and United Nations Office on Drugs and Crime, *Global Report on Cocaine 2023*.

55. Boekhout van Solinge, "Global Cocaine Flows."

56. Yarin Eski, "'Port of Call': Towards a Criminology of Port Security," *Criminology and Criminal Justice* 11, no. 5 (2011): 415-31; Eski and Buijt, "Dockers in Drugs"; Graham Farrell, "Routine Activities and Drug Trafficking: The Case of the Netherlands," *International Journal of Drug Policy* 9, no. 1 (February 1998): 21-32; Joras Ferwerda and Brigitte Unger, "Organised Crime Infiltration in the Netherlands: Transportation Companies Hiding

Transit Crimes," in *Organised Crime in European Businesses*, ed. Ernesto U. Savona, Michele Riccardi, and Giulia Berlusconi (Abingdon, Oxon., England: Routledge, 2016), 35–50; and Cyrille Fijnaut, Frank Bovenkerk, Gerben Bruinsma, and Henk van de Bunt, *Organized Crime in the Netherlands* (The Hague: Kluwer Law International, 1998).

57. Cláudia Costa Storti and Paul De Grauwe, "Globalization and the Price Decline of Illicit Drugs," *International Journal of Drug Policy* 20, no. 1 (January 2009): 48–61; Robby Roks, Lieselot Bisschop, and Richard Staring, "Getting a Foot in the Door: Spaces of Cocaine Trafficking in the Port of Rotterdam," *Trends in Organized Crime* 24, no. 2 (June 2021): 171–88; Vincenzo Ruggiero, "Organised and Transnational Crime in Europe," in *The Routledge Handbook of European Criminology*, ed. Sophie Body-Gendrot, Mike Hough, Klára Kerezsi, René Lévy, and Sonja Snacken (Abingdon, Oxon., England: Routledge, 2014), 154–67; and Anna Sergi, "Playing Pac-Man in Portville: Policing the Dilution and Fragmentation of Drug Importations Through Major Seaports," *European Journal of Criminology* 19, no. 4 (July 2022): 674–91.

58. Sampó and Troncoso, "Cocaine Trafficking from Non-Traditional Ports."

59. Marco Antonelli, "An Exploration of Organized Crime in Italian Ports from an Institutional Perspective: Presence and Activities," *Trends in Organized Crime* 24, no. 2 (June 2021): 152–70; and Anna Sergi and Anita Lavorgna, "Calabria and the 'Ndrangheta," in *'Ndrangheta: The Glocal Dimensions of the Most Powerful Italian Mafia* (Cham, Switzerland: Palgrave Macmillan, 2016), 13–32.

60. Adriana Ávila-Zúñiga-Nordfjeld, Hans Liwång, and Dimitrios Dalaklis, "Implications of Technological Innovation and Respective Regulations to Strengthen Port and Maritime Security: An International Agenda to Reduce Illegal Drug Traffic and Countering Terrorism at Sea," in *Smart Ports and Robotic Systems: Navigating the Waves of Techno-Regulation and Governance*, ed. Tafsir Matin Johansson, Dimitrios Dalaklis, Jonatan Echebarria Fernández, Aspasia Pastra, and Mitchell Lennan (Cham, Switzerland: Springer, 2023), 135–47; and Andrew O'Hagan and Chalkia Paraskevi, "Cocaine Trafficking Between South America and Greece and Methods of Concealment," *Forensic Research and Criminology International Journal* 10, no. 2 (2022): 37–43.

61. Boekhout van Solinge, "Global Cocaine Flows."

62. Sampó and Troncoso, "Cocaine Trafficking from Non-Traditional Ports."

63. Yarin Eski, "Customer Is King: Promoting Port Policing, Supporting Hypercommercialism," *Policing and Society* 30, no. 2 (2020): 153–68; and Anna Sergi, "Policing the Port, Watching the City: Manifestations of Organised Crime in the Port of Genoa," *Policing and Society* 31, no. 6 (2021): 639–55.

64. Russell Brewer, *Policing the Waterfront: Networks, Partnerships, and the Governance of Port Security* (Oxford: Oxford University Press, 2014); and Yarin Eski, *Policing, Port Security and Crime Control: An Ethnography of the Port Securityscape* (Abingdon, Oxon., England: Routledge, 2016).

65. European Union Drugs Agency, "EU Drug Market: Cocaine," Lisbon, 2022, https://www.euda.europa.eu/publications/joint-publications/cocaine-market_en.

66. United Nations Office on Drugs and Crime, *Global Report on Cocaine 2023*.

67. See, e.g., Giulia Berlusconi, "Come at the King, You Best Not Miss: Criminal Network Adaptation After Law Enforcement Targeting of Key Players," *Global Crime* 23, no. 1 (2022): 44–64; Calderoni, "The Structure of Drug Trafficking Mafias"; and Caulkins et al., "Modeling the Structure and Operation of Drug Supply Chains."

68. Fiamma Terenghi, "The Financial Management of Cocaine Trafficking in Italy," *European Journal of Criminology* 19, no. 6 (2022): 1501–20.

69. See, e.g., Francesco Calderoni, Giulia Berlusconi, Lorella Garofalo, Luca Giommoni, and Federica Sarno, "The Italian Mafias in the World: A Systematic Assessment of the Mobility of Criminal Groups," *European Journal of Criminology* 13, no. 4 (2016): 413–33; and Paolo Campana, "Eavesdropping on the Mob: The Functional Diversification of Mafia Activities Across Territories," *European Journal of Criminology* 8, no. 3 (2011): 213–28.

70. See, e.g., Aziani, *Violenza e mercati illegali*; and Gerell et al., "Open Drug Markets, Vulnerable Neighbourhoods and Gun Violence."

71. Letizia Paoli, "What Is the Link between Organized Crime and Drug Trafficking?," *Rausch: Wiener Zeitschrift für Suchttherapie* 6, no. 4 (2017): 181–89.

72. Reuter, "Drug Markets and Organized Crime."

73. Federico Sallusti, "Estimating the Cocaine Market in Italy: A National Accounts Framework," in *Illicit Drug Market and Its Economic Impact*, ed. Jiří Vopravil and Carla Rossi (Rome: Università di Roma, 2013).

74. Caulkins et al., "Modeling the Structure and Operation of Drug Supply Chains."

75. Commissione d'inchiesta sul fenomeno delle mafie e sulle altre associazioni criminali, anche straniere, "Relazione annuale sulla 'Ndrangheta (Annual Report on the 'Ndrangheta)" (doc. XXIII, n. 3, XV legislature, 2008); and Commissione d'inchiesta sul fenomeno delle mafie e sulle altre associazioni criminali, anche straniere, "Relazione conclusiva (Final Report)" (doc. XXIII, n. 38, XVII legislature, 2018).

76. See, e.g., Europol, "Threat Assessment: Italian Organised Crime," The Hague, 2013; and Francesca Calandra, "Between Local and Global: The 'Ndrangheta's Drug Trafficking Route," *International Annals of Criminology* 55, no. 1 (2017): 78–98.

77. United Nations Office on Drugs and Crime and Europol, *Cocaine Insights 1: The Illicit Trade of Cocaine from Latin America to Europe; From Oligopolies to Free-for-All?* (Vienna: United Nations, 2021), https://www.unodc.org/documents/data-and-analysis/cocaine/Cocaine_Insights_2021.pdf.

78. Reuter, "Drug Markets and Organized Crime."

79. Aziani, Berlusconi, and Giommoni, "A Quantitative Application of Enterprise and Social Embeddedness Theories"; Calderoni, "The Structure of Drug Trafficking Mafias"; Calderoni et al., "The Italian Mafias in the World"; Klaus von Lampe, *Organized Crime: Analyzing Illegal Activities, Criminal Structures, and Extra-Legal Governance* (Thousand Oaks, CA: SAGE Publications, 2016); and Zaitch, "From Cali to Rotterdam."

80. Baika and Campana, "Centrality, Mobility, and Specialization"; and Pearson and Hobbs, "Middle Market Drug Distribution."

81. Letizia Paoli and Peter H. Reuter, "Drug Trafficking and Ethnic Minorities in Western Europe," *European Journal of Criminology* 5, no. 1 (2008): 13–37; and United Nations Office on Drugs and Crime, *Global Report on Cocaine 2023*.

82. Michael Jerome Wolff, "Organized Crime and the State in Brazil," in *The Criminalization of States: The Relationship Between States and Organized Crime*, ed. Jonathan D. Rosen, Bruce Michael Bagley, and Jorge Chabat (Lanham, MD: Lexington Books, 2019), 323–40.

83. Paoli and Reuter, "Drug Trafficking and Ethnic Minorities."

84. Zaitch, "From Cali to Rotterdam."

85. Stephen Ellis, "West Africa's International Drug Trade," *African Affairs* 108, no. 431 (April 2009): 171–96.

86. Phil Williams, "Nigerian Criminal Organizations," in *The Oxford Handbook of Organized Crime*, ed. Letizia Paoli (New York: Oxford University Press, 2014), 254–69.

87. Paoli and Reuter, "Drug Trafficking and Ethnic Minorities."

88. United Nations Office on Drugs and Crime, *Global Report on Cocaine 2023*.

89. Aziani, Berlusconi, and Giommoni, "A Quantitative Application of Enterprise and Social Embeddedness Theories"; and Paoli and Reuter, "Drug Trafficking and Ethnic Minorities."

90. Letizia Paoli, "An Underestimated Criminal Phenomenon: The Calabrian 'Ndrangheta," *European Journal of Crime, Criminal Law and Criminal Justice* 2, no. 3 (1994): 212–38.

91. Campana, "Eavesdropping on the Mob"; Calderoni et al., "The Italian Mafias in the World"; and Anna Sergi, "Traditional Organised Crime on the Move: Exploring the Globalisation of the Calabrian 'Ndrangheta," in *The Dark Side of Globalisation*, ed. Leila Simona Talani and Roberto Roccu (Cham, Switzerland: Palgrave Macmillan, 2019), 123–45.

CHAPTER 11

Cocaine Trafficking and Criminal Organizations in Africa

Caroline Agboola

Historically, the role of Africa in the international cocaine supply chain was minor. West Africa, which is currently a key transshipment hub for cocaine trafficking between Latin America and Europe, witnessed extensive cocaine trafficking for the first time around 2004. The amount of annual cocaine seizures in West Africa increased rapidly from about one metric ton per year pre-2008 to between forty-six and three hundred tons by 2015.[1] This annual increase has continued over time through 2022.[2] The global increase in the use of cocaine has led to an increase in its production and trafficking,[3] with a ripple effect on the amount of cocaine that transits Africa. The exponential increase in the quantity of cocaine that is transshipped via Africa per year has resulted in the development of criminal networks of African and non-African descent who control the global trafficking of cocaine from Latin America to Europe, via Africa.

This chapter focuses on trends in cocaine trafficking, transshipment hubs, and routes in Africa, as well as the main actors in the trafficking of cocaine on the continent and how they operate. To understand cocaine trafficking in Africa, we must examine the nexus between Latin America and Africa because the two regions are interconnected in a supplier and transit relationship. This chapter will explain the role of Africa within the cocaine supply chain, with specific focus on the Latin American connection, the interrelatedness between the cocaine markets in Latin America and Africa, and the role of African actors in the Latin American cocaine landscape. In addition, the criminal organizations that control cocaine trafficking between Latin America and Africa will be discussed.

Departure Points:
From Latin America to Europe via Africa

There has been an increase in the use of cocaine worldwide.[4] The major global cocaine markets are South and Central America, the Caribbean, Western and Central Europe, and North America. Observers predict an expansion of the small cocaine markets in Asia and Africa because of the rise in the supply of the drug at its main source, Latin America.[5] The number of cocaine users is predicted to increase from an estimated 21.5 million users in 2020 to 55 million users by 2030 if the prevalence of cocaine use continues to rise in Africa, Asia, and some parts of Europe to match that of Western and Central Europe, and North America.[6]

According to the United Nations Office on Drugs and Crime (UNODC)'s 2013 report on the state of drug production and use worldwide, the main points of departure for cocaine in Latin America and the Caribbean bound for overseas markets were Brazil, Colombia, Argentina, the Dominican Republic, Venezuela, Peru, and Jamaica.[7] Ten years later, Brazil is the predominant departure point for cocaine trafficking from Latin America to Africa and Europe. The bulk of the cocaine that is trafficked globally originates from South America, particularly Colombia, Peru, and Bolivia. Of these three countries, Colombia accounted for up to 70 percent of the coca plants grown and two-thirds of cocaine manufactured between 2015 and 2020. Cocaine that is destined for the global market is trafficked from these three countries via several routes.[8] One of these routes is Africa.

Transit Routes: Africa as a Prominent Component of an Intercontinental Cocaine Trafficking Network

Africa occupies a key position in the cocaine supply chain. This is largely because of its crucial role as a transit and storage continent for cocaine being trafficked from Brazil to Europe. Similarly, there is a transit-destination relationship between Brazil and Nigeria.[9] Africa's prominence in the global cocaine market increased significantly during 2019-2021. This was evident by the large quantities of cocaine seized on the continent, which peaked in 2021. The outbreak of COVID-19 in 2020 resulted in a temporary decline in the amount of cocaine seized in Africa.[10] From 2019 to 2021, among the world's nine subregions as defined by the UNODC—Oceania, North America, South America, Central America, the Caribbean, Western and Central Europe, Eastern and Southeastern Europe, Asia, and Africa—Africa had the highest increase in cocaine seizures (almost 400 percent) compared to the period 2016-2018, more than doubling the growth rate registered in Asia.[11]

Cocaine is trafficked from Brazil to Africa and Europe across the Atlantic. Geographical and nongeographical considerations account for Africa's central role in the smuggling of cocaine from Brazil to Europe. First, because of their location, West and Central Africa are ideal passageways for cocaine being smuggled from South America, particularly Brazil, to Europe. The shortest distance between South America and Africa is between the easternmost point of Brazil and the coastlines of Senegal and Guinea-Bissau.[12] Second, the choice of trafficking cocaine through Africa is informed not so much by the continent's geographic location but by the ease with which drug cartels and other criminal organizations are able to navigate African countries without being caught. Sometimes, cocaine makes its way into West Africa, then transits through northern Mali, for instance, and exits the continent through Algeria[13] or elsewhere in North Africa.[14] Latin American criminal groups that control the movement of cocaine find cocaine trafficking through Africa more financially rewarding, and safer, than other routes.[15]

Seaports and airports, with weakened law enforcement structures, cheap bribes,[16] and lax security, constitute the entry points of cocaine into West Africa from Latin America.[17] Inadequate policing, corruption of border officials, and corrupt and ineffective criminal justice in West Africa have aided the growth of cocaine trafficking in the region.[18] Criminal networks involved in cocaine trafficking in Africa are rarely charged with crimes in court. Even when they are, their convictions are overturned without reason. For instance, in 2010 a Frenchman and his local accomplices were convicted in Nouakchott, Mauritania, for the transport of 760 kilograms of cocaine in a minibus, and the conviction was later reversed.[19] Other cases of members of drug cartels who are deliberately released by the African criminal justice system abound.[20] Poor law enforcement and corruption, particularly in West Africa—the ability to bribe those who control African bureaucracies, including government officials[21] and top politicians—have allowed cocaine trafficking on the continent to thrive. In Guinea-Bissau, Latin American criminal organizations bribe the military personnel who control the country. These bribes serve as a shield against prosecution.[22] In Ghana, which has more effective state institutions than Guinea-Bissau, Latin American criminal groups evade arrest by using local Ghanaian criminal actors as "shields of protection." Inevitably, the number of arrested small-time Ghanaian cocaine traffickers increases while the Latin American drug barons remain unscathed.[23] Criminal networks establish alliances with politicians—high cadre government officials and members of the criminal justice system—through bribery. They deploy such a strategy to maximize profits, as anti-cocaine smuggling state responses, whether heightened border security or increased prosecution of cocaine smugglers, result in an overall increase in the transportation costs of cocaine consignments and a corresponding decrease in profit for the smugglers.[24]

Cocaine Criminal Actors in Africa

Criminal actors in the cocaine trade are present throughout Africa; the African Organized Crime Index ranks African countries as follows, from most active in this trade to least: Guinea-Bissau, Cape Verde, Guinea, the Gambia, Ghana, Nigeria, Senegal, Angola, Benin, Kenya, Mali, Morocco, Niger, Lesotho, Liberia, South Africa, Côte d'Ivoire, the Republic of the Congo, Tanzania, Togo, Chad, the Democratic Republic of the Congo, Mauritania, Namibia, Sierra Leone, Burkina Faso, Ethiopia, Libya, Algeria, Botswana, Cameroon, Mauritius, Mozambique, Uganda, the Seychelles, Tunisia, Zambia, Zimbabwe, Eswatini, Burundi, Gabon, Madagascar, Malawi, Rwanda, Sudan, the Comoros, Egypt, Somalia, São Tomé and Príncipe, the Central African Republic, Djibouti, Equatorial Guinea, Eritrea, and South Sudan.[25] Although cocaine criminal actors are spread throughout the continent, Guinea-Bissau is the epicenter of drug trafficking in Africa. Indeed, this has been the situation since around 2005.[26]

In West Africa, there are cocaine hubs in Cotonou (Benin) and Abidjan (Côte d'Ivoire), and Nigeria is a major hub for cocaine trafficking.[27] Latin American criminal organizations partner with Nigerian actors. The Latin Americans establish their presence and ensconce themselves in the communities through a process that Henk van de Bunt, Dina Siegel, and Damián Zaitch describe as "embeddedness,"[28] which entails engaging in social interactions within local West African communities. Some interactions involve gaining legal residence in a given country by obtaining a resident permit. Thereafter, the Latin American newcomers can consolidate their presence in the local economy and with local cocaine actors by establishing companies, which act as a facade for cocaine trafficking in the region. Partnerships between Latin American cocaine organizations and Nigerians facilitate the establishment of storage outlets, banking services, and other services that promote cocaine smuggling and trafficking.[29] In addition to Latin American criminal organizations such as Mexican drug cartels (e.g., the Sinaloa cartel) and Venezuelan groups, others also operate in West Africa, including Italians and Surinamese.[30]

Like the structure of the Nigerian cocaine network in São Paulo, which is discussed in detail later in this chapter, West African criminal networks consist of small groups with a maximum of ten members, often of the same ethnic group. Recruitment into such an organization is strictly by invitation. Established members invite members of their family and their dependents to join their network.[31] The influence of the Nigerian cocaine networks extend beyond the African continent to Brazil, as discussed below.

The heavy presence of Nigerians in the African cocaine trafficking scene notwithstanding, the primary target of predator South American drug traffickers is Guinea-Bissau, because conditions in that country—extremely ineffective maritime security, unmonitored airspace, the absence of prisons, ill-equipped police vehicles, and a military and government that are easily bribed—allow cocaine trafficking to blossom, both within the country and transiting through.[32] This situation also allows Bissau-Guineans to become major actors as well, in collaborations with Malian criminal groups[33] and in the trafficking of cocaine throughout Africa, too. The prevailing conditions in Guinea-Bissau mark the country as a failed state; these include persistent political violence, the proliferation of criminal violence including drug trafficking, and porous borders.[34] In addition to Guinea-Bissau's extreme poverty, its distance from the region's major economic powers enables it to pass under the radar of European governments. The country has witnessed several cocaine seizures, one of the most famous being one that occurred in September 2019 where four thousand pounds of cocaine, millions of US dollars in bank accounts, and various goods were confiscated.[35] In Guinea-Bissau, cocaine actors include rich members of Colombian drug cartels, with lavish residences and luxurious cars that starkly contrast against the impoverished environment they are in; and poor locals. Guinea-Bissau functions as a storage and transshipment center for cocaine that is trafficked from South America to Europe by local drug mules on passenger flights, by ship, and across Morocco on land following the old cannabis route.[36] Guinea-Bissau has a thriving local cocaine market, too, with the drug being peddled from door to door; in 2008, a local restaurant owner complained to *The Guardian*: "A few weeks ago, the man who used to be my gardener knocked at the door and offered to sell me 7kg of cocaine."[37]

Cocaine Trafficking Networks in Brazil: Brazilian and African Interconnectedness

There is a high concentration of Nigerian cocaine traffickers in the city of São Paulo, Brazil. Other cocaine traffickers in Brazil include Lebanese, Kenyans, Angolans, and Mozambicans. Criminologist Jude Roys Oboh has identified six categories of players in the Nigerian cocaine trafficking scene within and outside Nigeria. These are large-scale smugglers, who are also referred to as *oga* or big men; small-scale traffickers or entrepreneurs; strikers; couriers or "suicide birds"; part-time couriers or freelance traffickers; and retailers. These actors have not developed large organizations in Brazil; instead, they often engage in solo work as cocaine traders or act in collaboration with other middlemen. They occupy the position of middlemen between the traffickers who dominate the cocaine scene in Brazil and the lesser-known cocaine traffickers. Collaborations between these Nigerian cocaine actors go beyond Brazil and extend to countries such as Colombia, Venezuela, Bolivia, and Argentina. Furthermore, the influence of Nigerian traffickers extends to carceral spaces when they are imprisoned. They continue to mastermind cocaine trafficking from inside Brazilian prisons using cell phones, which they purchase from imprisoned members of Primeiro Comando da Capital (PCC; First Command of the Capital) or from corrupt prison staff. While the Nigerian traffickers who belong to the oga category can single-handedly purchase individual cell phones for their use behind bars, small-time traffickers often contribute money to a joint fund to buy a phone for shared use among themselves. Prison inmates who cannot afford a cell phone buy a SIM card and then rent a phone from another inmate to make calls. During incarceration, Nigerian cocaine traffickers form alliances with imprisoned PCC members and other Brazilian and Latin American prisoners.[38]

In addition to cocaine trafficking, some Nigerian criminals in Brazil engage in regular business ventures such as retail businesses and services, and they may be looked down upon by local people. However, they remain susceptible to violence from local criminal groups in the Brazilian cocaine network because they do not belong to any dominant group, suggesting that "transplantation," using Federico Varese's term, is highly unlikely.[39] Instead, these Nigerian actors strive to consolidate their integration into Brazil through education and by marrying Brazilian women. Some maintain a strong bond to Nigeria, a high level of ethnic unity, an affinity for kinship ties, and international travel experience, among other attributes. Strong affiliations to ethnic groups and kinship ties are a major disadvantage for Nigerian cocaine traffickers in Brazil, because such affiliations may result in their easy arrest by the Brazilian police—and they can be a breeding ground for jealousy and dispute. The large numbers of Nigerian cocaine traffickers in Brazil notwithstanding, some who reside in São Paulo have legitimate livelihoods and distance themselves from their compatriots who are involved in cocaine trafficking in the city. More recent Nigerian migrants to São Paulo are recognized as being involved in cocaine trafficking in the city, as compared to long-standing migrants of Nigerian origin who emigrated to Brazil around the 1970s and actively participate in the local economy with respectable jobs as lawyers, engineers, lecturers, and medical doctors. Some Nigerian cocaine traffickers in São Paulo had intentions of being law-abiding residents when they first arrived in Brazil but got involved in cocaine trafficking due to insufficient opportunities in the country. Established cocaine traffickers in São Paulo recruit new members to their organizations, both Brazilian and Nigerian, by focusing on those from poor socioeconomic backgrounds.[40]

Sometimes, Nigerians are involved in the interregional shipment of cocaine between Latin America and Africa. For instance, in January 2013, Ghanaian authorities seized two hundred kilograms of cocaine at Tema Harbor, near Accra, that had been smuggled from Bolivia to Ghana by Nigerian traffickers. The apprehended cocaine had been transported in freight containers and concealed among several boxes of shampoo. Four Nigerian passports, which had four different names, were found on an arrested individual. This incident highlights the contention that criminals who claim to be Nigerian and who are in possession of Nigerian passports are not always Nigerian but in fact come from other African countries. Unscrupulous Nigerians sometimes issue bogus Nigerian passports to their accomplices.[41] Smuggling cocaine with bogus passports is not uncommon among cocaine traffickers. In March 2019, police in Guinea-Bissau intercepted a 789-kilogram cocaine shipment and arrested a Malian in connection with the seizure. The cocaine was on its way from Senegal to Mali, and the arrested trafficker had a Nigerian passport even though he was Malian.[42] Although only half of all Africans who reside in Brazil are Nigerians, most Brazilians refer to every African living in their country as Nigerian. A plausible reason for this faulty generalization could be because Nigerian cocaine traffickers in Brazil often attract the attention of Brazilian police, and the general public, through their incessant brawls; their high visibility perhaps leads Brazilians to generalize about Africans more broadly. The raucous nuisance incited by some Nigerian cocaine traffickers in Brazil is often an anathema to law-abiding Nigerians, who tend to dissociate themselves from such kinsmen.[43]

Not surprisingly, nearly all cocaine trafficking in Africa takes place in West Africa. A quick Google search on the phrase "cocaine trafficking in Africa" leads to websites about trafficking in West Africa. A small proportion of the search results mention Central Africa, East Africa, and Southern Africa. West Africa is a storage,[44] transit, and consumer location in the cocaine supply chain. The cocaine that is trafficked through Africa is produced in South America.[45] Prior to 2004, West Africa was insignificant as a cocaine trafficking route. Between 2004 and 2008, however, the region experienced a boom in this regard.[46] This was spurred on by a sharp decline in the US cocaine market, which began in 2006, and the simultaneous increase in the European cocaine market.[47] Data on cocaine seizures in West Africa has become increasingly comprehensive since 2005.[48] Now, the region plays a central role in drug trafficking, particularly cocaine. It is a transit region for cocaine between South America and Europe. About fifty-seven tons of cocaine were intercepted by law enforcement agencies in the region during the four-year period from 2019 to 2022.

This passage of illegal drugs through West Africa has transformed the drug landscape in the region, with the development of a homegrown market worth billions of dollars annually.[49] The large-scale local use of drugs in Africa, including cocaine, is projected to generate a 38 percent increase in the number of drug users on the continent between 2018 and 2030.[50] The drug-use problem in Africa is so great that one of the hardest-hit countries, Guinea-Bissau, has been declared Africa's first "narco-state"[51] ("narco" in this regard implying cocaine).[52] The production and trafficking of cocaine on the continent has culminated in a myriad of problems for African nations. These include the generation of funds for armed militias, with youth within these organizations being remunerated with cocaine; political instability and violence, which is sustained with the arms in circulation and the huge amounts of money generated by cocaine trafficking; and an increase in illicit drug use. These conditions are evident in countries that have suffered incessant coups, both failed and successful—Guinea-Bissau, Chad, Mali, Guinea, Sudan, and Burkina Faso.[53]

For more than a decade since around 2015, drug trafficking has steadily increased in West Africa, warranting the declaration of a drug epidemic in the region. The use of illicit drugs is deemed a public health problem, and it has affected nearly the entire adult population (those between the ages of fifteen and sixty-four). Prior to the advent of and upsurge in the trafficking of illicit drugs through West Africa, the region itself did not have a drug use problem among its own inhabitants.[54] In 2021, there were an estimated twenty-two million cocaine users worldwide.[55] While there is a paucity of data on the extent of cocaine consumption in Africa, the increased transshipment of cocaine through the continent has resulted in a corresponding increase in the use of illicit drugs there.[56] As much as 20 percent of cocaine that transits South Africa, for instance, is consumed locally.[57]

The West African country of Mali is another transit point for cocaine that is trafficked from Latin America to Europe.[58] Cocaine trafficking within Mali is carried out by local criminal groups and armed groups.[59] Some notable criminal groups are Groupe d'Autodéfense Touareg Imghad et Alliés (GATIA), Mouvement National de Libération de l'Azawad (MNLA), Mouvement Arabe de Libération de l'Azawad–Plateforme (MAA-PF), and Coordination des Mouvements de l'Azawad (CMA).[60] These armed groups provide protection, including armed escort services within Mali, for cocaine and related contraband in transit across the country;[61] they fund their purchases of weaponry and other activities with the money that is generated from these illicit endeavors.[62] Some of the armed groups enjoy the support of their communities because they provide those communities with social amenities such as water and electricity.[63] Sometimes, the Arab communities in Mali give support to armed groups, who are their kinsmen.[64] Money obtained from cocaine trafficking fuels intrastate conflict in Guinea and Guinea-Bissau as well as Mali.[65] Some of the major cocaine trafficking hubs in Mali are Tabankort, Lerneb, Tinzaouaten, Boughessa, Boujheba, Kidal, Talhandak, Anéfis, Tessalit, Taoudenni, Léré, Nioro du Sahel, Nara, Timbuktu, Labbezanga, Ber, Bourem, Gao, Menaka, Almoustarat, Tarkint, Anderamboukane, and In-Khalil.

In addition to West Africa, Central and East Africa are also transit zones for cocaine en route to European markets, with the countries having sea coasts accounting for the highest number of cocaine seizures. An emerging transit zone is found in South Africa, with its significant cocaine seizures and predicted rebound in its own local cocaine market. The East African countries of Kenya and Ethiopia are transit zones for cocaine, too, with stopovers on the journey to Europe. Brazilian criminal syndicates strategically pick out countries where Portuguese is spoken (e.g., Cape Verde, Mozambique, and Angola) as transit zones in the Europe-bound cocaine movements they control.[66] Henk van de Bunt, Dina Siegel, and Damián Zaitch show that criminal organizations tend to collaborate with those who speak the same language or share similar cultural and social codes of conduct.[67]

As noted, there is a dearth of data on the supply and demand of illicit drugs in Africa, and available estimates are steeped in great uncertainty. Moreover, data on the trafficking of cocaine is marred by methodical flaws such as inaccurate counting, nondisclosure by some countries, guesses, and estimations.[68] Imperfect as such statistics may be, they still provide insights into the scale of the activity, but they should by no means be regarded as an accurate numerical representation.[69] Large quantities of cocaine are seized along the shores of coastal African countries, especially Guinea-Bissau, Côte d'Ivoire, and the Gambia.[70] One of the largest illicit drug busts in Africa was carried out in Guinea-Bissau in 2019. A total of 1,910 kilos of cocaine were seized during this operation. Europe, via Mali, was the intended destination of the drugs. One Mexican citizen and three Colombians were among the twelve people who were arrested in this cocaine seizure. Cars and a speedboat were also recovered during the raid.[71] Speedboats are one medium of transportation for cocaine along maritime routes, which will be discussed later in this chapter.

Entry Points into Africa from Latin America

In Africa, the main points of entry of cocaine being transported from Brazil to Europe are Guinea-Bissau, Senegal, Cape Verde, the Gambia, and the Gulf of Guinea coastline (beginning from Côte d'Ivoire). The volume of cocaine-smuggling vessels that depart from Brazil have led to the important status of the Gulf of Guinea coastline as a stopover destination for cocaine being trafficked to Europe. The substantial traffic in smuggled cocaine in the Gulf of Guinea has led to equally substantial quantities of the drug being intercepted by authorities. From 2019 to 2021, West African coastal countries, including those along the Gulf of Guinea, recorded large cocaine seizures of 100 kilograms and above. These include the Gambia (3 tons), Senegal (5.1 tons), Côte d'Ivoire (6 tons), and Cape Verde's territorial waters and its surrounding areas (2.3 tons, 5.7 tons, and 9.5 tons).[72]

West Africa features prominently as a major point of entry for cocaine that is smuggled from Latin America. The scale and value of drug trafficking in West Africa is so great that it exceeds the national income of some countries in the region.[73] Within the West African cocaine trafficking industry, Nigeria is a key player—as an entry point into Africa, and a distribution point within and outside Africa. Cocaine is trafficked from Nigeria to countries in North Africa, other countries in West Africa, the Asia-Pacific region, the Middle East, and Europe. Nigerian cocaine traffickers work with cult groups in Europe and other Nigerian cocaine traffickers in countries outside Nigeria, particularly in Brazil. Moreover, Nigeria was the country with the highest number of citizens arrested for cocaine smuggling in Europe during the 2018–2020 period. During the same period, Nigeria was the number one African country in terms of individuals arrested worldwide for smuggling cocaine. Even though Nigeria features prominently in terms of arrests of cocaine traffickers, it is recognized as a midlevel and dealer-level cocaine trafficking constituent in the global cocaine market, and not a large-scale cocaine trafficking country. Brazil supplies most of the cocaine that is trafficked to Nigeria.[74]

Latin American criminal groups are able to take advantage of impoverished West African countries. As noted, this predator-prey relationship is enhanced by the poor security at the seaports and airports of many African countries, and by the unscrupulousness of government officials and security personnel. The police in transit countries are largely powerless in the face of the highly influential and financially buoyant drug lords.[75] Some criminal groups who are involved in cocaine trafficking domestically buy political protection and continue cocaine supply operations successfully.[76]

Within Africa, cocaine is distributed by land, air, and sea.[77] Cocaine makes landing into Nigeria via some seaports, international airports, and postal agencies in the country. Big vessels arrive at Tincan Island and Apapa in Lagos, and Onne near Port Harcourt. Cocaine also arrives on passenger flights landing in airports of major Nigerian cities, particularly Enugu, Lagos, Kano, and Abuja. In addition, cocaine moves across land borders and overland throughout the country via courier services and postal agencies. Even though sea routes are one means of entry of cocaine into Nigeria, they are not popular for trafficking cocaine to the country, because the country's trafficking networks are "loose, transactional structures, not the hierarchical organisations seen with some other national groups,"[78] such as

Colombian criminal actors. This implies that Nigerian criminal groups are not capable of the complex planning required to execute the smuggling of cocaine via maritime routes. However, the assumption that Nigerian drug networks lack the sophisticated knowledge and expertise needed to carry out complex criminal activities is incorrect. The adhocratic structure of Nigerian drug networks might lead one to underestimate their criminal capabilities.[79] Nigerian airport staff are bribed with or without their knowing what is contained inside the bags they are paid to ignore.[80] As Robby Roks, Lieselot Bisschop, and Richard Staring argue, corrupt airport staff are a metaphorical representation of "doors."[81] They function as two-way doors in their extortion of people who travel in and out of Nigeria via international flights.[82]

As discussed earlier, cocaine trafficking is common in Guinea-Bissau. Indeed, Guinea-Bissau as well as Ghana are two additional predominant entry points of cocaine into Africa from South America. From there, the drug is distributed to other African countries on its way to Europe.[83] Most of the illicit drugs that journey through Guinea-Bissau evade detection and seizure by the police. Guinea-Bissau is a financially struggling West African country with a population slightly above two million people. The thriving cocaine smuggling activities in the country since 2005 prompted the United Nations to declare the country a "narco-state," a label that is justified with an estimated ten tons of cocaine passing through the country annually en route to Europe.[84]

Cocaine Trafficking Methods: International Perspective

Among the methods of trafficking cocaine internationally are via international post, on passenger flights carried by drug mules, and in unescorted luggage or parcels. Cocaine is hidden inside seemingly innocent-looking objects such as religious artifacts, reading materials, and automobile spare parts to avoid scrutiny by law enforcement agents. The COVID-19 pandemic period witnessed an increase in cocaine trafficking via international courier and postal services. This was prompted by the global restrictions on international air travel during that time. Consequently, criminal organizations also relied more heavily on unaccompanied baggage as a means of transporting cocaine across international borders. Although the use of couriers and postal agencies to transport cocaine internationally peaked during the COVID-19 pandemic, criminal organizations were beginning to rely on this method even before the pandemic. During COVID-19, there was a corresponding increase in cocaine seizures globally. An increase in cocaine supply, or the increase in unaccompanied cocaine parcels worldwide, could be causes for this. In 2021, there was a spike in the farming of coca bush and the production of cocaine in Colombia by 43 percent and 14 percent, respectively. This trend coincided with the height of the pandemic and increased the supply of cocaine worldwide.[85]

Cocaine is also trafficked via maritime routes using speedboats,[86] sailing and fishing boats, shipping containers, merchant vessels, semisubmersible and water drones, and parasite modalities. Cocaine-trafficking groups have been able to leverage technological advancements to boost their trade. They have also devised various strategies in the maritime trafficking of cocaine. To avoid scrutiny, detection, and possible arrests and seizures at seaports in West and North Africa, cocaine traffickers often transfer the illicit drug from one vessel to another. This involves transfers from big vessels to smaller vessels such as fishing boats and smaller speedboats, and back to bigger vessels, for instance large speedboats and yachts, which carry the drug to the coastline of the destination country. A reason for these transfers is that some bigger vessels cannot navigate shallow water bodies. Ship-to-ship transfers may take place in the territorial waters of the destination country, or the transferred cocaine may then be delivered to another country. This ship-to-ship transfer method is commonplace in the Pacific islands, Central America, the Caribbean, and Africa. Sometimes cocaine that is trafficked from Brazil to Africa is transferred at sea to a boat registered in a third-party African country that is not the destination or transit country. Alternatively, a cocaine shipment may be dropped off by a container ship in a predesignated spot for later pickup by a speedboat. The trafficking of cocaine across the Atlantic Ocean from Brazil to Africa is sometimes done in shipping containers, or various types of vessels such as sailboats, merchant vessels, or fishing boats might be used.[87]

Scholars such as Anna Sergi,[88] Marleen Easton,[89] and Damián Zaitch[90] have shown that the use of shipping containers to smuggle cocaine is not a recent phenomenon, but it is growing in prominence and complexity. Cocaine can be introduced to a shipping container at various points, such as at a seaport, outside a seaport, en route to a seaport, or offshore. The cocaine that is trafficked inside the container is usually concealed within the body of the container in a cavity that is created solely for the purpose of cocaine trafficking,[91] or inside food commodities that will not attract suspicion from law enforcement agents. Smuggling cocaine in a shipping container may or may not involve the knowledge of the business that owns the container.

In addition to smuggling cocaine hidden with food items, the illicit substance is often trafficked by concealing it within seemingly innocent-looking nonfood materials such as charcoal, liquids, beeswax, animal skins, plastic materials, and fabrics (clothing items). This type of cocaine-trafficking medium is also not new, but it is being applied in more sophisticated ways. To later separate the trafficked cocaine from the mixture of nonfood items that have concealed it, an extraction process must be carried out. For this purpose, Colombian criminal organizations have set up large-scale laboratories, staffed with Colombian on-site chemical specialists with help from citizens of whichever country hosts the laboratory.[92]

Cocaine Trafficking Modus Operandi from Latin America to Africa

Cocaine is trafficked from Latin America to Africa via drug mules, postal services, and cargo or container shipments. Although traffickers use both maritime and air transportation to move cocaine from Latin America to Europe via West Africa, they rely more on maritime routes.[93] Seaports are two-way corridors for the entry and departure of illicit substances.[94] Nigerian cocaine traffickers in São Paulo export small and medium quantities of cocaine from Brazil to West Africa through human couriers or drug mules, postal services, and cargo or container shipments. The latter involves smuggling the drug inside travel luggage, or concealed among cargo items or inside shipping containers. While Nigerian cocaine traffickers are not in control of trafficking routes between Brazil and West Africa, they participate actively in the process. These routes are in the control of Brazilian criminal groups such as the PCC, corrupt Brazilian officials, and legitimate entrepreneurs. In smuggling cocaine from Latin America to West

Africa, Nigerian traffickers tend to avoid exporting from countries under high scrutiny for cocaine—Colombia, Ecuador, and Venezuela—and operate from Latin American countries under less scrutiny such as Paraguay, Argentina, and Uruguay.[95] The diversification of cocaine departure routes hinges on risk potential. Routes that offer the least risk are favored by traffickers.[96]

Cocaine is also smuggled via human couriers, or drug mules. This may entail swallowing cocaine pellets. There is a preference for male drug mules, because they can usually ingest more cocaine pellets than women. Of all male prisoners in Brazilian prisons who have been arrested for trafficking cocaine, most are drug mules. While some drug mules engage in cocaine trafficking willingly and with full knowledge of its associated risks, others do not and are tricked into being drug mules (e.g., when cocaine is hidden in their luggage without their knowledge). Some male Nigerian cocaine traffickers also recruit their non-Nigerian wives or girlfriends, as well as their friends and family members, to carry the drug; female prostitutes also partake in the smuggling of cocaine across international borders.[97]

Some Nigerians in Brazil smuggle small quantities of cocaine via postal services as a way of trying their luck in the smuggling enterprise. They might hide the drug in harmless-looking items, such as clothes. As for shipping cocaine in freight containers, Nigerian traffickers in Brazil purchase large quantities of goods from a reputable local wholesale company, then instruct the company to ship their purchase to West Africa in a freight container. The cocaine is concealed among the legitimate cargo with or without the knowledge of the wholesale company; this is carried out in collaboration between the Nigerian traffickers and Brazilian artisans who make replicas of the legitimate cargo items. If the wholesale company is not aware of the ruse, the cocaine is interspersed among the legitimate goods during the process of packaging the goods for shipment.[98]

Criminal Groups in Cocaine Trafficking: The Latin American and African Nexus

In Africa, the Brazilian PCC controls most of the supply of cocaine. The trafficking of cocaine to Africa is also carried out by small and medium-size Brazilian criminal organizations through partnerships with growing specializations. While some of the Brazilian criminal groups specialize in distribution logistics to Africa and Europe, others, particularly local groups and street gangs, focus on the sale of the drug locally within Brazil. The distribution logistics involve the collection of cocaine from African ports, the provision of onward transportation, and the protection of the illicit cargo locally. Payments for distribution logistics services might be in the form of cocaine or cash, and the amount of the payment depends on the size of the shipment. The payments are absorbed into the local cocaine markets of the transit countries.[99]

Nigerian criminal groups appear to dominate the cocaine trafficking scene in West and North Africa. The influence of these criminal organizations extends beyond Africa to the global cocaine smuggling arena, through networks of illicit drug couriers and Nigerians in the diaspora. These groups often smuggle small quantities of cocaine on passenger flights using drug mules. Nigerian cocaine trafficking groups are organized along tribal lines, with ties to larger cocaine syndicates outside Nigeria. The Nigerian cocaine industry is made up of small groups. Each of these groups usually consists of about five members, and their activities are compartmentalized in such a way that members do not know the associates of other small groups.[100]

The PCC controls the trafficking of cocaine along the smuggling routes between Brazil, Peru, and Colombia, and has a close working relationship with the Italian criminal group known as the 'Ndrangheta. Other Brazilian criminal groups that are involved in international cocaine trafficking are the Comando Vermelho, which is the PCC's main domestic rival, and the nascent Familia do Norte—these three criminal groups vie for control of cocaine trafficking in Brazil, Peru, and Colombia. Sometimes, there are international collaborations between the criminal groups. In September 2018, for example, the 'Ndrangheta, Camorra (another Italian group), and PCC, among other international collaborators, masterminded the trafficking of 1.2 tons of cocaine, which was seized in Abidjan, Côte d'Ivoire, as it was making its way from Brazil to Europe.[101]

Conclusion

In this chapter, I have examined cocaine trafficking in Africa and its relationship with trafficking in Latin America. Africa plays a crucial role in cocaine trafficking between Latin America and Europe. West Africa has dominated the African cocaine trafficking scene and emerged as a major player in the trafficking route between Latin America and Europe. In addition, data on cocaine seizures within Latin America and Africa provides insights into the scale of cocaine that is trafficked within those regions. Furthermore, poverty and corruption in these regions have been highlighted as major reasons why cocaine trafficking thrives there. Poverty and corruption, in this sense, are not limited to any one country but are noted as problems that encompass both Africa and Latin America more broadly. Also, the influence of cocaine criminal networks is seen to transcend geography, and locking gang members up in carceral spaces does not stop cocaine trafficking, because criminals can operate from inside prisons.

The supply and departure points of the cocaine that is trafficked in Africa have been traced to Latin America. This provides the basis for the interdependent relationship between Latin America and Africa with respect to the trafficking of cocaine. I have discussed transshipment hubs, departure points from Latin America, entry points into Africa, and transit routes within Africa, as well as the various methods by which cocaine is trafficked intercontinentally between the two locations, namely the use of drug mules, cargo and container shipments, and postal services. I have noted that cocaine is smuggled from Latin America to Africa inside a plethora of mundane items, with or without the knowledge of the wholesale companies from which these legitimate goods were bought in bulk.

I have identified the citizens of countries in Latin America and Africa as the main actors who are involved in the trafficking of cocaine both within and between these two geographical locations. Corruption, compromised and inefficient political structures, extreme poverty, and the desire for an affluent lifestyle are some of the fertile factors upon which intracountry and intercountry cocaine trafficking has flourished. Criminals engaged in the trafficking of cocaine between the two regions can be solo actors or members of organizations. However, criminal organizations based in the departure points in Latin America have exercised the greatest control and dominance over the cocaine transported between Latin America and Africa. Sometimes, these criminal groups form alliances and work together to traffic cocaine.

Notes

1. Olayemi Jacob Ogunniyi and James Onochie Akpu, "The Challenge of Drug Trafficking to Democratic Governance and Human Security in West Africa: A Historical Reflection," *Africa Development/Afrique et Développement* 44, no. 4 (2019): 29–50.

2. Stephen Kafeero, "Guide to Investigating Organized Crime in Africa: Chapter 6—Drug Trafficking," Global Investigative Journalism Network, December 16, 2022, https://gijn.org/2022/12/16/guide-to-investigating-organized-crime-in-africa-drug-trafficking/.

3. United Nations Office on Drugs and Crime, *Global Report on Cocaine 2023: Local Dynamics, Global Challenges* (Vienna: United Nations, 2023), https://www.unodc.org/documents/data-and-analysis/cocaine/Global_cocaine_report_2023.pdf.

4. United Nations Office on Drugs and Crime, *Global Report on Cocaine 2023*.

5. United Nations Office on Drugs and Crime, *Global Report on Cocaine 2023*.

6. United Nations Office on Drugs and Crime, *Global Report on Cocaine 2023*.

7. United Nations Office on Drugs and Crime, *Transnational Organized Crime in West Africa: A Threat Assessment* (Vienna: United Nations, 2013), https://www.unodc.org/documents/data-and-analysis/tocta/West_Africa_TOCTA_2013_EN.pdf.

8. United Nations Office on Drugs and Crime, *Global Report on Cocaine 2023*.

9. Jude Roys Oboh, *Cocaine Hoppers: Nigerian International Cocaine Trafficking* (Lanham, MD: Lexington Books, 2021).

10. United Nations Office on Drugs and Crime, *Global Report on Cocaine 2023*.

11. United Nations Office on Drugs and Crime, *Global Report on Cocaine 2023*.

12. United Nations Office on Drugs and Crime, *Global Report on Cocaine 2023*.

13. Peter Tinti, "Drug Trafficking in Northern Mali: A Tenuous Criminal Equilibrium," Research Paper, Enhancing Africa's Response to Transnational Organised Crime, September 2020, https://enact-africa.s3.amazonaws.com/site/uploads/2020-09-17-mali-drugs-research-paper.pdf.

14. United Nations Office on Drugs and Crime, *Drug Trafficking as a Security Threat in West Africa* (Vienna: United Nations, 2008), https://www.unodc.org/documents/data-and-analysis/Studies/Drug-Trafficking-WestAfrica-English.pdf.

15. Carolina Sampó, "El tráfico de cocaína entre América Latina y África Occidental," *URVIO: Revista Latinoamericana de Estudios de Seguridad* 24 (June 2019): 187–203.

16. Carsten Weerth, "Cocaine Smuggling by Help of Narco-Submarines from South America to Africa and Europe: A Call for a Higher Awareness of an Existing Smuggling Pathway," *Customs Scientific Journal*, no. 2 (2020): 33–49.

17. United Nations Office on Drugs and Crime, *Drug Trafficking as a Security Threat in West Africa*.

18. Sanjay Badri-Maharaj, "Cocaine Trafficking Between Latin America and West Africa," Manohar Parrikar Institute for Defence Studies and Analyses, Delhi, January–March 2016, https://idsa.in/africatrends/the-cocaine-trafficking-between-latin-america-and-west-africa_sbmaharaj_0316.

19. Federico Varese, *Mafias on the Move: How Organized Crime Conquers New Territories* (Princeton, NJ: Princeton University Press, 2011).

20. Ross Eventon and Dave Bewley-Taylor, "An Overview of Recent Changes in Cocaine Trafficking Routes into Europe," Background Paper, European Monitoring Centre for Drugs and Drug Addiction, Lisbon, 2016.

21. Tinti, "Drug Trafficking in Northern Mali."

22. Varese, *Mafias on the Move*.

23. Varese, *Mafias on the Move*.

24. Davin O'Regan, "Cocaine and Instability in Africa: Lessons from Latin America and the Caribbean," Africa Security Brief no. 5, Africa Center for Strategic Studies, Washington, DC, July 31, 2010, https://africacenter.org/publication/cocaine-and-instability-in-africa-lessons-from-latin-america-and-the-caribbean/.

25. African Organized Crime Index, "Ranking by Cocaine Trade," 2021, https://africa.ocindex.net/rankings/cocaine_trade.

26. Jason Eligh, "A Powder Storm: The Cocaine Markets of East and Southern Africa," Global Initiative Against Transnational Organized Crime, December 2022, https://globalinitiative.net/wp-content/uploads/2022/12/Jason-Eligh-A-Powder-of-Storm-The-cocaine-markets-of-East-and-southern-Africa-GI-TOC-2022.pdf.

27. Varese, *Mafias on the Move*.

28. Henk van de Bunt, Dina Siegel, and Damián Zaitch, "The Social Embeddedness of Organized Crime," in *The Oxford Handbook of Organized Crime*, ed. Letizia Paoli (New York: Oxford University Press, 2014), 321–39.

29. Ogunniyi and Akpu, "The Challenge of Drug Trafficking to Democratic Governance and Human Security."

30. Varese, *Mafias on the Move*.

31. Ogunniyi and Akpu, "The Challenge of Drug Trafficking to Democratic Governance and Human Security."

32. Ed Vulliamy, "How a Tiny West African Country Became the World's First Narco State," *Guardian*, March 9, 2008, https://www.theguardian.com/world/2008/mar/09/drugstrade.

33. Tinti, "Drug Trafficking in Northern Mali."

34. Jonathan Di John, "'Failed States' in Sub-Saharan Africa: A Review of the Literature," Real Instituto Elcano, Madrid, January 14, 2011, https://media.realinstitutoelcano.org/wp-content/uploads/2021/11/ari5-2011-dijohn-failed-states-sub-saharan-africa-literature-review.pdf.

35. Isabelle King, "Africa's Narco-State: An Attempted Coup and Drug Trafficking in Guinea-Bissau," *Harvard International Review*, April 13, 2022, https://hir.harvard.edu/narco-state-an-attempted-coup-and-drug-trafficking-in-guinea-bissau/.

36. Vulliamy, "How a Tiny West African Country Became the World's First Narco State."

37. Vulliamy, "How a Tiny West African Country Became the World's First Narco State."

38. Oboh, *Cocaine Hoppers*.

39. Varese, *Mafias on the Move*.

40. Oboh, *Cocaine Hoppers*.

41. "Nigerian Citizen Involved in Supplying Fake Passports, Visas Arrested," *The Print*, July 2, 2022, https://theprint.in/india/nigerian-citizen-involved-in-supplying-fake-passports-visas-arrested/1022094/.

42. Tinti, "Drug Trafficking in Northern Mali."

43. Oboh, *Cocaine Hoppers*.

44. Eventon and Bewley-Taylor, "An Overview of Recent Changes in Cocaine Trafficking Routes."

45. United Nations Office on Drugs and Crime, *Drug Trafficking as a Security Threat in West Africa*.

46. Ogunniyi and Akpu, "The Challenge of Drug Trafficking to Democratic Governance and Human Security."

47. United Nations Office on Drugs and Crime, *The Transatlantic Cocaine Market: Research Paper* (Vienna: United Nations, 2011), https://www.unodc.org/documents/data-and-analysis/Studies/Transatlantic_cocaine_market.pdf.

48. United Nations Office on Drugs and Crime, *Transnational Organized Crime in West Africa*.

49. Kafeero, "Guide to Investigating Organized Crime in Africa."

50. Kafeero, "Guide to Investigating Organized Crime in Africa."

51. King, "Africa's Narco-State."

52. Nicholas R. Magliocca, Diana S. Summers, Kevin M. Curtin, Kendra McSweeney, and Ashleigh N. Price, "Shifting Landscape Suitability for Cocaine Trafficking Through Central America in Response to Counterdrug Interdiction," *Landscape and Urban Planning* 221 (May 2022).

53. King, "Africa's Narco-State."

54. Vanda Felbab-Brown, "The West African Drug Trade in the Context of the Region's Illicit Economies and Poor Governance," paper presented at the Conference on Drug Trafficking in West Africa, Arlington, Virginia, October 14, 2010.

55. François Murphy, "Cocaine Market Is Booming as Meth Trafficking Spreads, U.N. Report Says," Reuters, June 26, 2023, https://www.reuters.com/world/cocaine-market-is-booming-meth-trafficking-spreads-un-report-says-2023-06-25/.

56. Eligh, "A Powder Storm."

57. Eligh, "A Powder Storm."

58. United Nations Office on Drugs and Crime, *The Transatlantic Cocaine Market: Research Paper*.

59. Traore Sekou Amadou, "Understanding Drug Trafficking and Organized Crime in Mali," *Advances in Applied Sociology* 9, no. 5 (May 2019): 143–52.

60. Tinti, "Drug Trafficking in Northern Mali."

61. Afua Hirsch, "Cocaine Flows Through Sahara as al-Qaida Cashes In on Lawlessness," *Guardian*, May 2, 2013, https://www.theguardian.com/world/2013/may/02/cocaine-flows-through-sahara-al-qaida.

62. International Crisis Group, "Drug Trafficking, Violence and Politics in Northern Mali," Report no. 267/Africa, December 13, 2018, https://www.crisisgroup.org/africa/sahel/mali/267-narcotrafic-violence-et-politique-au-nord-du-mali.

63. International Crisis Group, "Drug Trafficking, Violence and Politics."

64. Tinti, "Drug Trafficking in Northern Mali."

65. Collins G. Adeyanju, "Drug Trafficking in West Africa Borderlands: From Gold Coast to Coke Coast," *Journal of Liberty and International Affairs* 6, no. 1 (2020): 70–86.

66. United Nations Office on Drugs and Crime, *Global Report on Cocaine 2023*.

67. Van de Bunt, Siegel, and Zaitch, "The Social Embeddedness of Organized Crime."

68. Eventon and Bewley-Taylor, "An Overview of Recent Changes in Cocaine Trafficking Routes."

69. United Nations Office on Drugs and Crime, *Global Report on Cocaine 2023*.

70. "Drug Use High in West Africa and Central Africa, Trafficking Funds Conflict: U.N.," Reuters, June 27, 2022, https://www.reuters.com/world/africa/drug-use-high-west-central-africa-trafficking-funds-conflict-un-2022-06-27/.

71. "The Global Drugs Trade Shifts to West Africa," *The Economist*, November 21, 2019, https://www.economist.com/international/2019/11/21/the-global-drugs-trade-shifts-to-west-africa.

72. United Nations Office on Drugs and Crime, *Global Report on Cocaine 2023*.

73. United Nations Office on Drugs and Crime, *Drug Trafficking as a Security Threat in West Africa*.

74. United Nations Office on Drugs and Crime, *Global Report on Cocaine 2023*.

75. United Nations Office on Drugs and Crime, *Drug Trafficking as a Security Threat in West Africa*.

76. United Nations Office on Drugs and Crime, *Global Report on Cocaine 2023*.

77. United Nations Office on Drugs and Crime, *Drug Trafficking as a Security Threat in West Africa*.

78. Ifeoma Okeke, "Tackling Drug Trafficking at Nigerian Airports," *BusinessDay* (Lagos), May 5, 2019, https://businessday.ng/opinion/article/zainab-aliyus-ordeals-resonate-calls-for-improved-measures-to-tackling-drug-trafficking-at-nigerian-airports/.

79. Ogunniyi and Akpu, "The Challenge of Drug Trafficking to Democratic Governance and Human Security."

80. Okeke, "Tackling Drug Trafficking at Nigerian Airports."

81. Robby Roks, Lieselot Bisschop, and Richard Staring, "Getting a Foot in the Door: Spaces of Cocaine Trafficking in the Port of Rotterdam," *Trends in Organized Crime* 24, no. 2 (June 2021): 171–88.

82. Abdulqudus Ogundapo, "Corruption, Bribery Reign Inside Murtala Muhammed International Airport," Whistleblowing International Network, January 7, 2022, https://www.corruptionanonymous.org/corruption-bribery-reign-inside-murtala-muhammed-international-airport/.

83. United Nations Office on Drugs and Crime, *Drug Trafficking as a Security Threat in West Africa*.

84. "The Global Drugs Trade Shifts to West Africa."

85. United Nations Office on Drugs and Crime, *Global Report on Cocaine 2023*.

86. Carsten Weerth, "Cocaine Smuggling by Help of Narco-Submarines from South America to Europe and Africa: A Proven Case; A Last Wake-Up Call for Customs Services Around the World," *Customs Scientific Journal*, no. 1 (2020): 37–42.

87. United Nations Office on Drugs and Crime, *Global Report on Cocaine 2023*.

88. Anna Sergi, "Playing Pac-Man in Portville: Policing the Dilution and Fragmentation of Drug Importations Through Major Seaports," *European Journal of Criminology* 19, no. 4 (July 2022): 674–91.

89. Marleen Easton, "Policing Flows of Drugs in the Harbor of Antwerp: A Nodal-Network Analysis," in *Maritime Supply Chains*, ed. Thierry Vanelslander and Christa Sys (Amsterdam: Elsevier, 2020), 115–34.

90. Damián Zaitch, "From Cali to Rotterdam: Perceptions of Colombian Cocaine Traffickers on the Dutch Port," *Crime, Law and Social Change* 38, no. 3 (2002): 239–66.

91. Andrew O'Hagan and Chalkia Paraskevi, "Cocaine Trafficking Between South America and Greece and Methods of Concealment," *Forensic Research and Criminology International Journal* 10, no. 2 (2022): 37–43.

92. United Nations Office on Drugs and Crime, *Global Report on Cocaine 2023*.

93. Eventon and Bewley-Taylor, "An Overview of Recent Changes in Cocaine Trafficking Routes."

94. Carolina Sampó and Valeska Troncoso, "Cocaine Trafficking from Non-Traditional Ports: Examining the Cases of Argentina, Chile, and Uruguay," *Trends in Organized Crime* 26, no. 1 (January 2022): 235–57.

95. Oboh, *Cocaine Hoppers*.

96. United Nations Office on Drugs and Crime, *World Drug Report 2020*, vol. 3, *Drug Supply* (Vienna: United Nations, 2020), https://wdr.unodc.org/wdr2020/field/WDR20_Booklet_3.pdf.

97. Oboh, *Cocaine Hoppers*.

98. Oboh, *Cocaine Hoppers*.

99. United Nations Office on Drugs and Crime, *Global Report on Cocaine 2023*.

100. United Nations Office on Drugs and Crime, *Global Report on Cocaine 2023*.

101. United Nations Office on Drugs and Crime, *Global Report on Cocaine 2023*.

CHAPTER 12

The Cocaine Trade in Asia

Molly Charles

Cocaine is the only currently illegal drug that once claimed a spot as a global "wonder drug" with beneficial properties added to its profile. The most common of these purported benefits was the drug's effect as an energy booster, which was emphasized when it was used as an ingredient in the soft drink Coca-Cola. This drink was created when its precursor—Peruvian Wine Coca—was banned for its alcohol content in places like the United States and Peru, and there was a need for a nonalcoholic drink to serve the same purpose. Other competitors of Coca-Cola such as Wiseola, Celery Cola, Cafe-Coca, Kos-Kola, and Koca-Nola all contained cocaine. Koca-Nola, for example, had two milligrams of cocaine in a six-ounce soft drink. Coca or cocaine made the soft drink business lucrative. By 1903, Coca-Cola was making over $1 million in profit annually.[1] Other goods that added cocaine as an ingredient were toothache drops, hemorrhoid remedies, and corn cures. It was even seen as a cure for morphine addiction. Not surprisingly, dealing with cocaine was a viable venture for pharmaceutical companies in the United States, Europe, and Japan. It was a product they could market with limited restrictions on labeling, and they had the freedom to increase the potency of their products based on customer demand.[2]

From this environment, a move to control the freedom enjoyed by the pharmaceutical industries began to grow in the early twentieth century. Several factors contributed to strengthening negative attitudes toward coca and cocaine, including the growing number of users who were marginalized and dysfunctional as well as the discovery of a chemical alternative to cocaine (namely, novocaine) with no addictive characteristics for use as a topical anesthetic and for other medicinal purposes. As a result, research into the medical benefits of cocaine came to a halt.

The period between the marketing of cocaine as a wonder drug and its fall also saw changes in the production of cocaine from the coca plant. The demand from the United States and other countries ensured quality for Peruvian coca, while the long-distance transport to Germany made their product unusable, further solidifying Peru's dominance in coca. An expert committee convened in Lima in 1889 and concluded with an assurance to modernize production and ensure large-scale exports of *cocaína bruta* (crude cocaine) made in Peru, with inputs from the country's best medical minds.[3] In 1890, the Andean country exported approximately one thousand kilos of crude cocaine, and by the mid-1980s production had quadrupled. Economist José Rodríguez spoke glowingly of Peru's ensured monopoly over the coca plant, as attempts by other countries to acclimatize the Andean crop had failed.[4]

In 1878, a Belgian seed exporter sent the South American bush to a botanical garden in Java. In 1883, cultivation of the bush on that island proved successful. Three years later, commercial-scale planting started in Java, Madura, and to a lesser extent Sumatra. This was the beginning of the Asian chapter in coca cultivation and its trade in coca leaves, coca base, and cocaine.[5]

Asia is a continent rich in diversity in terms of culture, ethnicity, terrain, development models, political identity, language, religious or nonreligious affinity, extent of awareness about technology, and the degree of active participation in the digital age. Under these circumstances, there is also diversity in the use of psychoactive plants and their products. The region's fifty-odd countries—falling within the subregions of Central Asia, South Asia, East Asia, Southeast Asia, and Western Asia—have been exposed to the use of psychoactive plant products and synthetic drugs. While the use of the coca plant and cocaine in Asia has largely been restricted to the period between the world wars, the continent has witnessed new trade routes—or the revival of old areas of cultivation—and new drug products finding a market. Ultimately, changes occurred in the perceived utility of cocaine in a network comprising producers, suppliers, distributors, and users.

This chapter focuses on the use of and trade in cocaine in Asia. It presents a brief history of Asia's association with cocaine, its disruption after World War II, the drug trade before 2000, and the changes that have occurred in that trade in the new century. It also looks at the presence of mafias and other criminal groups, as well as corruption among state-level actors and other vulnerabilities that make the drug trade possible. Most importantly, this chapter attempts to explain why cocaine is not the favorite drug of Asia, as it largely occupies a position after cannabis, opiates/opioids, and synthetic drugs.

The Cocaine Trade and Its Usage: A Historical Perspective

In Asia, psychoactive plants like cannabis, poppy, datura, ephedra, and kratom have been used for centuries—their popularity changing with time. Yet the coca plant cultivated in Asia during World War I almost disappeared from the market after World War II. Indeed, the coca plant is presently not cultivated in Asia, at least not on a scale worthy of trade in any form. Coca cultivated in Asia between the world wars was traded by the Dutch, but it was Japan that subsequently came to play a crucial role in its cultivation, trade, and transportation.

Coca cultivation was initiated in Java by the Dutch in the 1870s, and they, along with Germans, were actively involved in its trade. The Germans had a strong grip over the cocaine trade undertaken with *Erythroxylon novogranatense*, which is the coca plant variety cultivated in Java. This variety has a higher alkaloid content of 1 to 2 percent, which is largely uncrystallized. The *Erythroxylon* coca Lamarck variety largely grown in Latin America has an alkaloid content of 0.5 percent—nearly all of it crystallizable. The German advantage came from their chemists having discovered and patented a way to synthesize crystallized cocaine from the uncrystallized alkaloid.[6]

As there was no agreement between the Netherlands and Germany, Dutch manufacturers ignored the patent and used the German process to synthesize coca they purchased from the Japanese (who bought it from growers in Java), for sale in Amsterdam. Many private Dutch entities entered the trade when the patent ran out. Yet their role was curtailed when the Netherlands signed the Second International Opium Convention in 1925, which restricted trade in opium, coca, heroin, and cocaine. As a result, Dutch growers in Java had to depend largely on Japanese buyers. As time passed, Japan put in trade regulations that were discriminatory toward coca plantations owned by non-Japanese individuals. Tokyo drug companies had their own plantations in Formosa (Taiwan), Iwo Jima, and Okinawa, and the produce from these plantations was able to meet their need for coca leaves. Two major players were the Japanese companies Sankyo Pharmaceuticals and Hoshi Pharmaceuticals, which earned a profit from coca cultivation, trade, and transportation. Sankyo Pharmaceuticals, for example, had gross sales of more than one million yen annually from their wholesale branch office in Formosa. However, the Japanese government largely ignored the trade, as the use of coca, cocaine, and opium was nonexistent in Japan, except for Japanese soldiers using cocaine to help them cope with trauma during World War II. In 1868 and 1870, Japan had passed laws against the use and trade of opium and other narcotics. The same laws were applicable to Formosa—then a colony of Japan—with a slight change. For opium use, the punishment could be a sentence of up to ten years of rigorous imprisonment. Yet for cocaine and heroin, control fell under a home office ordinance, and the maximum sentence for dealers of those two drugs was three months. This made coca cultivation and the cocaine trade possible.[7]

Meanwhile, cocaine was traded in small quantities in India, and its users there numbered far fewer than those of cannabis and opium. Cocaine use existed in parts of West Bengal and Bihar, and it spread around two main railway routes, one of them reaching towns like Benares, Lucknow, Rampur, Saharanpur, and Ambala. The other route reached Allahabad, Kanpur, Agra, Mathura, and Delhi. The estimate for usage in India in 1930 ranged from 250,000 to 500,000 individual users.[8] The spread of cocaine usage occurred in different ways. For example, medical professionals in Delhi prescribed it as a stimulant and tonic. Midwives also introduced women to the drug. Moreover, shawl merchants and dried fruit traders were responsible for trade to different towns. It is alleged that traders who purchased cannabis from Central Asia sold *charas* (hashish) at high prices in Bombay and Calcutta. They used part of the money to purchase cocaine and sell it in different towns.[9]

Cocaine that reached India through Japanese sources was adulterated. Local dealers increased their profit margins by adding phenazone, acetyl salicylate, or potassium nitrate. The drug was consumed across religious backgrounds and across class. Women from certain sections of society also used it. While generally a habit of the elite, as cocaine is expensive, individuals from lower economic strata of society (e.g., prostitutes) also used the drug.[10] Interestingly, during the 1950s, there were attempts to grow coca locally in India, including bringing the plant from Java. However, this was not successful. When the plant did grow in India, it hardly had any cocaine in it. Observers at the time said that coca plants only grew well on the hilltops of the Nilgiris (in South India)—yet even there the leaves did not have adequate cocaine content.[11]

Not surprisingly, cocaine did not gain a strong foothold in Asia. Unlike opium or cannabis, more recent estimates show the limited relevance of cocaine on the continent. In 1985, for example, authorities in the Philippines discovered and destroyed a small plot for coca cultivation and a laboratory.[12] There were no further reports of such facilities after that incident. This absence is also reflected in the United Nations Office for Drug Control and Crime Prevention's report of 1999, which indicates that seizures of cocaine were almost nonexistent in Asia during the mid-1990s.[13] National data from India for 1991–2002 indicates that cocaine was seized in small quantities, the largest seizure occurring in 1995 at 40 kilos.[14]

By 2007, the trade situation had changed with a seizure of two hundred kilos in Hong Kong and seventy-seven kilos in Syria. Other countries in Asia reporting cocaine seizures were Israel, Japan, Thailand, Malaysia, Iran, India, Jordan, Pakistan, Lebanon, Taiwan, Kazakhstan, Indonesia, Armenia, the Palestinian Territories, South Korea, the Philippines, and Georgia.[15]

Cocaine Trafficking in Asia

In Asia, the trafficking of large quantities of cocaine is largely routed through the African continent. In recent years, the evidence suggests that maritime nations in West Africa accounted for most of the seizures. Large-scale overseas trade is destined for Europe, Australia, and parts of Western Asia and East Asia. Yet for most Asian countries, domestic needs are taken care of by smaller quantities couriered through the air or trafficked overland, as indicated by seizure data.[16]

Cocaine seizures in most parts of Asia are smaller in size than seizures made in North America or Europe, especially western Europe. The largest seizure during the period 2016–2019 was reported in 2019, when 15,247.12 kilos were confiscated in Malaysia. During the same year, cocaine packed as bricks in the Philippines were reported to police by local individuals who found the bricks floating in the water off the coast. Other major counterdrug operations during the 2016–2019 period were 1,556.42 kilos seized in Hong Kong, 639.86 kilos in Japan, and 519.058 kilos in Saudi Arabia. In China, the largest seizure of cocaine was 1,329.56 kilos in 2018.[17]

In recent years, large seizures of cocaine have been made in Malaysia. In one instance, in August 2023, a seizure of 302.2 kilos was in fact meant to have been delivered to a port in Maharashtra, India. In June 2023, 88 kilos were seized from the KLIA Air Cargo complex in Kuala Lumpur. As mentioned earlier, the biggest counterdrug operation in Malaysia occurred in 2019, when 15,247.12 kilos of cocaine were seized; the drug was mixed in with sixty metric tons of coal. Under these circumstances, there is a concern that the drug syndicates are now turning Malaysia into a major hub in Southeast Asia for illicit drugs by using both air cargo and seaborne shipping containers. The majority of the actors involved in trafficking are foreigners, primarily from Nigerian criminal syndicates.[18] And criminals operating from Malaysia have expanded their drug-trafficking operations beyond Asia. For example, one mule who was arrested in Kuala Lumpur indicated that she had carried cocaine to Rome and Amsterdam on different occasions. She purchased cocaine in Brazil and then took a detour via Nepal to Europe. Within the region, Malaysia is a transit spot for cocaine being trafficked to Hong Kong and Qatar. Drugs have also been trafficked via Malaysia to Australia, South Korea, Taiwan, Indonesia, and New Zealand.[19]

As cocaine is not the main illegal recreational drug used domestically in Asia, it is often trafficked along with other illegal drugs. This was seen as early as the 1950s, when traders who dealt cannabis (especially hashish) and opium also trafficked cocaine. In India, the 2023 arrest of two Nigerian nationals along with three other individuals for carrying seventy-eight grams of cocaine, ten grams of hashish, and thirty blots of LSD is a more recent example. There have been other cases as well.[20]

In Asia, two common ways of trading in cocaine are trafficking large quantities of the drug in sea cargo containers and small quantities using human mules or air cargo. In recent years, large quantities of cocaine have been trafficked through busy cargo ports in forty-foot containers, especially those that are not clocked electronically. For trafficking by air, as will be seen in more detail below, Nigerian groups largely control the cocaine carried by human mules across parts of Asia.

Trafficking via Sea

It is extremely difficult for law enforcement authorities to find cocaine transported by sea because it is trafficked through busy cargo ports in large containers. Often there are agreements among the customs agencies of trading countries or trade zones for the smooth traffic of cargo, as delays create big losses for the companies and countries involved. Moreover, the United Nations Office on Drugs and Crime (UNODC) focuses on training human resources manning the borders, and the agency has specific programs for the Asian region to monitor the large volumes of trade. The goal is to train officials to profile and inspect high-risk cargo.[21] The large volume of normal trade means that only a small portion can be inspected by officials, whether at seaports, dry ports, or border control points.[22] Indeed, detailed scanning of all cargo is nearly impossible given the large quantities of goods transported. Traffickers have also improved their skills in camouflaging the cocaine trafficked (e.g., mixing liquid cocaine with oil or concealing the drug with perishable food items, which must be transported on time to avoid losses). This means that the detection of drugs should be based on workable information received in advance. While land borders that are not often traversed may be easy to control, monitoring every busy cargo port is a Herculean task for customs officials.

A ranking of the world's busiest cargo container ports shows that the top ports are in Asia. To put this in perspective, Rotterdam is eleventh and Antwerp thirteenth on the list. Recent large seizures in Malaysia occurred in or close to Port Klang, near Kuala Lumpur (the fourteenth busiest port) and Colombo in Sri Lanka (the twenty-fifth busiest). The consignments seized in both countries were destined for India. Recent seizures of large consignments within India were in Mundra port in Gujarat and Nhava Sheva port near Mumbai, placed at twenty-sixth and twenty-seventh, respectively, in the list. Nhava Sheva is an old port that has been used for drug trafficking.

When the focus is on maintaining a smooth flow of traffic, the checking of containers is not a priority, as it slows down all traffic and creates big losses because of delays. Only a small percentage of cargo can be set aside for inspection, and the selection of this cargo is based on information provided to enforcement agencies. Even opting to inspect "smart" containers—which keep a digital record each time the container is opened—is not a foolproof method, as the volume of cargo is too large. A shipload of cargo, for instance, might contain from fourteen thousand to twenty-four thousand containers.[23]

This mode of drug trafficking utilizes a well-organized system. The most common approach is to exploit a legitimate customer, which means the drug consignment may be attached to the container on the outside or kept in available free space inside, and there may not be any indication that the package has been couriered. Yet enforcement agencies may feel—given the detailed process required for trafficking drugs—that the chances of this happening without the knowledge of the crew or some staff members in the shipping company is slim. In effect, the contraband can be introduced at any time, at the beginning of or during transit.[24]

As shown in chapter 2 of this volume, drug transit along sea routes in Asia is seen as an attempt by traffickers to avoid the evolved detection systems adopted in countries like the United States and utilize ports that are monitored less frequently. Moreover, authorities in Asian countries have not prioritized the installation of testing kits for cocaine. Therefore, cocaine can be traded without much ado. For example, the seizure by Bangladeshi authorities of cocaine oil mixed with sunflower oil was considered a sign of shifting trade routes; or, the consignment may have been intended for the local domestic market in India, as it was to land in an Indian port via Bangladesh. The quantity of cocaine seized was estimated to be around 60 to 100 kilos, not large in comparison to the cocaine trade in many other countries. It is rare, however, to traffic cocaine in liquid form in Asia.[25] According to an Indian Directorate of Revenue Intelligence report, there has been an increase in seizures of cocaine by Indian authorities, from 8.7 kilos in 2021 to 310 kilos in 2022.[26]

Human Mules and Cargo

Cocaine is often trafficked in small quantities across Asia. In August 2023, for example, Malaysian customs officials seized, as air cargo, eighty-eight kilos of cocaine meant for domestic use. The cocaine was being transported along with vehicle parts; a fake recipient was indicated in the airway bill. Malaysia was the destination, and the consignment had been sent from the Netherlands.[27]

Nigerians play an important part in cocaine trafficking, not just in Asia but also as a link to Africa. Nigerians have a strong hold on trafficking in West and North Africa, and they generally utilize human mules for trafficking small quantities via commercial aircraft. Nigerian criminal groups are village- and kinship-based with a core group of three or four members; a core group will hire outside individuals for specific tasks, but these individuals have only a limited understanding of the core.[28] Enforcement agencies in Nigeria maintain that it is difficult to infiltrate these groups, as they have ethnic or cultural codes. There are also differences in dialects spoken across small geographic areas. This gives these groups a form of security against outsiders, allowing them to conduct their illicit activities.[29]

Another method of bringing cocaine to Asia is through human couriers. African groups, especially Nigerians, play a central role in trafficking through the air. In the early 2000s, Nigerians utilized air couriers to traffic drugs in Asia. Consequently, there were frequent arrests of Nigerian couriers who had ingested the drug—a method not many Indians want to try. Nigerians' role in the drug trade in India has been documented, as they often languish in Indian jails after arrest, waiting for their case to be heard.[30]

Moreover, Nigerians are involved in international cocaine trafficking to different countries in Asia: China, Hong Kong, India, Malaysia, Sri Lanka, Pakistan, Saudi Arabia, and the United Arab Emirates.[31] Nigerians have been executed for their role in drug trafficking in Singapore, Indonesia, Malaysia, Saudi Arabia, and the United Arab Emirates. In 2014, there were five hundred Nigerians behind bars in Thailand, as this country does not typically carry out capital punishment for drug trafficking as do some other Asian countries. Arrested individuals are sent back to Nigeria after serving a certain period of their sentence. Not surprisingly, Nigerians have managed to build social networks in different parts of Asia to facilitate their role as a connecting link between Latin America, Africa, and Asia.

Indeed, Nigerians have become powerful players in the regional drug trade. They hire Indians as couriers to carry drugs to and from India. Yet they deal with small quantities, as their focus is the use of human mules who travel on commercial flights. In India, Nigerians are also involved in the local transportation of drugs for domestic use, and their presence has even become a threat to local drug dealers. For instance, a Nigerian trafficker was killed by local drug dealers in Parra, a village in North Goa, a location that has become a hub of Nigerian criminal activity.[32]

The Socially Embedded Reality: Mafia or Criminal Groups and State Actors in the Drug Trade

Mafias are rarely created merely to assert power or come into conflict with the legitimate governance system. Rather, they are created when a governance system needs muscle power or the services of a criminal group to engage in criminal activities on its behalf—whether to silence the discontent of the masses or to maintain political power through a strategy of fear. This has been seen in Japan, India, China, Hong Kong, Macau, Taiwan, Pakistan, Lebanon, and Syria. While mafia groups may have been subdued in many countries, the link between them and state actors has not been eliminated.

Global initiatives against organized crime have examined different criminal activities carried out in various countries and the types of groups involved. According to the Global Organized Crime Index, one category used to calculate a country's level of criminality is the presence of criminal actors and their effect on governance. The Global Index maintains that the corruption of state-level actors is an important vulnerability for countries in terms of facilitating organized crime activities. This is evident in Central Asia, South Asia, and East Asia. In Western Asia, criminal networks play a major role in organized crime activities, and in Southeast Asia, foreign actors have greater relevance. In countries like Japan and South Korea, mafia-like groups play an important role. Elsewhere in Asia, mafia-like groups and criminal networks are not the main players—they are the second- or third-most significant source of criminal activities. In this context, it may be useful to look at some of the mafia groups and criminal networks—other than Nigerians—operating in Asia.[33]

The yakuza in Japan may have lost their earlier hold over most of the country's governance, as youth are less attracted to the group today than in the past. It is important to note that the yakuza is more than a crime group; in fact, more broadly, it is considered an influential subculture. In the late 1990s, it had eighty thousand members in three thousand different subgroups. According to the Japanese police, by 2017, membership decreased to thirty-five thousand. Yet older members continue to exert a strong influence over many aspects of the country's governance. The strength of the yakuza evolved over time because governing politicians seeking to remain in power wanted to silence protests from the masses demanding more rights. The yakuza were willing to do what was necessary as long as plans to restrict the power of crime groups through legislation were kept on hold. Finally, the yakuza have also been involved in overseeing the methamphetamine trade.[34]

Like the yakuza, the triads in China were created to address political concerns. They evolved from secret societies that branched out to achieve common goals. However, they soon degenerated into criminal groups that influence almost all spheres of Chinese governance, directly or indirectly. They have established overseas groups in Hong Kong, Macau, Thailand, and Myanmar, and have begun to take on any activity that raises money and enhances power. Their international influence has grown in Europe and Singapore, especially in the synthetic drug trade. The group in Hong Kong has focused more on the financial aspects of organized crime.[35]

Taiwan's organized crime originated with the Chinese Nationalist Party, the Kuomintang, who fled to Taiwan after the Chinese Revolution of 1949. The Kuomintang created different groups to carry out activities like assassinations, brutal attacks on dissidents, and theft. The Bamboo Union became the largest and most powerful group—a status it still retains. The second most powerful group is the Four Seas, and the third the Celestial Alliance. Criminal groups have thrived in Taiwan, and they have increased their hold on politics in the country. Activities they control include waste disposal, construction, stock trading, entertainment, debt collection, gambling, nightclubs, and newspaper chains. Unlike in other countries in the region, group members do not just have strong links with the governing party but often become parliamentary members. Some members also belong to legitimate business groups; they tend to settle disputes by assassination. The triads of Taiwan oversee poppy cultivation in

Laos, Myanmar, northern Vietnam, and Thailand, and are involved in heroin processing and distribution.[36]

In India, the connection between criminal gangs and political groups or parties is not as strong or visible as in some other countries. Mumbai has been a stronghold of many gangs. Today, gang fights are not as prominent as in the past, especially during the 1980s and 1990s. When gangs settled scores by killing out in the streets, the public began to protest and question the role of the police. The police were then forced to take strong action. Compounding the need for action was a series of bomb blasts in 1993 in multiple locations in Bombay (as the city was then called) and the strong indication that a criminal group led by Dawood Ibrahim—D-Company—was involved in the attacks. Most importantly, this event and the strong reaction against it also meant that the underworld in India no longer enjoyed the power they had prior to the blasts.

As in other countries, in India there were strong links between organized crime groups like D-Company, Haji Mastan's organization, Chhota Rajan's group, and Arun Gawli's gang. All these groups were involved in traditional activities of the mafia, although the older groups preferred to avoid trafficking hard drugs like heroin and cocaine. The groups were able to maintain their criminal activities because of corrupt police and other government officials. Except for Gawli, none of them could make much headway in traditional politics. Indeed, they emerged to address the gaps in governance, which affected the lives of many individuals, especially marginalized groups. Haji Mastan, for instance, addressed the issues of migrants from South India seeking employment in the northern part of the country. Similarly, Gawli's gang was allowed to grow in power as they were needed to break the workers union's stronghold on cloth mills in Mumbai, for political gain for local parties. Dawood, by contrast, extended his influence far beyond Mumbai, establishing strong links with cities in the Persian Gulf, especially Dubai. Gold smuggling, money laundering through the Hawala system of money transfer, real estate, smuggling, and drug trafficking were part of their work profile. Dawood was "street smart" but with a business sense; this helped him branch out into legitimate business activities, especially in the Gulf states. Even if Dawood did not enter politics, he remained the most successful and powerful underworld leader in India, who was smart enough to diversify and be successful in both legitimate and illegal activities.[37]

The Domestic Cocaine Market in Asia

Two major indicators help explain the domestic cocaine market in Asian countries: the prevalence rate for cocaine consumption and the seizure trends. When focusing on the cocaine trade in other regions, it is possible to look at different aspects such as cultivation, yield, processing labs, and the involvement of specific organized groups. Yet many of these aspects are not relevant in the Asian context, as coca cultivation does not occur there. Moreover, domestic trade in cocaine in Asia is far lower than that for other drugs.

The UNODC is the best source of information regarding the prevalence of drug use, including cocaine, in Asia. There is diversity in the primary drug of choice for individuals across countries. The main source for this data is the different regional treatment centers, assessments by drug experts, and other local studies. For example, a UNOCD report provides information on treatment demand in thirty-three countries in Asia from 1998 to 2002.[38] The report indicates that while 0 percent of treatment center clients in Asia sought care for cocaine use, in North America it was 29 percent, in South America 60 percent, in Europe 4 percent, and in Africa 9 percent. This, however, changed gradually over time. By 2020, 10 percent of global cocaine users were in Asia. Specifically, South Asia accounted for 5 percent of global cocaine use, East and Southeast Asia accounted for 4 percent, and Western and Central Asia 1 percent.[39]

Cocaine trafficking also increased, a trend illustrated by recent seizures of more than ten kilograms of the illicit drug reported in Malaysia, Japan, Hong Kong, and Thailand. By 2022, the flow of small quantities of cocaine was noted from East Africa to East and Southeast Asia. There were also traffic flows to the same destination from Mexico, Central America, and the Andean countries of South America. By 2022, a UNODC report was showing the presence of trade in cocaine in different parts of Asia, be it as transit points or as emerging domestic cocaine markets.[40]

From 2018 to 2021, large seizures were registered, largely near coastal South Asia (Sri Lanka, the Maldives, and Bangladesh), in Southeast Asia (Indonesia and Vietnam), in East Asia (Hong Kong, Macau, China, South Korea, and Japan), and in Western Asia (the United Arab Emirates, Israel, and Lebanon).[41] Furthermore, the seizure of smaller quantities occurred across Asia, including in Central Asia (Tajikistan), in South and Southeast Asia (across India and Pakistan, and in parts of the Philippines, Malaysia, and Thailand), and in Western Asia (Qatar, Yemen, Saudi Arabia, Jordan, Syria, Armenia, Georgia, and Azerbaijan).[42]

There is also continuity in the cocaine trade in the border areas of India and Pakistan, close to Jammu and Kashmir, a conflict area with a significant military presence on both sides of the border. This is not surprising, as officials from different enforcement agencies (e.g., army officials and police officers) have been caught facilitating drug trafficking on both sides of the border. In 2001, for example, court cases under the Narcotic Drugs and Psychotropic Substances Act in Rajasthan (India) show that a senior Border Security Force (BSF) official and his subordinates helped a Pakistani drug trafficker by picking up him and another person and driving them to Punjab (India). The drugs were to be transported from there to Mumbai.[43] Similarly, in 2023, a court in Jammu and Kashmir refused bail to an army official who had facilitated the narcotics trade in the area.[44] On the other side of the border, Pakistan's Anti-Narcotics Force busted a massive network smuggling drugs to India using drones. The head of the Lahore police department's anti-narcotics wing was arrested. Since 1994, he had been suspended forty-five times for his alleged drug-trafficking involvement. Yet he was still given the key post. He had amassed a significant amount of wealth, and he received payment for his services in Dubai.[45]

Ultimately, social contexts facilitate cocaine trafficking. The presence of mafia-like groups or criminal networks, along with corrupt state actors, increase the vulnerability of Asian countries to illicit trade. It is corruption that has promoted the passage of contraband through airports and seaports. Airline crew members, customs officials, and government officials have been arrested, indicating the role of corrupt state-level actors in facilitating the cocaine trade.

Why Cocaine Use Is Low in Asia

Through the years, drug lords have attempted to manufacture cocaine, boost trade, and increase the drug's domestic sales in Asia, but they have not been successful. In 2007, a group of individuals from Latin America tried to create demand for cocaine in China, but they were unable to reach the scale they had aimed for.[46] Yet there were seizures of laboratories or "kitchens" in Hong Kong producing crack and other cocaine products. In 2012, for example, nine labs were seized, and in 2021 lab seizures had increased to twenty-five. In Macau, seizure data and the number of drug users arrested for cocaine are higher than for other drugs, indicating significant domestic use. However, data from Macau's Central Registration System of Drug Abusers shows that methamphetamines are the first drug of choice.

This section explores some critical factors that explain why cocaine is not the favorite drug of Asia, as it largely occupies a position after cannabis, opiates/opioids, and synthetic drugs. Specifically, I will analyze cocaine's limited social embeddedness and availability, its higher price vis-à-vis other illicit psychoactive substances, and other key economic and geographic considerations.

Social Embeddedness, Availability, and Proximity to Place of Production

Latin American countries, directly or indirectly, have a long history of association with the coca plant for various cultural reasons, including its medicinal properties. Associations of various kinds with the plant were embedded in society through practice or observation. The perception of the coca plant purely as a cash crop emerged with foreign actors or countries expressing an interest in the plant, especially for the product that could be synthesized from it: cocaine. Similarly, in the United States, people have been familiar with the use of coca or cocaine as an energy booster and as a pain relief medicine since the 1800s. Thus, by the time medical professionals and energy drink manufacturers were told to disassociate from the use of cocaine as a medicine or as a component in their products, a market had already been created, ready for the illicit trade to tap into.

This was not the case in Asia. Here, cocaine needed to compete with mind-altering substances that were already widely available like cannabis, opium, and even heroin to create its niche. In Asia, opium and cannabis have a history of cultural use that goes back centuries, and not restricted to medicinal use. Furthermore, cocaine was not independently trafficked by specific groups, but rather existing dealers simply added it to the drugs they were already trading in. This was the case with the cocaine trade that occurred in India between the two world wars as well as in the more recent arrests of cocaine traffickers. According to the *World Drug Report 2019*, comparing stimulants across different regions of the globe, cocaine is the first substance of choice in North America, Latin America, the Caribbean, western and central Europe, and eastern and southeastern Europe. The situation is different in Asia, as the stimulant of choice is amphetamines in Central Asia and Transcaucasia, methamphetamines in Southwest Asia, East Asia, and Southeast Asia, and captagon, an amphetamine, in the Middle East.[47]

Not surprisingly, cocaine has not been considered part of the culture or health care in any part of Asia, but rather seen as a drug to increase stamina and as a sexual enhancer, especially in India. A small study conducted among two hundred Indian cocaine users in early 1900 indicated that cocaine was often taken at night, and at times more than once. Unlike cannabis, which has religious and cultural links, cocaine use is associated with sexuality and sexual enhancement. Prostitutes were a key group that actively sought new cocaine users among their clientele. However, this activity was discreet, as they may have faced strong negative associations due to India's traditional values.[48]

More recent evidence suggest that cocaine use in Asia is associated with leisure. A qualitative study conducted in 2022 with a small sample of twelve cocaine users in Kuala Lumpur found that cocaine is generally considered a party drug that users take to be alert and have a good time during long hours of partying. In India, by contrast, habitual male users fear that cocaine consumption might impact the nerves in the genital area and negatively affect sexuality. Cocaine users in Malaysia did not face any health issues, even though the average duration of use was more than four years.[49]

Today, cocaine in India is seen as a party mood setter, a drug for having a good time. Its use is no longer limited to rave parties, but it is also used at many small gatherings and get-togethers among select elites and professionals. Yet this is the experience of only a small segment of Indian society. For the majority, as across Asia, cocaine is not the drug of choice.

Cocaine Is Beyond the Reach of Many

In Asia, cocaine is an expensive drug for most individuals compared to other drugs. Cocaine is considered a stimulant. However, the continent offers an alternative stimulant drug: methamphetamines. This drug is extracted from the ephedra plant, which grows wild in many parts of Asia. Not surprisingly, many processing units for synthesizing methamphetamines can be found across the continent. In this context, the price of cocaine is relatively high. For example, in Armenia the price of a kilo of cocaine is US$700,000, which is double that of methamphetamines. Similarly, cocaine costs $155,186 per kilo in the UAE compared to $32,670 for methamphetamines. This is the reality not just in Western Asia but also in East Asia, Southeast Asia, and South Asia. This is only natural, as the cultivation of ephedra and the processing of methamphetamines occurs within Asia. The street price of cocaine, as summarized in table 12.1, indicates how expensive cocaine is for the local population.[50]

Cocaine in Asia is cheapest in Cambodia. However, it's still expensive for locals, as it costs 82,100 Cambodian riel per gram. When considering street prices in Europe and the United States, in India, Pakistan, Sri Lanka, Cambodia, and Malaysia, cocaine is sold at a cheaper price despite the greater distance from the source. In most countries in Europe, a gram of cocaine costs around US$74.70. In Denmark, for example, it costs around $100, and in Belgium, $58.10. In the United States, the street price of one gram varies from $80 to $100.

A qualitative study of cocaine users in Malaysia also corroborates the same: users purchase the drug through close contacts at US$150 per gram (more than triple the amount indicated by the UNODC as the street price) and use it only during parties or small gatherings with their friends.[51] In other words, it is not a drug for daily use, and this works to decrease the gross amount of cocaine needed for domestic use in Malaysia, and other Asian countries as well.

Table 12.1. Street Prices of Cocaine.

Region and country	Year	Price per gram (US$)	In local currency
CENTRAL ASIA			
Kazakhstan	2014	117.50	54,910.76 KZT
WESTERN ASIA			
Armenia	2017	400.00	1,53,539.12 AMD
Israel	2017	105.07	399.95 ILS
Kuwait	2019	323.60	100.11 KWD
Lebanon	2019	80.00	1,200,453.60 LBP
Oman	2017	129.88	49.93 OMR
State of Palestine	2018	78.77	299.84 ILS
EAST ASIA			
China	2019	120.60	877.28 CNY
Hong Kong, China	2019	150.00	1174.15 HKD
Macau, China	2019	413.00	3324.35 MOP
Japan	2017	135.24	19985.09 JPY
SOUTHEAST ASIA			
Indonesia	2019	179.00	2,750,693.00 IDR
Malaysia	2014	47.38	221.93 MYR
Philippines	2016	76.70	4350.08 PHP
Cambodia	2018	20.00	82,072.42 KHR
SOUTH ASIA			
India	2019	60.18	5000 INR
Pakistan	2019	53.98	16000 PKR
Sri Lanka	2018	55.79	18,000 LKR

Source: Created by the author with data from the United Nations Office on Drugs and Crime, "Drug Trafficking and Cultivation: Drug Prices," https://dataunodc.un.org/dp-drug-prices.

Disparity in Access to Wealth Within Asian Countries

Throughout Asia, there is a strong disparity in access to a nation's wealth; the bottom 50 percent of the population, in terms of income levels, have access to a little over 10 percent of the total national wealth. There is an interesting regional difference regarding the sharing of wealth by the middle group of 40 percent and top 10 percent of the population. In East Asia, while the bottom 50 percent share around 12 percent of the nation's wealth, the rest is shared by the middle and upper classes, with little discrepancy in their sharing of the remaining 88 percent. In South and Southeast Asia, on the other hand, the bottom 50 percent share around 11 percent of the national wealth and the middle group share around 30 percent. The top 10 percent, disproportionately, thus control over 55 percent of the national wealth.[52]

Given this disparity, and the fact that middle-income people enjoy a reasonable share of the national wealth only in East Asia, cocaine is expensive for Asians in most countries (except a few like Japan and Palestine, where heroin is more expensive than cocaine). In all other Asian countries, cocaine is far too expensive, priced outside the reach of a large segment of the population.

Asia: The Darknet and the Future of the Drug Trade

The digitization of trade in drugs and chemicals is an initiative that has gained momentum, especially during the COVID-19 pandemic. The UNODC has issued specific reports on this trend, indicating the presence and use of the darknet beginning in 2014 and its continued active relevance since then. Vendors who set up sites on the darknet often handle direct sales to users; transactions between dealers is rare. Several factors contribute to the secretiveness of the darknet, including the use of onion routers like Tor, which vendors use to keep their IP address in flux; mechanisms to deliver the product to a public spot (such as a post office) or a hidden location communicated to the client; the use of cryptocurrencies to make financial transactions; and the use of fake identities. By using cryptic messages, vendors can create a closed environment to address their clients' needs. In fact, even the surface web is being used to traffic drugs, with a high level of anonymity and scope for the rapid replacement of workers and agents in case of arrest. Thus, business carries on as usual.[53]

Currently, among the services provided on the darknet as per a study of four marketplaces, 68 percent of products fall within the category of drugs. From the various drugs sold, 30 percent are cannabis products, and the next largest category is stimulants, including cocaine, at 12 percent.[54] Indeed, drug sales through the darknet are only a fraction of all drug business worldwide, which is around $315 billion annually. Online vendors, to evade enforcement activities, sell drugs as "research chemicals" and advertise custom synthesis, whereby clients can ask for products not in the list. A legitimate practice in the pharmaceutical industry is thus misused by online drug vendors.[55]

When considering darknet use in Asia, in China, 9 percent of the country's drug trade is through the darknet, and in India 3 percent. In China, unlike in other parts of the globe, digital platforms are used to trade in what are referred to as "new psychoactive substances" (NPS).[56] Under these circumstances, it is possible that in the future the darknet in Asia may evolve to play a stronger role in drug trafficking. Cocaine will likely remain too expensive for most Asians, and crack, like heroin (often adulterated), may not find clientele on the digital platform. It is difficult to market heroin or an adulterated form (brown sugar) or crack (adulterated cocaine) online, as users may prefer to purchase from a visible contact in close proximity.

Conclusion

Cocaine is not a favorite drug of choice in most parts of Asia, even though it has carved out its niche among the elite, who associate the drug with socializing and partying. The reality is that, although coca was cultivated, synthesized, and traded in different parts of Asia between the world wars, its use remained confined to a small section of the population in a few territories of some countries. Since the original source of coca, South America, is distant from Asia, entrepreneurs attempted to grow the plant locally. Though successful, the local plants never produced a sufficient amount of the alkaloid needed to manufacture cocaine to be viable.

Apart from Asian coca's low alkaloid content, psychoactive plant cultivation is an illicit activity, and most Asian countries have strong penal sanctions against it. Thus, considering cultivation as an economic venture would be restricted to a small segment willing to take the risk. Even then, cocaine would have to compete with other drugs, especially methamphetamines, a stimulant synthesized from the ephedra plant, which has a strong local presence. Moreover, cocaine is the most expensive recreational drug in almost all Asian countries, which restricts the domestic market. The chance of cocaine becoming the "drug of choice" thus seems remote within the Asian reality, except among certain sections of the population.

Notes

1. Joseph F. Spillane, "Making a Modern Drug: The Manufacture, Sale, and Control of Cocaine in the United States, 1880–1920," in *Cocaine: Global Histories*, ed. Paul Gootenberg (Abingdon, Oxon., England: Routledge, 1999), 25.

2. Spillane, "Making a Modern Drug," 29.

3. Paul Gootenberg, "Reluctance or Resistance? Constructing Cocaine (Prohibitions) in Peru, 1910–50," in *Cocaine: Global Histories*, ed. Paul Gootenberg (Abingdon, Oxon., England: Routledge, 1999), 47.

4. José Manuel Rodríguez (1857–1936) was a self-taught economist from Peru. He criticized direct foreign investment and analyzed capital flight, and advocated selective protectionism in practice while increasingly favoring state intervention for development. He has been described as the first Peruvian economist. This information is from Nicola Miller, "How Latin America Reimagined Classical Economics," *Boston Review*, November 16, 2020, https://www.bostonreview.net/articles/nicola-miller-how-latin-america-reinvented-political-economy/.

5. Steven B. Karch, "Japan and the Cocaine Industry of Southeast Asia, 1864–1944," in *Cocaine: Global Histories*, ed. Paul Gootenberg (Abingdon, Oxon., England: Routledge, 1999), 148.

6. Karch, "Japan and the Cocaine Industry of Southeast Asia," 149.

7. Karch, "Japan and the Cocaine Industry of Southeast Asia," 152–53.

8. I. C. Chopra and R. N. Chopra, "The Cocaine Problem in India," United Nations Office on Drugs and Crime, January 1958, https://www.unodc.org/unodc/en/data-and-analysis/bulletin/bulletin_1958-01-01_2_page005.html.

9. Chopra and Chopra, "The Cocaine Problem in India."

10. Chopra and Chopra, "The Cocaine Problem in India."

11. Chopra and Chopra, "The Cocaine Problem in India."

12. International Narcotics Control Board, *Report of the International Narcotics Control Board for 1985* (Vienna: United Nations, 1985), https://www.incb.org/documents/Publications/AnnualReports/AR1985/AR_1985_English.pdf.

13. United Nations Office for Drug Control and Crime Prevention, *Global Illicit Drug Trends 1999* (New York: United Nations, 1999), 9, https://www.unodc.org/pdf/report_1999-06-01_1.pdf.

14. Molly Charles, "Drug Trade Dynamics in India," Mama Coca, 2004, http://www.mamacoca.org/FSMT_sept_2003/en/doc/charles_drug_trade_dynamics_in_india_en.htm.

15. United Nations Office on Drugs and Crime, *World Drug Report 2009* (Vienna: United Nations, 2009), 74–75, https://www.unodc.org/documents/wdr/WDR_2009/WDR2009_eng_web.pdf.

16. United Nations Office on Drugs and Crime, *World Drug Report 2021*, "Statistical Annex," https://www.unodc.org/unodc/en/data-and-analysis/wdr2021_annex.html.

17. United Nations Office on Drugs and Crime, *World Drug Report 2021*, "Statistical Annex, Drug Seizure Data 2015-2019," https://www.unodc.org/unodc/en/data-and-analysis/wdr2021_annex.html; and United Nations Office on Drugs and Crime, *World Drug Report 2022*, "Statistical Annex, Drug Seizure Data 2016–2020," https://www.unodc.org/unodc/en/data-and-analysis/wdr2022_annex.html.

18. Global Organized Crime Index, "Malaysia," https://ocindex.net/country/malaysia; "Customs Dept Scores Major Drug Bust, Seizes 88Kg Cocaine Worth RM17.6m at KLIA Air Cargo Complex," *Malay Mail* (Petaling Jaya), August 7, 2023, https://www.malaymail.com/news/malaysia/2023/08/07/customs-dept-scores-major-drug-bust-seizes-88kg-cocaine-worth-rm176m-at-klia-air-cargo-complex/83995; and Noah Lee and Ali Nufael, "Malaysian Police Seize 12 Tons of Cocaine Hidden in Charcoal Shipment," *Benar News* (Washington, DC), September 20, 2019, https://www.benarnews.org/english/news/malaysian/cocaine-charcoal-09202019143807.html.

19. United Nations Office on Drugs and Crime, *Global Report on Cocaine 2023: Local Dynamics, Global Challenges* (Vienna: United Nations, 2023), 124, https://www.unodc.org/documents/data-and-analysis/cocaine/Global_cocaine_report_2023.pdf.

20. "Cocaine Trafficking Network Unearthed, Three Persons Arrested," *The Hindu* (Chennai), July 28, 2023, https://www.thehindu.com/news/cities/chennai/cocaine-trafficking-network-unearthed-three-persons-arrested/article67131956.ece; and "Rs. 1,476 Crore Meth, Cocaine in Truck Carrying Imported Oranges in Mumbai," NDTV News Desk, October 1, 2022, https://www.ndtv.com/india-news/rs-1-476-crore-meth-cocaine-in-truck-carrying-imported-oragnes-in-mumbai-3395485.

21. United Nations Office on Drugs and Crime, "Port Control Units in the Region Demonstrate Results in Drug Seizures and Undeclared Consumer Goods," Tashkent, n.d., https://www.unodc.org/roca/en/news/port-control-units-in-the-region-demostrate-results-in-drug-seizures-and-undeclared-consumer-goods.html.

22. United Nations Office on Drugs and Crime, *Misuse of Licit Trade for Opiate Trafficking in Western and Central Asia: A Threat Assessment* (Vienna: United Nations, 2012), https://www.unodc.org/documents/data-and-analysis/Studies/Opiate_Trafficking_and_Trade_Agreements_english_web.pdf.

23. "How a Cocaine-Smuggling Cartel Infiltrated the World's Biggest Shipping Company," Money Control, December 19, 2022, https://www.moneycontrol.com/news/business/how-a-cocaine-smuggling-cartel-infiltrated-the-worlds-biggest-shipping-company-9722091.html; and Greg Miller, "20 Tons of Coke = 40+ Years in Prison for MSC Container-Ship Crew," FreightWaves, June 15, 2021, https://www.freightwaves.com/news/20-tons-of-coke-40-years-in-prison-for-msc-container-ship-crew.

24. United Nations Office on Drugs and Crime, *Global Report on Cocaine 2023*.

25. M. Abul Kalam Azad, "British Intel Helped Bangladesh Detect Liquid Cocaine Smuggling," *Daily Star* (Dhaka), June 29, 2015, https://www.thedailystar.net/country/british-intel-helped-bangladesh-detect-liquid-cocaine-smuggling-104632; "Three Held in Connection with Liquid Cocaine Haul," *Daily Observer* (Dhaka), July 1, 2015, https://www.observerbd.com/2015/07/01/97376.php; and "Huge Bangladesh Cocaine Seizure Points to Growing South Asia Drug Route," *Guardian*, July 13, 2015, https://www.theguardian.com/world/2015/jul/13/huge-bangladesh-cocaine-seizure-points-to-growing-south-asia-drug-route.

26. Press Trust of India, "Seizure of High-Value Drugs Rises Manifold in FY22: DRI Report," *Deccan Herald* (Bengaluru), December 6, 2022, https://www.deccanherald.com/india/seizure-of-high-value-drugs-rises-manifold-in-fy22-dri-report-1168974.html; and Haima Deshpande, "With Highest Drug Seizures in 2022, Gujarat Coastline Has Become Hotspot for Drug Trafficking," *Outlook* (New Delhi), December 20, 2022, https://www.outlookindia.com/national/how-drugs-seizures-and-arrests-reached-a-high-in-2022-and-how-gujarat-coastline-has-become-hotspot-news-246366.

27. "Customs Dept Scores Major Drug Bust"; and Zaihan Mohamed Yusof, "Malaysian Customs Seize 300kg of Cocaine in Port Klang in Container Loaded with Beans," *Straits Times*, June 12, 2023, https://www.straitstimes.com/asia/malaysian-customs-seize-300kg-of-cocaine-in-port-klang-in-container-loaded-with-beans/.

28. United Nations Office on Drugs and Crime, *Transnational Organized Crime in the West African Region* (Vienna: United Nations, 2005), 16, https://www.unodc.org/pdf/transnational_crime_west-africa-05.pdf.

29. United Nations Office on Drugs and Crime, *Transnational Organized Crime in the West African Region*, 17.

30. Molly Charles, K. S. Nair, Gabriel Britto, and Anthony A. Das, "The Bombay Underworld: A Descriptive Account and Its Role in Drug Trade," in *Drug Trafficking, Criminal Organisations and Money Laundering*, vol. 2 of *Globalisation, Drugs and Criminalisation*, ed. Christian Geffray, Guilhem Fabre, and Michel Schiray (Paris: UNESCO, 2002), 12–71.

31. United Nations Office on Drugs and Crime, *Global Report on Cocaine 2023*.

32. Sandeep Unnithan and Bhavna Vij-Aurora, "Ruthless and Organised, Nigerians Have Become the Biggest Players in India's Market for Hard Narcotics," *India Today*, December 2, 2013, https://www.indiatoday.in/magazine/special-report/story/20131202-nigerians-drugs-narcotics-goa-police-drug-trafficking-nigerian-murder-768812-1999-11-29; "List of Nigerians Executed for Drug Trafficking in Indonesia, Singapore, Malaysia and Saudi Arabia Combined," Naijadazz, April 14, 2011, https://www.naijadazz.com/nigerians-executed-for-drug-trafficking/; Neeraj Chauhan, "NCB Raises Issue of Nigerians Involved in Trafficking with Their Top Drug Cop," *Hindustan Times* (New Delhi), December 18, 2022, https://www.hindustantimes.com/cities/delhi-news/ncb-raises-issue-of-nigerians-involved-in-trafficking-with-their-top-drug-officer-101671298932891.html; and "Drug Trafficking: Over 500 Nigerians in Thai Prisons," Channels Television, July 31, 2014, https://www.channelstv.com/2014/07/31/drug-trafficking-over-500-nigerians-in-thai-prisons.

33. Global Organized Crime Index, "About the Index," https://ocindex.net/about.

34. Darlene N. Moorman, "The Yakuza: Organized Crime in Japan," *Downtown Review* (Cleveland State University) 7, no. 1 (2020), https://engagedscholarship.csuohio.edu/tdr/vol7/iss1/1/; Jake Adelstein, "The Yakuza Lobby," *Foreign Policy*, December 13, 2012, https://foreignpolicy.com/2012/12/13/the-yakuza-lobby/; "Yakuza and Organized Crime in Japan: History, Honor, Punch Perms, Pinkies and Tattoos," Facts and Details, https://factsanddetails.com/Japan/cat22/sub147/item811.html; and "Tentacles of Organized Crime Once Had Firm Grip on Japanese Politics," The Mob Museum, https://themobmuseum.org/blog/tentacles-of-organized-crime-once-had-firm-grip-on-japanese-politics/.

35. T. A. Bancroft, "The Triads: Past and Present," In *Investigating the Grey Areas of the Chinese Communities in Southeast Asia*, ed. Arnaud Leveau (Bangkok: Institut de Recherche sur l'Asie du Sud-Est Contemporaine, 2007); and Aadil Brar, "Glitz, Glamour and Gambling: Behind China's Secret Societies and Crime Syndicates," *The Print*, December 1, 2021, https://theprint.in/opinion/eye-on-china/glitz-glamour-and-gambling-behind-chinas-secret-societies-and-crime-syndicates/774483/.

36. Brent O'Halloran, "'It Will Weaken Our Democracy': Fears Powerful Taiwanese Gangs Are Controlling the Country's Leaders," Sky News Australia, March 7, 2023, https://www.skynews.com.au/world-news/it-will-weaken-our-democracy-fears-powerful-taiwanese-gangs-are-controlling-the-countrys-leaders/news-story/c9d713402ab3871a0c7e946bd2601cfd; and "Organized Crime in Taiwan," Facts and Details, https://factsanddetails.com/southeast-asia/Taiwan/sub5_1c/entry-3829.html.

37. Charles et al., "The Bombay Underworld."

38. United Nations Office on Drugs and Crime, *World Drug Report 2004*, vol. 1, *Analysis* (Vienna: United Nations, 2004), https://www.unodc.org/pdf/WDR_2004/volume_1.pdf.

39. United Nations Office on Drugs and Crime, *Global Report on Cocaine 2023*.

40. United Nations Office on Drugs and Crime, *World Drug Report 2022*, vol. 4, *Drug Market Trends: Cocaine, Amphetamine-Type Stimulants, New Psychoactive Substances* (Vienna: United Nations, 2022), 26, https://www.unodc.org/res/wdr2022/MS/WDR22_Booklet_4.pdf.

41. United Nations Office on Drugs and Crime, *World Drug Report 2022*, vol. 4, *Drug Market Trends*, 27.

42. United Nations Office on Drugs and Crime, *World Drug Report 2022*, vol. 4, *Drug Market Trends*, 27.

43. Charles, "Drug Trade Dynamics in India."

44. Jehangir Ali, "J&K Court Rejects Bail of 5 Army Men Who 'Ran Narcotics Racket' Along LoC," *The Wire* (New Delhi), February 13, 2023.

45. "Lahore Police's Anti-Narcotics Chief Heads Gang Smuggling Drugs into India," *India Today*, September 13, 2023, https://www.indiatoday.in/world/story/pakistan-cross-border-drug-smuggling-network-lahore-deluivers-narcotics-in-punjab-india-dsp-mazhar-iqbal-2435182-2023-09-13.

46. United Nations Office on Drugs and Crime, *Global Report on Cocaine 2023*.

47. United Nations Office on Drugs and Crime, *World Drug Report 2019*, vol. 4, *Stimulants* (Vienna: United Nations, 2019), 10, https://wdr.unodc.org/wdr2019/prelaunch/WDR19_Booklet_4_STIMULANTS.pdf. The UNODC defines "Southwest Asia" as

Pakistan, Afghanistan, and Iran, and the "Middle East" as all the Asian countries west of Iran, including the Arabian Peninsula.

48. Chopra and Chopra, "The Cocaine Problem in India."

49. United Nations Office on Drugs and Crime, *Global Report on Cocaine 2023*, 125.

50. United Nations Office on Drugs and Crime, *World Drug Report 2021* (Vienna: United Nations, 2019), "Statistical Annex: Price and Purities Data," https://www.unodc.org/documents/data-and-analysis/WDR2021/8.1_Prices_an_purities_of_Drugs.pdf.

51. United Nations Office on Drugs and Crime, *Global Report on Cocaine 2023*, 125.

52. World Inequality Report, "Executive Summary," https://wir2022.wid.world/executive-summary.

53. United Nations Office on Drugs and Crime, *World Drug Report 2020* (Vienna: United Nations, 2020), "In Focus: Trafficking over the Darknet," https://www.unodc.org/documents/Focus/WDR20_Booklet_4_Darknet_web.pdf; and Bindu Shajan Perappadan, "Youngest Age Groups Using Social Media to Purchase Drugs: Report," *The Hindu* (Chennai), June 30, 2023, https://www.thehindu.com/news/national/younges-age-groups-using-social-media-to-purchase-drugs-report/article67027185.ece.

54. United Nations Office on Drugs and Crime, *Darknet Cybercrime Threats to Southeast Asia 2020* (Vienna: United Nations, 2020), https://www.unodc.org/roseap/uploads/archive/documents/darknet/index.html.

55. United Nations Office on Drugs and Crime, *World Drug Report 2021*, vol. 1, *Executive Summary: Policy Implications* (Vienna: United Nations, 2021), 24, https://www.unodc.org/res/wdr2021/field/WDR21_Booklet_1.pdf.

56. European Union Drugs Agency, "New Psychoactive Substances (NPS)," Lisbon, n.d., https://www.euda.europa.eu/topics/nps_en.

CHAPTER 13

Cocaine Trafficking and Criminal Organizations in Oceania

Jose Sousa-Santos

Cocaine trafficking in Oceania—the expansive ocean continent comprising Australia, New Zealand, and the Pacific islands[1]—is on the rise. Situated along a maritime corridor utilized for legitimate trade between major economic markets on the Asian and American borders of the Pacific Rim, the region has become a principal transshipment hub for drugs, with significant implications for populations and communities from Sydney to Nuku'alofa. Oceania is strategically valuable as a transit route and occasional production site for Asian organized crime syndicates, European criminal syndicates including the 'Ndrangheta mafia, and Mexican and South American cartels. The targets are the lucrative markets in Australia and New Zealand, where the street value of cocaine—and other drugs such as methamphetamines—is among the highest in the world. In contrast, the scale of trafficking in the Pacific islands is comparatively low, although the impact on small Pacific populations is high.

Parallel to the increase in the trafficking of cocaine—and other illicit drugs such as methamphetamines—is the growth of criminal networks in the Pacific island countries and territories (PICTs) and the emergence of hybrid local-transnational networks. This chapter explores the rise of cocaine trafficking in Oceania by examining the political economy of the cocaine trade in the region including the evolving processes, mechanisms, and actors that interconnect and enable the cocaine supply chain.

Oceania is comprised of island nations with few shared land borders spread across the Pacific Ocean. The sovereign and self-governing states and territories are broadly grouped into four geopolitical subregions: Australia and New Zealand; Melanesia (Fiji, Papua New Guinea, New Caledonia, the Solomon Islands, and Vanuatu); Micronesia (Kiribati, the Marshall Islands, the Federated States of

Micronesia, Nauru, and Palau); and Polynesia (American Samoa, the Cook Islands, French Polynesia, Niue, Samoa, Tonga, Tokelau, Tuvalu, and Wallis and Futuna).

The vast maritime geography of Oceania plays a critical role as facilitator and enabler of transnational crime. The Pacific Ocean covers approximately 33 percent of the earth's total surface, and the exclusive economic zones of Oceanic states collectively equate to 30 percent of global exclusive economic zones. Accordingly, the Pacific islands are frequently referred to as "large ocean states." The PICTs are characterized by large geographic areas largely of ocean and relatively small populations scattered across multiple islands.[2]

The PICTs' strategic location along both licit and illicit trading maritime highways, vast and porous maritime borders, weak jurisdictions, and limited enforcement capabilities are key structural challenges and enablers to transnational crime. For criminal enterprises, under-resourced law enforcement and security agencies, the relatively low risk of detection of transnational and organized crime in this environment, and profitability all contribute to the growing attractiveness of the region as a potential crime hub.[3]

Transnational crime has long been recognized as an enduring threat to the security of Oceania. In 2018, the Pacific Islands Forum, the region's primary intergovernmental organization, identified four security challenges, in addition to climate change, facing the region: human security, environmental and resource security, transnational crime, and cybersecurity.[4] The importation, transshipment, precursor trafficking, peddling, and use of illicit drugs is the most prevalent transnational criminal activity in the region.[5]

The Pacific Islands Forum's Honiara Declaration (1992) recognized that "the potential impact of transnational crime was a matter for increasing concern to regional states and enforcement agencies" and called for a "more comprehensive, integrated and collaborative approach" across law enforcement to counter these threats.[6] Since around 2018, there has been a growing recognition that transnational crime can generate significant insecurity, disrupt traditional and cultural mechanisms, fuel corruption, weaken key security sectors, and undermine formal and informal governance.[7] Some Pacific islands are seeing the transshipment of narcotics through their territories devolving into a growing domestic demand for illicit drugs.[8] This has led to increases in addiction, mental health issues, crime, and violence, including domestic and sexual violence.[9] National security strategies, which Pacific Islands Forum members committed to under the Boe

Declaration, have sought to align domestic focus on transnational crime with the regional architecture. The national security strategies of the Cook Islands, Palau, Samoa, the Solomon Islands, and Vanuatu all identify transnational crime and the spillover of drug abuse into local communities as key security issues. Palau's national security strategy highlights the negative health effects of illicit drug abuse and the drain on the nation's health-care system.[10]

Illicit drugs—and transnational crime more broadly—are, therefore, a crosscutting threat to development, security, and governance in the Pacific. Put bluntly, the PICTs are casualties of the criminal greed of organized crime and the drug appetite of Australia and New Zealand.

Markets and Methods

The political economy of the illicit drug trade in Oceania is driven by Australia and New Zealand as high-value markets. The illegal drug trade in Australia is estimated to be worth AU$11.3 billion[11] and in New Zealand up to an estimated AU$1.86 billion per annum.[12] As noted, Australia and New Zealand pay some of the highest prices globally for cocaine. Between mid-2016 and 2018, cocaine accounted for the largest volume of seized illicit drugs transiting through the region, with a record of eight metric tons seized.[13]

Moreover, reflecting contemporary global trends, cocaine and methamphetamine usage has been steadily increasing in both Australia and New Zealand,[14] reaching record levels in April and June 2020 despite the disruption of supply chains due to COVID-19.[15] During the year ending August 2022, data from the Australian Criminal Intelligence Commission's National Wastewater Drug Monitoring Program indicated that more than 3.3 metric tons of cocaine had been consumed in Australia (down from 5.6 metric tons in 2020). The cocaine market started to rebound later in 2022. Throughout 2022 and the early months of 2023, authorities detected a series of attempted large cocaine importations, both onshore and offshore. According to the Australian Federal Police, this was due to two factors. First, Albanian crime networks have been flooding the Australian market with cheap cocaine in a bid to control the lucrative trade; and second, shipments of cocaine that were bound for Australia but backlogged due to the reduction in air and sea freight during the COVID-19 pandemic are now contributing to the oversupply.[16]

Consumers in Australia and New Zealand pay high prices for cocaine and methamphetamines: a kilogram of cocaine in Australia can cost as much as AU$400,000.[17] Notably, the demographic of domestic users of cocaine is broadening, and street prices for cocaine are increasingly cheaper than for crystal methamphetamine.[18]

While PICTs have previously been linked to transnational organized crime activities as transit points for the movement of illicit substances to larger markets such as New Zealand and Australia, domestic illicit drug markets have grown across the region since around 2010. It is important to note here that while the numbers may appear to be small compared to other regions in terms of scale, the impact of illicit drugs on Pacific communities is considerable. For example, in 2021 Fiji's director of public prosecutions, Christopher Pryde, claimed that funds from illicit drug activities were more than US$5 million per annum and that "local traffickers could make between US$2,500 and US$5,000 a day from the sale of cocaine and meth in the domestic market."[19]

As noted above, Australia and New Zealand are the principal markets in Oceania for cocaine. The majority of the cocaine reaching Australia and New Zealand originates in Colombia and is transported by cartels and syndicates in South and Central America.

The key regional transshipment hubs in Oceania for the Australian and New Zealand markets are Papua New Guinea, Fiji, and Tonga. Cocaine seizures since 2018 demonstrate that Papua New Guinea is currently a key transit route into Australia. These include attempts to traffic AU$90 million of cocaine through the Torres Strait, the channel of water between Australia and Papua New Guinea, in 2018 and the discovery in 2019 by a community on Budi Budi Island, in the Papua New Guinean province of Milne Bay, of eleven duffle bags of cocaine buried on a local beach worth AU$50 million, destined for the Australian market.[20] In 2020, a Cessna aircraft carrying over five hundred kilograms of cocaine destined for Australia crashed at a remote jungle airstrip about thirty kilometers from Port Moresby, the capital of Papua New Guinea. That morning, the aircraft had flown 878 kilometers from Queensland, Australia, to the airstrip near Port Moresby at three thousand feet to avoid detection. The aircraft crashed during its attempted takeoff from the airstrip due to being overloaded with cocaine. The cocaine seizure, with a street value of US$54 million, was Papua New Guinea's largest-ever cocaine haul. In 2022 Papua New Guinea's police commissioner, David Manning, referred to his country as a "safe house" for drug traffickers operating in the region.[21] For example, Port Moresby has become a site for Australian outlaw motorcycle gangs (OMCGs) to work with West African and Chinese criminal organizations engaged in laundering payments for drug shipments.[22]

In the case of Fiji, a joint operation between Fijian, Australian, and New Zealand authorities led to the interdiction of a yacht off the coast of Australia in 2017 carrying 1.4 metric tons of cocaine valued at AU$312 million. The yacht was believed to have transited through Fiji from South America, illustrating the role of Fiji as a transit point.[23]

Although the majority of illicit drugs in Oceania are trafficked by air, the COVID-19 pandemic reinforced the strategic value of the maritime drug highway. The pandemic halted global aviation and disrupted supply routes, which resulted in changing patterns in drug trafficking. In the Pacific, the maritime transport sector rose to become the main vector in drug trafficking. The Pacific is heavily dependent on maritime shipping, with more than 80 percent of all international cargo (both container and noncontainer) transported by ship.[24] Containerization is one of the primary modes of trafficking illicit drugs in the Pacific, with the trend likely to grow. Container tonnage in the Pacific is estimated to increase from the 1.7 million metric tons, or 12.1 percent of total seaborne cargo worldwide, it amounted to in 2000, to 4.2 million metric tons, or 19 percent, in 2030.[25] Moreover, although not new, the use of container vessels to conceal cocaine appears to be on the rise.[26]

In 2023, approximately 560 kilograms of cocaine were dropped overboard from a bulk cargo carrier off the coast of Western Australia.[27] Cocaine equaling 175 kilograms was seized at two New Zealand ports in 2023; in both instances, the containers concealing the drug had originated in or transited through Panama.[28] In 2022, New Zealand authorities seized 700 kilograms of cocaine transported in shipping containers from South America.[29] Scale, insufficient oversight within the maritime transport sector, corrupt officials, and disparities in port infrastructure compound the challenge of countering maritime drug trafficking.

As the United Nations Office on Drugs and Crime (UNODC) notes, while cocaine traffickers have long taken advantage of legal trade in containerized goods, their techniques of "contamination" (referring to placing drugs in a container) and concealment continuously evolve.[30] For example, a rising trend is the smuggling of drugs into Australia by hiding them underneath or below the waterline of cargo ships—in some cases to be retrieved by divers, a practice that has been known to be fatal.[31] In August 2023, approximately 200 kilograms of cocaine were discovered in the sea chest of a container ship docked in the port of Melbourne. In October that year, approximately 150 kilograms of cocaine concealed inside the hull of a cargo ship originating from South America were seized after the vessel docked in Melbourne.

Moreover, the logistics of container trafficking are becoming more complex and sophisticated, requiring a network of collaborators among port workers, transport companies, drivers, and customs officials.[32] This, in turn, suggests increased levels of corruption. In the Pacific, narco-corruption has compromised institutions and individuals across key agencies such as customs, police, and immigration, and, ultimately, undermined the rule of law. In 2019, for example, Tonga's "war on drugs" resulted in the arrests of a Tongan senior customs official and a police officer who were facilitating the trafficking of methamphetamines, cocaine, and illegal firearms from the United States.[33] Tonga's antidrug task force has carried out the suspension of twenty-eight police officers, with the country's police minister, Mateni Tapueluelu, warning others with status in Tongan society: "Don't think you can sit on some high places and think you're too high for the police to reach, it's just a matter of time. You deal, you pay."[34] Papua New Guinea's police commissioner, David Manning, has similarly highlighted the complicity of Royal Papua New Guinea Constabulary officers, affirming that "there are criminals in uniform" and that he is committed to ridding the force of these elements.[35] Concerns about the infiltration of criminals into security and law enforcement agencies were also shared by the head of Fiji's Police Drug Intelligence Unit, Anare Masitabua.[36]

The maritime drug trade is also facilitated by the use of yachts, called "blow boats," to transport cocaine across the Pacific. The scale of the yachting industry in the Pacific is considerable; for example, annual estimates suggest that approximately nine hundred yachts visit French Polynesia, seven hundred yachts visit Fiji, and five hundred visit Tonga. Reflecting on the challenges of countering drug trafficking by yachts, Fiji's Revenue and Customs Authority manager stated in 2020 that "it's like looking for the needle in the haystack.... [W]hen you go fishing you don't expect to catch all the fish in the ocean."[37]

The quantity of cocaine seized on board yachts indicates that this method of trafficking cocaine is highly effective, and the concealment methods are sophisticated. In 2013, 750 kilograms of cocaine were hidden in the lower engine compartments of a yacht and its keel area and sealed with rocks and concrete.[38] From December 2016 to November 2017, Pacific law enforcement agencies seized approximately 7.6 metric tons of cocaine on board eleven small craft believed to be bound for Australia, a significant increase in both the frequency and volume from previous years. In 2017, two yachts with a total of 1,400 kilograms of cocaine were apprehended in two different locations in French Polynesia.[39] In 2022, customs officials and police in French Polynesia seized 423 kilograms of cocaine hidden in a Swedish yacht that had sailed from Panama bound for Australia.[40] Furthermore, there is one publicly known case of a yacht, the New Zealand–registered *Elakha*, rendezvousing with a "mother ship" in the southern Pacific Ocean; 1.4 metric tons of cocaine were transferred from the yacht onto the *Elakha*.[41]

In addition to transporting cocaine via container ships and yachts, innovative methods have been developed to traffic cocaine at sea, including the use of floating drug nets. For example, in 2023 New Zealand police, defense, and customs agents seized 3.2 metric tons of cocaine valued at US$315 million packed into eighty-one bales and floating in nets—supported by flotation devices—in international waters northeast of New Zealand.[42] The cocaine had been trafficked from South America and was awaiting pickup at sea to be transported to Australia. On occasion, this method has resulted in drugs washing up on Pacific beaches, including fourteen kilograms of cocaine discovered on Tongan beaches in 2021.

Furthermore, remote Pacific islands have served as staging posts for drugs to be hidden prior to collection and onward trafficking. In one such case, as described above, eleven duffle bags containing sixty kilograms of cocaine destined for Australia were buried on a beach on remote Budi Budi Island in Papua New Guinea. This resulted in a confrontation between the villagers who discovered the bags and the drug traffickers, described as "heavily tattooed foreigners," who demanded their return.[43] Although the villagers were forced to hand back most of the duffle bags, they had concealed six parcels, which they handed over to the police.

Brothers of the Underworld: Oceania's Cocaine Traffickers

Although a comprehensive mapping of the principal criminal actors and networks involved in the trafficking of cocaine in Oceania has yet to be undertaken, several observations can be made. Here, I offer a broad typology of criminal actors and identify a number of characteristics of the criminal network in Oceania. For instance, on several occasions, organized criminal groups in Australia have adopted protectionist strategies and chosen cooperation over competition to protect their stakes in the domestic cocaine market. This type of cooperation reflects the value of the market.

Australia's cocaine market, for example, is dominated by "the Commission," a syndicate or cartel comprising the country's most prominent cocaine importers and dealers. The Commission is believed to have been established by senior members of the Comanchero outlaw motorcycle gang; it has engaged in protectionist activities on several occasions to exercise influence and control over Australia's lucrative cocaine market.

In 2023, for example, the Commission ordered cocaine dealers to freeze supply in a bid to reverse a slump in the price of cocaine because of Albanian and other (Canadian, British, and South American) criminal organizations attempting to flood the market and undercut local suppliers. The directive, delivered via an encrypted message, stated: "To my dear brothers of the underworld I need us all to sit back and stop all supply of bricks for four weeks and let me raise the market with a bit of patience."[44] The strategy outlined that dealers would be permitted to sell ounces and grams of cocaine, but bricks of cocaine would be held until the price stabilized above AU$200,000 per kilogram. The message was followed with another, warning that those who broke ranks with the Commission and continued to flood the market with cocaine would face serious consequences.[45] Notably, the messages identified a key dynamic in the supply chain, with one message stating: "The ounce people will raise the market for us," and that "[a]s the supply tightens there [sic] prices will rise from being where we are at now."[46] This example demonstrates the extent to which organized crime groups in Australia were willing to collude and cooperate in order to protect the cocaine market.

In another example of protectionism, the Commission issued a warning to domestic and international criminal gangs involved in the importation or sale of fentanyl in Australia. The encrypted message stated: "Those international syndicates, fishing around to bring Fentanyl into Australia. It's not going to happen. Australia will be a fentanyl-free nation, any attempts will be dealt with immediate WAR."[47] The Commission's bid to protect the cocaine market came too late. In 2020, New South Wales health officials warned that fentanyl-related substances were being sold as methamphetamines and cocaine powder.[48] In 2022, the largest shipment of fentanyl to Australia yet, equating to five million doses, was seized. Furthermore, wastewater analysis has similarly shown the rise of fentanyl usage in Australia.

Australian and New Zealand outlaw motorcycle gangs (OMCGs) are central actors in the cocaine trade in the Pacific. OMCGs are believed to be involved in up to half of the large-scale drug importations to Australia and in many of the large, clandestine manufacturing labs. From the mid-2000s, OMCGs such as the Australian Rebels and the New Zealand Head Hunters began establishing chapters in the Pacific islands, thereby enabling better control and facilitation of the trafficking of illicit drugs including cocaine into Australia and New Zealand. The Pacific island chapters effectively became nodes in a criminal network stretching across Asia, Europe, and North America linking the syndicates and cartels with Pacific trafficking routes, and with the Australian and New Zealand drug markets.

Fiji, for example, is a highly valuable transshipment point; in 2014, the Australian Crime Commission suspected that the Fiji chapters of the Rebels were a key port of call for drug shipments from South America to Australia and other countries in the region.[49] The Fiji chapters of the Rebels had been established in 2012 by expatriates linked to the Rebels' New South Wales chapter—the same year the Rebels opened a chapter in Lebanon. With chapters in Suva and Nadi, the Fiji Rebels comprise both Australian and Fijian nationals and are the largest Pacific-based OMCG.[50] Since 2016, there has been further growth in Australian and New Zealand OMCGs, who have expanded their activities offshore and into the Pacific—most prominently to the Cook Islands and Fiji.[51] From 2016 to 2018, the number of OMCG members traveling to Pacific destinations increased by more than 50 percent.[52] In response to the increased number of gang members such as the New Zealand–based Head Hunters traveling to the Cook Islands, Cook Islands Immigration began preventing the entry of overseas gang members and criminals, including nearly forty individuals in 2019.[53] The Head Hunters are particularly active in the Cook Islands; a senior Head Hunters member (of Cook Islander descent) resides there and is well connected across both the gang and the local community.[54]

The threat that OMCGs pose to the Pacific is highlighted in Samoa's national security strategy, which identifies OMCGs with links to organized crime as a concern across several Pacific countries and an "emerging threat" in Samoa.[55] As previously noted, the strategy of opening local OMCG chapters in the Pacific islands is intended to facilitate the trafficking of cocaine—and other drugs such as methamphetamines—to the Australian and New Zealand markets. It also enables OMCGs to recruit local players into the global drug trade. This, in turn, leads to the development of local criminal networks working in partnership with international drug syndicates. These local actors play a key role as facilitators and foot soldiers. The recruitment of local actors has, in some instances, been linked to economic insecurity and threatened livelihoods in some island nations. Government ministers from the Solomon Islands, Palau, and Kiribati have alleged that fishermen, unable to work due to low fish stocks caused by overfishing, have been recruited into running guns and drugs.[56] As resource exploitation and climate change further threaten livelihoods, it is possible that the recruitment of local actors will increase out of economic necessity.

Another category of local actors are criminal deportees. The criminal deportee policies of Australia, New Zealand, and the United States support the return of individuals with criminal records to their country of citizenship and potentially contribute to the growth of crime, including transnational crime, in the Pacific. The lack of reintegration support for deportees in their home countries means that some vulnerable individuals turn (or return) to crime. Evidence suggests that some criminal deportees are involved in the domestic drug scene. However, there is a lack of data about the relationship between deportees and offshore syndicates. Anecdotal evidence suggests that there are cases of deportees with links to criminal gangs introducing those relationships, skills, and tactics into the Pacific.

Lastly, Mexican and South American cartels and Asian syndicates (primarily Chinese triads such as the 14K Triad) are the principal actors in the regional drug market.[57] Anthea McCarthy-Jones notes that the presence of Mexican cartels in Australia first came to light in 2010 when several Mexican nationals with ties to cartels were arrested by Australian Federal Police during counternarcotics operations.[58] This was, McCarthy-Jones states, the first time that direct links between the activities of Mexican drug cartels and the Australian market for illicit drugs had been identified.[59] Currently, cartels such as Sinaloa and Jalisco New Generation are the largest suppliers of cocaine—and methamphetamines—to Australia,[60] in partnership with OMCGs and other criminal actors.

In addition to direct involvement in the trafficking of cocaine, in some cases members of Asian organized crime groups are engaged in laundering the proceeds of the drug trade through casinos such as those in the North Pacific. For example, the 14K Triad, one of the largest Chinese organized crime groups, is active in Palau. Wan Kuok-koi, known as "Broken Tooth," a 14K Triad senior figure, is president of the Palau China Hung-Mun Cultural Association, which attempted to build a casino in Palau—both he and the association are sanctioned by the US Treasury.

Other actors include the 'Ndrangheta mafia group[61] as well as other Italian crime groups based in Australia. The 'Ndrangheta is responsible for trafficking 70 percent of the world's cocaine and is, according to the Australian Federal Police, "pulling the strings of Australian outlaw motorcycle gangs."[62] Anna Sergi notes that the 'Ndrangheta, which has operated in Australia for more than a century, is deeply ingrained in Australian society and political life as well as the criminal world, and that the drug trade is fundamental to 'Ndrangheta wealth and power in Australia.[63] Indeed, the Melbourne-based criminal syndicate behind the attempted trafficking of more than five hundred kilograms of cocaine on board the Cessna that crashed outside Port Moresby in 2020, as discussed above, allegedly had links to Italian organized crime.

Conclusion

The growing cocaine trade in Oceania is driven by the lucrative markets of Australia and New Zealand and facilitated by a complex web of criminal actors and networks that stretch across the Pacific Ocean and beyond. These actors operate along the licit and illicit maritime corridors of the Pacific Ocean and take advantage of the porous borders of the Pacific islands, which serve as transshipment hubs and, increasingly, markets. This chapter has offered an exploration of the cocaine trade in Oceania including an outline of the political economy of the market, a broad typology of the principal actors, their key characteristics, and the ways in which criminal organizations have colluded to adopted protectionist strategies. The chapter has found that the growth in cocaine trafficking by transnational criminal actors has contributed to the rise of local niche markets and hybrid networks. This review of the cocaine trade in Oceania recommends the development of a research agenda to comprehensively map transnational criminal organizations and actors in the region across multiple crime types, and to trace the intersections between the various crime types to develop a nuanced understanding of a complex and opaque web of activity.

Notes

1. The Pacific islands comprise twenty-two countries and territories: American Samoa, the Cook Islands, Fiji, French Polynesia, Guam, Kiribati, the Marshall Islands, the Federated States of Micronesia, Nauru, New Caledonia, Niue, the Northern Mariana Islands, Palau, Papua New Guinea, the Pitcairn Islands, Samoa, the Solomon Islands, Tokelau, Tonga, Tuvalu, Vanuatu, and Wallis and Futuna.

2. Danielle Watson, Jose Luis Sousa-Santos, and Loene M. Howes, "Transnational and Organised Crime in Pacific Island Countries and Territories: Police Capacity to Respond to the Emerging Security Threat," *Development Bulletin* 82 (February 2021): 151–55.

3. Watson, Sousa-Santos, and Howes, "Transnational and Organised Crime in Pacific Island Countries and Territories."

4. Pacific Islands Forum, "Boe Declaration on Regional Security," September 5, 2018, https://forumsec.org/publications/boe-declaration-regional-security.

5. Pacific Islands Forum, "The 2050 Strategy for the Blue Pacific Continent," July 18, 2022, https://forumsec.org/publications/report-2050-strategy-blue-pacific-continent.

6. Pacific Islands Forum, "Honiara Declaration on Law Enforcement Cooperation," 1992, https://forumsec.org/sites/default/files/2024-03/1992_HONIARA%20Declaration.pdf.

7. Jose Sousa-Santos, "Drug Trafficking in the Pacific Islands: The Impact of Transnational Crime," Lowy Institute for International Affairs, Sydney, February 16, 2022, https://www.lowyinstitute.org/publications/drug-trafficking-pacific-islands-impact-transnational-crime.

8. "Opening Remarks by Interpol President Kim Jong Yang, 48th Pacific Islands Chiefs of Police Conference," *Samoa News*, August 22, 2019, https://www.samoanews.com/opinion/opening-remarks-interpol-president-kim-jong-yang-48th-pacific-islands-chiefs-police.

9. Madonna L. Devaney, Gary Reid, Simon Baldwin, Nick Crofts, and Robert Power, "Illicit Drug Use and Responses in Six Pacific Island Countries," *Drug and Alcohol Review* 25 (July 2006): 387–90.

10. Pacific Islands Forum, "The Pacific Security Outlook Report 2022–2023," 30, https://forumsec.org/sites/default/files/2023-12/Pacific-Security-Outlook-Report-2022-2023.pdf.

11. Australian Criminal Intelligence Commission, National Wastewater Drug Monitoring Program, Report no. 10, June 30, 2020, https://www.acic.gov.au/publications/national-wastewater-drug-monitoring-program-reports/report-10-national-wastewater-drug-monitoring-program.

12. Ministry of Justice, "Strengthening New Zealand's Response to Organised Crime: An All-of-Government Response," August 2001, 12.

13. Pacific Transnational Crime Network, *Transnational Crime Assessment 2017–2018*, 3.

14. Australian Criminal Intelligence Commission, National Wastewater Drug Monitoring Program, Report no. 11, October 29, 2020, https://www.acic.gov.au/publications/national-wastewater-drug-monitoring-program-reports/report-11-national-wastewater-drug-monitoring-program.

15. Australian Criminal Intelligence Commission, National Wastewater Drug Monitoring Program, Report no. 11; Australian Criminal Intelligence Commission, National Wastewater Drug Monitoring Program, Report no. 9, March 10, 2020, https://www.acic.gov.au/publications/national-wastewater-drug-monitoring-program-reports/national-wastewater-drug-monitoring-program-report-09-2020; New Zealand Police, National Wastewater Testing Programme, Quarter 2, 2019, https://www.police.govt.nz/about-us/publication/national-wastewater-testing-programme-quarter-2-2019; New Zealand Ministry of Health, "Annual Update of Key Results 2019/20: New Zealand Health Survey," November 14, 2019, https://www.health.govt.nz/publication/annual-update-key-results-2019-20-new-zealand-health-survey; and Shane Neilson, Principal Advisor, Drugs, "Media

Statement: Cocaine," Australian Criminal Intelligence Commission, May 19, 2023, https://www.acic.gov.au/media-centre/media-releases-and-statements/media-statement-cocaine.

16. Marta Pascual Juanola, Cameron Houston, and Chris Vedelago, "'Dear Brothers of the Underworld': Cartel Plots to Stem Cocaine Supply and Raise Prices," *The Age* (Melbourne), April 28, 2023, https://www.theage.com.au/national/victoria/dear-brothers-of-the-underworld-cartel-plots-to-stem-cocaine-supply-and-raise-prices-20230427-p5d3to.html.

17. Australian Federal Police News Centre, "Authorities Seize 700 Kilograms Cocaine in NSW, Worth $280 Million," August 6, 2022, https://www.afp.gov.au/news-centre/media-release/authorities-seize-700-kilograms-cocaine-nsw-worth-280-million.

18. Rebecca Peppiatt, "Biggest Drug Bust in Australian History: Cocaine Worth $1 Billion Seized in WA Sting," *The Age* (Melbourne), March 4, 2023, https://www.theage.com.au/national/western-australia/biggest-drug-bust-in-australian-history-cocaine-worth-1-billion-seized-in-wa-police-sting-20230304-p5cpdi.html.

19. Christine Rovoi, "Fiji's War on Drugs: Police Find Narcotics More Lethal than 'Ice,'" Radio New Zealand, February 26, 2001, https://www.rnz.co.nz/international/pacific-news/437202/fiji-s-war-on-drugs-police-find-narcotics-more-lethal-than-ice.

20. Kate Lyons, "Bust in Budi Budi: The Day a Fisherman Hauled In $50m Worth of Cocaine," *Guardian*, June 24, 2019, https://www.theguardian.com/world/2019/jun/24/bust-in-budi-budi-the-day-a-fisherman-hauled-in-50m-worth-of-cocaine.

21. Miriam Zarriga, "Police Charge Four Men Involved in Methamphetamine Bust," *Post-Courier* (Port Moresby), November 22, 2022, https://www.postcourier.com.pg/police-charge-four-men-involved-in-methamphetamine-bust/.

22. Peter Michael, "Queensland Bikies and Nigerian Crime Syndicates Team Up to Run Drugs out of PNG," *Courier Mail* (Brisbane), May 2, 2014, https://www.couriermail.com.au/news/queensland/queensland-bikies-and-nigerian-crime-syndicates-team-up-to-run-drugs-out-of-png/news-story/37b96409ed770427baa46690d06adf7a.

23. Timoci Natuva, "Fiji's 'Blue Economy' and the Importance of Maritime Security," Royal Australian Navy, *Sea Power Soundings*, no. 23, (2021), https://seapower.navy.gov.au/media-room/publications/soundings-papers-fijis-blue-economy-and-importance-maritime-security.

24. Takashi Riku, Ryuichi Shibasaki, and Hironori Kato, "Pacific Islands: Small and Dispersed 'Sea-Locked' Islands," in *Global Logistics Network Modelling and Policy: Quantification and Analysis for International Freight*, ed. Ryuichi Shibasaki, Hironori Kato, and César Ducruet (Amsterdam: Elsevier, 2021), 276.

25. Riku, Shibasaki, and Kato, "Pacific Islands: Small and Dispersed 'Sea-Locked' Islands," 276.

26. United Nations Office on Drugs and Crime, *Global Report on Cocaine 2023: Local Dynamics, Global Challenges* (Vienna: United Nations, 2023), 163, https://www.unodc.org/documents/data-and-analysis/cocaine/Global_cocaine_report_2023.pdf.

27. Rebecca Trigger and Cason Ho, "Trio Allegedly Smuggled 560kg of Cocaine into WA on Boat After Drugs Dropped Off Coast," Australian Broadcasting Corporation News, August 18, 2023, https://www.abc.net.au/news/2023-08-18/men-allegedly-smuggled-560kg-of-cocaine-into-wa-on-boat/102745622.

28. "140kgs of Cocaine Worth $63m Seized at Ports of Auckland," Radio New Zealand, October 27, 2023, https://www.rnz.co.nz/news/national/501144/140kgs-of-cocaine-worth-63m-seized-at-ports-of-auckland; and "Enough Cocaine for 350,000 Hits Found in Shipping Container at Port of Tauranga," Radio New Zealand, November 14, 2023, https://www.rnz.co.nz/news/national/502403/enough-cocaine-for-350-000-hits-found-in-shipping-container-at-port-of-tauranga.

29. "Customs Seize 700 Kilograms of Cocaine in Shipping Container from South America," Radio New Zealand, March 16, 2022, https://www.rnz.co.nz/news/national/463410/customs-seize-700-kilograms-of-cocaine-in-shipping-container-from-south-america.

30. United Nations Office on Drugs and Crime, *Global Report on Cocaine 2023*, 163.

31. Sarah Keoghan, "Police Say Diver Left for Dead During Argentinian 50kg Cocaine Drop Gone Wrong," *Sydney Morning Herald*, May 10, 2022, https://www.smh.com.au/national/nsw/police-launch-investigation-after-body-of-diver-found-with-50kg-of-cocaine-in-newcastle-20220510-p5ajwq.html.

32. United Nations Office on Drugs and Crime, *Global Report on Cocaine 2023*, 163.

33. "Tongan Police Arrest Customs Official After Drug Bust," Radio New Zealand, April 27, 2019, https://www.rnz.co.nz/international/pacific-news/387885/tongan-police-arrest-customs-official-after-drug-bust.

34. Barbara Dreaver, "Tonga Steps Up War on Meth Trade with Multiple Arrests, over 30kg of Drug Seized," 1News, Television New Zealand, July 22, 2019, https://www.tvnz.co.nz/one-news/world/tonga-steps-up-war-meth-trade-multiple-arrests-over-30kg-drug-seized.

35. "Manning to Rid Constabulary of 'Criminals in Uniform,'" *Post-Courier* (Port Moresby), September 10, 2020, https://postcourier.com.pg/manning-to-rid-constabulary-of-criminals-in-uniform/.

36. "Fiji's High Tide," *Dateline*, Season 2020, Episode 3, Special Broadcasting Service (Australia), March 10, 2020, https://www.sbs.com.au/ondemand/video/1702315075823.

37. Sousa-Santos, "Drug Trafficking in the Pacific Islands."

38. "$370m Worth of Cocaine Found on Yacht Bound for Australia," *Australian Broadcasting Corporation News*, August 23, 2013, https://www.abc.net.au/news/2013-08-23/massive-drug-haul/4907052.

39. "French Polynesia Customs Nets 1.4 Tonnes of Cocaine," *Radio New Zealand*, January 26, 2017, https://www.rnz.co.nz/international/pacific-news/323147/french-polynesia-customs-nets-1-point-4-tonnes-of-cocaine.

40. "Huge Cocaine Shipment Seized in Tahiti," *Radio New Zealand*, September 26, 2022, https://www.rnz.co.nz/international/pacific-news/475485/huge-cocaine-shipment-seized-in-tahiti.

41. New Zealand Customs Service, "Australia's Biggest Cocaine Interception," February 6, 2017, https://www.customs.govt.nz/about-us/news/media-releases/australias-biggest-cocaine-interception/.

42. Charlotte Graham-McLay, "New Zealand Intercepts 3.2 Tonnes of Cocaine Worth $500m Floating in Pacific Ocean," *Guardian*, February 8, 2023, https://www.theguardian.com/world/2023/feb/08/new-zealand-intercepts-cocaine-3-tonne-500m-floating-pacific-ocean.

43. Bethanie Harriman, "PNG Fisherman Uncovers 60 Kilograms of Suspected Illicit Drugs Buried on Remote Beach," *Australian Broadcasting Corporation News*, May 11, 2018, https://www.abc.net.au/news/2018-05-11/png-fisherman-uncovers-60-kilograms-of-suspected-illicit-drugs/9752676.

44. Juanola, Houston, and Vedelago, "Dear Brothers of the Underworld."

45. Juanola, Houston, and Vedelago, "Dear Brothers of the Underworld."

46. Juanola, Houston, and Vedelago, "Dear Brothers of the Underworld."

47. Freddy Pawle, "Aussie Cocaine Gangs Declare War on Smugglers Who Want to Flood the Country with American 'Zombie Drug,'" *Daily Mail*, December 19, 2023, https://www.dailymail.co.uk/news/article-12883021/Aussie-cocaine-gangs-declare-war-smugglers-American-zombie-drug-fentanyl.html.

48. Alexandra Voce and Tom Sullivan, "Is There Fentanyl Contamination in the Australian Illicit Drug Market?," Australian Institute of Criminology, Statistical Bulletin no. 21, March 2020, https://www.aic.gov.au/sites/default/files/2020-05/sb21_is_there_fentanyl_contamination_in_the_australian_illicit_drug_market.pdf.

49. Stephen Drill and David Hurley, "Bikie Drug Lords' Deadly Network Expands Overseas," *Herald Sun* (Melbourne), November 16, 2014, https://www.heraldsun.com.au/news/law-order/bikie-drug-lords-deadly-network-expands-overseas/news-story/3e0b37a19d489fc85e6e3fb03c9133b2.

50. Pacific Transnational Crime Network, *Transnational Crime Assessment 2017–2018*, 16.

51. Pacific Transnational Crime Network, *Transnational Crime Assessment 2017–2018*, 16.

52. Pacific Transnational Crime Network, *Transnational Crime Assessment 2017–2018*, 16.

53. Katrina Tanirau, "Cook Islands Stops NZ Leader Because of Gang Connections," *New Zealand Herald* (Auckland), December 8, 2019, https://www.nzherald.co.nz/nz/cook-islands-stops-nz-leader-because-of-gang-connections/UB4B757KFHRFQDAA7D5S2PMEJE/.

54. Pacific Transnational Crime Network, *Transnational Crime Assessment 2017–2018*, 16.

55. Government of Samoa, "Samoa National Security Policy: Building a Secure and Resilient Nation," Ministry of the Prime Minister and Cabinet, Apia, 2018.

56. Karen McVeigh, "Drug Trafficking at Sea Is Devastating Island States, Ministers Say," *Guardian*, October 16, 2018, https://www.theguardian.com/environment/2018/oct/16/drug-trafficking-at-sea-is-devastating-island-states-ministers-say.

57. New Zealand Police, "Transnational Organised Crime in New Zealand: Our Strategy, 2020–2025," September 2020, https://www.police.govt.nz/sites/default/files/publications/transnational-organised-crime-in-new-zealand-our-strategy-2020-to-2025.pdf.

58. Anthea McCarthy-Jones, "Mexican Drug Cartels and Dark-Networks: An Emerging Threat to Australia's National Security," Working Paper, Strategic and Defence Studies Centre, Australian National University, April 2016, 2.

59. McCarthy-Jones, "Mexican Drug Cartels and Dark-Networks," 2.

60. Mahmood Fazal, Amos Roberts, and Dylan Welch, "Mexican and South American Cartels Penetrating Australian Border Security to Import Tonnes of Cocaine, Underworld Figure Tells Four Corners," Australian Broadcasting Corporation News, May 22, 2023, https://www.abc.net.au/news/2023-05-22/cartel-cocaine-import-australia-border-workers-/102370986.

61. Anna Sergi, "The Evolution of the Australian 'Ndrangheta: An Historical Perspective," *Australian and New Zealand Journal of Criminology* 48, no. 2 (June 2015): 155–74; and Australian Federal Police News Centre, "AFP to Target Italian Organised Crime and Money Laundering a Year On from Operation Ironside," June 7, 2022, https://www.afp.gov.au/news-centre/media-release/afp-target-italian-organised-crime-and-money-laundering-year-operation.

62. Australian Federal Police News Centre, "AFP to Target Italian Organised Crime and Money Laundering."

63. Anna Sergi, "A Flurry of Attention, Then Collective Forgetfulness: 100 Years of the 'Ndrangheta Calabrian Mafia in Australia," *The Conversation*, June 21, 2022, https://theconversation.com/a-flurry-of-attention-then-collective-forgetfulness-100-years-of-the-ndrangheta-calabrian-mafia-in-australia-184835.

Conclusion

Jonathan D. Rosen and Sebastián A. Cutrona

This volume has sought to provide valuable insights into the global cocaine supply chain. This diverse group of authors from around the world have analyzed the trends in criminal actors, markets, and routes, and the major challenges that exist. The authors come from an interdisciplinary background, which has provided a unique perspective to understanding this complicated phenomenon. In this concluding chapter, we propose some theoretical and methodological points to consider. We also highlight the main findings of the chapters.

The Perpetual Balloon Effect

One of the defining features of cocaine production and trafficking routes has been their changes over time. Various authors discuss how the balloon effect has occurred in the Andean region. In the 1980s, for example, Peru and Bolivia were the leading coca producers. By the year 2000, Colombia had become the leader in coca cultivation, cocaine production, and trafficking.[1] In 2011, Peru surpassed Colombia as the world's major coca-cultivating country. In 2015, however, Colombia regained its status as the premier coca-cultivating country.[2]

Susan Brewer-Osorio demonstrates that the balloon effect has been largely a result of interdiction efforts. In effect, it could be thought of as unintended consequences, or the collateral damage of the role of the military and police in the drug war. Drug traffickers must adapt and shift their routes to avoid seizure and interdiction. As Carolina Sampó and Valeska Troncoso reveal, efforts to shut down certain routes result in traffickers changing their supply chain, even if the new "counterintuitive" alternatives do not respond exclusively to the lowest cost–greatest profit dynamic. The balloon effect is the closest thing in the study of drug trafficking and organized crime to a theory, given that it has been proven over space and time. There are countless case studies that show how trafficking routes have changed. Thus, this is a problem that is not going to disappear.

Methodological Challenges to Studying the Cocaine Trade

Another big challenge scholars face studying cocaine trafficking is methodological in nature. Cocaine seizures are estimates. Some governments have been less than transparent in the publication of statistics and access to information. International organizations like the United Nations Office on Drugs and Crime (UNODC) have continued to produce annual reports about cocaine trafficking. Debates, however, exist among scholars and policymakers about methodologies and calculations. For instance, the US State Department and the UNODC produce different measurements about coca cultivation in the Andean region.[3]

Scholars also face a challenge in how to analyze the data. As access to information improves and technological techniques become more sophisticated over the years, these innovations can help scholars seeking to quantify the drug trade and some of its associated problems. Yet it is important to remember that any statistical model is only as good as its assumptions. If the data inputted are flawed, then the model is based on flawed data.[4]

Intricately related to the issue of data is the question of how policymakers can measure success. Should success be measured based on the number of hectares of coca sprayed with herbicides in the Andes? Should success be measured based on the number of seizures?[5] Should success be measured in terms of the number of kingpins imprisoned or killed? Are overcrowded prisons an indicator of success? Some scholars note that the decrease in supply will only increase the price of illicit drugs, making it a lucrative enterprise for drug traffickers.[6]

Cocaine Markets and Routes

This volume reveals that the cocaine markets have shifted over time. In 1999, David F. Musto published a book titled *The American Disease*.[7] The cocaine problem is no longer an "American phenomenon." Instead, there has been a globalization of consumption. Alberto Aziani and Jose Sousa-Santos demonstrate that European countries and Oceania have become consolidated markets. Similarly, Michael Jerome Wolff shows the increasing domestic use of cocaine in other American countries like Brazil. The global demand for this product has fueled a litany of actors working in the cultivation, production, and trafficking of cocaine around the globe.[8]

Furthermore, the chapters in this volume shed light on the shifting routes of cocaine. Ninety percent of the cocaine arriving in the United States still comes from Colombia. However, the routes have altered over the years. Ivelaw Griffith shows that in the 1980s, for instance, the Caribbean and Miami were major hubs for cocaine trafficking. Large numbers of traffickers from John Roberts to Griselda Blanco moved cocaine in South Florida.[9] But the launching of the South Florida Task Force by the Ronald Reagan administration shifted these cocaine routes. The cocaine supply chain has continued to shift over time, in large part due to the various law enforcement and military campaigns of governments.

Criminal Actors and the "Cartel" Phenomenon

The chapters in this book reveal the complex nature of criminal actors involved in the cocaine supply chain. This volume has shown that there is not one megacartel dominating the entire global cocaine trade. Even just defining the criminal actors in the cocaine trade presents a challenge. Steven Dudley, for instance, has noted that the word "cartel" is used endlessly by US lawmakers.[10] However, not all criminal organizations are drug cartels. As Michael Paarlberg notes in his chapter in this volume, MS-13 meets the classic definition of a street gang and is not a major player in the international cocaine trade. Yet politicians like Donald Trump refer to MS-13 as a ruthless cartel that poses one of the top security threats to the United States. But in reality MS-13 is only one of tens of thousands of gangs operating in the US.[11]

The chapters in this book attempt to shed light on the different criminal actors involved in the cocaine trade and how they work together. Daniel Pontón C. shows, for instance, that Ecuador is considered a strategic site of cocaine trafficking due to alliances of convenience between local gangs such as Los Choneros and more powerful transnational organized crime groups operating in Mexico. Thus, it is a misconception that there is a megacartel dominating the international cocaine trade. Alberto Aziani shows in his chapter that the 'Ndrangheta groups and their control over the cocaine supply chain is not absolute. He maintains that these criminal organizations are among numerous other actors competing in the cocaine market, as indicated by the low price of cocaine. Geography and competition make it nearly impossible for one actor to control the entire cocaine supply chain. The numerous groups competing for domination and territory make controlling the global cocaine trade an impossible task. Consequently, transnational organized crime groups have a transactional relationship with numerous actors in the cocaine supply chain, and these alliances can shift over time.

Scholars and other observers must continually shed light on the actors involved in the cocaine trade. Some criminal organizations have disappeared, while others have emerged out of the fragmentation of larger criminal groups (e.g., the collapse of the Beltrán Levya organization in Mexico).[12] These criminal actors continue to evolve. Groups that are more sophisticated are better at subcontracting other actors (e.g., gangs) as enforcers and microtraffickers. Some criminal groups (e.g., the Sinaloa cartel) have been able to penetrate the state apparatus and increase their power.[13]

Yet this volume shows that the territorial control of criminal organizations is something that needs to be analyzed in further detail. The chapters reveal that in most cases—perhaps with the exception of the PCC in Brazil—criminal actors are not relocating beyond their borders. There is debate, for instance, about the presence of Latin American drug traffickers in the United States. Some reports have indicated that Mexican cartels have a presence in each major city around the country.[14] A more nuanced view, however, requires examining the notion of "presence." As Marten Brienen shows, criminal organizations in the United States tend to be relatively fragmented, and groups like the Sinaloa cartel work with gangs and other criminal actors to move and distribute drugs in strategic locations like Chicago and New York City.[15]

Finally, more research is needed on the evolving nature of criminal organizations. Some criminal organizations have continued to diversify their illicit endeavors, partaking in not only drug trafficking but extortion, oil theft, and kidnapping. As Nathan P. Jones and Gary Hale show in their chapter, some Mexican cartels have diversified their portfolios and traffic not just cocaine, but synthetic drugs like fentanyl. It is highly likely that more criminal organizations will compete for the lucrative drug trade, which could result in more violence, as actors fight for control of territory.

Borders, Cocaine, and the Supply Chain

Borders will continue to be an important security issue. Alberto Aziani's chapter on Europe sheds light on the interconnectedness between the European Union countries. Globalization and interconnectedness, however, also benefit actors trafficking illicit products like cocaine. Molly Charles shows that even highly militarized borders, such as those between India and Pakistan, are porous, especially if corrupt law enforcement officials can facilitate trafficking. In this context, countries will continue to face pressure to strengthen their borders. For instance, there have been intensive debates in the United States for decades about the country's southern border. In 2023, some members of the Republican Party spoke in favor of sending troops into Mexico to stop the drug trade.[16] This extreme rhetoric ignores the importance of Mexico as a vital ally of the United States, as well as the long and complicated history between the two countries.

The focus on border security has also led to increased rhetoric and often discrimination against immigrant populations. Caroline Agboola claims that the heavy presence of Nigerian cocaine traffickers in countries like Brazil sometimes obscures the role of law-abiding Nigerians in Brazil who have legitimate livelihoods. Similarly, we have seen this in the extreme rhetoric in the United States by individuals like Donald Trump as well as in Europe by right-wing politicians. Such discourse has been utilized by populist leaders who vow to increase border security through misguided strategies such as building a wall between Mexico and the United States.[17]

Institutional Weakness, Corruption, and the Cocaine Trade

Another major emphasis of this book is the role of corruption. It would not be possible for drug traffickers to participate in the cocaine trade without corruption. Unlike terrorist groups, drug-trafficking organizations need the state to survive.[18] They do not want to destroy the state but rather seek to penetrate the state apparatus. Scholars have written extensively on the state–organized crime relationship. For example, Juan Orlando Hernández, the former president of Honduras, was arrested and extradited to the United States for cocaine trafficking in April 2022. His brother, Tony Hernández, a former congressman, is serving a life sentence in the United States for cocaine trafficking.[19]

Héctor Alarcón Barrera and Juan Albarracín show that state actors are crucial in shaping forms of regulation of illicit markets. The varying relationship between state and criminal actors is seen as a key variable in explaining forms of criminal governance in places like Colombia. Not surprisingly, scholars like Roberto Zepeda Martínez argue that combating corruption requires reforming multiple institutions.[20] In other words, simply reorganizing the police will not solve the problem unless systematic structural reforms occur in the prison and judiciary systems. The failure of some countries to effectively reform institutions at different levels of government has enabled organized crime to flourish. In the case of Mexico, Genaro García Luna, the secretary of public security during the Felipe Calderón government, was convicted in court in February 2023 for facilitating the operations of the Sinaloa cartel and taking bribes from them.[21]

Combating cocaine trafficking—and organized crime in general—requires strengthening the state apparatus. While many politicians have delivered a litany of discourses about being tough on crime, countless cases and examples reveal that fragile states serve as fertile grounds for organized crime. Strengthening the state cannot be a "smoke and mirrors" experience, but rather it requires deep-seated structural reforms. These reforms, which are often unpopular, will not occur overnight and require political will.[22]

Furthermore, combating cocaine production and trafficking requires cooperation between producing, transit, and consumption countries. This is often an arduous task, but it is essential when seeking to implement drug policies. Scholars argue that the "blame game" is often implemented by politicians (e.g., blaming countries in Latin America for trafficking drugs to the United States).[23] Ultimately, cooperation requires working together and implementing well-designed security strategies.

Conclusion

This volume has sought to contribute to the field by shedding light on the cocaine trade and the numerous criminal actors involved in this illicit activity. The authors writing herein show that the criminal landscape is diverse, as there is not one megacartel dominating the cocaine trade, for instance, from Colombia to Italy. The kingpin strategy, militarization, and competition have led to the fragmentation of organized crime.[24]

This work also shows that states play an integral role in the drug trade. It is not possible, for instance, to understand the drug trade without examining the role of state fragility. Corrupt states plagued by impunity and the lack of rule of law serve as fertile ground for drug trafficking and organized crime. Combating the cocaine trade requires not empty discourse but rather political will among states and significant efforts to make structural reforms in fragile states. The country case studies herein have shown numerous examples of high-level officials with intricate connections to the criminal actors involved in the cocaine trade.

Notes

1. Bruce Michael Bagley, "Drug Trafficking and Organized Crime in the Americas: Major Trends in the Twenty-First Century," Woodrow Wilson International Center for Scholars, Latin American Program, August 2012, https://www.wilsoncenter.org/sites/default/files/media/documents/publication/BB%20Final.pdf.

2. David Gagne, "Colombia Overtakes Peru as World's Top Coca Cultivator: UN," InSight Crime, July 17, 2015, https://insightcrime.org/news/analysis/is-peru-no-longer-world-top-cocaine-producer/.

3. For more, see Jonathan D. Rosen, *The Losing War: Plan Colombia and Beyond* (Albany: State University of New York Press, 2014); and Daniel Mejía and Carlos Esteban Posada, "Cocaine Production and Trafficking: What Do We Know?," World Bank Policy Research Working Paper no. 4618, May 1, 2008, https://papers.ssrn.com/sol3/papers.cfm?abstract_id=1149121.

4. For more, see Mejía and Posada, "Cocaine Production and Trafficking"; Dermot O'Connor, "The Political Economy of Colombia's Cocaine Industry," *Papel Político* 14, no. 1 (2009): 81–106; Peter H. Reuter and Victoria A. Greenfield, "Measuring Global Drug Markets: How Good Are the Numbers and Why Should We Care About Them?," *World Economics* 2, no. 4 (October–December 2001): 159–73; and Peter H. Reuter and Mark A. R. Kleiman, "Risks and Prices: An Economic Analysis of Drug Enforcement," *Crime and Justice* 7 (1986): 289–340.

5. Bruce Michael Bagley and Jonathan D. Rosen, eds., *Drug Trafficking, Organized Crime, and Violence in the Americas Today* (Gainesville: University Press of Florida, 2015).

6. For more, see Ted Galen Carpenter, *Bad Neighbor Policy: Washington's Futile War on Drugs in Latin America* (New York: St. Martin's Press, 2003); and Ted Galen Carpenter, *The Fire Next Door: Mexico's Drug Violence and the Danger to America* (Washington, DC: Cato Institute, 2012).

7. David F. Musto, *The American Disease: Origins of Narcotic Control* (New York: Oxford University Press, 1999).

8. Bagley, "Drug Trafficking and Organized Crime"; and Bagley and Rosen, *Drug Trafficking, Organized Crime, and Violence*.

9. Jonathan D. Rosen, *The U.S. War on Drugs at Home and Abroad* (Cham, Switzerland: Palgrave Macmillan, 2021).

10. Steven Dudley, "After US Hearing on Fentanyl, Is It Time to Retire the Word 'Cartel'?," InSight Crime, February 22, 2023, https://insightcrime.org/news/after-us-hearing-fentanyl-time-retire-word-cartel/.

11. For more, see Steven Dudley, *MS-13: The Making of America's Most Notorious Gang* (New York: Hanover Square Press, 2020); and Thomas W. Ward, *Gangsters Without Borders: An Ethnography of a Salvadoran Street Gang* (New York: Oxford University Press, 2013).

12. Bagley, "Drug Trafficking and Organized Crime"; and Laura H. Atuesta and Yocelyn Samantha Pérez-Dávila, "Fragmentation and Cooperation: The Evolution of Organized Crime in Mexico," *Trends in Organized Crime* 21, no. 3 (September 2018): 235–61.

13. For more, see Stephen D. Morris, "Drug Trafficking, Corruption, and Violence in Mexico: Mapping the Linkages," *Trends in Organized Crime* 16, no. 2 (June 2013): 195–220; Malcolm Beith, "A Broken Mexico: Allegations of Collusion Between the Sinaloa Cartel and Mexican Political Parties," *Small Wars and Insurgencies* 22, no. 5 (2011): 787–806; and John Bailey and Matthew M. Taylor, "Evade, Corrupt, or Confront? Organized Crime and the State in Brazil and Mexico," *Journal of Politics in Latin America* 1, no. 2 (2009): 3–29.

14. National Public Radio, "Mexican Drug Cartels in the U.S.," 2009, https://legacy.npr.org/news/graphics/2009/mar/mexico_cartel/index.html.

15. Nathan P. Jones, "Why the US Doesn't Have Mexico-Style Drug Cartels ... Yet," InSight Crime, August 16, 2011, https://insightcrime.org/news/analysis/why-the-us-doesnt-have-mexico-style-drug-cartels-yet/; and Fred Rosen, "*Capos* and Capitalists: An Interview with Mexican Political Analyst Sergio Aguayo About the Rise of the Drug Trade in Mexico," *NACLA Report on the Americas* 48, no. 2 (2016): 173–76.

16. Jonathan Swan, Maggie Haberman, Charlie Savage, and Emiliano Rodríguez Mega, "Trump Wanted to Fire Missiles at Mexico. Now the G.O.P. Wants to Send Troops," *New York Times*, October 3, 2023, https://www.nytimes.com/2023/10/03/us/politics/trump-mexico-cartels-republican.html.

17. For more, see Sarah Pierce and Andrew Selee, "Immigration Under Trump: A Review of Policy Shifts in the Year Since the Election," Policy Brief, Migration Policy Institute, December 2017, https://www.migrationpolicy.org/research/immigration-under-trump-review-policy-shifts; and Guadalupe Correa-Cabrera, "Migration, Border Security, and New Forms of Resistance in the Age of Trump," *Sicherheit und Frieden* 38, no. 2 (2020): 100–105.

18. Raúl Benítez Manaut, "Mexico-Colombia: U.S. Assistance and the Fight Against Organized Crime," in *One Goal, Two Struggles: Confronting Crime and Violence in Mexico and Colombia*, ed. Cynthia J. Arnson and Eric L. Olson with Christine Zaino (Washington, DC: Woodrow Wilson International Center for Scholars, 2014), 53; and Carolina Sampó,

"Porque no todo es terrorismo: Notas sobre la actividad del crimen organizado en España," *Relaciones Internacionales* 25, no. 51 (2016): 129–42.

19. Jeff Ernst and Elisabeth Malkin, "Honduran President's Brother, Arrested in Miami, Is Charged with Drug Trafficking," *New York Times*, November 26, 2018, https://www.nytimes.com/2018/11/26/world/americas/honduras-brother-drug-charges.html; and US Department of Justice, "Juan Orlando Hernandez, Former President of Honduras, Extradited to the United States on Drug-Trafficking and Firearms Charges," Press Release, US Attorney's Office, Southern District of New York, April 21, 2022, https://www.justice.gov/usao-sdny/pr/juan-orlando-hernandez-former-president-honduras-extradited-united-states-drug.

20. Jonathan D. Rosen and Roberto Zepeda Martínez, "La guerra contra las drogas y la cooperación internacional: El caso de Colombia," *Revista CS*, no. 18 (January–April 2016): 63–84.

21. US Department of Justice, "Ex-Mexican Secretary of Public Security Genaro Garcia Luna Convicted of Engaging in a Continuing Criminal Enterprise and Taking Millions in Cash Bribes from the Sinaloa Cartel," Press Release, US Attorney's Office, Eastern District of New York, February 21, 2023, https://www.justice.gov/usao-edny/pr/ex-mexican-secretary-public-security-genaro-garcia-luna-convicted-engaging-continuing.

22. For more, see Susan Rose-Ackerman and Bonnie J. Palifka, *Corruption and Government: Causes, Consequences, and Reform*, 2nd ed. (New York: Cambridge University Press, 2016); and Peter Eigen, "Measuring and Combating Corruption," *Journal of Policy Reform* 5, no. 4 (2002): 187–201.

23. See: Ethan A. Nadelmann, "Criminologists and Punitive Drug Prohibition: To Serve or to Challenge?," *Criminology and Public Policy* 3, no. 3 (July 2004): 441–50; Ethan A. Nadelmann, "Global Prohibition Regimes: The Evolution of Norms in International Society," *International Organization* 44, no. 4 (Autumn 1990): 479–526; and Peter Andreas and Ethan Nadelmann, *Policing the Globe: Criminalization and Crime Control in International Relations* (New York: Oxford University Press, 2008).

24. Bagley and Rosen, *Drug Trafficking, Organized Crime, and Violence*.

Selected Bibliography

Andreas, Peter. *Smuggler Nation: How Illicit Trade Made America*. New York: Oxford University Press, 2013.

Andreas, Peter, and Ethan Nadelmann. *Policing the Globe: Criminalization and Crime Control in International Relations*. New York: Oxford University Press, 2008.

Arias, Enrique Desmond. *Drugs and Democracy in Rio de Janeiro: Trafficking, Social Networks, and Public Security*. Chapel Hill: University of North Carolina Press, 2006.

Atuesta, Laura H., and Yocelyn Samantha Pérez-Dávila. "Fragmentation and Cooperation: The Evolution of Organized Crime in Mexico." *Trends in Organized Crime* 21, no. 3 (September 2018): 235–61.

Aziani, Alberto. *Illicit Financial Flows: An Innovative Approach to Estimation*. Cham, Switzerland: Springer, 2018.

Aziani, Alberto. "Violent Disequilibrium: The Influence of Instability in the Economic Value of Cocaine Markets on Homicides." *Crime, Law and Social Change* 74, no. 4 (October 2020): 245–72.

Bagley, Bruce Michael. "The Evolution of Drug Trafficking and Organized Crime in Latin America." *Sociologia, problemas y práticas*, no. 71 (2013): 99–123.

Bagley, Bruce Michael, and Jonathan D. Rosen, eds. *Drug Trafficking, Organized Crime, and Violence in the Americas Today*. Gainesville: University Press of Florida, 2015.

Baika, Laura, and Paolo Campana. "Centrality, Mobility, and Specialization: A Study of Drug Markets in a Non-Metropolitan Area in the United Kingdom." *Journal of Drug Issues* 50, no. 2 (2020): 107–26.

Barnes, Nicholas. "Criminal Politics: An Integrated Approach to the Study of Organized Crime, Politics, and Violence." *Perspectives on Politics* 15, no. 4 (December 2017): 967–87.

Bewley-Taylor, David R. *International Drug Control: Consensus Fractured*. Cambridge: Cambridge University Press, 2012.

Brewer-Osorio, Susan. "Turning Over a New Leaf: A Subnational Analysis of 'Coca Yes, Cocaine No' in Bolivia." *Journal of Latin American Studies* 53, no. 3 (August 2021): 573–600.

Britto, Lina. *Marijuana Boom: The Rise and Fall of Colombia's First Drug Paradise*. Oakland: University of California Press, 2020.

Broséus, Julian, Natacha Gentile, and Pierre Esseiva. "The Cutting of Cocaine and Heroin: A Critical Review." *Forensic Science International* 262 (May 2016): 73–83.

Calandra, Francesca. "Between Local and Global: The 'Ndrangheta's Drug Trafficking Route." *International Annals of Criminology* 55, no. 1 (2017): 78–98.

Calderoni, Francesco. "The Structure of Drug Trafficking Mafias: The 'Ndrangheta and Cocaine." *Crime, Law, and Social Change* 58, no. 3 (December 2012): 321–49.

Carpenter, Ted Galen. *Bad Neighbor Policy: Washington's Futile War on Drugs in Latin America*. New York: St. Martin's Press, 2003.

Carpenter, Ted Galen. *The Fire Next Door: Mexico's Drug Violence and the Danger to America*. Washington, DC: Cato Institute, 2012.

Castells, Manuel. *The Information Age: Economy, Society and Culture*. Vol. 3, *End of Millennium*. Hoboken, NJ: Blackwell, 1998.

Caulkins, Jonathan P., Emma Disley, Marina Tzvetkova, Mafalda Pardal, Hemali Shah, and Xiaoke Zhang. "Modeling the Structure and Operation of Drug Supply Chains: The Case of Cocaine and Heroin in Italy and Slovenia." *International Journal of Drug Policy* 31 (May 2016): 64–73.

Correa-Cabrera, Guadalupe. "Migration, Border Security, and New Forms of Resistance in the Age of Trump." *Sicherheit und Frieden* 38, no. 2 (2020): 100–105.

Costa Storti, Cláudia, and Paul De Grauwe. "Globalization and the Price Decline of Illicit Drugs." *International Journal of Drug Policy* 20, no. 1 (January 2009): 48–61.

Cruz, José Miguel, and Angélica Durán-Martínez. "Hiding Violence to Deal with the State: Criminal Pacts in El Salvador and Medellín." *Journal of Peace Research* 53, no. 2 (March 2016): 197–210.

Customs and Tariff Bureau, Government of Japan. *Trends in Smuggling in Japan ("White Powder and Black Firearms" Report)*. 2022 ed. Tokyo: Ministry of Finance, 2022.

Daly, Sarah Zukerman. *Organized Violence After Civil War: The Geography of Recruitment in Latin America*. Cambridge: Cambridge University Press, 2016.

Dávila, Anayansi, Nicholas Magliocca, Kendra McSweeney, and Ximena Rueda. "Spatialising Illicit Commodity Chains: Comparing Coffee and Cocaine." *Area* 53, no. 3 (September 2021): 501–10.

Dudley, Steven. *MS-13: The Making of America's Most Notorious Gang*. New York: Hanover Square Press, 2020.

Duncan, Gustavo. *Beyond "Plata o Plomo": Drugs and State Reconfiguration in Colombia*. Cambridge: Cambridge University Press, 2022.

Eski, Yarin. *Policing, Port Security and Crime Control: An Ethnography of the Port Securityscape*. Abingdon, Oxon., England: Routledge, 2016.

European Monitoring Centre for Drugs and Drug Addiction. *European Drug Report 2022: Trends and Developments*. Luxembourg: Publications Office of the European Union, 2022.

Farah, Douglas, and Kathryn Babineau. "The Evolution of MS 13 in El Salvador and Honduras." *PRISM* 7, no. 1 (2017): 58–73.

Felbab-Brown, Vanda. "The Political Economy of Illegal Domains in India and China." *International Lawyer* 43, no. 4 (2009): 1411–28.

Felbab-Brown, Vanda. *Shooting Up: Counterinsurgency and the War on Drugs*. Washington, DC: Brookings Institution Press, 2010.

Ferreira, Marcos Alan. "Brazilian Criminal Organizations as Transnational Violent Non-State Actors: A Case Study of the Primeiro Comando da Capital (PCC)." *Trends in Organized Crime* 22, no. 61 (June 2019): 148–65.

Frank, Dana. *The Long Honduran Night: Resistance, Terror, and the United States in the Aftermath of the Coup*. Chicago: Haymarket Books, 2018.

Gibbon, Peter and Stefano Ponte, *Trading Down: Africa, Value Chains, and the Global Economy*. Philadelphia: Temple University Press, 2005.

Giommoni, Luca, Giulia Berlusconi, and Alberto Aziani. "Interdicting International Drug Trafficking: A Network Approach for Coordinated and Targeted Interventions." *European Journal on Criminal Policy and Research* 28, no. 4 (2022): 545–72.

Gootenberg, Paul. *Andean Cocaine: The Making of a Global Drug*. Chapel Hill: University of North Carolina Press, 2008.

Gootenberg, Paul. "Cocaine's Long March North, 1900–2010." *Latin American Politics and Society* 54, no. 1 (Spring 2012): 159–80.

Gootenberg, Paul. "Peruvian Cocaine and the Boomerang of History." *NACLA Report on the Americas* 47, no. 2 (Summer 2014): 48–49.

Gootenberg, Paul. "The 'Pre-Colombian' Era of Drug Trafficking in the Americas: Cocaine, 1945–1965." *The Americas* 64, no. 2 (October 2007): 133–76.

Griffith, Ivelaw Lloyd. *Drugs and Security in the Caribbean: Sovereignty Under Siege*. University Park: Pennsylvania State University Press, 1997.

Gugliotta, Guy, and Jeff Leen. *Kings of Cocaine*. New York: HarperCollins, 1990.

Kleiman, Mark A. R., Jonathan P. Caulkins, and Angela Hawken. *Drugs and Drug Policy: What Everyone Needs to Know*. New York: Oxford University Press, 2011.

Lessing, Benjamin, and Graham Denyer Willis. "Legitimacy in Criminal Governance: Managing a Drug Empire from Behind Bars." *American Political Science Review* 113, no. 2 (May 2019): 584–606.

Lovato, Roberto. *Unforgetting: A Memoir of Family, Migration, Gangs, and Revolution in the Americas*. New York: HarperCollins, 2020.

May, Channing. *Transnational Crime and the Developing World*. Washington, DC: Global Financial Integrity, 2017.

Mejía, Daniel, and Carlos Esteban Posada. "Cocaine Production and Trafficking: What Do We Know?" World Bank Policy Research Working Paper no. 4618, May 1, 2008. https://papers.ssrn.com/sol3/papers.cfm?abstract_id=1149121.

Mieczkowski, Thomas M. "The Prevalence of Drug Use in the United States." *Crime and Justice* 20 (1996): 349–414.

Mintz, Sidney W. *Sweetness and Power: The Place of Sugar in Modern History*. Harmondsworth, England: Penguin, 1986.

Mora, Frank O. "Victims of the Balloon Effect: Drug Trafficking and U.S. Policy in Brazil and the Southern Cone of Latin America." *Journal of Social, Political, and Economic Studies* 21, no. 2 (Summer 1996): 115–40.

Musto, David F. *The American Disease: Origins of Narcotics Control*. New York: Oxford University Press, 1999.

Nadelmann, Ethan A. "Criminologists and Punitive Drug Prohibition: To Serve or to Challenge?" *Criminology and Public Policy* 3, no. 3 (July 2004): 441–50.

Nadelmann, Ethan A. "Global Prohibition Regimes: The Evolution of Norms in International Society." *International Organization* 44, no. 4 (Autumn 1990): 479–526.

Oboh, Jude Roys. *Cocaine Hoppers: Nigerian International Cocaine Trafficking*. Lanham, MD: Lexington Books, 2021.

O'Connor, Dermot. "The Political Economy of Colombia's Cocaine Industry." *Papel Político* 14, no. 1 (2009): 81–106.

Ogunniyi, Olayemi Jacob, and James Onochie Akpu. "The Challenge of Drug Trafficking to Democratic Governance and Human Security in West Africa: A Historical Reflection." *Africa Development/Afrique et Développement* 44, no. 4 (2019): 29–50.

Perl, Raphael F. "United States Andean Drug Policy: Background and Issues for Decisionmakers." *Journal of Interamerican Studies and World Affairs* 34, no. 3 (Autumn 1992): 13–35.

Reuter, Peter. *Disorganized Crime: The Economics of the Visible Hand.* Cambridge, MA: MIT Press, 1983.

Reuter, Peter. "Systemic Violence in Drug Markets," *Crime, Law and Social Change* 52, no. 3 (September 2009): 275–84.

Reuter, Peter, and John Haaga. *The Organization of High-Level Drug Markets: An Exploratory Study.* Santa Monica, CA: RAND Corporation, 1989.

Rose-Ackerman, Susan, and Bonnie J. Palifka. *Corruption and Government: Causes, Consequences, and Reform.* 2nd ed. New York: Cambridge University Press, 2016.

Rosen, Jonathan D. *The Losing War: Plan Colombia and Beyond.* Albany: State University of New York Press, 2014.

Rosen, Jonathan D. *The U.S. War on Drugs at Home and Abroad.* Cham, Switzerland: Palgrave Macmillan, 2021.

Ruiz, Jason. *Narcomedia: Latinidad, Popular Culture, and America's War on Drugs.* Austin: University of Texas Press, 2023.

Saab, Bilal Y., and Alexandra W. Taylor. "Criminality and Armed Groups: A Comparative Study of FARC and Paramilitary Groups in Colombia." *Studies in Conflict and Terrorism* 32, no. 6 (2009): 455–75.

Sampó, Carolina. "El tráfico de cocaína entre América Latina y África Occidental." *URVIO: Revista Latinoamericana de Estudios de Seguridad* 24 (June 2019): 187–203.

Sampó, Carolina. "Porque no todo es terrorismo: Notas sobre la actividad del crimen organizado en España." *Relaciones Internacionales* 25, no. 51 (2016): 129–42.

Sergi, Anna. "The Evolution of the Australian 'Ndrangheta: An Historical Perspective." *Australian and New Zealand Journal of Criminology* 48, no. 2 (June 2015): 155–74.

Sergi, Anna. "Playing Pac-Man in Portville: Policing the Dilution and Fragmentation of Drug Importations Through Major Seaports." *European Journal of Criminology* 19, no. 4 (July 2022): 674–91.

Skarbek, David. "Governance and Prison Gangs." *American Political Science Review* 105, no. 4 (November 2011): 702–16.

Stahlberg, Stephanie G. "From Prison Gangs to Transnational Mafia: The Expansion of Organized Crime in Brazil." *Trends in Organized Crime* 25, no. 2 (April 2022): 443–65.

Tate, Winifred. *Drugs, Thugs, and Diplomats: U.S. Policymaking in Colombia.* Stanford, CA: Stanford University Press, 2015.

Thoumi, Francisco E. "Illegal Drugs in Colombia: From Illegal Economic Boom to Social Crisis." *Annals of the American Academy of Political and Social Science* 582, no. 1 (July 2002): 102–16.

United Nations Office on Drugs and Crime. *Global Report on Cocaine 2023.* Vienna: United Nations, 2023.

United Nations Office on Drugs and Crime. *World Drug Report 2021.* Vienna: United Nations, 2021.

Valero, José Luis Gil. "The Western Balkan Organised Crime at European Union: The Albanian Mafia—Does It Pose a Real Threat?" *European Law Enforcement Research Bulletin* 22 (Summer 2022): 79–99.

Varese, Federico. "How Mafias Migrate: Transplantation, Functional Diversification, and Separation." *Crime and Justice* 49, no. 3 (June 2020): 289–337.

Varese, Federico. *Mafias on the Move: How Organized Crime Conquers New Territories.* Princeton, NJ: Princeton University Press, 2011.

Wallerstein, Immanuel. *The Modern World-System I: Capitalist Agriculture and the Origins of the European World-Economy in the Sixteenth Century.* New York: Academic Press, 1974.

Ward, Thomas W. *Gangsters Without Borders: An Ethnography of a Salvadoran Street Gang.* New York: Oxford University Press, 2013.

Williams, Phil. "Nigerian Criminal Organizations." In *The Oxford Handbook of Organized Crime*, edited by Letizia Paoli, 254–69. New York: Oxford University Press, 2014.

Wolff, Michael Jerome. "Building Criminal Authority: A Comparative Analysis of Drug Gangs in Rio de Janeiro and Recife." *Latin American Politics and Society* 57, no. 2 (2015): 21–40.

Zaitch, Damián. "From Cali to Rotterdam: Perceptions of Colombian Cocaine Traffickers on the Dutch Port." *Crime, Law and Social Change* 38, no. 3 (2002): 239–66.

Zaitch, Damián. *Trafficking Cocaine: Colombian Drug Entrepreneurs in the Netherlands.* The Hague: Kluwer Law International, 2002.

Zavala, Oswaldo. *Drug Cartels Do Not Exist: Narcotrafficking in US and Mexican Culture.* Translated by William Savinar. Nashville: Vanderbilt University Press, 2022.

Contributors

Editors

Sebastián A. Cutrona is a senior lecturer in criminology and program lead for the MRes in Transnational Crime at Liverpool Hope University, United Kingdom. He earned his PhD in international studies from the University of Miami. His work has been published in *Latin American Politics and Society*, *Trends in Organized Crime*, *Law and Social Change*, among others. His most recent book is *Drug Policy Revolutions: Trajectories in Argentina, Portugal, and Uruguay*, which was published by Bristol University Press in 2025. Dr. Cutrona has taught drug trafficking, organized crime, and Latin American politics at O. P. Jindal Global University (India), Universidad de San Andrés (Argentina), and the University of Miami (United States). His research interests mainly consist in organized crime, drugs, and Latin American politics.

Jonathan D. Rosen is an assistant professor in the Professional Security Studies Department at New Jersey City University. Dr. Rosen earned his master's in political science from Columbia University and received his PhD in international studies from the University of Miami in 2012. His research focuses on drug trafficking, organized crime, and security. He has published more than twenty books with Routledge, Lexington Books, Palgrave Macmillan, the University Press of Florida, and the State University Press of New York. He has published journal articles in *Trends in Organized Crime*, *The Journal of Criminal Justice*, *Deviant Behavior*, *International Journal of Offender Therapy and Comparative Criminology*, *Contexto Internacional*, and *Revista CS*, among other journals. He has participated in grant-funded research studies in El Salvador, Guatemala, Honduras, Nicaragua, Colombia, and Mexico. In 2017, for example, Jonathan and his colleagues at Florida International University interviewed and surveyed nearly 1,200 active and former gang members in El Salvador.

Contributors

Susan Brewer-Osorio is an assistant professor of Latin American studies and political science at the University of Arizona. Her research lies at the intersection of security studies, public policy, violence, and peacebuilding with a regional focus on Andean South America. Susan completed her PhD at the University of Virginia in 2014 and was a 2021 US Fulbright Fellow to Colombia and a 2023 Fellow of the Udall Center for Studies in Public Policy at the University of Arizona.

Carolina Sampó is a professor, researcher, and academic coordinator in the Department of Criminology and Security, Universidad Camilo José Cela, Spain. She earned her PhD in social sciences from the University of Buenos Aires and her master's degree in international studies from the Universidad Torcuato Di Tella, Argentina. Dr. Sampó was a postdoctoral fellow at the Latin American and Caribbean Studies Center at the University of Maryland. Her research focuses on organized crime, violence, criminal organizations, and gender in Latin America. Dr. Sampó is an international consultant working for international institutions such as the Organization of American States, United Nations Office on Drugs and Crime, and Global Initiative Against Transnational Organized Crime, among others.

Valeska Troncoso is a professor at the University of Santiago de Chile. She has a master's degree in international studies from the University of Santiago de Chile and is a PhD candidate at the University of Buenos Aires. Valeska Troncoso is an international consultant and has worked for international institutions such as the Global Initiative Against Transnational Organized Crime. She has also participated in the Voluntary Pilot Initiative for Chile coordinated by the Civil Society Unit of the United Nations Office on Drugs and Crime. Her research focuses on criminal organizations in South America, gender, organized crime in the Tri-Border area between Chile, Peru, and Bolivia, and cocaine trafficking routes and ports from Latin America to Europe and Asia.

Héctor Alarcón Barrera is a Colombian graduate student at the PhD program in political science and a teaching assistant at the University of Illinois Chicago. He has worked as a consultant in the Superintendence of Industry and Commerce of Colombia and as a teaching assistant and research assistant at the Universidad de los Andes in Bogotá, where he graduated in economics and political science. His academic interests focus on the political economy of development and the political and social legacies of civil wars. Currently, he is working on the effect of civil wars on people's identity and political preferences; in particular, the relationship between the violence of civil war and the level of political polarization. He has received the support of the Fulbright Commission in Colombia and the Universidad de los Andes to complete undergraduate and postgraduate studies in the United States and Colombia.

Juan Albarracín is an assistant professor in the Department of Political Science at the University of Illinois Chicago. Prior to coming to UIC, Dr. Albarracín was a visiting assistant professor in the Keough School of Global Affairs at the University of Notre Dame (2021–2022) and an assistant professor and director of the Political Science Program at Universidad Icesi in Cali, Colombia (2018–2021). His research focuses on threats to political and civil rights in cases of mass-scale violence and extralegal governance. In this sense, his work lies at the intersection of studies of democratization, criminal and political violence, criminal governance, and political institutions. He employs multiple methods ranging from experiments and quantitative analysis with observational data to case studies based on extensive fieldwork.

Michael Jerome Wolff earned his PhD in political science from the University of New Mexico and joined the faculty at Western Washington University in 2016. His research focuses on organized criminal violence and policing in Latin America and seeks to understand how state policy and behavior shape the development of different types of criminal groups, as well as how organized crime and violence influence politics. Dr. Wolff currently has ongoing research projects in Mexico and Brazil. He teaches a range of courses in the subfields of comparative politics and international relations. Special course topics include civil wars and political violence, gangs and organized crime, development and inequality, the politics of Brazil and Mexico, and comparative border studies.

Daniel Pontón C. is a professor at Universidad de Posgrado del Estado IAEN, Ecuador. He was dean of the School of Security and Defense of the same institution. Currently, Dr. Pontón also works as a part-time professor at the Universidad Central del Ecuador. He taught at several public universities for nineteen years. Dr. Pontón worked in the public sector with several state portfolios in advisory and management positions, and he managed several public policy projects. His areas of research and work are violence, organized crime, prisons, citizen security, police, and drug policy. He has also been an international consultant in several projects related to subjects such as the Organization of American States and the Inter-American Development Bank.

Ivelaw Lloyd Griffith is a fellow of the Washington, DC, think tanks Global Americans and the Caribbean Policy Consortium. A senior associate with the Center for Strategic and International Studies, he is an expert on Caribbean security, drugs, and crime who has published extensively on the subject, including the books *Strategy and Security in the Caribbean* (Praeger, 1991), *The Quest for Security in the Caribbean* (M. E. Sharpe, 1993), *Drugs and Security in the Caribbean* (Pennsylvania State University Press, 1997), *The Political Economy of Drugs in the Caribbean* (Macmillan, 2000), *Caribbean Security in the Age of Terror* (Ian Randle, 2004), and *Challenged Sovereignty* (University of Illinois Press, 2024). He has testified before the US Congress and has been a visiting scholar at security institutes in the United States, Canada, and Germany, and a consultant to several governmental and international organizations. Dr. Griffith also has served as a professor and an academic leader for several decades, including as a dean at Florida International University, provost at Radford University and at York College of the City University of New York, president of Fort Valley State University, and vice chancellor (president) of the University of Guyana. He is the recipient of the Dr. William J. Perry Award for Excellence in Security and Defense Education, named in honor of former US defense secretary Dr. William Perry and conferred by the Perry Center for Hemispheric Defense Studies at the National Defense University.

Michael Ahn Paarlberg is an associate professor in the Political Science Department at Virginia Commonwealth University. He studies migration and security issues in Latin America and the United States. Dr. Paarlberg is also an associate fellow at the Institute for Policy Studies in Washington, DC, and served as chief Latin America policy adviser to Senator Bernie Sanders during his 2020 presidential campaign. He is a former journalist for *The Guardian* and regularly publishes his work in news outlets such as *Foreign Policy*, *Slate*, *El Faro*, and *The Washington Post*. He has consulted for the US Department of State, the Norwegian Ministry of Foreign Affairs, and the Organization of American States, and also serves as an expert witness in US immigration courts. Prior to coming to VCU, Dr. Paarlberg was a postdoctoral fellow at the University of Pennsylvania's Center for the Study of Ethnicity, Race, and Immigration. He earned his PhD in political science from Georgetown University.

Nathan P. Jones is an associate professor of security studies in the College of Criminal Justice at Sam Houston State University. He is the author of *Mexico's Illicit Drug Networks and the State Reaction* (2016) with Georgetown University Press. His areas of interest include organized crime violence in Mexico, drug-trafficking organizations, social network analysis, border security, and the political economy of homeland security. Dr. Jones is also a senior fellow with the *Small Wars Journal–El Centro*, a nonresident scholar at Rice University's Baker Institute for Public Policy in drug policy and Mexico studies, and the book review editor for the *Journal of Strategic Security* and the *International Journal of Police Science*.

Gary Hale was appointed in 2010 as a nonresident fellow in drug policy and Mexico studies at the James A. Baker III Institute for Public Policy, US-Mexico Center. From 2000 to 2010, he held the position of chief of intelligence in the Houston Field Division of the Drug Enforcement Administration, from which he retired in July 2010. Hale joined the DEA in 1979 while serving as a task force agent and narcotics officer detached from the Laredo Police Department. From 1979 to 1987, he held posts with the agency in New Orleans, El Paso, and Boston. He was the embassy intelligence coordinator at the US Embassy in La Paz, Bolivia, from 1987 to 1990, during which he spearheaded the arrest of Roberto Suárez Gómez, Bolivia's "King of Cocaine." In 1989, he led DEA operations in Panama during Operations Blue Spoon and Just Cause, which led to the arrest of Panamanian dictator Manuel

Noriega. From 1990 to 1997, Hale had various assignments in Washington, DC, including serving as chief of the Heroin Investigations Support Unit, chief of the Dangerous Drugs Intelligence Unit, and liaison to the National Security Agency. During this period, he also served a tour of duty at the US Embassy in Bogotá, Colombia, and participated in the hunt for Medellín cartel leader Pablo Escobar. During 1997–1998, Hale was assigned as the DEA's chief of intelligence at the US Embassy in Mexico City. In 1990, Hale received the DEA Administrator's Award, the agency's highest recognition, for work that led to the seizure of hundreds of general aviation aircraft involved in the cocaine transport airbridge throughout Bolivia, Peru, and Colombia. In 1995, he was recognized by Attorney General Janet Reno as a "Hispanic Hero Serving America." Hale is a decorated veteran with six years of service in the US Army Security Agency during the Vietnam War. He has a bachelor of science in computer science and a master's in law and judicial policy (LLM). Hale is an alumnus of the Harvard University Kennedy School of Government and the University of Virginia's Darden School of Leadership.

Marten Brienen is an associate professor in the School of Global Studies and Partnerships at Oklahoma State University. Dr. Brienen taught in both the African and Latin American Studies Programs at the University of Miami from 2004 to 2013. From 2011 to 2013, he served as the director of the Latin American Studies Program at the University of Miami. While he has worked on a variety of subjects, the fundamental principle that binds them together is his ongoing interest in the struggle between marginalized populations and the interests of states in the process of national construction in Africa and Latin America. From that perspective, he has in recent years focused primarily on energy security, drug trafficking, and complex emergencies. His publications include two volumes coedited with Jonathan D. Rosen: *New Approaches to Drug Policies: A Time for Change* (New York: Palgrave Macmillan, 2015), and *Prisons in the Americas in the Twenty-First Century: A Human Dumping Ground* (Lanham, MD: Lexington Books, 2015). More recent publications include the book chapters "Throwing Away the Key: *Mano Dura* with Bolivian Characteristics," in *Mano Dura Policies in Latin America*, ed. Jonathan D. Rosen and Sebastián A. Cutrona (New York: Routledge, 2023); and "'The Police Are Involved in Everything': Corruption and the Corrupt in Bolivia," In *Corruption in the Americas*, ed. Jonathan D. Rosen and Hanna Samir Kassab (Lanham, MD: Lexington Books, 2020).

Alberto Aziani is an associate professor of criminology at the University of Milano-Bicocca. His work focuses on illegal markets, transnational trafficking, and organized crime, with particular attention to cocaine trafficking in Europe. Dr. Alberto has collaborated with international and supranational organizations like the United Nations Office on Drugs and Crime and the European Commission, contributing to research on illicit financial flows and organized crime. He has published extensively on these topics and participates in various academic and policy-oriented projects in the field.

Caroline Agboola is a full professor at the Jindal Institute of Behavioural Sciences, O. P. Jindal Global University, and a Senior Research Fellow at the University of Johannesburg, South Africa. Her multidisciplinary professional experience cuts across the fields of sociology, criminology, and education. She earned a PhD in sociology from the University of South Africa (UNISA). Her PhD thesis is titled "A Qualitative Analysis of Women's Experiences Before, During, and After Imprisonment in South Africa." She was a National Research Foundation Scarce Skills Postdoctoral Research Fellow at the University of Johannesburg, South Africa, and an Open Distance Learning Postdoctoral Research Fellow at the University of South Africa. She serves as a reviewer for several peer-reviewed journals. She has published several papers in accredited journals.

Molly Charles is a blogger and a consultant for research and for monitoring and evaluation (M&E); her work has been largely in the areas of drug policy, drug trade, organized crime, HIV, and development issues with respect to vulnerable populations. Dr. Charles is a founding member of the National Addiction Research Centre, Mumbai, and was the center's deputy director until 2001, subsequent to which she has worked as a consultant for national and international agencies. Some of her recent publications include: Letizia Paoli, Victoria A. Greenfield, Molly Charles, and Peter Reuter, "Should Afghanistan Enter the Licit Opium Business? Lessons from India's Experience," *Addiction* 104 (2009): 347-54; and Molly Charles and Letizia Paoli, "India: The Third Largest Illicit Opium Producer," in *The World Heroin Market: Can Supply Be Cut?*, edited by Letizia Paoli, Victoria A. Greenfield, and Peter Reuter (New York: Oxford University Press, 2009).

Jose Sousa-Santos, an associate professor of practice, is the convenor of the Pacific Regional Security Hub at the University of Canterbury. He was formerly senior fellow and Pacific Policy Fellow with the Australia Pacific Security College at the Australian National University. His area of expertise and research is transnational crime, regional security, and nonstate actors in the Pacific islands and Southeast Asia. In June 2021, he was appointed to the Global Initiative Against Transnational Organized Crime panel of experts. Dr. Sousa-Santos has previously held positions as the subject matter expert (transnational crime and terrorism) with the executive cadre for the US Pacific Command, Special Operations Command Pacific's Cooperation Against Transnational Threats program, and the Pacific Area Security Sector Working Group (2015–2019).

Index

Page numbers in *italic* text indicate figures or tables.

14K Triad, 340–41

ABC Corridor, 161
Abuja, 2, 9, 292
aerial spraying, 245
Afghanistan, 159
Africa, 1–2, 8, 11–12, 15, 18, 33,
    49–51, 67, 70, 72–74, 76–77, 79, 111,
    119, 122–23, 155, 161, 164, 263–64,
    281–84, 286, 288–98, 309, 313, 317
Agosto, Jose Figueroa, 171
airports, 161, 266, 283, 292, 318
Albanian gangs, 12
Algeria, 73, 283, 285
Alto Huallaga Valley, 6
Amazon region, 209
Andean Ridge, 1–2, 7, 9, 208, 257
Andes, 5, 14–15, 27, 29, 31–34, 37, 45,
    49–50, 52, 87, 209, 233, 349
Angola, 285, 290
Anslinger, Harry J., 236–38
Antwerp, 7, 12, 76, 110, 122,
    139, 264, 268, 311
Argentina, 11, 28, 45–46, 49–51,
    69, 91, 263, 282, 287, 296
Armenia, 309, 318, 321–22
Asia, 1, 8, 12, 15, 18, 33, 42, 51, 67, 68, 70–71,
    73–76, 79, 111, 123, 155, 203, 220, 264,
    282–83, 292, 306–14, 317–24, 339
Autodefensas Unidas de Colombia (United Self-Defense Forces of Colombia—AUC),
    10–11, 39, 47–48, 181, 268
Australia, 1–2, 12, 17, 19, 74, 77, 164, 166,
    203, 258, 260, 270, 309–10, 331, 333–42
Azerbaijan, 318

balloon effect, 9, 32, 134–35, 209,
    213, 217, 244, 348–49
bandas criminales (BACRIM), 10, 39, 181–82
Bangladesh, 312, 317
Barrio 18 (18th Street gang), 16,
    177, 183–84, 188, 192, 194
Benin, 73, 264, 285
Blanco, Griselda, 350
Bolivia, 6, 8–9, 14, 27–31, 33–37, 39–46,
    48, 50–52, 66, 69, 77, 90–94, 98, 121,
    131, 207–10, 233, 236–38, 243–46,
    248–49, 257, 282, 287–88, 348
broker, 2, 12–13, 52, 157, 178, 269, 271
Burundi, 285

Cali cartel, 7, 9–10, 33, 37, 44, 46–47, 89,
    92, 97, 203, 207–9, 213, 242, 248
Camacho, Marcos Willians Herbas
    "Marcola," 118–19, 121, 123
Cambodia, 321–22
campesinos, 2, 5–6
Cameroon, 73, 285
cannabis, 113, 224, 286, 306–8,
    310, 319–20, 324
Cape Verde, 263, 285, 290–91
Caribbean, 7, 10, 15–16, 32, 46–47,
    49–50, 74, 92, 97, 121–22, 134, 155–56,
    160–61, *163*–64, 166–68, 170–73, 202,
    208–9, 212–13, 215, 217, 239, 242,
    263, 266, 282–83, 294, 320, 350
Cartel Jalisco Nueva Generación (Jalisco New Generation cartel—CJNG), 13,
    71, 142, 146, 202, 204, 218–20, 224
cartelitos, 10, 247
casinos, 341
Central Corridor, 161

Chad, 285, 289
Chapare, 6, 34, 36–37, 39, 41, 43–44, 209
chemical precursors, 1, 6, 41, 44, 131, *133*, 215, 220, 224, 257
Chile, 28, 42, 49–51, 70, 72, 74, 76, 78, 91, 104, 236, 238
China, 14, 68, 73–75, 195, 203, 224, 309, 313–15, 317, 319, *322*, 324, 341
Clan del Golfo (Gulf Clan), 13, 100–101
clicas, 186
coca bush, 1, 66–69, 93, 155, 233, 294
coca cultivation, 2, 5, 9, 32, 34–37, 43, 48, 50–51, 93, *95*, 98–101, 105, 135, 143, 207, 236, 244, 257–58, 261, 306–9, 317, 348–49
coca eradication, 98
coca leaves, 6, 10, 40, 93, 211, 257, 306–7
Coca-Cola, 29, 234, 305
cocaine hydrochloride, 1, 6, 10, 27, 29, 33, 44, 68, 155, 208–9, 211, 234, 239, 262
cocaine markets, 1, 8, 12, 16–17, 49, 53, 68, 79, 87, 122–23, 177, 212, 222, 255, 268, 281–82, 297, 317, 350
cocaine paste, 6, 30, 87, 89, 91–93, 208, 211, 257
cocaine production, 8, 10, 14, 27–31, 33, 40–46, 48, 66, 68, 88–92, 97–98, 100, 111, 121, 123, 135–*36*, 139, 143–44, 221, 239, 257, 348, 354
cocaine retail, 12, 145
cocaine smugglers, 30, 45, 52, 284
cocaine supply chain, 2, 3, 5–9, 12–18, 27–28, 37, 45, 68, 87–89, 91–93, 101, 104–5, 111, 119, 121–22, 129–30, 140, 142, 147–48, 182, 203, 209, 211, 217, 220, 257, 281, 283, 289, 331, 348, 350–51
cocaine trafficking, 1–2, 7, 11, 13, 15–19, 36–37, 40, 45–46, 67–68, 70, 73–75, 77, 80, 98, 123–24, 129–30, 134, 142, 146, 148, 165, 169, 178, 185, 202, 204, 207, 255–56, 260, 263–65, 267–71, 281–90, 292–98, 313, 317–18, 331, 342, 349–51, 353
Coke, Christopher, 172
Colombia, 6, 8–11, 13–15, 27–28, 30–45, 47–48, 50–52, 66, 68–69, 72, 74, 76, 78, 87–89, 91–*94*, *96*–105, 110, 119–21, 124, 129–37, 139–40, 142–43, 145, 159, 166, 171, 180–82, 188, 203, 207–11, 218, 220, 224, 238–39, 242, 244–46, 248, 257, 262, 268–69, 282, 287, 294, 296–97, 334, 348, 350, 353–54
Colombia Peace Accord, 39, 121, 135
Comando Vermelho (Red Command—CV), 11, 15, 52, 113–18, 120, 297
Comoros, 285
Congo, 285
consolidated markets, 1–2, 68, 70–71, 80, 350
consumer markets, 5, 7, 9, 49, 51, 66, 79, 92, 105, 110–11, 123, 263
containers, 7, 50, 72–74, 78, 110–11, 122, 164, 170, 262, 265, 288, 294–96, 310–12, 335
contractors, 12–13
Cook Islands, 332–33, 339–40
Costa Rica, 52
COVID-19, 2, 48, 50, 67, 139, 261, 266, 283, 293–94, 323, 333–35
crack cocaine, 8, 17, 115, 233, 239–40, 242, 261
criminal deportees, 340
criminal governance, 15, 88, 101, 103–5, 214, 353
criminal organizations, 2, 3, 7–19, 46, 66–73, 75–76, 79–80, 87–89, 92, 101, 105, 110–11, 123–24, 132–33, 140, 143, 146, 148, 180–81, 202–3, 214, 224, 242–43, 246, 248–49, 256, 258, 263, 267–68, 270–71, 281, 283–85, 291, 293–95, 297–98, 335, 338, 342, 350–52
Cuba, 91, 159, 160, 170

de Carvalho, Sergio Roberto, 173
dealers, 2, 8, 114, 119, 222, 240, 258–59, 267, 308, 314, 320, 323, 338
Djibouti, 285
Dominican Republic 52, 161, 169–71, 213, 217, 282
drug cartel, 2, 8–11, 13, 38, 47, 91, 178, 180, 204, 215, 224, 242–43, 245. 283–86, 341, 350
drug interdiction, *133*, *216*
drug policies, 105, 354
drug-related violence, 14, 39, 46
drug seizures, 74, 78, 131, *133*, 135, 167
Drug Trafficking Organization (DTO), 97–98, 101, 178–81, 188, 190
drug-trafficking routes, 146

Eastern Corridor, 161
Ecuador, 11, 15, 28, 45, 66, 72, 74, 76, 78, 93, 100, *128*, 135, 137–39, 140–48, 163, 203, 207–8, 262, 296, 351
Ejército de Liberación Nacional (National Liberation Army—ELN), 10, 110, 245
El Mencho, 219
El Salvador, 177–79, 181–83, 185–87, 189–91, 193–95, 203
emerging markets, 5, 18, 45, 122
ephedra, 307, 321, 325
epidemic, 8, 202, 240, 242, 246, 248, 289
eradication, 1, 9, 31–32, 37–38, 50, 89, 91, 93, 98, 100, 105, 135, 239, 244, 246, 257
Eritrea, 285
erythroxylon coca, 307
Escobar, Pablo, 10, 46–47, 97, 203, 142, 180, 207, 242
Eswatini, 285
Ethiopia, 73, 285, 290
Europe, 1–2, 7–8, 10–12, 15–18, 29–30, 33, 48–52, 70–74, 77–78, 80, 110–11, 119, 121–23, 129, 132–35, 139, 144, 146, 148, 155–56, 161, 163–64, 166–67, 170, 173, 203, 215, 217, 255, 256–64, 266–71, 281–83, 286, 289–93, 295, 297–98, 305, 309–10, 315, 317, 320–21, 339, 352
European Monitoring Centre for Drugs and Drug Addiction (EMCDDA), 260, 274
Europol, 11

failed state, 35–37, 286
Familia do Norte (FDN), 120, 298
Federal Bureau of Narcotics (FBN), 236, 238
fentanyl, 17, 73, 76, 202, 219–22, 224, 246–47, 249, 339, 352
Fiji, 31, 334–36, 339
French Guiana, 160, 166–67, 170
Fuerzas Armadas Revolucionarias de Colombia (Revolutionary Armed Forces of Colombia—FARC), 10, 15, 38–39, 41, 44, 89, 97–98, 100–101, 110, 119, 121, 135, 143–44, 245
Fujimori, Alberto, 244, 248

Gallardo, Miguel Ángel Félix, 11, 180, 218
gangs, 12, 15–16, 19, 40, 111, 113–16, 129, 145–46, 148, 177–81, 183–86, 188–91, 193–96, 217, 297, 316, 335, 338–41, 351–52
Georgia, 309, 318
Ghana, 18, 73, 264, 284–85, 288
go-fast boats, 7, 50, 167
Guadalajara Federation, 11
Guatemala, 66, 74, 76, 78, 80, 177, 182, 185, 203, 218
guerrilla organizations, 8
Guinea-Bissau, 18, 73, 283–86, 288–91, 293

Gulf cartel, 11, 212
Guzmán, Joaquin "El Chapo," 143, 171, 204, 247

Haiti, 160–61, 169
heroin, 161, 204, 224, 234–35, 237–39, 243, 248–49, 307–8, 316, 320, 323–24
Honduras, 48, 66, 74, 76, 177–78, 185, 190, 193, 195, 203, 215, 353
Hoshi Pharmaceuticals, 307

illicit drugs, 5, 12, 111, 131, *133*, 290–91, 293, 310, 331–35, 339, 341, 349
India, 1, 14, 68, 73, 76–77, 203, 224, 308–14, 316–18, 320–22, 324, 352
Indonesia, 309–10, 313, 317, 322
interdiction, 7–9, 47, 92–93, 97, *133*, 141, 161, 170, 204, *216*, 263, 335, 348
Iran, 309
Israel, 309, 317, 322
Italy, 17, 170, 255–56, 259–60, 265, 267–68, 270, 354

Japan, 14, 18, 68, 74, 78–79, 234, 305, 307–9, 314–15, 317, 322–23
Java, 18, 29, 306–7
Jordan, 309, 318

Kazakhstan, 309, 322
kingpin strategy, 217, 242, 247, 354
Kiribati, 331, 340
Kuwait, 322

laboratory, 1, 211, 295, 309
Latin America, 1, 11–12, 18, 46, 49–50, 72, 74–75, 78, 80, 95, 99, 122, 129, 145, 161, 170, 208, 238, 259, 261–63, 270, 281–83, 288, 290, 292, 295, 298, 307, 313, 319–20, 354

Lebanon, 309, 314, 317, *322*, 339
Lesotho, 285
Liberia, 285
Libya, 73, 285
Los Chapitos, 219
Los Choneros, 15, 143, 145–46, 351
Los Lobos, 146
Luna Garcia, Genaro, 215, 353

Madagascar, 285
Malawi, 285
Malaysia, 309–11, 313, 317–18, 320–22
Mali, 18, 73, 283, 285, 288–91
Mara Salvatrucha (MS-13), 16, 177–79, 181, 183–84, 186–87, 189–94, 350–51
maras, 16, 177–96
maritime corridors, 331, 342
Marshall Islands, 331
Mauritania, 73, 284–85
Mauritius, 285
Medellín Cartel, 32, 36, 43, 46–48, 97, 103, 180, 207, 242
Melanesia, 331
methamphetamines, 202, 219, 224, 236, 246, 261, 319–21, 325, 331, 334, 336, 339–41
Mexican Mafia, 178, 184, 186–87
Mexico, 4, 11, 13, 16, 66–67, 71–72, 74, 76, 78, 89, 92, 98, 124, 171, 177–78, 180–81, 202, 204, 208–9, 211–15, 217–18, 220–22, 224, 243, 263, 317, 351–53
Miami, 10, 17, 92, 160–61, 163, 237, 239, 350
Middle East, 17–18, 33, 258, 292, 320
money laundering, 52, 104, 132, 140, 155–56, 160, 171, 173, 178, 195, 316
Morales, Evo, 31–32, 244
Morocco, 4, 73, 264, 266, 285
motorcycle gangs, 19, 335, 339, 341
Movimiento al Socialismo (Movement for Socialism—MAS), 31
Mozambique, 77, 123, 263, 285, 290
Mumbai, 1–2, 9, 311, 316, 318

mules, 72, 142, 167, 286, 293, 295–8, 310, 313–4

Nauru, 332
narco-bourgeoisie, 42–44
narcogenerals, 141, 144
narcoterrorism, 98
narco-submarines, 72–73
Nariño, 6, 37, 93, 100, 131, 135
'Ndrangheta, 2, 11–13, 17, 122, 265, 268, 270, 297, 331, 341, 351
Nepal, 14, 68, 77, 310
Netherlands, 12, 164, 166–67, 170, 215, 234, 255–56, 260–61, 263–64, 269–70, 307, 313
New York, 1, 9, 92, 172, 194, 209, 211, 215, 236, 245, 352
New Zealand, 19, 203, 310, 331, 333–35, 337, 339–40, 342
Niemann, Albert, 29, 234
Nigeria, 18, 73, 264, 266, 269, 283, 285, 287, 292–93, 297, 313
Nigerian criminal organizations, 18
Niue, 332
Nixon, Richard, 17, 91, 233, 237–38, 240
nontraditional markets, 1
nontraditional routes, 11
Norte del Valle cartel, 97
Norte de Santander, 6, 37, 93, 100
North America, 1, 15–16, 29–30, 111, 121, 134, 155, 160–61, 163, 238, 256, 260, 282–83, 309, 317, 320, 339
Northern Triangle, 16, 177, 184–85, 188

Oceania, 8, 19, 73, 75, 283, 331–35, 338, 342, 350
Operation Screaming Eagle, 210
Organized Crime Groups (OCGs), 17, 49, 202–4, 213–14, 217–18, 224, 316, 338, 341, 351
OxyContin, 249

Pacific islands, 19, 164, 294, 331–32, 337, 339–40, 342
Philippines, 74, 309, 318, 322
Paisas, 10, 46
palabreros, 186
Palau, 332–33, 340–41
Pakistan, 309, 313–14, 317–18, 321–22, 352
Paraguay, 7, 50, 119, 296
paramilitary groups, 38–39, 89, 97, 100–101, 143
Parana-Paraguay waterway, 7
pasta base, 1, 6, 238, 244, 257
Peralta, Cesar "The Abuser," 171–72
Peru, 6, 8–9, 14, 27–40, 42–46, 48, 50–52, 66–67, 69, 72, 74, 77, 78, 91, 93–94, 98, 112, 120–21, 130–31, 133, 135, 146, 207–9, 236–38, 244–45, 248–49, 257, 282, 297, 305–6, 348
Petro, Gustavo, 105
Plan 503, 187
Plan Bitter Tears, 187
Plan Colombia, 9, 32, 37, 98, 131, 134, 143, 181, 245–46, 248
Plan Dignidad, 244
Plan Orphan Children, 187
Polynesia, 332, 336–37
Port Moresby, 334–35, 341
port of Busan, 75–76
port of Guayaquil, 144
port of Yokohama, 75–76
Portugal, 170, 260, 262–63, 269
Prado Álava, Édison Washington (Gerald), 142
Primeiro Comando da Capital (First Command of the Capital—PCC), 2, 11, 13, 15, 18, 52, 71, 111, 115–24, 269, 287, 295, 297, 351
prison gangs, 15, 111, 113–16, 184–85
prison violence, 146
Pure Food and Drug Act, 235
Putumayo, 6, 37, 93, 100, 131

ranfla, 187, 192–93
Rastrojos, 100, 143
Reagan, Ronald, 213, 240, 242, 350
Rio de Janeiro, 11, 46, 111–16, 118, 120
Rodríguez Orejuela brothers, 10, 207
Rota Caipira, 119
Rota Solimões, 120
Rotterdam, 2, 7, 9, 12, 110, 122, 264, 268, 311

Samoa, 332–33, 340
Sánchez Farfán, Wilder Emilio "El Gato," 142
Sankyo Pharmaceuticals, 307
São Paulo, 11, 77, 111–12, 114–18, 120, 122, 285, 287–88, 295
seaports, 7, 12, 15, 17, 111, 119, 122, *138,* 161, 256, 265–66, 268, 271, 283, 292, 294–95, 311, 318
semisubmersible, 7, 72, 161, 294
Sendero Luminoso (Shining Path) movement, 38, 244
Sinaloa Cartel, 17, 71, 142–43, 146, 166, 181, 202, 204, 215, 218–20, 224, 285, 351, 353
sindicatos, 6
Singapore, 313, 315
South Africa, 2, 73, 76–77, 285, 290
South America, 7, 13, 15–16, 27, 33, 66, 68, 72, 74–75, 110–11, 120–22, 124, 145, 155, 160–61, 166, 171, 202, 208, 224, 255–59, 260, 264–65, 267–68, 282–83, 286, 289, 293, 317, 324, 335–37, 339
South Florida Task Force, 7, 350
South Korea, 14, 68, 73, 75–77, 79, 309–10, 314, 317
Southern Cone, 7, 11, 91, 263
Soviet Union, 10, 242
Spain, 161, 170, 255–56, 260, 262–65, 266, 269–70
Sri Lanka, 76, 311, 313, 317, 321–22
Suárez, Roberto, 43–44, 46, 207
subcontractor, 2, 7, 177
Sydney, 1, 9, 331
synthetic drugs, 73, 79, 161, 202, 219–20, 224, 306, 319, 352

Taiwan, 29, 234, 307, 309–10, 314–15
Tajikistan, 317
Texis cartel, 178, 194, 195
Thailand, 74, 77, 309, 313, 315–18
The Commission, 19, 338–39
three-strikes law, 240, 242
Tiguerones, 145–46
Tijuana Cartel, 218
Tonga, 332, 334, 336
Tuvalu, 332
trafficking routes, 7, 10–11, 16–18, 38, 92, 104, 146, 165, 185, 209, 242, 255–56, 262–63, 269, 271, 295, 339, 348–49
Tranquilandia, 92
transit country, 15, 51, 75, 129, 132–*133*, 148, 221, 294
traquetos, 13
Transnational Criminal Organizations (TCOs), 110–11, 123, *133*, 146, 148, 202–3, 224–25, 243, 246, 249, 342
transshipment hub, 11, 19, 263–66, 281, 298, 331, 334, 342
transshipment points, 73–74, 79, 215

United Kingdom, 3, 170, 255–56, 260–61, 264
United Nations Office on Drugs and Crime (UNODC), 1, 66, 110, 129, 163, 282, 311, 335, 349
United States, 4, 7–11, 13–15, 17, 29–33, 42, 46–50, 52, 70–72, 74–75, 77, 80, 87, 89, 91–92, 97–98, 101, 103, 105, 132–35, 139, 142, 157, 159, 160–61, 163, 166, 169, 171–72, 177–78, 181, 183–87, 189, 191–92, 196, 202–4, 207–9, 212–15, 217–18, 220–22, 224, 233–39, *241*–49, 255, 259, 264, 270, 305, 312, 319, 321, 336, 340, 350–54
Uribe, Alvaro, 39, 89, 98, 100, 245
Uruguay, 49, 70, 104, 296

Vanuatu, 331, 333
Venezuela, 11, 48, 52, 72, 93, 100–101, 121–22, 161, 167, 195, 262, 282, 287, 296
vessels, 7, 50, 72, 111, 122, 134, 142, 161, 163–64, 265, 291–92, 294
VRAEM, 6, 35, 37–38, 40, 51

Wallerstein, Immanuel, 3–4
War on Drugs, 32, 87, 130, 132, 134, 148, 233, 237, 239, 245, 247, 336
wastewater analysis, 339
West Africa, 11, 18, 73, 123, 263–64, 281, 283–85, 289–90, 292, 295–96, 298, 309

World-Systems Theory, 3–5, 259
World War I, 17, 307
World War II, 29, 306–8

Yakuza, 180, 315
youth subculture, 179, 191
Yungas, 6, 28, 36, 39

Zambia, 285
Zero Coca campaign, 248
Zimbabwe, 285

www.ingramcontent.com/pod-product-compliance
Lightning Source LLC
Chambersburg PA
CBHW020634230426
43665CB00008B/165